Teaching French Women Writers of the Renaissance and Reformation

Modern Language Association of America
Options for Teaching

For a complete listing of titles,
see the last pages of this book

Teaching French Women Writers of the Renaissance and Reformation

Edited by

Colette H. Winn

The Modern Language Association of America
New York 2011

Library of Congress Cataloging-in-Publication Data

Teaching French women writers of the Renaissance and Reformation / edited by Colette H. Winn.
p. cm. — (Options for teaching ; 31)
Includes bibliographical references and index.
ISBN 978-1-60329-089-0 (hardcover : alk. paper) —
ISBN 978-1-60329-090-6 (pbk. : alk. paper)
1. French literature—Women authors—Study and teaching. 2. French literature—16th century—Study and teaching. 3. French literature—17th century—Study and teaching. I. Winn, Colette H.
PQ149.T33 2011
840.9'9287071—dc22 2011014867

Options for Teaching 31
ISSN 1079-252

Cover illustration of the paperback edition:
Plaque of Margaret of France, by Jean de Court (1555). By kind permission of the Trustees of the Wallace Collection, London.

Published by The Modern Language Association of America
26 Broadway, New York, NY 10004-1789
www.mla.org

Contents

Comparative Contexts and Strategies

Part IV: Current Resources

Colette H. Winn

Introduction

In 2007 the volume *Approaches to Teaching Marguerite de Navarre's* Heptameron, which I edited, was published by the MLA. One may thus wonder, Why devote a second volume to the teaching of French women writers of the Renaissance and Reformation? Perhaps the most compelling reason is the recent rediscovery of early modern women writers. Marguerite de Navarre has long been a canonical figure in Renaissance studies and teaching, but we know today of many other long-neglected women authors of the period who are also worthy of scholarly and pedagogical attention.

Indeed, French women of the Renaissance and Reformation wrote about anything and everything, including law and customs, motherhood, education and the care of children, health and medicine, religion, politics, and aesthetics. They tried their hand at nearly every type of writing and literary form: moral advice literature and marriage manuals (Anne of France, Marie de Romieu, Madame and Philipe Du Verger); drama (Catherine de Parthenay, Catherine Des Roches); epics (Gabrielle de Coignard); letters (Jeanne d'Albret, Charlotte de Bourbon, Hélisenne de Crenne, Catherine and Madeleine Des Roches), lyric and devotional poetry (Pernette Du Guillet, Louise Labé, the Dames Des Roches, Gabrielle de Coignard, Anne de Marquets, Anne Picardet); memoirs and religious history (Jeanne d'Albret,

Charlotte Arbaleste de Mornay, Marie Dentière, Jeanne de Jussie, Margaret of Valois); philosophical treatises and political pamphlets (Marie de Gournay, Marie de Romieu, Margaret of Valois), and so on. While some engaged in activities considered appropriate for women—cultivating frivolous poetic forms like the chansons, rondeaux, complaints, and debates (e.g., Madeleine de L'Aubespine, Margaret of Austria) or translating scriptural texts (Gabrielle de Coignard)—others devoted themselves equally to scholarly pursuits. Catherine Des Roches and Marie Le Gendre composed several dialogues, a favorite humanist genre. Marie de Cotteblanche took an interest in scientific subjects and gave the first French translation of the Spanish *Coloquios* or *Dialogos* of the cosmographer Pero Mexia or Mejia (in 1579). Madeleine de L'Aubespine, Catherine de Parthenay, and Catherine Des Roches published translations of classical works into the vernacular, thus partaking in the erudite craft that was primarily the domain of the male humanists. Others distinguished themselves as pioneers in the introduction of new forms or in the transformation of older ones. Hélisenne de Crenne wrote the first sentimental novel in France (*Les angoysses douloureuses qui procedent d'amours* [1538]). Georgette de Montenay composed the first book of Christian emblems ever written in any language by a woman (*Emblèmes ou devises chrestiennes* [1566]). The Dames Des Roches published the first collection of private letters by women in France (*Les missives* [1586]). Margaret of Valois composed, before 1600, the first full-length woman's memoirs in the French language, and Marie de Gournay won fame for her pioneering work in translation, editorial practices, and poetic theories.

Changes in the Literary Canon and the Academic Curriculum

With the rediscovery of writings by early modern women, the literary canon has changed considerably.[1] Before the 1980s, few early women writers, if any, were included in reading lists for preliminary and oral exams, and it was not until 2000 that Marguerite de Navarre's *Heptameron* was featured on the program for the *agrégation* (Louise Labé had to wait until 2005). Early women were as scarcely represented in anthologies as in the academic curriculum. André Lagarde and Laurent Michard, in their manual designed for students preparing for the *baccalauréat*, mention in passing Marguerite de Navarre as the sister of King Francis I and the protectress of Clément Marot. Pernette Du Guillet receives attention merely as the muse of Maurice Scève. While the name of Louise Labé is cited in relation to the École de Lyon, her works are summarized in one line: "[ses] sonnets sont remarquables par la *sincérité* des sentiments" ("her sonnets are remarkable for their impression of emotional sincerity"; 31).

Since the 1980s, the continued interest generated by the study of French women of the Renaissance and Reformation and the growing accessibility of texts in both modern editions and English translations (see Winn, "Print Resources for Teaching and Further Study," in this volume) have led to the creation of many exciting courses. These courses will not take the place of the standard Renaissance courses but nonetheless enrich the curriculum by offering alternative perspectives on familiar topics as well as new texts by a hitherto nearly unrepresented segment of the population.[2] Today, undergraduate survey courses on French literature and courses on literary genres are partially focused on women. In courses specifically devoted to French women writers, women of the Renaissance and Reformation are generally read with works that precede and follow so that students can examine the major cultural, intellectual, and artistic movements in ancien régime France (the courtly tradition, Petrarchism and Neoplatonism, humanism, *préciosité*, the Enlightenment) along with recurrent debates over women's education and the development of a "feminist" consciousness. In the multidisciplinary courses so popular these days, these French women writers are taught in English alongside their European counterparts (mostly Italian, Spanish, and English). Topics courses tend to concentrate on fewer significant examples to give a representative sample of women's contributions to a particular question (e.g., the centuries-long gender debate known as the *querelle des femmes*) or a particular theme (love, marriage, friendship, education, religion, etc.).

Works by women are generally read in relation to works written by men so that students may gain a good understanding of the sociohistorical and cultural contexts in which these various texts were written and a much richer and more accurate picture of the past. When compared with male historical accounts, writings by women often reveal alternative views on social, political, and religious issues and events of the time. Written in the late 1590s but not published until 1628, the *Mémoirs* of Margaret of Valois gives us valuable insight from a privileged woman's point of view into the workings and intrigues of the Valois court during its twilight years. Published posthumously in 1623, the *Mémoirs* of Charlotte Arbaleste de Mornay, wife of the famed Huguenot leader Philippe Duplessis-Mornay, tells us of the various ways in which religious changes brought about by the

Reformation and Counter-Reformation affected women's lives and their devotional practices. Accounts of the Saint Bartholomew's Day Massacre, written by Margaret of Valois; Charlotte Arbaleste de Mornay; and Renée Burlamacchi, Théodore-Agrippa d'Aubigné's second wife, indicate how three women from different socioeconomic backgrounds experienced this bloody episode of French religious history.

Furthermore, reading male and female writings in dialogue with each other makes for animated class discussion and gives students an understanding of gender issues in the early modern period. If texts written by moralists and theologians of the time provide ample evidence of common assumptions about women and the repressive nature of French social codes, writing by women brings to light women's responses to traditional images of them and to the constraints placed on them. Students can see, for example, how Marguerite de Navarre's *Heptameron* (1559) presents, in reaction to the consistently stereotyped features attributed to women (fickleness, lustfulness, shamelessness, adulterousness, etc.), models of women who reject adulterous liaisons to preserve their honor and their family's cohesion. In her *Apologie pour les dames* (1602), Jacqueline de Miremont likewise offers examples of ancient heroines who sacrificed all for their husbands and children as a response to traditional notions concerning women's inherent moral weakness. Male educators recommended that women be humble in their behavior, modest, and silent. Catherine Des Roches dares to question the true purpose of such prescriptions. In the preface to the *Œuvres* she admits that bashful silence, "ornament de la femme" ("the ornament of women"), will avoid scandal or blemish to her sex, but she also notes that it will not bring women any honor (79 [1993]). In her prose dialogues ("Dialogue de Placide, et Severe," "Dialogue d'Iris, et Pasithée"), she challenges education that aims solely at preparing women to become well-informed and pleasant companions to their husbands, good mothers and caretakers, and ethical and pious Christians. As for Louise Labé, in her dedicatory letter to her noblewoman friend, Clémence de Bourges, she urges women to abandon gendered occupations and ornaments and envision more lasting pleasures for themselves such as reading and writing, which were supposedly encouraged by the humanist educational program.

Finally, reading women's writing alongside texts by their male contemporaries illuminates new aspects of the writing of both sexes and encourages students to analyze women's works in aesthetic terms: How did men and women interact in the fashioning of literary taste? What impact, if any, did women have on the male writers that constitute the current canon of French authors?

In sum, a gender-sensitive approach encourages a revisionist appreciation of the current literary canon and gives students the broadest possible view of early modern French society and letters.

The Challenge of Teaching Early Women Writers

Since most of our students in French are female, they are intrigued to learn about the history of early women. However, early modern classes are a challenge for undergraduates. The language is difficult and the world that is introduced to them is drastically different from theirs. Many aspects of the early modern period—views, ideals, expectations regarding gender, and even the very nature of its literature—are so alien to them that they constantly risk mistaking the meanings, intentions, and implications of any given work. It is imperative to begin with an introduction to the political, religious, and sociocultural background and to place gender issues in their historical context. Instructors may want to engage their students to further explore the question of gender and have them ponder on what it means in terms of aesthetics, literary production, and textual representation (see the essays by Alduy and Chang in this volume, as well as McManus). An obvious advantage is that students will grapple with the theoretical notions of voice, gender, and authorship instead of focusing on questions of sincerity and authenticity. This should enable them to better differentiate between the authorial voice of the text and the genuine voice of the writer.

When I present the historical background, I find it important to keep in mind our students' frame of reference, and I usually insist on those areas that prove most alien to them and therefore more difficult for them to absorb.

Laws and Common Views Regarding Gender

It is useful to begin by bringing the class to understand how both religious and social institutions helped construct gender as a social category.[3] Gender definitions derived from indisputable authorities: scriptural, patristic, and scientific writings, as well as ancient Greek sources like Galen, Hippocrates, and Aristotle (who was by far the most influential non-Christian source for ideas in many fields up to the seventeenth century). These provided the basis for law codes that attempted to regulate behavior and determine gender roles in society. Following Aristotle's dualities, male was commonly associated with form, completion, order, and control, whereas female was linked with matter, incompletion, disorder, and nature. In Aristotelian terms, woman was an error of nature, an incomplete or imperfect version of the man (*De generatione animalium* [*On the Generation of Animals*], bk. 4, ch. 6). She was thought to be equipped with the same genitalia as man but unable to fully develop her sexual organs and push them outward because of her inherent weakness and the lack of heat in generation, a belief that was embraced by such notorieties as the French physician and prolific writer Ambroise Paré and Laurent Joubert, the chancellor of the School of Medicine of Montpellier. Much debated also were the roles of male and female in the process of conception. Aristotle claimed that it was only the male who contributed by his seed or semen to the process of conception and the formation of the embryo, whereas women served as incubators, furnishing the fetus a warm place to develop (*Generation*, bk. 4, chs. 1, 4).[4] Another widespread belief was Galen's claim that human beings' psychological attributes were determined by the combination of bodily humors (*The Soul's Dependence on the Body*, esp. chs. 4, 5, 7). According to Galen, if hot and dry humors dominated in man, generating the qualities of strength, courage, reason, order, and control, the cold and moist humors that reigned supreme in woman were responsible for her weak, passionate, irrational, and fickle nature. Moisture was thought to prevent reason from developing fully. Because woman was weaker than man physically, she was perceived to be inferior to him morally and intellectually.

Salic law denied woman access to the throne, although some women like Catherine de Médicis managed to exercise considerable political power.[5] Roman laws that were influential during the early modern era generally had a negative impact on women's civil legal status. Unwed adult women enjoyed certain legal rights, but because of women's alleged incapacity and ignorance, they were usually given male guardians. A married woman, on the other hand, ceased to have legal existence: she could not act as an independent person, could not make contracts or go to court without her husband's approval, and was therefore excluded from politics and public affairs in general. Property and goods she brought to the marriage became her husband's property. Only in very special cases (e.g., for fear that an irresponsible husband might squander the conjugal estate) was she allowed to retain partial control over them. When her husband died, the widow became head of the household and the legal guardian of her children if she renounced remarriage. Free of male control, she could run her estate as she saw fit. However, if widowhood gave a few women greater autonomy and power, it was accompanied for the vast majority of them by extreme hardship (impoverishment, abandonment by kin, isolation).[6]

Today's French women enjoy full legal rights, as do other women in Western societies, but the fact that this is a relatively recent phenomenon (they obtained the right to vote in 1945, the right to open a checking account in 1965, and so on) indicates how deeply engrained gender assumptions were in French society.

The Prospect before Her

Students are puzzled to realize the extent to which gender conditioned an individual's expectations and life experiences in the early modern period. Also, living as they do in an era of greater and more complex choices for young people, they find it difficult to imagine a time when the prospect before a young lady was either marriage or the convent.[7] Celibacy, except for nuns in convents, remained a notable exception. Catherine Des Roches's choice never to marry in order to pursue a life of learning and writing in the company of her mother was frowned on by her male contemporaries.

Marriage patterns differed greatly according to social class, rank, family circumstances, education, religious affiliation, and place of residence (urban as opposed to rural settings). However, alongside these differences, there were many constants. Marriage marked the official entrance into social adulthood. For a woman, it meant taking charge of running the household, raising the children, and supervising the servants, including any other household dependents like journeymen or apprentices. Parents played a major role in choosing a woman's mate. With the exception of widows and women whose parents had died, women seldom had a say in when and whom to marry. In the upper classes, it was fairly common for a girl to be married at a young age to an older man already established in society. The main consideration in making a match was economic: economic survival and the rearing of children at one end of the social spectrum; lineage and patrimony, wealth, social prestige, and political power at the other end. In getting married the new bride promised to obey her master. Indeed, law and religion reinforced the common view that the husband was superior to his wife in authority and judgment. This is not to say that mutual affection and respect did not exist between spouses. Charlotte Arbaleste de Mornay and her husband greatly enjoyed each other's company and shared genuine affection. She accompanied him on his diplomatic missions and, when she could not go, carried out his duties. Philippe Duplessis-Mornay entrusted her with maintaining his alliances at home, communicating important information to members of his party, and even publishing his work. He greatly valued her advice on both domestic and public matters.

Marriage was generally followed by repeated pregancies and births, a prospect the young wife approached with much apprehension (mortality in childbirth was a major cause of death among women).[8] Viewed as an indissoluble sacrament by the Catholic Church, marriage was almost impossible to undo. However, annulment or separation might be conceded in cases of prolonged absence or abandonment, adultery, impotence, unjustified violence, heresy, or proof of the existence of an earlier marriage. In such cases the Protestant Church, starting in 1559 with John Calvin's *Discipline* (ch. 13), allowed the possibility of divorce followed by remarriage (Garrisson 84–85; Watt 130–37). The marriage of Jeanne d'Albret to the Duke of Clèves as part of the political maneuvering of Francis I against Charles V was annulled when this alliance was no longer needed, on the grounds that the marriage had never been consummated. Jeanne, who was twelve years old at the time, had composed a written protest in which she claimed that she had obeyed under threat. Margaret of Valois's union to Henri IV was likewise annulled in 1599 because it did not produce children.

The convent remained an alternative to marriage for those who were drawn to religious life.[9] It was mostly available to women of the upper classes who did not wish to marry or remarry (in the case of widows), who were unsuitable for the marriage market because of their physical appearance or poor health, or who did not have a dowry and therefore could not be married properly (convent entrance fees cost far less than dowries). Social hierarchy remained important inside convent walls. While women of the nobility had access to positions of power (many were appointed abbesses), lower-class women became lay sisters or servant nuns, positions similar to those that were available to them in the secular world. The convent clearly imposed particular constraints, but it also offered distinct advantages, both socially and culturally, and often allowed women to transcend gender limitations. Above all, convents offered women the opportunity to receive an education, to read and write. While some nuns were appointed to document the history of their foundations, others would relate the lives of saints for the edification of their sisters. Soon after she entered the convent of Saint Clare in 1521, the Franciscan nun Jeanne de Jussie became its official writer and record keeper. Free from family responsibilities, nuns also had the opportunity to engage in creative activities such as composing devotional literature, practicing music, and so on. When Protestantism began to spread, convents found themselves embroiled in religious controversy; many were dissolved along with their governing theology or had to be relocated. When the reformed faith penetrated the city of Geneva, the sisters of Saint Clare were forced to leave and resettle in Annecy. Jeanne de Jussie wrote a powerful narrative (*Petite chronique* [*Short Chronicle*]) on the vehement reaction of her community when two prominent reformers, Guillaume Farel and Pierre Viret, came to the Franciscan convent to convert the nuns.

The Place of Religion in Women's Lives

It can be difficult for many students today to absorb the place religion occupied and the role it played in the lives and education of people of this era, women's lives in particular. When reading, for instance, Anne of France's *Enseignements* (1504/1505), students seldom note the admonition to fear and love God or the frequent reference to the everlasting torments of hell awaiting the sinner and fail, therefore, to understand the impact religious beliefs had on women's views of things and on their actions. Religion was at the center of a woman's life (see Broomhall, *Women and Religion*), and the fear of hell provided a strong incentive for good conduct.

Religious turmoil in early modern France had a great impact on women's lives. From the start, women of the upper classes showed strong sympathies for the Reformation movement.[10] Some of them like Renée of France and Georgette de Montenay embraced the new faith, whereas their husbands remained devout Catholics. In the 1530s and 1540s Renée of France engaged openly in reformist activities at the court of Ferrara until her husband confined her to the ducal palace. After his death in 1559, she moved to Montargis, her place of birth, and continued to devote herself to the Protestant cause. In 1571 Charlotte de Bourbon fled the convent of Jouarre, where she had been placed by her father, in order to adopt the Protestant faith. Other women converted before their husbands did and, in all likelihood, influenced other family members to follow. Such was the case of Charlotte de Laval, wife of the Huguenot leader Gaspard de Coligny. As for Charlotte Arbaleste de Mornay, she ensured that her first and only surviving son be instructed by a humanist reformed preceptor. Calvin, who was quick to realize the potential such women might have for the advancement of his cause, initiated a correspondence and maintained connections with several important figures of the day like Renée of France (see Blaisdell). The Protestant Reformation created opportunities for women to receive limited instruction so they could read and interpret scripture alongside their husbands. However, most male reformers agreed on the need to keep women from preaching publicly or holding authoritative positions (see Mentzer), and thus attempts such as Marie Dentière's were doomed to fail. In 1539, Dentière had addressed an "epistre tresutile" ("*very useful epistle*") to Marguerite de Navarre, in which she claimed that women were entitled to interpret scripture and had the obligation to preach, at least to one another.[11] Read as an attack on the current leadership in Geneva (and rightly so), the pamphlet was immediately seized by the council of the city of Geneva.

A handful of women were able to take part in public life as supporters of the reform and even to play key roles in its major events. Although she remained outwardly obedient to Catholicism, Marguerite de Navarre supported attempts to reform the church. Between 1521 and 1524 she corresponded with the bishop of Meaux, Guillaume Briçonnet, who was also the leader of the *évangéliques.* Even after the Placards affair in 1535, when posters attacking the Catholic dogma of transubstantiation appeared in major cities in France as well as on the door of Francis I's bedchamber, causing the king to change his attitude toward the reformers, she continued to offer protection to evangelical reformers (Clément Marot, Jacques Lefèvre d'Étaples, Gérard Roussel) and remained highly committed to their cause. In her works, Marguerite de Navarre addressed various controversial religious matters (grace, faith, and free will). When reprinted in 1533 along with her *Dialogue en forme de vision nocturne* ("Dialogue in the Form of a Nocturnal Vision"), her *Miroir de l'âme pécheresse* ("Mirror of the Sinful Soul") was censured by the Sorbonne theologians before her brother, King Francis I, intervened. Éléonore de Roye intervened on two occasions and used her influence to free her husband, the noted Huguenot activist Louis de Bourbon, prince of Condé. Jeanne d'Albret, queen of

Navarre, established Calvinism in her lands but always insisted on religious tolerance. Other women won fame as martyrs of their faith.[12] Not only did Protestantism advance new spiritual values, it brought women a new domestic ethic. The new theology promoted mutuality as the main component of marriage, but historians differ about whether it fostered this or created additional constraints in the family.[13]

Meanwhile, the Catholic reform movement established new female orders to address special needs.[14] Most of these were dedicated to the education of young women outside convent walls. Especially notable are the Ursulines, founded in Brescia in the 1530s by Angela Merici; the Compagnie de Marie-Notre-Dame, founded in 1607 by Jeanne de Lestonnac (Michel de Montaigne's niece); the Visitandines, established in 1610 by François de Sales and Jeanne-Françoise de Chantal; and the Filles de la Charité, created in 1633 by Vincent de Paul and Louise de Marillac. The founding of such orders provided a great opportunity for women to experience new forms of spirituality as well as an active religious life in the community, but such autonomy of action came to an end when the Council of Trent imposed enclosure of all women religious (see Medioli).

In sum, both institutions of Christianity (Protestant and Catholic) provided early modern women opportunities, although brief and limited, to venture into uncharted territory.[15]

Sex Denied

Today, when many students believe in the individual's right to bodily autonomy and the pursuit of sexual pleasure, one may well imagine students' bewilderment at early modern sexual ideals and practices. The religious virtue of chastity that had its roots in the first Christian centuries weighed heavily on the early modern era.[16] Both church and society viewed virginity as the most desirable state. This ideal was presented to women as a means to overcome their allegedly insatiable lust. The Catholic Church held up the exemplar of Mary, the ideal of holy virginity, while condemning Eve as the source of all sexual evil. The story of Eve's eating the forbidden fruit was interpreted as a sexual story, and Eve was viewed as the sexual temptress. It was felt that because innocence was constantly endangered by woman's natural weakness, female agency in both important and unimportant matters should be closely supervised, as evidenced by the myriad prescriptions commonly found in advice literature: how to speak, how to walk, how to dress, how to think, how to be a good wife and mother, how to serve God, and so on.[17]

Daughters were required to remain virgins until they married. In lineage alliances, the virginity of the bride was crucial to ensure the legitimacy of the heir. Virginity was always linked to the concept of honor. A daughter's loss of virginity (whether through rape or seduction) brought shame on the girl and on her family. Idealized constructs of female virtue were promoted through sermons, hagiographic writings, catalogs of famous women worthies, advice literature, and tales of women winning fame for self-sacrifice and self-motivation in defense of chastity (e.g., tales 2 and 10 of the *Heptameron*). Since chastity embodied the ideal of woman, women became the guardians of chastity. Hence women who wrote of erotic love—a topic deemed inappropriate for a woman's speech—typically appealed to an audience of women, reminding them of the vulnerability all women shared and thus cautioning them against quick judgment and blame (e.g., "Helisenne aux lisantes" ["Helisenne to female readers"] in part 1 of Hélisenne de Crenne's *Angoysses douloureuses*; Louise Labé's third elegy, lines 1–8 [*Complete Poetry* 167–71]).

Marriage was viewed by the church as a device to control the irrational force of male sexual desire, although preachers cautioned their parishioners against the sins of the flesh, urging them to practice "chaste marriages," which meant that they should engage in sexual intercourse only on rare occasions. At the beginning of the sixteenth century, the sexual act, even in marriage, was to be joyless, and its performance restricted exclusively to the function of procreation. However, much later sexual activity not solely for the purpose of conception and moderate sexual pleasure came to be permitted in marriage. It was not the sexual act itself that was held sinful but the pleasure derived from it. Other forms of physical enjoyment (eating, dancing) were also condemned, as was any type of amusement that might be conducive to impure thought, like novel reading or theater. Just as damnable was the sensation of desire for a person of the opposite sex, even when unconsummated. For a woman, adultery was a crime severely condemned by the community and sometimes punished by unusual cruelty or even death. The Catholic Church honored widowhood as the state closest to virginity, hence the intense surveillance over widows and the pressure exerted by both church and society urging them to occupy their time in charitable activities or join a convent or religious community.

The Female Author in a Male-Dominated World

In today's world, writing and publishing have become the prerogative of each and every one of us. It is therefore difficult for our students to grasp the social and cultural conditions that surrounded literary production in early modern times or simply what was at stake for a woman to enter the public sphere of print.

Illiteracy remained high in the early modern period (among men as well), although access to learning was facilitated by the advent of printing; the reform movement; and, above all, the humanists who believed that education led to virtue and consequently placed new emphasis on educating both men and women.[18] However, education for women did not become a social reality before the seventeenth century, when female orders dedicated to the teaching of women flourished.[19] The humanists, for the most part, shared the mind-set of their time on gender difference. Skeptical of woman's mental capability, they thought education should serve strictly utilitarian goals and prepare women for the domestic roles they were expected to fill as wives, mothers and providers of moral and religious instruction, and widows.[20] Women were barred from access to universities simply because the learning dispensed in such institutions prepared one for public service, an area that was denied to females. Michel de Montaigne claimed that "la plus utile et honnorable science et occupation à une femme, c'est la science du mesnage" ("the most useful and honorable knowledge and occupation for a woman is the knowledge of housewifery"; "De la vanité" 952). A woman's education was typically limited to reading, writing, and a little arithmetic. Rhetoric, logic, astrology, and theology were judged irrelevant to the identity of womanhood. Few women were taught Latin, and even fewer managed to attain literacy in it. Marguerite de Navarre did not read Latin easily, and she did not know Greek. On the other hand, Antoinette de Loynes and Catherine de Clermont Retz, who were both early initiates in reading Latin, had the ability to converse and entertain a correspondence in Latin. Hélisenne de Crenne gave a translation of Vergil, and Camille de Morel won fame for her Latin eloquence. The reading of Christian writers was advocated in preference to pagan classics, with the exception of Cicero, Seneca, Plutarch, and Xenophon because they offered examples of proper behavior, lessons in the seven virtues, as well as a specific program for training a wife. A common concern was the possible effect of educating women. A woman's learning could interfere with household tasks and distract her from raising her children, and, most disturbing of all, it could alter her view of the world and her place in it. Thus education for women was designed to sustain the patriarchal family structure. As such, it underscored the importance for a woman of being chaste, silent, and obedient, and it aimed at moral improvement and stronger faith.

Women who were born into a wealthy and powerful family usually received a finer education, comparable with that of males of equal social status, and so did those who grew up in a specific cultural environment, such as the printing milieu or an urban community, that was more cosmopolitan and therefore more favorable to the new learning.[21] The cities of Paris, Lyon, and Toulouse were important centers of humanist writing and publishing. Typically the learned woman was one who had received special attention from either her parents or a friend. Camille de Morel's highly learned mother, Antoinette de Loynes, made sure her daughter was taught by the most outstanding tutors of their time: Charles Utenhove and his noted pupil Jean Dorat. Catherine Des Roches was likewise tutored by her mother and the leading humanists of Poitiers. Louise Labé owed to her liberal father, who was a wealthy rope maker, her unusually rich classical education. The gifted linguist and translator Marie de Cotteblanche was taught Italian by her friend and patron Marguerite de Saluces. Marie de Gournay, on the other hand, had to teach herself Latin by comparing Latin texts with their French translations. She was forced to do it secretly when she had a little time to herself, because her mother had great distaste for any kind of formal education for girls besides the womanly arts required to attract suitable husbands.

Among the privileged few who had access to learning and enjoyed free time, a good number wrote, as the listings of female authors in early modern biobibliographical compilations indicate. These women typically wrote for family and friends with no intention of publishing. They circulated their writings in intimate circles. Catherine d'Amboise's devotional works are thought to have been intended as gifts for family members. The prologue of Marguerite de Navarre's *Heptameron* suggests that the collection was intended as a gift for a group of intimate friends at the royal court. In all likelihood, Gabrielle de Coignard began writing after her husband died and with the hope of passing on to her daughters the fruits of her spiritual meditations. Clearly the real challenge for the lettered woman was not the writing itself but making her writing public.[22] Indeed, how was she to legitimize her self-publication to a suspicious audience? How was she to establish herself as a writer in a world dominated by men who were not only writers themselves but also mentors, readers, and critics?[23] And where would she find literary models to make herself intelligible? In brief, what price would she have to pay for transgressing gender boundaries or for just being an exception?

In entering the public arena, women risked social and literary censure. This may be why some works remained unpublished while others appeared pseudonymously or posthumously. In early modern society, female silence was inevitably linked to chastity, open speech to a lack of chastity. Therefore, the female author had to find ways to compromise with interdictions. One way was to construct a persona that earned her the right to publish.[24] Catherine Des Roches's insistence on chastity was an attempt to escape gender constraints and justify herself as a writer. Aware of the social usefulness of humility, the female author generally assumed a feminine posture of humility by reworking to her advantage conventional authorial admissions of self-doubt or inadequacy to cope with the subject matter. Another technique to circumvent social disapproval was the claim that writing was done after all domestic tasks were attended to and with the sole intention of avoiding idleness, which was then thought to be the source of all evil.[25] Once she had constructed an acceptable self-representation, the female author still had to justify her "monstrous nonconformity."[26] By breaking silence and seeking visibility as a writer, she crossed gender boundaries. (In humanist culture, participation in public discourse was the elite male prerogative, and eloquence the male's most praised attribute.) She needed to minimize the uniqueness of her female endeavor and often ended up declining responsibility for it, pretending that it was a parent or a friend who urged her to publish but that she would have been just as content had her work remained unknown.[27] In a world where authority was male, she felt she needed to define herself through her relationship to a male already established in the literary community. Pernette Du Guillet fashioned a persona in dialogue with a male mentor, whereas the Dames Des Roches authorized themselves through the theme of mother-daughter bonding.

Last but not least were the constraints and contradictions associated with writing itself. How could the female author situate herself within a literary-rhetorical framework that was either male authored or had an unmistakably masculine perspective built into it (see Jones, *Currency*)? Furthermore, imitation, which in the humanists' view was an intrinsic and inevitable part of literary production, promoted male solidarity by engaging the male writer to stand in discourse with his spiritual forefathers. Thus male authors could assume their vocation with confidence, placed as they were as legitimate heirs in a long and prestigious line, whereas the female author found herself in isolation.

When dealing with writings by early modern women, the instructor needs to clarify for students the cultural gender constructions (gender expectations and constraints) in effect when these texts were produced along with the discursive framework (predominantly male) from which such women had to speak. Only then will students be able to understand the ways in which sociocultural and literary-rhetorical discourse was used by the early female writer to construct her authorial subjectivity.

The Present Volume

Given the rapidly expanding field of gender and women studies in the early modern period, the present volume responds to the need felt by both teachers and scholars for a critical reappraisal of important issues, as well as tips on how to use current resources and instruction guidance. For teachers planning to incorporate women writers into their courses, it gives background on the lives of French women of the Renaissance and Reformation, shedding light on the historical and cultural contexts in which gender issues ought to be placed, and discusses specific authors and various works and genres practiced by French women writers. It also presents successful teaching experiences in a variety of disciplines, at different levels, and in different contexts.

Part 1 is intended to provide background and information on various contexts, which are appropriate both as introductory readings or subsequent readings in a course on early modern French women. The first essay, by Brigitte Roussel, examines the way Nicole Estienne, the daughter of the reputed French physician Charles Estienne, represents in her *Misères de la femme mariée* gender and domestic relationships, notably patriarchal authority, its use and abuse, and the duties of the wife in the fulfillment of Christian marriage values.[28] The following essay, by Kathleen Wilson-Chevalier, focuses on early modern women's responsibilities as caretakers, educators, patrons, and writers, demonstrating at the same time how sixteenth-century visual art may enhance our understanding of these various roles. The next essay considers the role of religion in early modern women's lives as well as the specificity of their experience of the Reformation. Carrie F. Klaus reveals how Jeanne de Jussie experienced the Reformation from inside the convent of Saint Clare in Geneva and the active part she took as champion of the Catholic faith and bitter opponent of its enemies. Taking Hélisenne de Crenne as a case in point, Diane S. Wood and Laura B. Bergman demonstrate the impact humanism had on women's lives and writings. The last four essays in part 1 examine the challenges faced by women writers and the strategies and techniques they used to negotiate their entry into the world of print. Susan Broomhall studies women's access to paid and professional status in the larger context of gendered labor in the early modern period. François Rigolot discusses the cultural conditions that in the France of the 1550s allowed some women to go into print. In the light of Clément Marot's *blasons*, famous poems by Pierre de Ronsard and Joachim Du Bellay, and Pierre de Bourdeille, seigneur de Brantôme's humorous *Vies des dames galantes,* Dora Polachek invites us to rethink what constitutes desirability in the early modern period in order to show "what women's writing was responding to and against." Finally, Ann Rosalind Jones examines the strategic value Neoplatonism offered women and the way early modern women poets not only in France but also in Italy and Great Britain used Neoplatonic conventions to overcome gender restrictions.

Part 2 focuses on specific authors, the type of works French women of the Renaissance and Reformation produced, and the forms or genres in which they wrote. Two essays focus on Renaissance women's love lyrics. Zeina Hakim determines the specificity of Louise Labé's poetic voice through insight gained from an analysis of the past female exemplars Labé incorporates in her elegies. Danielle Trudeau reassesses Pernette Du Guillet's place in the poetic trends of her day and examines her novel approach to the chanson. Women's contributions to the epistolary form is the subject of Jane Couchman's essay. The next two essays examine the feminine devotional discourse that developed toward the end of the sixteenth century. Carla Zecher, in her essay on the Protestant Georgette de Montenay, and Edith Joyce Benkov, writing on the Catholic Anne de Marquets, pay special attention to the genres and forms (emblems and pasquins) these writers employed to express their faith. Finally, Jean-Philippe Beaulieu suggests exposing students to Marie de Gournay's *Discours sur son livre* as an entryway into her enormous and complex oeuvre.

Part 3 is divided into two sections. The first describes a variety of critical approaches and methodologies that have proved particularly useful in the classroom. As an introduction to Louise Labé's poetic world Leslie Zarker Morgan examines with her students the sociocultural changes that took place in Renaissance Lyon and the vogue of Italianism that marked the period. In reconsidering the *Heptameron* of Marguerite de Navarre, Carla Freccero offers several examples of the kind of reading that is enabled by feminist and queer literary criticism and theory. Nancy Frelick suggests reading Hélisenne de Crenne's *Angoysses douloureuses* with an awareness of "transference," which, in Frelick's view, yields greater insight into the complexities of this text—for example, the contradictory points of view expressed by Hélisenne and the dialogistic role of various intertexts and exempla. Cécile Alduy advocates an interdisciplinary approach in a course on Petrarchan lyrics (Labé, Scève, Ronsard) and examines various discourses that shed light on the social, cultural, and literary codes within which women poets maneuvered. Claude La Charité outlines the specific challenges of teaching early modern women poets, one being the tendency our students have of labeling as "autobiographical" every poem written in the first-person singular. In an attempt to refute such preconceived ideas, he offers a subtle analysis of Marie de Romieu's poetic practice, expanding on the concept of androgynous writing quite common in the Renaissance as demonstrated by the next essay. This is indeed usefully exemplified by Leah Chang, who suggests including men writing as women in a course devoted to Renaissance women writers in order to encourage students to question notions of gender and ideas about the meaning of male and female in Renaissance France.

The second section in part 3 demonstrates the pedagogical benefits of literary rapprochements like teaching an assigned work alongside related works by another author or alongside other works by the same author. Both Anne R. Larsen and Gary Ferguson deem it essential to familiarize their students with the sociohistorical contexts within which early modern women were able to write—contexts that fostered female associations of one form or another where women may have found support and inspiration as well as the convent, the court, and the city. Larsen cites the case of Catherine Des Roches to address the question of influence within Renaissance female communities. When including selected poems by Anne de Marquets in his poetry courses, Ferguson reads Marquets in conjunction with other women who engaged in religious polemic to bring out the similarities and differences in the articulation of their literary voices. Mary McKinley recommends reading side by side Marie Dentière's *Epistle to Marguerite de Navarre* and Marguerite de Navarre's *Heptameron* as a way of considering the significance of the Protestant Reformation for women and the different roles they played in that reform. Colette H. Winn shows how the reading of Gabrielle de Coignard's spiritual sonnets may be enhanced by comparing them with Louise Labé's love sonnets, which students usually enjoy reading. Obviously this comparative approach permits a broader perspective on women's contributions to a specific genre. Finally, Deborah Lesko Baker addresses the common challenge of teaching texts in Middle French. She recommends reading Louise Labé's prose texts—the dedicatory letter to Mademoiselle Clémence de Bourges and *The Debate of Folly and Love*—together and suggests teaching these texts in French and English at the same time to maximize students' understanding and enjoyment.

Part 4 consists of four essays. The first one, by Winn, provides information on editions, translations, groundbreaking studies published since 1980, and various resources for teaching and further study. The second one, by Winn, surveys publishers, special organizations, and conferences devoted to the study of early modern women writers. Next Graziella Postolache and Winn discuss specific Web sites and online resources on early modern women and individual authors. The last essay, by Karen Simroth James and Mary McKinley, "Rare Books and Web Pages," lists the online resources made available as part of *The Renaissance in Print: Sixteenth-Century French Books in the Douglas Gordon Collection* and offers specific suggestions for putting them to use in a variety of class settings.

As demonstrated in this volume, much has been accomplished in the last thirty years, yet much remains to be done. It is to be hoped that this endeavor will encourage future generations of scholars and teachers to engage in the pursuit of retrieving lost or neglected works by women and to shape new questions and methods to pass on what they have learned to their students.

Notes

1. On the question of canon formation, especially in the case of early modern women's writing, see Jones and Vickers.

2. In saying this I do not mean to suggest that those works that have withstood the test of time and are conventionally known as the Renaissance canon should be eliminated from our literary curriculum. One can hardly imagine, for example, courses in humanism in which Marie Le Gendre's moral *discours* would replace Michel de Montaigne's essays or courses on French poetry of the Renaissance in which Pernette Du Guillet's *Rymes* would supplant Maurice Scève's *Delie* or Pierre de Ronsard's *Amours.*

3. On the notion of gender and contemporary attitudes toward gender, see, among others, Maclean; Wiesner, *Women and Gender*.

4. On early modern medical theories concerning women, see Berriot-Salvadore, *Corps*. On the tendency among early modern medical men to use woman's reproductive system as a means of social control, see Dixon.

5. On gender and power, see Davis, "Femme"; Haase-Dubosc and Viennot; as well as Viennot's site, *La France*.

6. On the legal status of married women and widows and for a more nuanced view of widowhood, see Beauvalet-Boutouyrie; Cavallo and Warner; and Winn and Pellegrin.

7. For more on this question, see the section on background studies in Winn, "Resources for Teaching and Further Study," in this volume.

8. For more on pain and death in childbirth, see Shorter, part 2, chapter 5.

9. Rapley's study would be a good starting point on this subject.

10. On the appeal of Calvinism to French noblewomen and the active role women in high places took in the French Reformation, see Bainton ("Role"); and Roelker, "Appeal" and "Role."

11. On Dentière's activism, see Head, "Propagandist"; Skenazi.

12. The French Protestant martyrologist Jean Crespin recounts their stories in his *Histoire des vrays tesmoins/History of True Testimonies*. See Shepardson on the ways in which these images of women martyrs were constructed to fit within the larger ideological framework of the reformed movement.

13. Both Davis (in her essay "City Women and Religious Change" from *Society and Culture* 65–95) and Crété underscore the positive impact Protestantism had for women in the household; Bainton speaks of "a personalization of marriage" ("The Role of Women in the Reformation" 141). In recent years, however, critics have expressed a more nuanced view regarding the changes the reform movement brought about in women's domestic lives. See, more particularly, Mentzer; Roper.

14. For a broad overview of these new religious orders and the question of *clausura*, see Stier and *Les religieuses dans le cloître et dans le monde*.

15. On the ways in which women benefited from the various reform movements, see Head, "The Religion of the Femmelettes."

16. For a broader view on the question of sexuality, see Foucault, *History*, and G. Taylor. On the exaltation of virginity, sexual relations within marriage, and adultery, see Matthews Grieco, "Corps."

17. In upper-level classes, it was not uncommon for a mother to write a book of lessons. Conventional advice typically found in these books could indicate how patriarchal discourse might have been unconsciously internalized and perpetuated. It also provides a good example of the ambiguous position in which the woman writer frequently found herself. Indeed, her maternal role offered the woman an enabling subject position in allowing her the privilege of speaking and writing, but at the same time it posed a serious threat to her agency. On motherhood as a source of female authority, see Lerner, chapter 6. On the contradictions associated

in mothers' advice books with the simultaneous construction and destruction of women's subjectivity, see Wayne.

18. For more on women's education, see the section on background studies in Winn, "Resources for Teaching and Further Study," in this volume.

19. On the teaching religious orders instituted by the Council of Trent and their impact on the instruction of girls, see Wiesner, *Women and Gender* 196–203; and *Les religieuses enseignantes.*

20. On mothers as agents of religious instruction, see Delumeau.

21. Both Marguerite de Navarre and Marie de Romieu had the same preceptor as their brothers.

22. For more on the contexts of female publication, see Broomhall, *Women and the Book Trade*, chapters 3 and 4.

23. Few women in early modern France made a career of writing. After Christine de Pisan, the Dames Des Roches and Marie de Gournay were the only ones, as far as we know, to live by the income of their pen.

24. For more on the strategies used by women to legitimize their self-publications, see Broomhall, *Women and the Book Trade*, chapters 5–7; on prefatory strategies, see Larsen, " 'Un honneste passetems' "; Rigolot and Read; and C. Winn, "Femme écrivain"; on strategies in love lyrics, see Jones, *Currency of Eros.*

25. On the ideological conflict between the distaff, emblem of housewifery, and the pen or the lyre, symbolic of unconventional literary ambitions, see Mathieu-Castellani. For many women, the decision of taking up the life of the intellect had to be postponed until they were freed from family responsibilities and had time to themselves to pursue their literary endeavors. Widowhood offered such opportunity.

26. The expression comes from Jones, *Currency of Eros* 29. In early modern society, the learned woman was commonly viewed as some kind of monster for transgressing expected gender roles, which the following exchange from Catherine Des Roches's *Dialogue between Placide and Severe* shows (Des Roches and Des Roches, *From Mother* 219): "PLACIDE. 'Whether Women seem foolish or wise to you, I think that we should allow them to read, so that the foolish ones can become a bit less foolish, and the wise ones even wiser, thanks to the books which are very necessary for them if only to keep them at home alone where they would remain otherwise idle.' SEVERE. 'O what misfortune it is to see a learned Woman!' PLACIDE. 'Oh? What's that? Please explain.' SEVERE. 'Why, she's a monster!' " (219).

27. This was frequently the case. Georgette de Montenay, for example, published her *Emblemes ou devises chrestiennes* with support and encouragement from Jeanne d'Albret and perhaps even financial assistance. For a more extensive discussion on Renaissance women patronage, see Stephenson, *Power.*

28. Nicole Estienne published under her married name, Mme Liebault.

Part I

Background and Contexts

Brigitte Roussel

Nicole Estienne's *Les misères de la femme mariée* and the Marriage Controversy in the Second Half of the Sixteenth Century

Among the numerous French texts that addressed the question of women's place and role during the sixteenth century, a good number focused on the question of marriage, especially after the 1560s. These endemic polemics surged at crucial moments of women's social history and often developed into literary "quarrels," responding to one another, reviving a literary practice started in the medieval period when Christine de Pisan took on Jean de Meun for his misogynist treatment of women in *The Romance of the Rose.*

A new valuation of marriage took place in Renaissance Europe, as Erasmian humanists, who wished to bring about new institutions, insisted that the marriage-family structure ought to prevail (Margolin 181). By limiting women's roles to the domestic sphere, these moralists, jurists, and theologians perpetuated fundamental inequalities between the sexes. They had recourse to what they defined as the moral vocation of women to ensure a massive adhesion to their restructuring of this early modern society. They prescribed that wives ought to have qualities such as chastity, humility, modesty, perseverance, temperance, piousness, humanity, courtesy, courage, equity, prudence, and knowledge. Although these virtues had always been deemed desirable in both men and women, the humanist writers of the sixteenth century focused their concerted efforts on developing them among women. The reformers especially valued a good housekeeper, using sacred texts to justify these requirements (Margolin 395–96). Luther emphasized women's mastery of domestic qualities, asserting that outside the domestic realm they had little to offer. Men, on the other hand, were made for conducting wars, creating policies, and enforcing authority (Albistur and Armogathe, *Histoire* 118–19; Ridé 229–32). The sixteenth century provided rational arguments to promote this new ideology: God's law and the guarantee of social stability.

Nicole Estienne, also known as Olympe following the moniker accorded her by Jacques Grévin in his 1560 *L'Olimpe* (Yandell, "Raconter" 5, 51) was the daughter of the French physician Charles Estienne and granddaughter of the renowned printer Henri Estienne and stands out as a writer who defended women's intellectual equality with men and who wrote about the dire hardships that befell her fellow women in marriage.[1] She was considered highly accomplished and gained an honorable reputation among her contemporaries (Lavaud 350–51). The works attributed to her, written under her married name, Mme Liebault (Yandell, "Raconter" 51), include *Stanzes*, which exists in manuscript form and constitutes a response to the *Stances du marriage*, by Philippe Desportes; *Le mépris d'Amour*; and the prose *Apologie ou défense pour les femmes contre ceux qui les meprisent*. None of these works seem to have been published, and no manuscripts of the last two have been found (Zinguer 49).

Les misères de la femme mariée, a series of *stances* distinct from those mentioned above and written later, was published in Paris by Pierre Mesnier after it was prepared for publication by Claude Le Villain. The exact date of its first appearance is not known but is thought to be 1587, the year Mesnier established himself as a printer at the address posted on the manuscript.

Desportes's *Stances* offers a mundane literary satire of marriage similar to other misogamist pieces that were read in the salon of Mme de Retz (Berriot-Salvadore, *Femmes dans la société* 47–48; Sabatier 242–43). Nonetheless, it provoked a number of literary retorts by persons who considered marriage a sacred institution. Nicole Estienne's response addressed each *stance* one by one in tight arguments to show that, contrary to Desportes's portrayal, marriage was a sound and desirable situation. It is surmised that Nicole Estienne's response was an early work; although the date is not known, it was probably written around 1573 (Lavaud 346).

On the other hand, *Les misères de la femme mariée* seems to contradict its author's previous assertions, since it presents a dark, unhappy tableau of married women's lives. This work, compared with Nicole Estienne's response to Desportes, is not so much an exercise in virtuosity in the vein of the rhetorical art of persuasion so enjoyed by salon writers in the Renaissance; instead, it presents a realistic description of women's entrapment in marriage and its inescapable consequences. However, in both her sets of *stances*, Nicole Estienne highlights the sweet disposition, compassion, and resourcefulness of women.

Composed of thirty-five six-line stanzas in alexandrine verse, the *Misères* is organized in six distinct parts to systematically unveil the deliberate pattern of social corruption of an institution that ought to preserve the natural relationship between men and women. Instead of underscoring her previous defense of marriage, Estienne invites her readers to witness the consequences of the absolute domination of husbands over their wives, not only when that domination is obtained by force but also when it is secured by appealing to women's sense of moral obligation. In stanzas 1 through 5, the main themes of the poem are introduced—the torments, woes, punishment, and inequality endured by married women as payment for their sweet, loyal, faithful, and loving disposition. Stanzas 6 through 12 portray courtship as a calculated deceit to catch young women like birds and cage them. In stanzas 13 through 18, the author's denunciation of marriages contracted for property and lineage points to a situation where many young women married older men who were free to abuse them sexually, physically, and mentally. In stanzas 19 through 22, an ideal husband is imagined as educated, discreet, and reasonable; as naturally inclined to look for similar qualities in a wife; and even as thankful to get such a graceful companion. But reality, the book asserts, makes this occurrence a rare find. Stanzas 23 through 31 describe the hopeless situations in which women fall, whether they marry a young, handsome man or a rich or a poor one; no matter how hard a wife works at making her husband comfortable and happy, he will cheat on her, be jealous and treat her harshly, or even glorify himself as the breadwinner and act with a miserly disposition toward her. Stanzas 32 to 35 depict wives as hopelessly miserable; no matter from which angle their condition is considered, they are subject to the whims of their ruthless husbands, since men are free to create unjust laws or to break existing ones. Thus a married woman's only way out might be death. The sad situation of pregnant women and the dangers of childbirth do not seem to bring a lull in the torment a wife endures. The *Misères* ends with a short address to the Muses who were invoked at the beginning. Estienne solicits them like any other poet of the period but uses them here as an embedded female presence who witnesses what plagues her real-life sisters (Yandell, "Raconter" 53). Identifying the carefully crafted structure of the text enables readers to detect an overlap between three literary genres: the poetic, with the voice of the persona sustaining a convincing tone during the long address to prestigious figures; the dramatic, with the image of the sun lifting the curtain of the night in the second stanza used as if to position the readers in front of a stage for a visual representation that will shed light on a variety of marital scenes; and the narrative, with the unfolding of tales that highlight the scandalous realities of married women's daily lot.

Because the *Misères* focuses on women's sad fate by listing a host of woes, standing in stark contrast to the first series of Estienne's *Stances*, critics were not sure what to make of her endeavor in this poem. Some were puzzled by this spirited and realistic account of married life, so they concluded that Estienne changed her mind because she was unhappy with her own husband, regretting not marrying the poet who courted her in her youth and gave her the name Olympe in his laudatory verse. Albert-Marie Schmidt, for instance, drew biographical conclusions that were not matched by any findings (Yandell, "Raconter" 52). Thus critics, such as Régine Reynolds-Cornell, in "*Les misères de la femme mariée*: Another Look at Nicole Liebault and a Few Questions about the Woes of the Married Woman," speculated on whether there was any possibility of an autobiographical account of Estienne's life in the *Misères* and examined a host of fascinating archival documents to determine what could be surmised in the "rapprochement" between the two. Yet others found her changed rhetoric not revolutionary enough because, by creating concise stanzas within the constraints of the genre, she merely described women's fate in marriage but did not promote an explicit political platform for change (Berriot-Salvadore, *Femmes dans la société* 463; Jordan 280–81).

However, since documents concerning Estienne's life are scant and since literature was almost the only avenue of public expression for women of the period who wanted to draw attention to political, social, cultural, or judicial issues, scholars returned to the *Misères* and other contemporary texts in the same vein to scrutinize their rhetorical devices in order to see whether, by comparison, the *Misères* could reveal more subtle and fruitful aspects of the author's views that had not yet been discovered.

Because the Renaissance inherited a satirical poetry both misogamist and misogynist that was enriched by the tradition of the legal debate, literary quarrels reproduced a well-established structure for codified court games in which virtuosity was often the main objective, although a few such texts by men delivered a sincere message in favor of the "sacred nature" of marriage. By the second half of the sixteenth century, women writers such as Estienne, aware of the enormous impact of the new social order, entered the literary contests on the topic of marriage and chose *stances* as their medium to evoke married women's woes. Jacques Scherer defined *stances* as a certain number of lines containing a particular theme and arranged in a particular manner throughout a poem. In the theater, *stances* present themselves as a versified monologue marked by a particular rhythm. The term comes from the Italian *stanza*, which means "dwelling," because there needs to be a completed thought and a complete rest or stop at the end of each stanza. In serious and spiritual topics, *stances* are the equivalent of verse in songs and stanzas in odes (Scherer, app. 1). Although *stances* had long existed, they first became extensively used in literature written in French during the second half of the sixteenth century, and they abounded during the seventeenth (Larousse 1053). Thus through a medium newly experienced and in exchange with others around her who used *stances*, Estienne chose to express her voice and to discuss a topic that solicited her utmost attention. Her exploration is analogous to that of Louise Labé, who used the sonnet, still a new form in the 1550s, to express a major concern of Renaissance women—the intellectual pleasure of experimenting with literary creation. Later, when Estienne wrote, the focus of women's writing was inequality in marriage (Berriot-Salvadore, *Femmes dans la société* 455).

It is significant that Estienne chose a medium of expression that, by definition, overlaps the poetic voice, narrative sequence, and dramatic crescendos so she could present a provocative account of married women's lives. She held her own in her response to Desportes. But she did not stop there: by writing the *Misères*, she went further, subverting the rules of the game by commenting on the reality of marriage, not on its principles. Women were truly burdened by huge duties and suffered a high death rate (Hufton, "Women" 26–30). Therefore, instead of merely responding to Desportes, Estienne used moral arguments and reason to show that in daily life marriage was a torment for women when it ought to have been blissful, since it was created by God. It was to be a "sacrée alliance" ("sacred alliance") filled with pleasure, grace, and sweetness. There is no trace of Eve's original sin in Estienne's works. Equality between man and woman is a natural given. If marriage turned into a torment, the fault was that of "l'homme audacieux" ("the audacious man") who changed "tes douces loix en dure tyrannie" ("your fair laws in harsh tyranny"; 33).[2] Following in the footsteps of Marguerite de Navarre (Febvre 271–73, 292–97) and the Dames Des Roches, Estienne unmasks the lure of courtly codes that allowed men to prey on women and encouraged families to entice women into marriage to satisfy familial dynastic ambitions and greed because, as Évelyne Berriot-Salvadore has shown, "to plan a marriage / one thinks only of property and lineage" ("pour faire un mariage / On songe seulement aux biens et au lignage"; Estienne 35, qtd. in "Évocation" 216). Madeleine Lazard, in *Images littéraires de la femme à la Renaissance* (129), demonstrates that Estienne and the Dames Des Roches use similar arguments to express their discontent at men's tyrannical laws. When she is married, woman becomes a prisoner of domestic chores, leading a life of sacrifice: "La femme prend le soin d'apprester les viandes / Qui au goust du vieillard seront les plus friandes, / Sans prendre aucun repos ny la nuict ny le jour" ("The wife carefully prepares the morsels / So as to please the old man's palate, / Without ever taking a rest at night or during the day"; 36). To show women's complete lack of freedom in marriage, Estienne describes their forced submission to the will of their husbands by alluding to the physical violence that must have prevailed: "Rien de plus misérable, et de plus tourmenté, / Que la femme subjette à ces hommes iniques, / Qui despourvueuz d'amour, par leurs loix tiraniques / Se font maistres du corps, et de la volonté" ("Nothing more miserable, and more tormented, / Than woman subjected to these unfair men, / Who, incapable of love, with their tyrannical laws / make themselves masters of their wife's body and mind"; 32). This submission was also sexual, considering "how much the young woman / Endures a torment to both body and soul / Subjected to an old man filled with cruelty / Fulfilling his lust at leisure with such a young thing" ("combien la jeune femme / Endure de tourment, et au corps et à l'âme / Subjette à un vieillard remply de cruauté / Qui jouit à son gré d'une jeunesse telle"; 35). Estienne uses the repetitive structure of the genre of the stance to convey the circularity, continuity, and infernal cycle that truly imprisoned wives in an inescapable way as long as the harsh laws of men were to prevail. Cathy Yandell's "Raconter le temps," an insightful study of time and repetition in the *Misères*, highlights Estienne's treatment of the theme of endless suffering and utter circularity of married women's daily lives. By pretending to imitate the traditional masculine lyrical voice expressing undying love and intense suffering to a distant muse, Estienne enacts a deliberate parody of that voice and a legitimization of real women's voices. She highlights this idea in a few concise statements: "Les travaux continus, et le cruel martyre, / Qui sans fin nous tallonne en ce joug nuptial" ("The continuous chores, and the cruel suffering, / Which pile up on us ceaselessly under this marital yoke"; 32); "Et un seul petit mot promis à la légère / Nous fait vivre à jamais en peine et en misère / En chagrin et douleur par un tard repentir" ("And because of one single little promise carelessly uttered / We are to forever live in grief and misery"; 34).

Thus, by shifting from her first *stances* in favor of marriage to a set of *stances* showing the woes it created for women, Estienne unveils the paradox between the principle of marriage and the reality of it, which points to the fact that she might have been in favor of reforming the institution rather than turning against it. By alternating her denunciation of inequality with suggestions for improvement, she uses judicial-legal terminology throughout the *Misères* to substantiate her position. She shows that men broke God's will and took over the charge of making laws guaranteeing their own freedom while taking away woman's natural freedom. The stanzas are replete with phrases such as "femme subjette," "hommes iniques," "loix tiraniques" ("subjected wives," "unfair men," "tyrannical laws"; 32). Estienne emphasizes men's subversion of God's law by addressing God directly: "tes douces loix en dure tyrannie" ("your fair laws in harsh tyranny"; 33). She describes the wedding day as "desguisé de fraude et tromperie" ("disguised with fraud and deceit"; 34) and the epoch as "ce temps corrompu" ("this corrupted time"; 37), where man is "corruptible" ("corruptible"; 37). Her use of judiciary terminology in the *Misères* is not just a convention of the medieval debate. It becomes an opportunity for Estienne to comment on the new social order that altered the legal status of married women. Dorothea Nolde explains that laws had changed over the sixteenth century as the humanist machinery not only redefined woman's role within marriage but enacted unjust and inequitable laws. Estienne depicts married life as a formidable power relationship of which violence was an essential characteristic. Wives were supposed to submit to their husbands in all spheres of life, including sexually, and husbands could chastise their wives physically, while the reverse was not permitted. Any woman brought to trial for having disobeyed or used violence as a counterpower against her husband was accused on two counts: for violating the law (especially if she committed murder) and for transgressing the role of a wife submitted to her husband's authority. But, even more pernicious, as Dorothea Nolde points out, the key factor in the success of this new repression was not so much force as it was the willing submission of the wife. Theologians and moralists stressed the idea that the wife's consent was the foundation of the marital relationship.

Nicole Estienne thus uses the concept of "natural law" to illustrate that women deserve to be equal companions in marriage (Jordan 273): "Tu luy donnais la femme en beautés excellentes / Pour fidèle compagne et non comme servante, / Enchargeant à tous deux un amour mutuel" ("You gave him [man] an exquisitely beautiful woman / To be his faithful companion and not his servant, / Charging them both with mutual love"; 33); "quelque femme gentille, / Sage, de rare esprit et de bon jugement" ("some kind woman, / Wise, with exceptional mind and good judgment"; 39). As Yandell shows, Estienne provides a valuation of the moral qualities that women display but that are normally not appreciated. This role reversal displays women's courage and resourcefulness and highlights men's lack of consideration, thus providing an effective strategy to empower women (57). Having validated her point, Estienne can now offer a real suggestion, based on reason, for improving how marriages are entered into: "Il serait donc besoin de grande prevoyance / Ainsi que faire accord d'une telle importance, / Qui ne peut seulement que par mort prendre fin" ("It would therefore be necessary to plan / As well as get the parties to agree for such important choice, / Which can only end when death strikes"; 37). Passion did not motivate Estienne's desire for change. Many treatises of the period warned young women against entering a marriage based on passion, arguing that doing so did not guarantee a successful marriage. But neither did forced and arranged marriages guarantee success. Estienne advocated mutual respect and support, shared intellect, and social graciousness—a major change in cultural attitudes. Possibly for her, this change was an important aspect of promoting other changes, such as in the laws.

By contrasting the natural law that ought to prevail between husband and wife with the unnatural laws created by men, she shows that the situation of married women was cultural and not natural and was, therefore, changeable. Her text shows a strong desire to work within the institution of marriage to improve women's lot, to move toward a more equitable sharing of marital duties, and to promote a genuine respect for women. Interestingly, the editor of the *Misères*, Claude Le Villain, dedicated the book to a nun in Rouen, praising her for choosing, in accordance with the teachings of God and Saint Paul, a life of contemplation over an active one and for taking the right path despite the difficulty of sustaining a life of celibacy based on prayer, fasting, and solitude. In this light, because social expectations of the time did not leave respectable alternatives for women other than marriage or convent life, the choice of Catherine Des Roches to remain single and stay close to her mother, herself a widow, a closeness that allowed the women to protect each other's freedom, represents an interesting break from the social mold.

Les misères de la femme mariée can be considered not only a three-pronged "spirited indictment of *arranged* marriages, of the *institution of marriage*, and of *men* as the authors and the beneficiary of its laws" to denounce a "hierarchical system of socio-economic oppression of which women are the victims" (Reynolds-Cornell 37). It can also be considered Nicole Estienne's appropriation of a three-pronged medium to depict marital issues of violence, injustice, and domination: stances in poetry form to provide the voice, a narrative to tell the story, and the theater to reverse the role play.

Notes

1. Nicole Estienne published under her married name, Mme Liebault.

2. Citations to the *Misères* are from Zinguer's edition. All translations in English are mine.

Kathleen Wilson-Chevalier

Picturing Great Ladies of the Renaissance Who Helped Pave the Literary Way

In our gender studies–inflected age, prerevolutionary France appears tainted by the infamous Salic law, fabricated in the waning Middle Ages to prevent women from ascending to the throne. Imagery from the late fifteenth to the late sixteenth century, however, opens a series of windows onto the regents, queens, royal mistresses, and great ladies who attained exceptionally high political and cultural visibility during the Renaissance and Reformation age. Unique depictions created for traditional surfaces such as canvas, fresco, stained glass, vellum, and so on (in churches, castles, manuscripts, etc.), eventually flanked by multiple reproductions from proliferating printing presses, provide ample evidence—twentieth-century claims to the contrary notwithstanding—that this was an exceptional age for the then oft-decried "weaker sex." The visual offers a fecund means of envisioning the passage from "the exceptional woman" to "the learned woman" (Rang); for understanding how princesses and aristocratic ladies, a number of whom were writers themselves, opened the road for women from lower rungs of the social ladder who were then engaged in forging their literary sense of self.

Women in High Places and Their Politico-Cultural Roles

Saints and Sibyls

The theme of Saint Anne educating the Virgin is emblematic of the early age of Renaissance humanism, when the church was still one (Sheingorn; Orth, "Madame Sainte Anne"). Power and intellectual pursuits were increasingly complementary; households were being intellectualized; and amid the ruling elites, education was made a priority even for girls (MacDonald). Although they were not the sole tutors of their progeny, princesses and great ladies occupied a privileged place in the transmission of knowledge, not only down bloodline generations but also out into the world beyond. The library constituted by Queen Charlotte of Savoy (Legaré), who is but one early example of a large contingent of upper-class bibliophiles (Beaune and Lequain), draws attention to the ties between culture and politics. The queen's books functioned as tools for shaping the fine mind of her daughter Anne of France, named regent for her underage brother King Charles VIII on their father's death in 1483. Anne, and in her wake Anne of Brittany and Louise of Savoy, the other two most powerful female political figures of the first phase of the French Renaissance (Matarasso; Tolley), laid some of the bricks that turned the royal house into the "supreme academy . . . of the realm" (MacDonald 293). Homonyms or not, all three bowed to Saint Anne.

Anne of France, who owed her name to this patron saint of fertility and education (L'Estrange, "Sainte Anne"), identified with Saint Anne for as long as she lived (fig. 1). In keeping with the pattern of intergenerational book giving that tended to mark the rite of passage of youthful elite maidens into their virtually inevitable political marriages, Anne had received from her learned mother an abundantly illustrated book of hours (Pierpont Morgan Lib. MS 677). As the years passed, the real Anne morphed into the imaginary leader of pious and forthright ladies projected on folio 272v. Once a key political protagonist of the realm, she in turn mentored the major French-speaking female political figures of the dawning age: Margaret of Austria, future regent of the Netherlands; Anne of Brittany, twice queen of France; Louise of Savoy, ever-present adviser to her son, King Francis I, and officially twice regent of the realm; and Diane of Poitiers, mistress and political protagonist during the reign of the next king, Henry II.

Although programmed to become a governor of ladies, Anne of France proactively crossed gender boundaries and governed men too. So when

Figure 1. Jean Hey, *St. Anne Presenting Anne of France and Her Daughter Susanne de Bourbon*, c. 1497, right wing of the Moulins Triptych, Moulins, Cathedral of Notre-Dame (© F. Buffard)

the time came to mark her own daughter Suzanne's passage into marriage, this champion tennis player, capable of defeating her major male political peers on the court (Wilson-Chevalier, "Art Patronage"), appropriated the secular medieval genre of educational treatises, formerly a preserve of male authors (De Gendt), to produce a text of her own—the *Enseignements.* This vernacular courtesy book, which Anne addressed to her daughter by name, eventually found its way into print (Anne, Enseignements [2006]), with the consent of the mother-daughter pair (presented together by Saint

Anne in fig. 1). In the upper echelons of society, private and public spheres were inextricably intertwined.

Anne of Brittany, credited with having magnified the presence of women at court, owed her name to and modeled her pious persona on the very same Saint Anne (L'Estrange,"Mécénat"). When Jean Bourdichon depicted the Breton's patron saint in her luxurious *Large Book of Hours* (which Louis XIV was still proud to own), the artist spotlighted close intellectual contact between the generations for this strong and finely educated duchess-queen (fig. 2). In other volumes of Anne's huge library (1,300–1,500 books), which sought to rival that of a king (Thibault), her male literary suitors were bent on lending a gender slant to their production in hope of pleasing the queen (Brown, "Mécénat"). When, for instance, the anonymous French translator of Giovanni Boccaccio's *De claris mulieribus* (*On Famous Women*) dedicated his text to Anne, it appeared with a recurring woodcut intentionally conflating her with a selection of Boccaccio's protagonists: Semiramis, Juno, and Cleopatra, to name but three (see Boccaccio, *Livre*). The ambitious Parisian printer Antoine Vérard, always attentive to the desires of his prospective patrons, offered Anne a superior vellum volume that included Christine de Pisan's *Treasure of the City of Ladies*, and his dedicatory illumination pictured the queen. Around 1506, Antoine Dufour had surely assimilated Christine de Pisan's lesson when he too rewrote Boccaccio's text to cater to Anne. And was it by chance that his *Vies des femmes célèbres* (Cassagnes-Brouquet; Szkilnik) culminated with a miniature of the militant Joan of Arc, the final heroine of Christine de Pisan's life? Remarkably, Jean Marot, father of the renowned poet Clément, translated the epistles of Saint Jerome—a female favorite, for Jerome had energetically furthered the education of the women in his circle—and posthumously dedicated them to Queen Anne. Three surviving primers bear witness to the close eye Anne had kept on her children's education (Wieck); and at such a late date, Marot could only have been targeting her elder daughter Claude, by then another pious and learned queen of France and the sovereign duchess of Brittany in her mother's stead.

The tragically short-lived (because highly fertile) Queen Claude had inherited six tapestries woven for her mother after Christine de Pisan's *Book of the City of Ladies* (Bell). Hence it was under their aegis, and with her mother's fine library at hand, that Claude in turn kept a court of educated women alive. In the daughter's entourage, however, learned great ladies were treading in Anne of France's footsteps and donning their plumes. The poetess and bibliophile Anne of Graville, like Christine de Pisan and

Figure 2. Jean Bourdichon, *St. Anne Teaching the Virgin to Read*, c. 1505, from the *Grandes Heures d'Anne de Bretagne*, Paris, Bibliothèque Nationale de France, ms. Latin 9474, f° 197v (© BNF)

Antoine Dufour before her, took up the task of recomposing earlier texts written by men: Boccaccio's *Theseida* and Alain Chartier's *La belle dame sans mercy.* On the exquisite dedicatory page adorning Paris, Bibliothèque de l'Arsenal manuscript 5116 (fig. 3), Anne staged herself gifting the volume to Queen Claude, enthroned above ladies-in-waiting caught in animated conversation—literary conversation, I presume. Within the book held forth, Chartier's merciless lady had transmuted into a woman intent on reconfiguring her lover, who, in the image of Baldassare Castiglione's well-bred gentleman, knew how to respect women (C. Müller). This preoccupation with culture as a civilizing tool would dutifully be transmitted down both Queen Claude and Anne of Graville's dynastic lines. The family library inherited by the kneeling author passed into the hands of her son-in-law, Claude d'Urfé, then on to his grandson Honoré d'Urfé, author of the famed *Astrée.*

As Graville's manuscript was being produced, the well-read Claude, whose progeny included both the future king Henry II and the future major literary patron Margaret of France, Duchess of Savoy, found herself reigning alongside particularly formidable great ladies of rank. The mother of Claude's husband, King Francis I, was the bibliophile Louise of Savoy (Orth, "Louise de Savoie"; M. B. Winn), so well groomed at Amboise by her aunt, Anne of France, that she was quickly appointed regent by her trusting son. Claude's sister-in-law, the third member of the Angoulême "royal trinity," was none other than Marguerite de Navarre, another of Anne of Graville's friends, destined to become a shining star of the sixteenth-century literary scene.

Five years after Claude's death at age twenty-four, the political career of Francis's precious mother-sister team reached its peak: Louise and Marguerite negotiated the Ladies' Peace with Margaret of Austria, who, like Louise, was groomed by the savvy Anne of France. The Hapsburg Margaret had evolved into a highly skillful regent, too, but she was charged with governing the Netherlands in the name of her nephew—Francis I's most tenacious enemy—the Holy Roman Emperor Charles V. In an age when the political rivalry of nations in the making was being played out on battlefields and in the cultural realm alike, powerful women were simultaneously active on both of these planes.

Margaret of Austria was another important bibliophile, a composer of music, and one of the most important female patrons of the age (see the items in Eichberger's exhibition catalog). Over the last decade and a half of her life, she devoted much effort to erecting the church of Brou as a

Figure 3. *Anne of Graville Presenting Her Text to Queen Claude de France*, c. 1520–21, manuscript illumination, from the *Roman de Palamon et Arcita*, Paris, Bibliothèque de l'Arsenal, ms. 5116, f° 1v (© BNF)

Figure 4. Workshop of Louis van Beghem, *Sibyl* from the Tomb of Philibert of Savoy, before 1522, Brou, Church of St. Nicholas of Tolentino (Bourg-en-Bresse) (photo Kathleen Wilson-Chevalier)

mausoleum for herself, her last husband (Louise of Savoy's brother), and her mother-in-law (Louise's own mother), in view of consolidating the hostile Hapsburg imperial presence in Louise's native Savoy. At Margaret's behest, Flemish artists produced a masterpiece series of sibyls to adorn the niches encircling her deceased husband Philibert's centrally situated tomb (fig. 4). Christine de Pisan had made these female counterparts of the Old Testament prophets and New Testament apostles the subject of the first chapter of the second part of her seminal *Book of the City of Ladies*, owned by Margaret and nearly all her female peers. It hence comes as no surprise that the Brou sibyls, in the image of Christine's, form a cohort of not twelve but ten. Once again, this referential path had already been trodden by the mentor Anne of France (Lequain). When seeking protection for his *Louanges*, Jacques de Brézé had sensed that by dubbing Anne "the wisest sibyl," he would please the powerful regent of the realm. Demoted when her brother King Charles VIII took the reins of power from her hands,

Figure 5. *Symphorien Champier Presenting His* Nef des dames vertueuses *to Anne of France*, 1503, dedicatory page, Paris, Bibliothèque Nationale de France, Vèlins 1972 (Lyon, Jacques Arnollet)(© BNF)

Anne rebounded by sidestepping into her position as Duchess of Bourbon. In 1503, it was in Lyon, the capital of the Bourbon duchy, that Symphorien Champier published his *Nef des dames vertueuses.* Champier had himself shown on the dedicatory page in the traditionally humble manner offering his volume to Anne (fig. 5). The proffered *Nef* may or may not be open to chapter 3, with its text on the sibyls written by Anne's poet-officer Jean Robertet. Yet to be sure, two years later Benoît Montenat composed a "treatise on the conformity of the prophets and sibyls with the twelve articles of faith" at the dowager duchess Anne's request.

With Francis I's accession to the throne in 1515, Louise of Savoy emerged victorious from the clash that had involved most of these high-profile princesses over who would (and could) conceive the next Salic-law king. Her prize was a political seat on her son's privy council. The following year, Symphorien Champier undertook a side step of his own when he had his *Great Chronicles of Savoy* printed in the capital city of Paris rather than the more peripheral Lyon. As evidence that supreme power had now changed hands, Champier's dedicatory page now showed him ostensibly offering his luxury vellum volume (Bibliothèque Nationale de France, Ms Vélins 1173) to the new Queen Mother, bypassing in a most unprecedented manner the twenty-two-year-old king seated to her right. As the Renaissance marched forth, politico-cultural battles were undermining the feudal system of power, as they were being hiked up a notch to a more broadly based geopolitical plane. All the while, women held firm on the front line.

But how exactly did the content of elitist libraries filter down to the population residing outside castle walls? As Margaret of Austria was installing magnificently carved sibyls in the sanctuary of the Hapsburg-sponsored church of Brou, Louise of Savoy was patronizing the *Mystery of the Sibyls* in the streets of the nearby Valois realm (Evain). Apparently the first French play dedicated to a woman, it was also the first and only religious play in which these pagan figures commanded center stage on urban scaffolds. The fame of the sibyls, credited with having foreseen practically every minute detail of the coming of Christ, was exceptionally widespread. Moreover, Marsilio Ficino, whose Neoplatonic thought system was tingeing the intellectual debates of both sexes, had cited these ancient heroines among the classical stepping stones that lined his upward-rising syncretic Christian worldview. By the mid–sixteenth century, when the French Pléiade poets were making themselves heard, the sibylline gift of prophecy and the frenzy of poetic inspiration had converged (Joukovsky-Micha).

Women in High Places Scaling the New Olympus

Louise of Savoy is regularly cited for having favored her son-cum-king. Yet the fact that she employed her manuscript illuminator, Robinet Testart, to illustrate the *Louange du muliebre et femynin sexe* (*Dialogue in Praise of the Female Sex*), destined for her daughter, Marguerite, at the moment of Marguerite's engagement to the Duke of Alençon in 1509, is a sign that this tale can also be told with a different slant. Before this first major turning point in the young princess's trajectory, Marguerite had frequented an empowering series of texts and images in her mother's cherished library (Orth, "Manuscrits"). There, in particular, lay a translation of Ovid's *Epistres d'Ovide*, which the same Testart had adorned for Louise around the turn of the century. Childhood visions of its alignment of famous ancient ladies engaged in epistolary activities—among whom Penelope, shown writing at a window sporting Louise of Savoy's coat of arms (fig. 6)—surely encouraged Marguerite to feel authorized to pick up the quill.

Today, Marguerite de Navarre's literary persona looms large among French Renaissance authors, male and female alike. The time she expended on writing, as well as on her many political and humanist activities, which included proactive support for university learning (Stephenson, "'La protection'"; Reid 2: 516–19), seems to have held her engagement with pictorial artists in check. In the realm of books, Marguerite prioritized content over decoration, beyond the shadow of a doubt. Hence her decision to invest both funds and energy on the embellishment of a text of her own, *La coche*, in which an all-female cast grapples with the theme of love, strikes the historian all the more. Written and produced at a moment of crisis, 1541–42, the manuscript edition currently at Chantilly sports a dedicatory image in which Marguerite tenders her volume to her brother's mistress Anne de Pisseleu, the powerful Duchess of Étampes (fig. 7). In sharp contrast to the hierarchical inflection of the dedicatory illumination offered by Anne of Graville to Queen Claude, a sense of equality informs Marguerite's impressive courtly vision of female writer and female recipient, notable dissimilarities between the two ladies aside. Moreover, the itinerary of this text marks a watershed. After the initial manuscript version(s), *La coche* was inserted into the *Marguerites de la Marguerite des princesses* toward the end of the 1540s; accompanied by more modern woodcut illustrations (fig. 8), it embarked on a second, more communal life in print.

By the time Jean de Tournes published this two-volume selection of Marguerite's texts, women at court were more and more often being equated with the Muses, as evidenced by a print (one of three and related to Francesco Primaticcio's frescoes) for the vault of the Gallery of Ulysses

Figure 6. Robinet Testart, *Penelope Writing an Epistle to Ulysses*, c. 1500, from the *Epistres d'Ovide*, Paris, Bibliothèque Nationale de France, ms. Fr. 875, f° 1 (© BNF)

Figure 7. Master of François de Rohan, *The Queen of Navarre Offering* La coche *to the Duchess of Étampes*, 1541–42, Chantilly, Musée Condé, ms. 522, dedicatory page (© Réunion des Musées Nationaux/Art Resources, NY Photo René-Gabriel Ojéda)

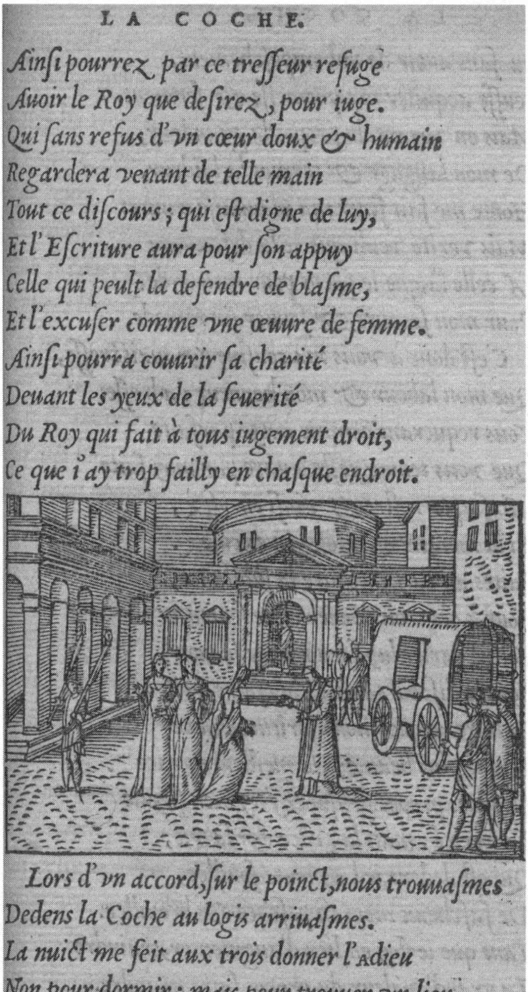

LA COCHE.

Ainſi pourrez par ce treſſeur refuge
Auoir le Roy que deſirez, pour iuge.
Qui ſans refus d'vn cœur doux & humain
Regardera venant de telle main
Tout ce diſcours; qui eſt digne de luy,
Et l'Eſcriture aura pour ſon appuy
Celle qui peult la defendre de blaſme,
Et l'excuſer comme vne œuure de femme.
Ainſi pourra couurir ſa charité
Deuant les yeux de la ſeuerité
Du Roy qui fait à tous iugement droit,
Ce que i'ay trop failly en chaſque endroit.

Lors d'vn accord, ſur le poinct, nous trouuaſmes
Dedens la Coche au logis arriuaſmes.
La nuict me feit aux trois donner l'Adieu
Non pour dormir; mais pour trouuer vn lieu,

Figure 8. Woodcut from *La coche: Lady Arriving at Court*, from the *Marguerites de la Marguerite des Princesses*, Jean de Tournes, 1547, from the Bibliothèque Municipale de Lyon, Rés 373734, II, p. 319 (© Bibliothèque Municipale de Lyon, Didier Nicole)

at the castle of Fontainebleau (Béguin, Guillaume, and Roy; see fig. 9). This reproductive engraving by the Italian artist Giorgio Ghisi hoists the viewer up into the new Olympus, which from the age of Francis I onward reigned sovereign in humanist milieus. Literary topoi (Joukovsky-Micha) amply reinforce classical imagery of this sort, while dedications of printed works

Figure 9. Giorgio Ghisi after Francesco Primaticcio, *Three Muses and a Putto with a Lyre*, 1540s, from the Galerie of Ulysses at Fontainebleau, Paris, Bibliothèque Nationale de France, Cabinet des Estampes (© BNF)

prove that concrete women were stepping into the sandals of Apollo's Muses in real life. Many a male author in search of financial remuneration for poetry and prose (Martin-Ulrich) and/or theatrical plays (Evain) placed himself under the protective mantle of the lords and ladies of the realm. The phenomenon, of course, was far from new. Yet the power of the printed word enhanced the social visibility of the contingent of female benefactors who, like early-century sponsors of scribes and illuminators, were bent on pursuing their ever-important civilizing task.

Neoplatonic debates about love (i.e., the gendered interrelations between women and men) were rife in the air, both at court and in the major urban centers of the realm; and it was the publisher Jean de Tournes who brought the two arenas together most remarkably at the thriving crossroads of Lyon. Before including *La coche* in the *Marguerites de la Marguerite* and before putting to press the local female author Louise Labé's love sonnets in 1555, Jean de Tournes printed François Habert's *La nouvelle Venus*, a text ostensibly promoting the new Venus of chaste love, dedicated by its author to Catherine de Médicis, "dauphine." By the time Habert's promise of immortality in exchange for protection reached the public, though, in 1548, his dedicatee had risen to become the most stately muse of the realm. The scramble for Catherine's support picked up pace, and the city's Italian merchants and bankers were soon beseeching the new Franco-Italian queen's liberality, too. In her honor they commissioned the first comedy *à l'antique* to be performed in French: Bernardo Dovizi da Bibbiena's *La Calandria*—the content of which, in this instance, was most unchaste. Renaissance spaces left room for a wider range of female deportments than the contemporaneous terms of *honest* and *dishonest* imply. Shortly thereafter, the dominant discourse would be modulated by the published voice of "Louise Labé lyonnaise." An assessment of this small sampling of Jean de Tournes's production in the 1540s and 1550s indicates a trend: "exceptional" learned ladies of high rank would increasingly be finding themselves flanked by learned townswomen, too. Nonetheless, the visual projection of Louise Labé, known through the portrait Pierre Woeiriot engraved to accompany her poetic works (fig. 10), proves that it was still very much the grandes dames who were setting the tone.

The very year that Louise Labé's poetry entered the public sphere, Jean de Court's only signed and dated enamel (fig. 11) cast Margaret of France, Queen Catherine's erudite sister-in-law, as Minerva (Higgott and Biron), the Olympian goddess of wisdom, war, and peace. Ronsard joined a polyphonic chorus of poets to christen Margaret "a wise Minerva," too. For a princess instructed in Italian, Greek, and Latin and whose (Latin) motto translated as "Wisdom, guardian of the world," no classical parallel could have been more fitting. Moreover, the line of transmission from our wise sibyls of the early century was physical and direct. Decades earlier, Symphorien Champier had sought to flatter Margaret's grandmother Louise of Savoy by anointing her "a princess of peace . . . another Pallas and very wise Minerva" (Lecoq); and the parallel had also been invoked any number of times to honor Margaret's aunt, Marguerite de Navarre. Margaret of France owed much of her quality education to her namesake aunt, whose pedagogical tools were creative to the hilt. Did not Margaret the aunt tailor for Margaret the niece a role alongside the spirited Duchess of Étampes and other ladies of rank? In his funeral oration eulogizing

Figure 10. Pierre Woeiriot, *Portrait of Louise Labé*, 1555, etching, Paris, Bibliothèque Nationale de France, Cabinet des Estampes Ed 5b Rés fol. 41 (© BNF)

Figure 11. Jean de Court, *Margaret of France as Minerva*, 1555, London, The Wallace Collection (by kind permission of the Trustees of the Wallace Collection, London)

Marguerite de Navarre, Charles de Sainte-Marthe sketched a picture of her as an ideal literary patron whose liberality was royal in scope. During the age of the Pléiade, Margaret the niece would thus "naturally" become the second-most-sought-after patron of poets (among whom are Du Bellay, Mellin de Saint-Gelais, Ronsard, Charles Fontaine); George Buchanan would thus "naturally" dedicate to her, in Latin, his Latin translation of Euripides's *Alcestes*. Furthermore, Du Bellay's epithalamiums for Margaret of France afford a supplementary example of communication up and down the social ladder. The female poets Camille, Diane, and Lucrèce de Morel, whose Parisian home, rue Pavée, drew together many of the writers benefiting from Princess Margaret's protection, were entrusted with acting them out (Evain; Ford). Finally, when the author Étienne Jodelle relates Margaret and Catherine de Médicis to tragedies and comedies that the religious wars had prevented him from staging, he leads us into the last act of Renaissance performances—those held in the amphitheater of the ever-growing religious divide. The aforementioned image of an exemplary princess in Anne of France's hours makes it clear that the church had long been a site deemed appropriate for women. Therefore the positioning of ladies on or around the socioreligious battlegrounds that marred much of the last half of the century will come as no surprise.

Women of Rank as Literary Protagonists in the Reformation Age

Both Louise of Savoy, somewhat unwittingly, and her daughter, Marguerite de Navarre, much more consciously, contributed to demolishing the (strongly female) cult of Saint Anne around which this essay first untwined. As early as 1518, one of Louise's most devoted literary servants saw that she was kept abreast of the ideas of Jacques Lefèvre d'Étaples, Marguerite's soon-to-be protégé who had just attacked head-on the very core of the widespread popular devotion that had been constructed around the legend of Anne (Orth, "Madame Sainte Anne"). From this point on, ladies in high places would be cultivated by the men promoting the Reformation (Jenkins Blaisdell) or combatting it, as the social fabric of France was slowly being ripped apart.

A verbal sketch has come down to us of two erudite ladies, Marguerite de Navarre and Jeanne de Genouillac, engaged in deep conversation as they wandered through the ancient ruins of Nîmes. Jeanne, the nearly forgotten but highly independent daughter of the famed artillery master Galiot de Genouillac, inherited the military skills of her father and proceeded to use them to transform his castle of Assier into the center of a Protestant stronghold in the Quercy (Wilson-Chevalier, "Introduction"). If Marguerite clung to the notion of tolerance until the day she died, her daughter Jeanne d'Albret, instead, was destined to play an even greater role as a leader of Protestant forces. Not loath to taking up her mother's pen or to defending the Huguenot cause, Jeanne of Navarre was conversely the recipient of many an homage from the writers and playwrights active in her religious camp. How fitting, then, that it was in Jeanne's entourage that Georgette de Montenay took it upon herself to make a foray into a genre that had formerly been a male preserve: the emblem book. Fellow Huguenot Pierre Woeiriot, the creator of the aforementioned portrait of Louise Labé, supplied the illustrations for Montenay's *Emblemes ou devises chrestiennes*, initially published in 1571 (Matthews Grieco, "Georgette de Montenay"), the year preceding the most disastrous massacre of the age. Woeiriot's etched portrait seats the author behind her desk, where a real woman with a specific name is proudly presented with pen in hand—the first such image of all those mentioned in this essay. It is no longer a mystery that virtually all the great Renaissance ladies owned or had access to the content of Christine de Pisan's books. Hence when Montenay's pen along with one of Woeiriot's depictions traces the image of a queen (by implication, Jeanne d'Albret) laying the bricks of a new holy temple, both the debt and homage to Christine de Pisan are crystal clear. However, the queen of Navarre's bricks were being set into the weak mortar of a realm that was at least as terrifyingly disarticulated as the one that Christine was watching disintegrate as she composed her last poem in honor of Joan of Arc. On the opposite shore of theological territories, Guise men and Guise women, no less than Jeanne d'Albret and her allies, were busy mustering troops (Munns and Richards; Grand-Dewyse; Polachek, "Mécénat meurtrier"). About a decade earlier, the enamel artist Léonard Limosin had gone so far as to picture the Duchess of Guise, Antoinette de Bourbon, as the very incarnation of the militant Catholic faith (fig. 12). As Montenay prepared her emblem entitled "Fainete Religion," she was thus retweaking the theme of the Catholic Church as the whore of Babylon to counter those who envisioned the heads of Huguenot heros being squelched beneath the wheels of an ultra-Catholic cart.

As a consequence of King Henry II's accidental death in 1559, Catherine de Médicis had gradually been propelled to the true summit of royal power, by her childrens' side. The Queen Mother was a highly cultivated,

Figure 12. Leonard Limosin, *Triumph of the Eucharist and of the Catholic Faith*, enamel, c. 1561–62, New York, The Frick Collection (© The Frick Collection New York)

deeply political being whose Neoplatonic worldview, genetically descending from her Florentine forebears, had been further honed at the sophisticated French Renaissance court (Crouzet). Once at or near the helm of the ship of state, she unceasingly reiterated her dream of the victory of concord over discord in every artistic medium she could find (ffolliott, "Reine"; Odde; Zum Kolk; Turbide; Zvereva; Bimbenet-Privat; Michahelles). The earlier illumination of Penelope made for Louise of Savoy (fig. 6) is a semiotic sign that the epistolary genre was dear to the hearts of ladies of rank (Pascal, "Princesses épistolières"), whose exogamous marriages programmed them to be mediators throughout their lives. Catherine's epistolary activity was unusually prodigious, and thousands of her letters have weathered the passage of time. Their overriding raison d'être, for thirty long, trying years, was linked to her struggle for the survival of a unified Valois realm.

Since a number of the writers discussed in this volume were writing their works as Catherine de Médicis and her sons were doing their best

Figure 13. Léonard Limosin, *Allegory of Catherine de' Medici as Juno*, 1573, enamel, The J. Paul Getty Museum 86.SE.536 (© J. Paul Getty Museum)

to rule over an unruly realm, it seems logical to conclude this essay with a second portrayal by Léonard Limosin (fig. 13) in which the Queen Mother is allegorized on a chariot of a different type (Grand-Dewyse). While her son Charles IX is cast in a pendant image as Mars, symbolizing the neutralization of all possible threats, Catherine plays the role of the supreme Olympian goddess Juno, her arrow pointed down in sign of peace, her emblem, Iris's rainbow of hope, by her side. Catherine's socially conspicuous agency was comforted by the high visibility of the many cultivated princesses who preceded, surrounded, or would soon succeed her. On the bottom line, no doubt whatsoever can be entertained. The dissimilar voices of these (and other) great ladies paved the way for the cohort of female writers who came to imagine how to trace their own paths into this book.

Carrie F. Klaus

Jeanne de Jussie, the Convent of Saint Clare, and the Reformation of Geneva

For the Poor Clares of Geneva, the Protestant Reformation was a devastating event, disrupting the rhythm of their lives; challenging the beliefs for which they had sacrificed family, friends, and the world; and driving them from their home forever. Jeanne de Jussie (1503–61), the secretary of the Genevan convent of Saint Clare, recorded her experience of the Reformation—beginning with Geneva's alliance with the Swiss cantons of Bern and Fribourg in 1526 and culminating in its acceptance of the Reformation and the Poor Clares' departure from the city in 1535—in an animated and engaging narrative that includes a wealth of historical detail and offers rare insight into the lives and minds of early modern religious women. First published in 1611 as *Le levain du Calvinisme, ou commencement de l'heresie de Geneve* (*The Leaven of Calvinism; or, Beginning of the Heresy of Geneva*), Jussie's text has reappeared, in whole or in part, in the original language or in translation, at least thirteen times over the centuries, most recently in full-length editions in French, German, and English.

Born in 1503 in Jussy-l'Évêque, a village about fifteen kilometers from Geneva, Jeanne was the daughter of land-owning nobles Louis and Jeanne de Jussie (or Jussy). We know little about her childhood, although she indicates in two separate passages of her chronicle that she attended school in Geneva. In August 1535, when the Genevan council member Claude Bernard visits the convent to try to persuade Jussie—who is gravely ill at the time, she points out—to abandon the religious life and to offer her a choice of husbands, he flatters her by saying “que par aultant quelle avoit este leurs escolliere et estoit leur circumvoisine, lavoiens aultant chiere que les fille de ville” (“that because she had been their schoolgirl and was their close neighbor, she was as dear to them as the Genevan girls”; *Petite chronique* 242; *Short Chronicle* 153). Not surprisingly, Jussie, who portrays herself and the rest of the Poor Clares—with the notable exception of Blaisine Varembert, who had left the convent shortly before Bernard’s visit—as deeply devoted to God and unswayingly loyal to the church, sends Bernard away, telling him firmly that her only desire is “destre espouse amon dieu” (“to be the bride of my God”; 243; 154). Still, financial considerations surely played a role in Jussie’s decision to become a nun. She was the youngest of six children in her family to reach adulthood and thus poorly positioned to attract a suitor of appropriate standing. Moreover, after her father’s death in 1519, her uncle, Amédée de Jussie, put forth his own sons as heirs to the castle of Jussy, setting off a costly legal battle that ultimately ruined the family. In 1521, the eighteen-year-old Jeanne de Jussie took religious vows and entered the Convent of Saint Clare.

The Order of Saint Clare was founded in 1212 by Saint Clare of Assisi, a follower of Saint Francis. Reforms in the fifteenth century by Saint Colette of Corbie had revitalized the order in Savoy and in surrounding regions. The convent in Geneva was established in 1477 by Yolande of Savoy, the widow of Duke Amédée IX of Savoy and sister of King Louis XI of France; at the time, there were also Poor Clares in nearby Chambéry (in another convent established by Yolande of Savoy), Orbe, and Vevey. Not long after Jussie entered the convent, the political and religious situation in Geneva became tense. In 1526, to defend its autonomy against the encroaching powers of Charles III, Duke of Savoy, and of Pierre de la Baume, prince-bishop of Geneva, Geneva joined Bern and Fribourg in the *combourgeoisie*. In 1528, Bern officially adopted the Reformation and soon began sending Reformed preachers to Geneva. The first envoys met with resistance: Jussie notes with obvious satisfaction that the distinguished Reformer Guillaume Farel had to steal away by boat early one morning in October 1532. However, amid fervent public preaching and carefully orchestrated debates, as well as violent confrontations and more than a few executions, the Reformation steadily gained ground in Geneva.

In 1535, the celebration of Mass was suspended in the city. In August that year, under the protection of the Duke of Savoy, the Poor Clares left Geneva and traveled by foot to Annecy, where they moved into the abandoned Augustinian Monastery of the Holy Cross. It was no doubt in Annecy that Jussie composed her chronicle, perhaps integrating pieces of earlier writing, such as letters she had written to the Duke and Duchess of Savoy and other protectors informing them of events in Geneva. Jeanne de Jussie was elected abbess of her convent in 1548 and held the position until her death in 1561. The Poor Clares, who continued to refer to themselves as the "Sœurs de Sainte-Claire de Genève refugiez à Annecy" ("Sisters of Saint Clare of Geneva in refuge in Annecy"; xix; 12), remained in Annecy for two and a half centuries, until their convent was dissolved in 1793 in the wake of the French Revolution (see the introductions to the editions of her text by Feld and Klaus; Backus, "Les Clarisses"; Ganter; and Roth).

With her narrative, Jeanne de Jussie provides teachers and students with an extraordinary opportunity to observe the lives of early modern monastic women and to consider these women's understanding of the Reformation and of the world. Her text is incredibly rich, since she writes not only of the Reformation's impact on her convent but also of contemporary events in Geneva (fighting in the streets, executions of presumed heretics, the theological disputation at the Rive monastery in spring 1535), in the Swiss-Savoy borderlands (the duke's attempts to assert his authority, acts of iconoclasm, pillaging and burning of castles), and in Europe more generally (the spread of Lutheranism, battles between Christians and Muslims, negotiations involving France, the empire, and Rome) (see Feld). In this essay, I consider two topics that can be explored in the classroom: the significance of the convent itself as a physical space and the roles and responsibilities of nuns in their community.

Jussie's chronicle is particularly illuminating with regard to the convent building, shedding light on the material world in which the Poor Clares lived and that thus shaped their sense of reality (see Klaus, "Architecture"). The only women's religious house within the Genevan city walls, the Convent of Saint Clare—the full name of which was the Monastère Jésus de Bethléem (Jesus of Bethlehem Monastery)—was located prominently on the busy place du Bourg-de-Four, at the top of the rue Verdaine and not far from the cathedral, where the Palais de Justice now stands. It would have been a conspicuous sight; at one point, Jussie mentions the "grand croix qui estoit deuant le conuent et le beaux crucefix dussus le portal a lentree du conuent" ("large cross in front of the convent and the handsome crucifix above the door at the entrance to the convent"; 24; 49). This entrance on the place du Bourg-de-Four led into a corridor that opened, on the left, into the church and cloister and, on the right, into the wing occupied by the Poor Clares' lay brothers. The church was the convent's only public space; visitors were welcomed there to hear offices or Mass. Jussie stresses repeatedly the importance of her convent's church to the inhabitants of Geneva. When Swiss troops occupy the city in October 1530, she notes that the observation of Mass is suspended everywhere except for at the Convent of Saint Clare:

> Le londy suvuant bien matin furent fermees toutes les esglise vnyuersellement de la cite, et ny fust dict messes ne seruice diuin hault ne bat, durant que ses fault suysses heretiques y furent, si non ou couent de madame saincte clere, que lesglise ne fut a nulz denie. (22)

> The next Monday, early in the morning, all the churches in town were closed, and there was no Mass or divine service, high or low, observed in them while those false heretical Swiss were there, except in the convent of Madame Saint Clare, whose church was closed to no one. (48)

Throughout her narrative, Jussie stresses the exceptional status of her convent and of the devoted women inside it, who are increasingly at odds with policy and practice in Geneva.

The nuns themselves remained in the cloister at all times; they did not enter the public space of the church, but rather heard Mass, chanted offices, and worshipped the sacrament on the altar from inside their choir, which hung over the back of the nave and was reachable from inside the cloister. An iron grille separated the nuns' choir from the church. When granted permission, visitors to the convent could speak to the nuns through this grille, accessible by means of a stairway in the back of the church that led up to a small landing. One of their only points of contact with persons outside the convent, the grille was thus tremendously important to the Poor Clares. Jussie mentions it many times in her chronicle. It is at the grille that the Poor Clares ask the Swiss soldiers to protect them, listen to their confessors' accounts of public disputations, and negotiate with city leaders. The nuns maintained full control of the use of the grille. When the Reformed Genevan woman Hemme Faulson—sister of the apostate Blaisine Varembert—comes to the convent to preach to the Poor Clares, they quickly close the wooden door on their side of the grille so they will not have to listen to her. Jussie expresses sympathy for the Poor Clares in Orbe who are not allowed to do the same when Guillaume Farel comes to their convent. In Orbe, she says, "les seurs estoien contraintes de sonnes le sermons et di asister en la treille le drap leuez. Qui leur estoit bien griefz, il nen fault doubter" ("the sisters were forced to ring the bell for the sermon and to listen at the grille with the curtain raised, which caused them much grief, there can be no doubt"; 55; 64). The deficiency of the grille is one of the chief hardships that Jussie notes as the Genevan nuns settle into the monastery in Annecy: "Et combien qui li avoit vne treille ferre, ny avoit encore nulle porte ny drapt deuant et de hors nulz degre ny plangier" ("And even though there was an iron grille, there was not yet a door or curtain in front of it and there were no steps or landing outside of it"; 303; 185). The adverb *encore* (yet) suggests that improvements to the grille would be one of the Poor Clares' first renovations to their new home.

The other main space of the convent allowing some access to the outside world was the nuns' garden, which lay on the side of the cloister opposite the church and was bound on one side by the city wall. Jussie writes frequently of the garden as well. It is from it that the astonished nuns view the burning of the Abbey of Bellerive, near Geneva, in October 1530. At about this time, when the Poor Clares are obliged to quarter thirty-five Swiss soldiers (and six horses!) during the occupation of Geneva, Jussie writes that the barefoot nuns walk in procession into their garden each day, despite the cold weather, to recite a litany and beg God for mercy. Threats to the garden by the Bernese, who in September 1534 attempt to break through the adjacent city wall, are the subject of a long episode in the chronicle. Later, Jussie reports that "heretics" who climb up on this wall to taunt the nuns and to throw stones at them force the women to withdraw definitively into their cloister. She states sadly, "Et furent contraintes de clourre la porte et de non plus y allez, pour neccessitte que fut pour y labouree, curtiuez ny cuylly herbes, et avoien bien indigence" ("They had to close the gate and not go there anymore to work, garden, or gather herbs, which caused them great poverty"; 173; 119). The lack of privacy in the garden of their new convent is another complication the nuns encounter in Annecy: "la place por fere le jardin subget ala ville et trois porte ouuerte por entraige atous venant" ("the place to make their garden was subject to the city and had three open gates by which anyone could enter"; 304; 185). Presumably, modifications to this garden would be another early convent-improvement project.

Jussie's chronicle also provides valuable information about roles and responsibilities inside the convent. Twenty-four regular nuns—twenty-three after Blaisine Varembert's departure—resided in the Genevan Convent of Saint Clare during the years of which Jussie writes. There were also lay sisters and brothers, who acted as servants, and two confessors. Jussie refers to a variety of offices held by the regular nuns: discreets appointed as advisers to the abbess, a bursar, cooks, a nurse, and herself, the convent secretary. It is the portresses, the abbess, and the vicaress, however, who play the most significant roles in Jussie's text. These women were responsible for dealing with the world outside the convent, a charge that became distinctly more critical as the Reformation gained a hold on Geneva.

At any given time, one of three portresses tended a turning window at the entrance to the cloister, serving as a buffer between the Poor Clares and the outside world and, thus, as their first line of defense. (Jeanne de Jussie's aunt, Guillaume de Villette, was one of these portresses.) The portress would receive any monetary donations to the convent and would carry messages to the nuns. With the approval of the abbess or vicaress, she could also grant permission for visitors to approach the grille. Jussie repeatedly praises the portresses' sound judgment, particularly in dealing with Reformers. She writes, "Mais la mere portiere estoit atrempes et discrette et ne leur tenoit point long porpost, quelle ne fermat son tornoit, et se force estoit de respondre, faisoit venir la mere abbesse et mere vicaire, et les seurs se mettoiens en oraison" ("But the mother portress was sensible and discreet and did not talk long to them before closing the turning window; and if a response was necessary, she would call for the mother abbess and the mother vicaress and the sisters would pray"; 204; 134). Jussie is well aware of the power of words and knows how carefully they must be chosen, since her convent's future hangs in the balance.

The climactic moment of Jussie's tale occurs when a horde of Reformers, infuriated by the nuns' refusal to listen to or speak with them, finally break into the convent, tearing apart the turning window. Jussie underlines the drama of this event by focusing on the portress at the precise instant in which the intruders penetrate the nuns' hitherto unviolated space. She writes:

> La portiere voiant tomber et escartelle le tornoit, vat barre la porte contre et couttoit de son dos por garde de louurit. Mais lon deulx vat fraper de son hachon si fierement, qui le my bien avant, et peu faillir, qui ne le my ou dos de la portiere. Mais dieu le createur la reculla miraculeusement. (214–15)

> When the portress saw the turning window collapse and break into pieces, she barred the door to them and braced it with her back to keep them from opening it. But one of them hit it so hard with his axe that

> the axe sank in and nearly went into the portress's back. But God the Creator miraculously moved her away. (139–40)

With the turning window and door destroyed, the portress no longer has a meaningful function, and she runs to join the rest of the nuns prostrate in the choir. After smashing statues, chairs, and pulpits the iconoclastic pack finally leaves the convent, and the nuns find themselves exposed. Two police officers are sent to stand guard at the broken turning window in the place of the portress. Six days later, the Poor Clares leave Geneva.

The abbess of the Genevan convent of Saint Clare from 1528 until 1538 was the aged and ailing Louise Rambo. Jussie presents the abbess as admirable but naive. When Guillaume Farel first comes to the convent to try to convert the Poor Clares, the abbess summons the nuns to hear him. Later, when Hemme Faulson (just one week after giving birth!) brings a group of Reformed women to the grille to preach to the nuns, the abbess listens carefully and begins to answer their accusations—"La mere abbesse bien sachant de la sainte escripture leur respondoit viuement" ("The mother abbess knew the Holy Scripture well and gave a spirited response"; 203; 134)—prompting the more decisive vicaress to take the abbess by the arm, tell her the nuns should not hear such words, and slam closed the door on the inside of the grille. Still later, the ever-credulous abbess allows the nuns to speak to the Reformer Pierre Viret and his associates: "La bonne mere abbesse soit confiant aleur parolle de menterie, leur comanda parler aeulx" ("The good mother abbess, trusting their lying words, ordered the sisters to speak to them"; 240; 152). Under different circumstances, the abbess's unsuspicious nature would be laudable. As the scales tilt toward the Reformation in Geneva, however, it places the Convent of Saint Clare in great peril.

Fortunately for the Poor Clares, the abbess is seconded by the shrewd and daring vicaress. Indeed, it is the vicaress who emerges as the great hero of Jussie's story. She assists and often stands in for the abbess, bargaining with city leaders, rallying the support of secular Catholic women, and diverting Reformers in their attempts to gain access to the nuns and convert them. She risks her life to try to keep Blaisine Varembert from leaving the convent—"Et il prirent de grosse esclapes des formes et cuiderent fendre la teste amere vicayre, qui la volloir retires aforce" ("They took a great shard of wood from the chairs and almost struck mother vicaress's head as she was trying to pull her away forcibly"; 222; 143–44)—then skillfully represents the Poor Clares in negotiations with Varembert's family in their attempts to reclaim a dowry that the vicaress insists was never paid. Most notably, she prevails over male figures of civic and religious authority in two dramatic episodes in the chronicle.

In May 1535, city leaders come to the convent to order the nuns to attend the Rive Disputation, which ends up being the deciding event in Geneva's adoption of the Reformation. Without a moment of hesitation, the vicaress blocks each of the arguments the men put forth to try to convince them to come, telling them the nuns must uphold their vow of seclusion, are forbidden by the church to debate scripture, are busy at complines, cannot take time away from their penance and prayers, and so on, even going so far as to call the men wicked harassers and to suggest they are agents of the devil. "Et leur parlat si viuement," Jussie write, "que tous estoiens esmerueilliez" ("She spoke to them so forcefully . . . that they were all astonished"; 186; 125). When the irate city leaders direct vague threats at the vicaress, she tells them they may punish her all they like, then states her name boldly: "Et si je dict rient, qui vos de plaise, jen veult porter la poine seulle, et affin que mieulx sachee, que je suis, et que les aultres ne aient de plaisir pour moy, je me nomme seur pernette de monloix ou de chastiaux fort" ("And if I say anything that displeases you, I wish to suffer alone for it; and so that you may know better who I am and so that others will not suffer in my place, I tell you my name, which is Sister Pernette de Montluel ou de Châteaufort"; 186–87; 125). In the end, she wins. The men leave the convent, and the nuns do not attend the disputation.

In July of the same year, the city leaders bring a group of Reformers, including Guillaume Farel and Pierre Viret, to the convent to preach to the Poor Clares. Against the vicaress's better judgment, the abbess allows them to enter. When Farel begins to condemn seclusion, pointing out that even the Virgin Mary did not lead a life of solitude, the vicaress leaps to her feet and calls the Reformers "maulues seducteurs" ("wicked seducers"; 197; 130). She is thrown out of the room but continues to make a great commotion, shouting and pounding on the wall. The nuns, surely roused by the vicaress, tell Farel he speaks lies, spit on him, then stuff their ears with wax so they will not have to hear him. Ultimately, the Reformers leave the convent, led by Farel, who vows never to return. Jussie writes, "Et voiant, que de rien ne profitoint et ne gagnoien que de grans injures, se vont retires dehors, et se meschant faret courut pour estre le premier et se vat lauer les mains hastiuement por soit refrescher, croiant qui bruloit de rage" ("When they saw that it was doing no good and that they were gaining nothing but great insults, they went outside, and that criminal

Farel ran to be the first one out; he washed his hands impatiently to cool himself because he felt like he was burning with rage"; 201; 132). Here Jussie creates, surely, one of the most memorable portraits of the eminent Reformer.

It is the vicaress who orchestrates the Poor Clares' departure from their convent. When the situation in Geneva has become untenable for the nuns, she secures from the city leaders permission to leave and a promise of safe conduct, as well as cloaks, coats, veils, and shoes for the journey. As the women leave the convent, she lines them up in pairs, entrusting weaker nuns to stronger ones, and instructs them all to keep utterly silent. She even gives orders to the city leaders, telling them to forbid anyone to speak to the nuns and shouting at them to maintain order when the townspeople try to provoke them; the leaders respond immediately, threatening with death anyone who moves, and the Poor Clares finally leave Geneva. The vicaress continues to guide the women on their journey, finding shelter for them in La Perrière at the castle of her cousin, Baron Michel de Viry, and ultimately leading them safely to Annecy.

Jussie's chronicle offers many other avenues of inquiry that would be fascinating to consider in the classroom. One might discuss the nuns' understanding of the theological issues at stake in the Reformation, such as the status of miracles and women's right to interpret scripture (note, above, the vicaress's selective use of the Pauline injunction to silence). The Poor Clares' understanding of the larger world would be another intriguing topic, particularly Jussie's comments on Jews and on the Ottoman Empire, including an extended description of "le mode de turquie" ("Turkish ways"; 68; 70) that was omitted from early editions of the chronicle. Jussie also offers a look at the specificity of women's experience of the Reformation. She writes not only of the Poor Clares but of secular Catholic women, who pull their babies from the arms of Reformers who attempt to baptize them; who are beaten, banished, or imprisoned by Reformed husbands and fathers; who join in armed skirmishes; and who furtively aid a jailed theologian from the Sorbonne. She also writes of Reformed women who sit in their windows spinning wool during processions, who do laundry on feast days, and, of course, who come to the Convent of Saint Clare to preach to the nuns. Students might also examine the literary qualities of the text. Despite its serious nature, Jussie's tale is lively and even humorous, with comic and satirical aspects; her style is unpretentious and direct, with colorful, image-filled language. Students could identify these elements as well as the shape Jussie gives to her story, its cast of characters and deliberate narrative structure, along with the larger point she aims to make.

Jussie may be approached from a variety of disciplinary perspectives, including history, religious studies, women's studies, and literature. Her work is easily adaptable to different levels of the curriculum and may be taught in French or in translation. It may be studied fruitfully alongside works by other male and female writers of the Reformation; the *Epistle to Marguerite de Navarre*, by Marie Dentière, the outspoken and eloquent Reformed woman who visited the Genevan convent of Saint Clare and appears in Jussie's text, is surely the most obvious pairing, but many others are possible as well.[1] Jussie's remarkable chronicle is an essential text for understanding the importance of the Reformation in French-speaking Europe.

Note

1. For a discussion of teaching Jussie in conjunction with Arcangela Tarabotti and Marie Dentière at the early undergraduate level, see Klaus, "Reading Jeanne de Jussie's *Short Chronicle*." Lazard ("Deux sœurs ennemies") writes specifically about the clashes between Jussie and Dentière.

Diane S. Wood and Laura B. Bergman

Humanism and Women's Writing: The Case of Hélisenne de Crenne

Hélisenne de Crenne, the pseudonym of Marguerite Briet, was a convent-educated intellectual whose love of reading determined her path to creating four seminal works: *Les angoysses douloureuses qui procedent d'amours* (*The Torments of Love*), the first French sentimental novel; *Les epistres familieres et invectives*, the forerunner of the epistolary novel; *Le songe*, a polemic on the question of women; and *Les Eneydes*, the first translation into French prose of Vergil's *Aeneid*, books 1–4. Her writings reflect her taste for popular fiction of the time, including Italian and Spanish novels, as well as protofeminist polemics and epic literature. While her books have been studied from the angle of narrative technique, the *querelle des femmes*, and affairs of the heart, much remains to be said about the humanist tendencies reflected in her prose, not only in her translation of Vergil but also in her novel, especially part 2. Modern interest in her writings stems from both her literary innovations and her thematic concerns. The avid sixteenth-century French readers who purchased her best-selling novel, reprinted eight times from 1538 to 1560, probably recognized and enjoyed the intertextual richness of her prose, since it reflected the penchants of their literary milieu. For twenty-first-century readers, these allusions prove more difficult to grasp. Hélisenne makes no direct reference to contemporary authors besides Marguerite de Navarre and Clément Marot, both of whom she lauds in her "Fourth Invective Letter." The names of the great humanists of her time—Jacques Lefèvre d'Étaples, Guillaume Budé, and Desiderius Erasmus—are not to be found in her pages, yet their interest in rediscovering antiquity, in reading and translating classical authors, nonetheless lies beneath the surface of the chivalric quest of the *Angoysses.*

While her long narrative is not a formal treatise, questions of leadership posed by humanists do find their way into her novel in an oblique manner, mainly through Jacopo Caviceo's *Le peregrin*, translated into French in 1527. This work models the general contours of part 2's construct of intertextuality, and Hélisenne selected from it passages that reflected princely humanism, the dominant political thought of the time (Nelson 319). Following Petrarch's lead, many philosophers offered a *speculum principis* ("a mirror for princes"), outlining the virtues necessary for good princely government. High on the list were generosity and clemency (Nelson 320–23). Erasmus's *Institutio principis christiani* (1516) and Budé's *Livre de l'institution du prince,* published in 1547, nearly a decade after the *Angoysses*, bear witness to the continuing importance of the *speculum principis* in the sixteenth century. Hélisenne inserted reflections of the humanist concerns of her day into her texts with great care and made them her own. This essay first underscores the connection between the chivalric quest of part 2 of the *Angoysses* and the Trojan epics and then untangles the threads of Renaissance humanism woven into this second part of the novel.[1]

Hélisenne's preoccupation with antiquity centers on her interest in the Trojan War, especially as inscribed in Caviceo's *Le peregrin*, Jean Lemaire's *Les illustrations de Gaule et singularitez de Troie* (1510–13), and the anonymous compilation *Le grant Olympe des histoires poétiques* (1532). Extensive footnotes to editions of Hélisenne's writings document her borrowings from Caviceo's plot devices and Lemaire's descriptions of mythological figures. Beginning with the prologue to part 2, Hélisenne conflates the chivalric with the epic, as in her statement that knights will find her narrative useful in the same manner that Homer's *Iliad* benefited Alexander the Great: "cette assiduité de lire, l'instiguait l'efficace et émotion de chevalerie que les choses par écrit rédigées lui pouvaient causer" ("this assiduity in reading inspired his deeds and the inclination to chivalry which things written down could cause"; 148; 77).[2] Indeed, she believed that her novel would have the same effect on her contemporaries. Thus, from the outset, the author specifically links the aim of her project in the *Angoysses*, part 2, to Homer's epic. Hélisenne probably did not know Greek, but the *Iliad* was available to her in French through Jehan Samxon's translation (1530). A competent Latinist, she would have read the *Aeneid* in the original in one of the several editions available in Paris at the time, perhaps supplemented by Octavien de Saint-Gelais's verse translation (1509), the only French translation of the epic until Hélisenne's own (1541) prose translation of the first four books.

Whereas allusions to the epics of the Trojan War colored all of Hélisenne's writings, her novel opens on a confessional note. Hélisenne, an unhappily married woman who falls hopelessly in love with the young and handsome Guénélic, narrates the first-person account in the *Angoysses*, part 1. Confined in a tower by her irate husband, she writes her memoirs. While this sentimental part of the novel will probably remain the most popular among modern readers, the chivalric quest of part 2 offers a journey shaped by lofty, epic aspirations, since Guénélic, along with his faithful friend Quezinstra, proposes to surpass Odysseus in search of his beloved (163–64).

Hélisenne carefully structures the adventures of part 2 so that the three major cities visited present an ever-increasing set of experiences for the two young men. The first city, Goranflos, provides the model for good civic leadership in the person of the Duke, whose domain is orderly and well run. The Duke himself is the personification of princely virtues, displaying both politeness and generosity. Guénélic and Quezinstra become knights with the Duke's help, a vital first step in their quest. Ever an extraordinary combatant, Quezinstra wins the Duke's tournament, earning two prizes: Hercules's sword and a beautiful damsel. The sword serves him well in subsequent battles. He has no personal desire for the young woman but, instead, generously bestows her on the man she loves. This love match and marriage unite two well-suited young people and offers a sharp contrast to the mismatched situation in the next city.

Leaving Goranflos, the narrative echoes the Homeric epic with a brief stop at Troy, where the questing knights visit the graves of Hector, Achilles, and Polyxena, after which they arrive at Elivéba, the second major stop. Once again, the newcomers are welcomed with the grace expected of an exemplary Renaissance leader, this time a female ruler, the Princesse Monarque. Hélisenne compares the princess's poise and beauty with those of Diana, Juno, and Dido (240, 128; 246, 132; 259, 139). Monarque fulfills the expectations of the *speculum principis* in all ways, except for her gender. Her city is flourishing, and her people love her. She possesses administrative talents in abundance. Hélisenne's princess steps from the catalogs of exemplary female rulers in Giovanni Boccaccio's *De muliberius claris* (1362) and Christine de Pisan's *La cité des dames* (1405). She faces a threat no male counterpart would have had to deal with, an outraged suitor whom she describes as "cet amiral (homme scélère et inicque)" ("this admiral—a scoundrel, and a wicked man"; 246; 132). Hélisenne endows her princess with the agency to act on her own behalf to select a spouse, and the princess rejects the unsuitable man, not only on personal grounds but also for the benefit of her kingdom, since he intends to "renverser et totalement ruiner cette très fluente et populeuse cité" ("reverse and totally ruin this prosperous and populous city" 243; our trans.). She suggests to her faithful citizens that he is unfit to rule and that his laws would be unjust and difficult for them to bear:

> Et aussi, [vous] devez être timides que ne soyez régis et gouvernés sous prince mal conditionné, qui pourrait instituer lois iniques et mauvaises. Parquoi vous succomberiez en si grosse molestie de coeur que ce vous serait chose griève à supporter. (246)
>
> You should also fear that you might be ruled and governed by an ignoble prince who might institute iniquitous and evil laws, whereby you would succumb to such great heart-sickness that you would find it a very painful thing to endure. (132)

The admiral's irascible and unreasonable temper recalls François Rabelais's Picrochole, and his precipitous siege illustrates Erasmus's comment, "when kings go mad, the people are smitten" (175). The townspeople rally to support her because she exemplifies the humanist ideal of good leadership and has earned their trust. The siege of the town recalls that of Troy, and Quezinstra, identified as a French Hector, becomes the city's most dangerous defender (253–54; 136).

The Princesse Monarque governs with the aid of trusted advisers and thoughtful deliberation. At the suggestion of settling the dispute by single combat, she becomes "merveilleusement pensive, puis après à son parler donna tel principe, et dit à ses familiers que c'était chose très urgente de bien consulter cette affaire, à ce que lon prît sur ce faire bonne délibération" ("extraordinarily pensive; then she began to tell her counselors that it was very urgent to discuss this affair to be sure that they made the right decision"; 258; 139). Her counsel comprises "les plus expérimentés et savants" ("[t]he most experienced and wise"; 258; 139) men, who discuss the situation and agree with the wisdom of limiting bloodshed. The princess then acts quickly to solicit Quezinstra's help. On the enemy side, the admiral's brother provides wisdom lacking to his brother and refuses to support poor judgment and unreasonableness. His speech encapsulates the qualities expected of a good Renaissance prince: "de tel prince . . . devrait être l'ire tardive et l'audience légère, le jugement franc, le conseil mûr, la passion rejetée et la justice présente" ("such a prince . . . should be slow to anger and willing to listen, with unfettered judgment, mature counsel, setting aside passion and keeping his eyes on justice"; 254; 136). The two champions resemble heroes of epic poetry: "Beau faisait voir la singulière magnanimité des deux nobles chevaliers, desquels la valeur était si grande que mille langues de poètes ne la sauraient exprimer" ("It was wonderful to see the exceptional magnanimity of the two knights, whose valor was so great that the tongues of a thousand poets could not express it"; 261; 140). Quezinstra triumphs, and even the old admiral realizes that the princess has been totally justified in declining his suit and waiting for a satisfactory match such as the one Quezinstra had arranged in Goranflos.

The third and last major stop of the *Angoysses*, part 2, is Bouvaques, whose citizens are described as "pervers et iniques, lesquels ne voulaient obéir ni avoir de supérieur" ("perverse and iniquitous people who did not want to obey or have any superior"; 269; 145). The Bouvaques episode lacks the love interest of the two previous stops but does feature another wise monarch. Guénélic and Quezinstra hear of a prince whose citizens are in revolt and decide to come to his aid even before they meet him. After much fighting, the rebels capitulate but are to be severely punished. This time, Quezinstra acts as the spokesperson for reason and defends the notion of clemency for those he has been battling, using terms akin to the *speculum principis.* His long speech to the Prince of Bouvaques offers Julius Caesar as a role model for leniency and ends with an appeal to the prince's noble heart:

> Bien vous l'ai voulu remémorer, très illustre prince, afin de vous exciter à extirper toute rigueur de votre noble coeur, à ce que cette vertu de clémence, que bien est convéniente à vostre altissime noblesse, y puisse retrouver le lieu de son accoutumée résidence, qui par ire a été de rigueur occupé. (273)
>
> I have desired to remind you of this, illustrious prince, in order to urge you to extirpate all inflexibility from your noble heart, so that this virtue of clemency, which well befits your noble heart, so might find there its accustomed place of residence which through wrath has been occupied by rigorous severity. (147)

Hélisenne's notion of clemency in this episode closely aligns with the philosophy of Rabelais's *Gargantua*, which, in turn, has been traced back to

Erasmus (*Gargantua* 171n1). Hélisenne's chapter heading, "La débonnaireté d'un prince envers ses sujets . . . " ("The gentleness of a prince toward his subjects . . ."; 274; 148), underscores the goodness of the ruler. A rebel spokesman recognizes the prince's virtues: "en ces considérations, pouvons juger très félice le peuple sur lequel tel prince domine" ("given these considerations, we can deem very fortunate the people who live under such a prince's authority"; 275; 148). Quezinstra stresses the need for the citizens to be grateful toward their monarch, implying that such positive feelings would, perhaps, alleviate future conflicts.

With the peaceful resolution of the siege of Bouvaques, the political discussions come to an end and the focus of the chivalric quest in part 3 turns from heroic exploits of epic proportions back to its original purpose of finding the missing Hélisenne. In fact, the prince initiates the transition back to the quest. Alluding to the *Odyssey*, he attempts to convince Guénélic to abandon his ardent passion for Hélisenne: "plus n'ensuivez cette effrénée lascivité, délaissez cette immodérée rage, qui très facilement peut les hommes transformer comme les compagnons d'Ulysses" ("pursue no longer this unrestrained lustfulness, leave off this immoderate madness that can very easily transform men as the companions of Ulysses were transformed"; 278; 150).

The allusions to Vergil and Homer subside in the latter portion of the novel only to become central once again in the epilogue. As the quest draws to an end, humanist meditations on leadership give way to concern about the souls of the main characters. Hélisenne prepares the way for her passionate lovers to be reunited for eternity without tarnishing the purity of their love in adultery. Part 3 reconciles their ardor with Christian values, thereby resolving their "angoysses douloureuses" with a tragic finality redeemed in a socially acceptable manner.

An examination of the chivalric quest in Hélisenne de Crenne's *Angoysses*, part 2, reveals the author's concern with the same questions of good government that preoccupied Renaissance philosophers of her day. Rather than a treatise on princely humanism, the novel incorporates models of wise leadership into the narrative, creating situations where rationality and clemency prevail.

In part 2 of the *Angoysses*, Hélisenne de Crenne transforms a traditional chivalric quest into a meditation on leadership. Starting from the treatises on princely humanism written by Renaissance thinkers, she deftly inserts a new possibility into the debate, that of female leadership and female rationality. Hélisenne's Princesse Monarque possesses all the qualities expected of an ideal Renaissance sovereign along with the authority to determine her own future. Thus Hélisenne breathes new life into the dominant philosophical discussion by presenting an innovative example of female empowerment. With her pen, she redraws the humanist model of virtuous leadership to permit a woman to claim the mantle of power to govern a city-state. By including this passage, Hélisenne offers her readers a twofold act of empowerment. She publishes her own writing and creates a strong female character who is worthy of her position of authority. Hélisenne's carefully crafted demonstration of princely humanism hereby embodies a strong feminist principle, that women are fully capable of ratiocination and of wielding the reins of power.

Notes

1. This essay contains material adapted from Wood, *Hélisenne de Crenne: At the Crossroads* 121–31.

2. All references to the *Angoysses* are made to the edition *Angoisses* (2005), edited by Beaulieu. Unless otherwise noted, the translations are from Neal and Rendall's edition, *Torments of Love.* Christine de Buzon's edition contains extensive notes and documentation for advanced readers.

Susan Broomhall

Production and Reproduction: Contextualizing Women's Writing as Labor

One of the assumptions that arise when we teach women writers of the early modern period is that we share their understanding of what it meant to be an author and of the status that it brought to writers of manuscript and printed texts. Particularly when we teach courses on women who participated in publication culture as "female authors," we may be giving students a false impression that these women thought of themselves as writers, or that their contemporaries thought of them thus. Naturally, the concept of authorship is a critical aspect for students to explore, since it was an intellectual notion that embedded gendered understandings of authority and public speech (as the following essay by François Rigolot will examine). However, students are often unfamiliar with the broader social, cultural, and practical contexts that were equally important factors informing both female experiences as writers and the expression of their ideas in textual domains. Could women be authors in a professional sense? Which kinds of women could be engaged in this textual enterprise? Was being "a writer" a meaningful part of the identity of women whose writing appears in manuscript and print? What kind of labor did they see themselves conducting when they wrote? What kind of "work" did contemporaries consider that their writing constituted?

Bibliographical Contexts

A useful starting point to engage students in this discussion may be to consider how women's compositions came to be included in manuscript and printed texts of the early modern era. Sometimes it appears that women's works were incorporated into text without their knowledge or regardless of their intentions. The writings of some women were included posthumously. It was the "affectionnées remonstrances de son dolent mary" ("affectionate pleas of her sorrowful husband"; my trans.) that apparently persuaded Antoine Du Moulin to publish Pernette Du Guillet's verses in 1545 (preface, *Rymes*, fol. a2r). Significantly, most women whose writings were published in the sixteenth century in France were included in collective anthologies or at the margins of texts composed by others to which they contributed such compositions as prefaces and laudatory verses (Broomhall, *Women and the Book Trade*). This fact does not necessarily mean that such women did not see themselves as part of a literary community in their lifetime; indeed, many of these women were. However, it may provide contexts for reconsidering the intentionality that we attribute to both the work and the identities that women created as authors.

Moreover, for another group of women, having their writings circulated in manuscript or print occurred because of their experiences outside the literary sphere. Some women wrote texts that transmitted knowledge that they gained in other occupational contexts. For example, after many years of experience, the royal midwife Louise Bourgeois composed medical advice texts and professional memoirs that were widely disseminated in print after 1609. Women working in print trades too might become involved in the composition of texts that appear as prefaces for editions published under their name. Charlotte Guillard used a 1552 preface to defend the quality of a scholarly dictionary that appeared in print under her Parisian imprint, anticipating criticisms that might be generated by the involvement of a female in its production. Two entreaties by Charlotte de Minut, the abbess of a Poor Clare convent in Toulouse, in which she sought patronage from the pope and Catherine de Médicis to support her community were published as the prefaces to posthumous 1587 editions of her brother's work. She argued that, being unable to create her own work of a publishable standard "à cause de mon sexe, de mon insuffisance incapable de la discipline des lettres . . . ie me veux aider pour cest effect du labeur d'un mien frère" ("because of my sex, my insufficiency incapable of the discipline of letters . . . I want to be aided in this by the labor of my brother"; "A nostre Sainct Pere" 4–5; my trans.). Such women become authors as a direct result of a distinctive occupational or professional identity, rather than an obvious acquaintance with a literary milieu or a desire to fashion an identity as a literary author. It was in fact their labor in or duties to these vocations that occasioned their compositions.

Women's Productive and Reproductive Labor

In addition to learning about these bibliographic contexts, students may need to consider some of the realities of women's lives in the early modern period to understand the writings women produced and the topoi commonly found in them. This includes giving some consideration to the kinds of work that women undertook. Women were often engaged in paid labor. Service in the craft guilds, especially the textile trades, were particularly important sources of income for women (Davis, "Women in the Crafts"; Loats; Lanza). However, these women, who were often illiterate, were not typically of the same status as women writers. Bourgeois, a guild-licensed midwife, was an exception to the typical profile of an early modern female author, and even she began publishing only after her clientele extended to the royal court. Some women whose works were circulated or published did identify themselves as belonging to more genteel occupations. Mme Du Verger, the author of a 1595 child-rearing manual apparently edited and extended by her daughter, was a Parisian governess to the daughters of elite families. Most women writers were literate and often learned women of wealthy or aristocratic origins for whom association with paid labor was degrading to their own, and their family's, social identities.

Just as critical to women's lives were contemporary expectations about forms of unpaid female labor. All women, irrespective of their status, were responsible for the performance of household tasks or the supervision of the performance of others. How then could women find time to write if doing so took them away from one of their primary duties? Students will be able to identify the echoes of the expectations placed on women throughout their writings. Female authors used a number of common rhetorical strategies to explain why their composition would not jeopardize their moral reputation as responsible women, whether daughters, wives, mothers, or widows. Students can be encouraged to understand such statements as topoi that, regardless of an author's particular circumstances, reflect significant contexts and sometimes constraints for their compositions.

For some authors, a response to the expectation of domestic labor was expressed through recognition of a rushed or disordered literary production. Some literary women emphasized a sense of the deficiency of their works that was a result of their inability to devote sufficient time to their composition. Marie de Romieu expressed precisely this sentiment in 1581 when presenting her "brief discours . . . composé assez à la haste, n'ayant pas le loisir, a cause de nostre mesnage, devacquer . . . à chose si belle & divine que les vers" ("brief discourse . . . composed in some haste, not having the leisure, because of our household to attend . . . to a thing as beautiful and divine as verse"; *Premières œuvres* [1581] fols. Aiiv–Aiiir; my trans.). Catherine Des Roches reminded her readers outright that she had not neglected her needlework and other accomplishments as a result of her writing (Larsen, "Catherine De Roches" 63). Even men who supported women's attempts to write still acknowledged expectations of female domestic responsibilities. Jacques de Rochemore lamented in 1573 that Marguerite de Cambis lost time for her composition while she tended to her household responsibilities: "me semble feries aussi grant tort a votre prompt, & gentil esprit, si l'employez totallement au seul menage de votre maison: Bien que, comme I'ay asses conneu, prouvoies fort bien, & a votre grand honneur" ("it seems to me that you commit a great wrong to your quick and gentle spirit, if you employ it totally to the management of your household: even though, as I know well enough, you run it very well and to your great honor"; *Propos amoureux* 8; my trans.). Antoine Du Moulin, who was responsible for editing the posthumous works of Pernette Du Guillet, was careful to indicate the state in which he had found her papers: "parmy ses brouillas en assés poure ordre," "de divers lieux, & plusieurs papiers confusément extraictz" ("among her muddle in quite poor order," "in diverse places, and several papers confusingly removed"; *Rymes* [1545] 5; my trans.). While emphasizing his own role in organizing her work, Du Moulin was also protecting Du Guillet's reputation by implying that she gave precedence to her domestic labor over her literary works, just as a good woman should.

Another aspect of women's unpaid labor that was of pivotal importance to elite families was reproductive labor. Women's production of healthy children protected the family lineage, making their role as the bearers, nurturers, and educators of future generations particularly important. These assumptions too find resonance within women's compositions (see, e.g., Miller and Yavneh's collection). The daughters of Gabrielle de Coignard, who secured the publication of her devotional poetry in 1594, were careful to emphasize that she attended to her duties of family and household before her writing: "durant son vefvage ayant à commander des filles, & à gouverner sa maison sceut si bien mesnager, & les heures du iour . . . qu'elle en fit ces vers Chrestiens tesmoins des vertueuses pensees dont elle entretenoit son esprit, & son loisir" ("during her widowhood, having to command her daughters and govern her household, [she] knew so well how to manage the hours of the day . . . that she wrote these Christian verses, witnesses of her virtuous thoughts, with which she occupied her mind and leisure"; *Œuvres chrestiennes* [1595] 4; my trans.). For some women, joint publications as mother and daughter were valorized as a form of educational responsibility (Sankovitch; Winn, "Mère/fille/femme/muse"). Madeleine Des Roches, the mother in one of perhaps the most famous mother-daughter collaborations in early modern France, suggested that it was her maternal responsibility to accompany her daughter into print: "Mamie, ie sçay que la reuerence, l'amour, & l'honnete pudeur, ne vous permetent étre sans moy au papier des Imprimeurs, & qu'il vous plait mieux que ie suiue mon devoir, mon desir, & ma coutume" ("My dearest, I know that reverence, love, and chaste modesty would not permit you to be without me on printers' paper, and that it pleases you better that I follow my duty, my desire, and my custom"; Des Roches and Des Roches, *Les secondes œuvres* [1583]; my trans.). Learning about the social responsibilities of elite women to their families and households will enable students to make sense of the justifications that pepper their work, as well as the particular choice of themes that commonly emphasize maternal and housewifery duties or role models.

Authors could combine a number of these expectations of women's productive and reproductive labor in inventive ways. Philippe Du Verger, who composed a manual on child-rearing with her mother, describes the act of editing and composition through a metaphor of tending the orchard, which was a play on the name of the authors, the locale in which the text was set, as well as common imagery used to describe the training of children and youths:

> [A]yant leu & releu ce commencement, iay pris resolution de refraichir & reverdir ce Verger fertile . . . de ma tres-honoree Dame & mere, & l'orner & augmenter de plusieurs sortes d'arbres, plantes, compartimens, . . . qui peuvent servir à son enjolivement rapportant tout le

> devoir du iardinier au devoir de ceux qui prennent la charge de cultiver, arrouser, dresser & gouverner la petite & delicate jeunesse.
> (Du Verger and Du Verger *Le Verger fertile* [1595], sig. Aiiir)

> Having read and reread the beginning, I decided to refresh and make green again this fertile orchard . . . of my honored lady and mother, and to adorn and add to it with several sorts of trees, plants, compartments . . . that can serve its embellishment relating all the duty of a gardener to the duty of those who take charge of cultivating, watering, raising, and training the little and delicate young. (my trans.)

For Philippe Du Verger, the act of publication represented a form of matrilineal heritage, and each generation added an element to the final text: "y apportant quelque chose du mien ne faire du labeur de la mere & de la file qu'un mesme œuvre & un mesme livre" ("bringing to it something of mine, make the labor of the mother and daughter only a single work and a single book"; sig. Aiiir; my trans.). Du Verger even conceptualized the text as an infant when she apologized for the work that was "ce que la petitesse de mon esprit peut enfanter" ("what the smallness of my mind can give birth to"; sig. Aiiiv; my trans.). In such ways, the productive labor of writing could become for elite women a form of reproductive labor.

Unsurprisingly, female labor of these kinds, which women authors knew intimately from their own experiences, was a considerable focus of their writings. It reflected in part what matters women thought were important to discuss and disseminate as well as what information or themes copyists, printers, and publishers considered merit worthy or marketable to a broader public. Conduct texts about women's responsibilities at court or in households by authors such as Christine de Pisan and Anne de Bourbon were recovered or transferred from manuscript in the early period of print publication. Advice manuals about gestation, infant care, and child rearing by Louise Bourgeois and the Mesdames Du Verger emerged toward the end of the sixteenth century. For such women it was precisely their occupational experience that conveyed expertise and authority to provide advice to other women. Bourgeois's printed works even included an author portrait, as did the texts of her male scientific and medical counterparts (McTavish). Yet it was not simply practical prose texts that examined women's labor. In literary works too, elite women's experiences as wives, mothers, or widows managing estates, households, family, and children or as nuns were commonly integrated as themes in poetry and prose. The meditative works of Catherine d'Amboise, which exhorted patience in her readers, described "lenuy daulcunes femmes maries voyre qui sont de grosse maison qui aulcunefoys mal sont traictez" ("the troubles of some married women even of great houses who are sometimes mistreated"; *Traicté de morale* fol. 7r; my trans.). Later in the century, Nicole Estienne's versified lament on the position of the "femme mal mariée," a popular literary genre, remarkably highlighted both the sexual and reproductive labor expected of elite women in arranged marriages with older men: "On ne sçauroit penser combien la jeune femme / Endure de tourment, & au corps & à l'âme / Subiette à un vieillard remply de cruauté" and "l'incroyable tristesse / que cette pauvre femme endure en sa grossesse / Le danger où elle est durant l'enfantement / La charge des enfans si penible & fascheuse" ("One cannot imagine how much torment the young wife endures, with both body and soul subject to an old man full of cruelty who enjoys her youth at his will"; "the incredible sadness that this poor woman endures in her confinement, the danger she is in during childbirth, the charge of children so tedious and tiresome"; [c. 1600], fols. Bv and Biiiv; my trans.).[1] However distinct individual female authors' experiences were, the expectations that shaped their lives also informed the kind of intervention that their writing could make in public discourses.

Female Negotiations in Publication Culture

By providing broad gendered and class contexts for understanding women's labor in the period, instructors can help students better appreciate a further set of issues surrounding the presentation of individual female writers' identities as participants in publication culture. How did women negotiate their status as authors with publishers and readers? For women, there was more at stake than simply their literary standing. Their moral reputation was at risk if their words were misrepresented or poorly edited in a sloppy production.

These relationships among female authors, texts, and their wider audience could be very different in manuscript, incunabula, and later printed texts. Christine de Pisan was the only female author whose works were published in incunabula in France, and she had been dead for many years. The first authors of the print era were typically classical and church fathers, and it thus fell to printers to fashion the presentation of their writings in print. It was therefore male printers who first developed a framework for the concept of female print authorship. Antoine Vérard selected Christine de Pisan's *Livre des faits d'armes* to publish in 1488 as *Lart de chevalerie selon Vegece*, with no reference to the sex of its author. Where *Christine* appeared in the original as an interlocutor in the text, Vérard replaced it with the male *l'aucteur*. Specific references to Christine's position as a female author were effaced from the text's first chapter (Wareham). Some fifty years later, Etienne Groulleau, who published Christine's *Le chemin de long estude* in 1549, indicated through the work's preface his assumption that the very notion of a professional writer such as Christine might need some explanation to contemporaries. He found it through a careful explanation of her activity as a virtuous avoidance of vice: "il te faut entendre qu'apres le trespass de son mary, ne voulant demourer oysive . . . composa ce present œuvre . . . qui signifie le bon vouloir qu'elle avoit de soy ocuper aulx lettres sacrées, et prophanes" ("you should understand that after the death of her husband, not wanting to remain idle . . . she composed this present work . . . that demonstrates the praiseworthy desire she had to occupy herself with sacred and profane learning"; fol. Aiiiv; my trans.). The first print presentations of Christine's de Pisan's work would serve as a reflection of publishers' notions of female authorship, with which later female authors would have to contend.

As living authors became increasingly common, printers and publishers were required to learn to negotiate the presentation of an author's work. Students can still study some of the relationships between female authors and publishers through tracing the editions of particular works, as well as in prefaces and copyright statements. With every new copy of a manuscript, changes might creep in beyond the control or knowledge of the author. Print might represent some security against this as a standardized version but risked disseminating errors far and wide if a female author could not control the production. Typically it was the printers or publishers who sought protection for their economic investment in the production of a text, through the mechanism of the royal privilege. A number of women writers, however, responded to their concerns by securing the privilege for their text themselves, thus retaining control over the choice of publisher and the final printed version. Louise Labé is one example. The granting of the privilege included in the 1556 reedition of her poetic works indicated that

> elle auroit des long temps composé . . . plusieurs Sonnets, Odes & Epistres . . . & iceus encores non parfaits, publiez en diuers endroits. Et doutant qu'aucuns ne les vousissent faire imprimer en cette sorte, elle les ayant revuz & corrigez à loisir les mettroit volontiers en lumiere, à fin de supremer les premiers exemplaires.

> she long ago composed . . . several sonnets, odes and epistles . . . and those not yet perfected, were published in diverse places. And doubting that anyone would want to have them printed in this way, she having reviewed and corrected them at leisure put them willingly in print, so as to suppress the first versions.
> (*Euvres . . . Revues et corrigees*, n. pag.; my trans.)

Securing privilege provided one means for some women to take a degree of control over their words in print, but it was dependent on financial and physical access to the kings and courts who were responsible for their issue.

Students might be asked to consider the ways in which manuscript offered an alternative or complementary mode of literary publication for a select group of women writers. Particular salons circulated verses that were later compiled into manuscript and printed anthologies (see Catherine de Clermont, countess of Retz, as one example). Manuscript as well as print could publicize the work of a particular female author. The rhyming and translated versions of popular texts composed by Anne of Graville, a lady-in-waiting to Queen Claude, enjoyed scribal circulation at court in multiple copies. Graville's version of Boccaccio's *Teseida delle nozze d'Emilia* was evidently commissioned by the queen, and one copy includes an image of Graville presenting the finished text to the queen (MS 5116, fol. 1v, Bibliothèque de l'Arsenal, Paris; see fig. 3 of Wilson-Chevalier's essay). Yet other versions make no reference to her name, demonstrating the ways in which women's identities as authors of texts (just as men's) could be effaced from the literary record.

Manuscript and print also allowed access to different groups of women. Circulation of female writings in manuscript was often dependent on women's access to discrete communities such as literary salons and court environments where manuscripts operated as a form of limited dissemination. Print could, however, circumvent barriers of distance or class by transmitting a woman's works and thus her literary reputation far and wide. Women were not typically able to travel as freely as men because of social and financial restrictions, which limited their ability to secure forms of patronage from centers of literary activity. In such cases, print might be an instrumental strategy to develop networks. Madeleine and Catherine Des Roches, who resided in Poitiers, published some of their works in Paris, where opportunities for their writings to be exposed to a wider literary circle were greatly enhanced. When the poetic works of Marie de Romieu, from Viviers, were published in Paris, print was seen by contemporaries as a means of her introduction into French literary culture. As one admirer wrote in her honor: "tes vers eurent si bonne grace . . . Que tous disoient qui est ceste Romieu. /L'on leur respond, c'est une Vivaroise/Qui se fait voir en la terre Francoise,/Gloire des siens & de son petit lieu" ("your verses were of such good grace . . . that everyone asked, Who is this Romieu? 'She's a Vivaroise,' came the reply, 'who makes herself known in French lands, glory of her loved ones and of her little place' "; Les premières œuvres poetiques [1581], fol. Aiiiv; my trans.).

Some female authors embedded aspects of the processes of print authorship directly into their texts. Catherine Des Roches published some of her correspondence with her Parisian publisher, Abel L'Angelier, in the very text about which she was corresponding. This included notifying the publisher of the progress of her latest work: "moy, qui ay transcrit les deux premiers livres de Claudian, esperant d'achever bien tost le troisiesme" ("I have transcribed the first two books of Claudian, hoping to finish the third very soon"; my trans.). She also included a letter in her published correspondence in which she debated the most appropriate title for the work: "Nommez-le donc ainsi que bon vous semblera, du tiltre de Missives, ou de Lettres, ou d'Epistres: pource que la curiosité des homes en rendra peut ester la depesche plus prompte" ("name it thus as you see fit, as Missives, or as Letters or Epistles, so that readers' curiosity will perhaps make it sell more quickly"; Des Roches and Des Roches, *Missives* [1586], fol. 40r; my trans.). The public presentation of Des Roches's relationship with L'Angelier highlighted above all her intellect and her learned networks but, significantly, did not occlude her aspiration to be seen publicly as an author.

In summary, it is clear that female authors of early modern manuscript and printed texts conceived of the labor associated with their efforts in wide-ranging ways. For some women, the composition of works in manuscript or print was a form of professional work, as they strove to gain a living from patronage or recognition as participants in literary or intellectual cultures. Others found in writing simply a forum in which to present their occupational expertise beyond it, marketing their abilities for future work opportunities or stamping their authority on the nature of public discussion of that field. For a broad array of female authors, writing enabled them to present their own experiences or ideal models of paid or unpaid forms of labor to a wider audience. For all, expectations about women's responsibilities to household and familial cares formed an integral component of the assumptions that female authors brought to their writing and that governed their reception. With some knowledge of the contexts in which women labored for money, for reputation, and for status as befitted their individual circumstance and social position in the early modern period, students will be better placed to appreciate the techniques and strategies of women as writers of manuscript and published compositions, as well as the topoi of industry, production, and reproduction within them.

Note

1. Nicole Estienne published under her married name, Mme Liebault.

François Rigolot

The Invention of Female Authorship in Early Modern France

In Ovid's *Metamorphoses*—one of the great best sellers of all times—some of the most powerful myths have to do with abused women turned into artists. In one tale (6.144–45) Arachne, a low-born girl who has gained fame in the art of tapestry, daringly challenges Athena, Jupiter's daughter, who identifies with Olympian authority, to a weaving contest. Arachne is punished by the infuriated goddess, who transforms her into a spider, thus condemning her derisively to continue her art as an insect weaver, in a cruelly depreciated mode. In another tale (1.625–67), Princess Io, after being seduced and cowardly abandoned by Jupiter, is transformed into a heifer by her tormenter, who fears his wife's vengeance. Deprived of human speech and thus unable to denounce the Olympian god's abuse, she manages to trace letters on the sand with her foot and reveals her identity and the story of her misfortune. Philomela (6.571–646) offers another horror story with a similar theme and denouement. After being raped by Tereus, her tongue is cut off by the criminal so she will not reveal the name of her assailant. She nevertheless finds a way to alert the outside world: by weaving her tragic story into a tapestry, which she smuggles off to her sister.

Although these powerful myths have often been interpreted by feminist critics as emblems of masculine silencing strategies toward talented women (Nancy Miller, "Arachnologies"; Joplin), they may also have served as exemplary models for female authors who, in the face of adversity, read them as a source of inspiration to fight for their legitimate rights, take an assertive stand, use their imagination, and produce works of art and literature. As Louise Labé wrote in the 1550s, the creative female response is meant to show men "all the wrongs they have done to the other sex" and, at the same time, how women, when allowed to make use of their creative powers, can contribute significantly to humanist culture and civilization (*Œuvres complètes* 41; my trans.). Yet Renaissance women were also encouraged to become themselves published authors by the exemplary real role models provided by formidable predecessors. One of them was the Italian-born *femme de lettres* of the late Middle Ages, Christine de Pisan. At the dawn of the fifteenth century, myth became reality. In *Le livre de la Cité des Dames* (*The Book of the City of Ladies* [1405]) Christine de Pisan used the well-established convention of allegory to celebrate the achievements of the female sex and systematically record the wrongs done to women from classical time to her medieval society. A widow and a foreigner at the royal court of Charles VI, the mad king, Christine was doubly suited to speak out about female marginality and "self-consciously construct a gendered authoritative voice within the rhetorical strictures of late medieval literary cultures" (Desmond, "Gender, Authorship" 123; see also Kellogg; Quilligan, *Allegory*).

The Renaissance did not forget such an extraordinary role model. Editions of Christine's works were regularly printed throughout the sixteenth century (Brown, "Reconstruction"). In addition to her *Cité des Dames*, which was translated into English in 1521, one of her most widely read works was the *Epistre Othéa*, also known then as *Les cent hystoires de Troye*. It was translated three times in English (Yenal). A rhymed fictional letter in the manner of Ovid's *Heroides*, it was supposedly written by Othéa, the goddess of wisdom. Addressed to a young man, the fifteen-year-old Hector, it offers a highly complex text (with a mix of verse, gloss, and allegory) and uses the epistolary form to recount and comment on one hundred mythical stories for the education of the future Trojan hero (Hindman). Truly, Christine made no mystery of her intentions: passing herself off as a double of the goddess of wisdom, she transformed the Greek myths to suit her goals and used her fictional frame to paint a positive portrait of women for the future leaders of French society (Brown-Grant; Huot, "Seduction"; Reno; Richards, "Medieval *Femme-Auteur*").

As the revered Minerva of French letters, Christine was widely acknowledged by later writers, and her name remained an obligatory reference in the profeminine literary tradition (Willard). In the sixteenth century, she was repeatedly quoted, always approvingly, in works as diverse as Symphorien Champier's *Ship of Ladies* (1503), Jean Marot's *The Truespeaking Advocate of Ladies* (1530–35), and Jean Bouchet's *Poetical Judgement of Feminine Honor* (1538). In a popular tract, *On the Evil and Virtue of Women*—a major feminist document in the *querelle des femmes*, which had six editions between 1564 and 1586—Jean de Marconville, an outspoken defender of women, assigned Christine the first place among writers of both sexes.

Yet one should not be blinded by the recurring mention of Christine's name and the constant eulogy of her fame throughout the Renaissance. When, some forty years before Marconville, Clément Marot, the witty court poet, mentions Christine's name, his tribute sounds considerably restrictive. In the rondeau he composed for Jeanne Gaillarde, a learned woman from Lyon, he contrasts Christine's knowledge and erudition with Jeanne's and declares that Jeanne's more refined eloquence certainly qualifies her to earn the prize (*Œuvres complètes* 140). Obviously the times had changed. For a new generation of writers, although "la Cristine" represented the highest ideals of feminine learning, her language had become old fashioned and her poetic style could no longer rival the inventive rhythms and vivid eloquence of Renaissance writers. Christine was still an unparalleled figure of learning, but her stature as a *femme auteur* was doomed to wane, as new talented women writers came into the limelight, ready to have their works published and praised by posterity (Richards, "Medieval *Femme Auteur*"; Sommers).

In his famous letter to Pantagruel, old Gargantua deplored the lack of opportunities he himself had had to face in his youth, and he confessed his amazement at the social and cultural progress accomplished since then, which made it so much easier for children like his son to receive a decent education: "Le temps n'estoit tant idoine ne commode ès lettres comme est de present. . . . Maintenant toutes disciplines sont restituées" ("The times were not as fit and favorable for learning as they are to-day. . . . Now every method of teaching has been restored"; Rabelais, *Pantagruel* 243; *Complete Works* 160). And the good old king added, with a slightly ironical twist, "Que diray-je? Les femmes et les filles ont aspiré à ceste louange et manne celeste de bonne doctrine" ("What am I to say next? Women and girls have aspired to this celestial laud and manna of good learning"; 243;

160). Coming from a writer like François Rabelais, whose male chauvinistic tendencies can be amply documented, such a statement is all the more remarkable. The education of women had certainly made enormous progress since the end of the One Hundred Years War. Rabelais's position is echoed by humanists like Desiderius Erasmus, Juan Luis Vives, and many others. They concur in recognizing the need for a cultivated female elite, not only in the aristocratic courts of Europe (Rabelais himself dedicated his *Tiers livre* to Marguerite de Navarre, the learned sister of King Francis I) but also in the middle-class families of major cities (Read).

In his famous literary manifesto *La deffence et illustration de la langue françoyse* (1549), Joachim Du Bellay recalled Greek and Roman cultural achievements and urged modern poets to imitate them by enriching the French language and contributing their talents to French greatness. At one point, the Pléiade's spokesman marvels at classical times, when "even women" ("les femmes mesmes") shared the scholarly ideals of their male counterparts. He cites Sappho, Corinna, Cornelia, "and a thousand others, whose names fully belong to the memory of Greeks and Romans" (81–82).[1] To be sure, Du Bellay's advice was heeded, and by 1584 the number of talented women writers had become so impressive and their contribution to French literary life so respectable that a late-sixteenth-century bibliographer, François Grudé La Croix du Maine, proposed to create a special collection of books exclusively devoted to the French and Latin writings of contemporary women writers: "une Bibliotheque à part, contenant leurs vies et leurs compositions tant Latines que Françoises" ("A separate library, containing their lives and works, both in Latin and French"; 284; my trans.).

Most scholars agree today that the Renaissance, no matter how we may define it, was not only a great cultural movement by men for men in the service of patriarchal power (Rigolot, "Écrire au féminin"). It also witnessed the unprecedented development of a feminist consciousness, especially in mid-cinquecento Italy, when a "collective process of publication" in salon circles was led by the female patrons of the Colonna d'Aragona family (Robin). In northern Europe a similar phenomenon was nurtured by humanist thought and the liberal, antiestablishment aspects of the Reformation. In those days, as Merry E. Wiesner reminds us,

> the best life, the one which earned oneself and one's family the most honor, was that which included not only scholarly activity, but also political and public service. Such a life was impossible for women, however,

> not only because of the realities of Renaissance politics, but also because for a woman, a public reputation was dishonorable, a sure sign of immorality and scandal. ("Women's Defense" 12)

While numerous women openly engaged in authorship, many were reluctant to go into print. Manuscript circulation was a much preferred medium: for women it provided "a readership outside the home, control over the work, and a reputation as poet-scholar, or controversalist without a word having been published" (Ezell 83).

In *Histoire de la vie privée*, Roger Chartier cites a Latin proverb about why women should refrain from going into print: "Est virgo haec penna, meretrix est stampificata," which could translate, "with a pen, she is a virgin; once published, she turns a whore" (123). Yet despite such a serious threat, some women writers still decided to choose publication over manuscript circulation. What was their motivation? In his groundbreaking *Bibliotheque françoise* (1584), La Croix du Maine gives some useful statistics and makes some perceptive remarks. La Croix du Maine observes that, "while a significant number of women writers participated in the intellectual life of the times, less than half published their manuscripts" (qtd. in Larsen, "'Un honneste passetems'" 13). Anne Larsen further notes that "of the forty-five sixteenth-century literary women he mentions . . . , only fourteen published books, and another four had their pieces printed in miscellanea, leaving twenty-seven who did not publish" (13). In keeping with the Pléiade poets' drumming up for French greatness, La Croix du Maine encouraged literary women to publish their works because they would contribute to the national effort toward the "deffence et illustration de la langue françoyse." The French bibliographer was himself deeply concerned about women writers' literary survival:

> He forcefully argue[d] that women should get their works into print, rather than merely circulate their manuscripts, so that, if not at present, at least some day in the future a more enlightened reader [could] rightfully judge without sexual prejudice the excellence of their inventions. (14)

About Suzanne Habert, a little-known writer whose works were still unavailable in print, La Croix du Maine wrote:

> Je n'ay encores rien veu imprimé de ses escrits et compositions mais quand il luy plaira de les mettre en lumiere, elle montrera que les hommes se sont jusques icy vantez de surpasser les femmes en inventions de plusieurs beaux escrits, et toutesfois le jugement en sera delaissé à

> juger à la posterité, qui n'aura esgard aux personnes mais aux effects de la chose. (461)
>
> I still have not seen any writings and compositions [by Suzanne Habert] in print; but, when she wishes to publish them, she will demonstrate that men have always boasted to surpass women in inventing several fine written works, and yet it will be left to posterity to pass judgment, not on the basis of gender but by looking at facts. (my trans.)

In other words, future readers should not be blinded by gender expectations but judge for themselves on the sole basis of literary excellence. In Elizabeth Eisenstein's words, "the preservative power of print could insure the survival of literary endeavors in a market economy in which, by 1550, manuscripts were relegated to second place in most libraries" (113). But, more important perhaps, the desirability of going into print resulted from a new, pervasively rising awareness of the social rewards of literary authorship.

In early modern Europe, for both sexes, the development of a literary consciousness was linked to a series of complex factors: the changing nature of the notion of authorship; the evolution of the writer's social function; and, more generally, the question of the rise of individual values in society (Blumenberg; Burckhardt; Cassirer; Garin; Renaut; Simonin; C. Taylor; Toulmin; Viala). Historically, literary subjectivity was mostly fashioned through traditional linguistic and rhetorical models that, as Roland Barthes ("Mort") and Michel Foucault ("Auteur") have shown, were themselves influenced by powerful ideological constructs. In the Middle Ages, bards and minstrels, clerks and copyists, *acteurs* and jongleurs represented various aspects of the creative process, and the modern concept of authorship remains largely inadequate to describe the complex performative process through which literary works were produced and transmitted (Zumthor). Beginning with the fifteenth century, however, some crucial changes can be observed with major writers like Guillaume de Machaut, Jean Froissart, Charles d'Orléans, and Christine de Pisan (Brownlee; Cerquiglini; Huot, "Seduction"). Beneath the universal thrust of their productions looms an unconcealed claim to individual intellectual ownership. As writers, the onus is on them to give evidence that their authority is justified and deserved. At the same time, as the manuscript culture recedes, a new legal system develops to insure protection of authors and publishers from unlawful imitations and forgeries. In France, the granting of a privilege ensured copyright guarantees that, in turn, fostered an increased awareness of and desire for literary property (Brown, *Poets* and "Reconstruction"; Marc Rose).

Yet many early modern writers continued to believe that their legal rights would be better preserved by seeking the protection of powerful aristocratic patrons. In the early 1500s, court poets did not really care to rush into print as long as they could be assured that their position was solidly anchored and they would continue to enjoy their patrons' liberal generosity (Brown, *Poets* 21). At the same time, as books became economic products with a market value and the lure of profitability, writers and publishers entered into a new style of relationship. The authors' names began to appear on title pages, in *incipit* and *explicit* formulas or in the form of special emblems and signatures (Fraenkel). At the court of Burgundy, a chronicler named Jean Molinet represented himself quite candidly as a *moulinet*, that is, literally, as a small mill grinding away the grains of rhetoric for the pleasure of wealthy patrons always eager to savor his most ornate "flours of speech" (Rigolot, *Poétique* 28–30).

Regardless of these new markings of individuality, however, the Renaissance author, lauded by generations of scholars as the autonomous and self-made *uomo universale*, was in fact constructed by collective agency. The seemingly individualistic creation of identity on the part of Renaissance artists and writers may best be understood as the result of a collaborative process. Clément Marot dedicated his first collection of poems, *L'adolescence clementine*, to other poets who shared his love for poetry and whom he addressed affectionately as his "brothers," all of them "Apollo's children" (*Œuvres complètes* 35). Yet the corporate spirit that pervades Marot's literary production does not clash with his claim to utter singularity: Marot is an "Autheur" who has a personal reputation to defend and intends to have his talents recognized by posterity. Marot's ambivalence is significant. His decision to go to print has both a collective and an individual side: it is meant as a monument to poetic brotherhood as well as a personal reaction against the printers' sloppiness and the booksellers' greed. Here the medieval tradition of scholarly brotherhood (*confrérie*) becomes conflated with a new humanist sense of intellectual solidarity and exchange (*sodalitas*): the individual rights of the "Autheur" can best be recognized within a renovated republic of letters.

Unsurprisingly, a similar motivation can be observed with women writers who emulate their male counterparts, either by responding collectively to the clerical establishment or by presenting their individual works with the approval of a supportive intellectual community (Solterer). Since, for a woman, going into print constituted a transgression of the patriarchal order, the need for group support became essential. Allusions to the communal origins of women's literary projects are often thematized as such in fictional texts. Thus Marguerite de Navarre's *Heptameron*, a collection of seventy-two tales united by a frame story, is a case in point. The conception of the book is explicitly presented as a collective, historical one. In the prologue we learn that the idea of rewriting the *Decameron* in French was first entertained at the court of Francis I as a collective intellectual pastime. In Marguerite's Boccaccian imitation, travelers are stranded by spring flooding in the Pyrenees. As they wait for the waters to subside and a bridge to be built, Parlamente, one of the *devisants* who serves as the fictional double of the author, proposes to take up the aborted courtly project. Clearly, the fictional names of the five women and five men who serve as storytellers point, although sometimes deceptively, to the real aristocrats who initiated the project at the French court. Also, the "truthfulness" ("la verité") of the stories about to be told is dramatically emphasized in the prologue by Parlamente, who claims that unlike Boccaccio's *brigata* the small *compagnie* will only recount things that have *really happened* (*Heptaméron* [1998–99] 9). In sum, while presenting herself as an individual and autonomous author, Marguerite stresses the collective nature of her work. At the same time, she establishes a "communal spirit," which justifies her claim to individual authorship. One can fathom the hidden political implications of such a strategy. In a different national context, one could also look at Edmund Spenser's *Faerie Queene* and Philip Sidney's *Arcadia* as extraordinary attempts to displace into fiction similar problems of female sovereignty (Patterson; Doody).

The case of Louise Labé is even more significant in the role played by a local intellectual community in the publishing of women's works. Labé's *Euvres*, printed in 1555, are often read as the product of a lone dissident who dramatically challenged the patriarchal order in her home city of Lyon. Yet one wonders how this low-born daughter and wife of rope makers was able to persuade Jean de Tournes, one of the most famous humanist printers of the time, to publish her "feminist" manifesto and passionate love poems. To answer this question, one must recontextualize Labé's works within the intellectual community of a progressive, forward-looking city, located at the crossroads of French and Italian cultures (Romier; Saulnier, *Maurice Scève*).

In a recent highly controversial study, Mireille Huchon, a respected professor at the Sorbonne, defended the intriguing thesis that Louise

Labé's work was a hoax ("une supercherie"), a literary fabrication cooked up by male writers eager to play a monumental joke on naive readers by giving real life to a mythical female author. Although some of Huchon's arguments raise interesting questions, they only amount to mere conjectures that leave many readers unconvinced. On the positive side, Huchon's "paper tiger" reinforces the sound belief that any claim to authorship must be carefully recontextualized, not in terms of an abstract and vague zeitgeist but in the light of the specific conditions that made it possible for a woman to become a published author. Obviously, in their open rivalry with the northern Pléiade poets, Lyon's literary circles needed a remarkable woman writer to boost their own reputation. After all, the works of Sappho, the Greek poet of Lesbos, had just been rediscovered and made available in print (Rigolot, *Louise Labé* 31–67). In the context of Lyon's claim to cultural supremacy, Labé's talent was a great opportunity to show that the voice of Sappho could be successfully reanimated in French. Thus Labé's feminist bravado cannot be viewed as the product of a lone visionary or foolhardy individual inexplicably ahead of her times. It must be reread historically as mirroring the major concerns of an ambitious intellectual and political community eager to present itself as the true reenactment of the idealized Greek elite, with a new extraordinary Sapphic presence in their midst.

Finally, one must consider the theoretical question of sexual difference in the elaboration of group identity as a key to early modern authorship. It could be construed, of course, that, in any patriarchal society, women's drive for social cohesion is an ideological maneuver tied to their symbolic status and political subjugation. Yet the fact that, in the Renaissance, both male and female writers felt the same urge for group support runs contrary to a gender-based theory. It seems safer to steer clear of a certain kind of feminist psychoanalytic position which posits that the female self is essentially less individuated than the male self and that, as a consequence, women have less rigid boundaries than men and exhibit a greater propensity for nurturing and caring for others. Historically, in the case of generic authorship, this is simply not true (Chodorow; Dinnerstein; Kristeva; Bruneau).

What may be true, however, is the importance of "homosocialness" for the emergence of published authors. Under Foucault's influence we have grown accustomed to defining the literary critic's mission as one that makes silence speak. It has become crucial to uncover what meanings were suppressed by the "homosocial" force of desire. If Eve Kosofsky

Sedgwick is right—and indeed she may be—in a patriarchal environment men really desire nothing more than one another, but society's prohibition against homosexuality forces them to repress that desire (*Between Men*). Instead, they recognize women as love objects and in the literary pantheon channel their homosexual impulses into keeping women writers subordinate while using token recognition as a means to bond with one another for social as well as political advantage.

In early modern France—and probably mutatis mutandis in the rest of Western Europe as well—all signs point to consider female authorship as a male invention, which came about because an elite, trained in the classics, needed it for their own gratification. In most situations governed by Girardian mimetic and triangular desire, implicitly or explicitly women were offered pseudopartnerships that were meant to consolidate male "homosocial" bonding and political entitlements. The only chance for women writers to become published authors was gleefully to join the theocentric order established by men, often with the complicity of female sovereignty. This certainly does not mean that women did not produce great works of art under such constraints. But they were most successful when they were clones of Athena, directly born of Jupiter's brains, and ready to punish female dissidents who did not conform to that Olympian order. The triumph of Arachne as an artist remained repressed and concealed in the most remote recesses of the collective unconscious. From Pisa to Navarre, from Lyon to Paris and beyond, a foundational mythical story seems to have repeated itself endlessly. Princess Io's letters and Queen Philomela's tapestry continued to reflect the tragic impulse that lies at the heart of creativity and that accounts for a relentless anxiety toward authorship. No wonder Ovid's *Metamorphoses* remained for a long time on the best sellers' list.

Note

1. I cite Chamard's edition.

Dora E. Polachek

Brantôme's Women: Revising the Masculine Point of Reference

To get a full grasp of what early modern women authors were responding to—that is, what they incorporated into their creations and what they put into question—I designed a semester-long upper-level undergraduate French seminar that cast a wide net and included more than female-authored texts. Laughing at Love, Sex, and Marriage: Renaissance Perspectives was offered for the first time in 2006, with the goal of making accessible a complex and varied corpus of readings in French that was held together by the guiding question, What were the defining features of the erotically attractive female as figured in predominantly male texts? Formulating a new course is always a challenging enterprise. When I was in the preliminary planning stages, I realized that almost all the texts I was including were not part of the canonical readings that constituted my undergraduate education. Many of them remained unknown to me even during my graduate school days. As with many American scholars of early modern French literature, I was formulating a course based on subsequent discoveries made through participation in National Endowment for the Humanities summer institutes and seminars, professional conferences, as well as explorations of texts that resonated with my interest in gender, sexuality, and the comic in the early modern period. Will this course fly? is what we always ask ourselves. Will the readings be linguistically accessible to students who are taking an advanced-level seminar but whose individual preparation varies wildly? What kinds of prereading guiding questions will need to be posted on *Blackboard* to deal with any language issues that could be stumbling blocks to understanding and therefore to discussions in class? Furthermore, texts that we find particularly rich and fruitful in our personal exploration for presentation at academic conferences and in professional journals are not necessarily those that will speak to our students in the same way that they speak to us.

But I wanted to perform a pedagogical experiment and introduce on the undergraduate level texts that would get students thinking about the kinds of issues that are still strongly debated today and to make students see that many of our current stereotypes about women and their erotic desirability have a long literary history. The attempt to subvert these stereotypes has an equally long history, and, on the basis of my belief that humor was then and remains even now one of the most effective methods of unsettling the foundations of certain commonplaces, I decided to introduce relevant sections of the physician Laurent Joubert's 1579 *Traité du ris* ("Treatise on Laughter") so students would have a theoretical framework with which to work. I have also found that the comic offers a familiar point of entry to new material, since humor is such a staple of American youth culture.

Besides three novellas from Marguerite de Navarre's *Heptameron* and two sonnets of Louise Labé, the texts I chose were written by men. Among the texts relevant to the focus of this essay are Pierre de Ronsard's famous sonnet for Hélène (Sonnet XLIII) "Quand vous serez bien vieille" ("When you will be very old") and two of Clément Marot's anatomical *blasons*, both entitled "Le tétin" ("The Breast"), but the first better known as "Le beau tétin" ("The Beautiful Breast") and the second as "Le laid tétin" ("The Ugly Breast"). Serving as opposite sides of the same coin, these two poems were meant to show what qualities a woman's body had to possess to merit praise and what metamorphosis that same part needed to undergo to provoke disgust. I also included the anonymous *blason* "Le con de la pucelle" ("The Maiden's Twat") so students could see that even the most private of a woman's body parts—her genitals—could be the focus of the male gaze and the literary creation that was born of it.

By beginning with these texts, students saw immediately that youth, beauty, and virginity were the operative elements in the tropes of erotic desirability in the male fantasies that these readings provided. With Ronsard's poem, students became aware of how the carpe diem motif functioned as a male seduction strategy that depended on instilling fear of aging in the woman. Painting a vivid picture of what old age will look like for her (she will be a hag, stooped, sitting by the fire to warm her cold body), the male voice in the poem makes clear that a woman's desirability is time bound and that her only chance for "surviving" lies exclusively in the hands of the poet. To share in the immortality that the poet assures the young woman that he will attain, he proposes a tit-for-tat exchange: literary immortality for the woman can be obtained only if she allows herself to be physically had.

Students often laugh when they see what constitutes these male fantasies of female desirability and to what ends they are employed. But they laugh even more when they confront with this preliminary background knowledge Brantôme's second volume of his *Recueil des dames* (*Book of the Ladies*), better known as *Les vies des dames galantes* (commonly translated as *Lives of Fair and Gallant Ladies*). In his dedicatory letter to François, duc d'Alençon, the brother of King Henry III, Brantôme states explicitly that the work's sole goal is to amuse: "C'est assez parlé des choses serieuses, il faut un peu parler des gayes" ("Enough with serious matters; it's time to speak of merrier things"; Brantôme, *Recueil* 236; my trans.).

When students focus their attention on the table of contents of the work, they see immediately how Brantôme plays with the form of the philosophical treatise by dividing into "discours" ("discourses") his associative accumulation of hundreds of titillating anecdotes revolving around the sexual goings-on in the Valois court. Here is a sampling of his subdivisions: "Discours sur les dames qui font l'amour et leurs maris cocus"; "Discours sur le sujet qui contente plus en amours, ou le toucher, ou la veue, ou la parole"; "Autre discours [sur la beauté de la belle jambe, et la vertu qu'elle a]"("Discourse on Ladies Who Make Love and Their Husbands Cuckolds"; "Discourse on the Question of Which Gives the Greatest Satisfaction in Love: Touching, Seeing, or Speaking"; "Other Discourse on the Beauty and Power of Shapely Legs"; Brantôme, *Recueil* [1629]; Brantôme, *Tales* n. pag.).[1] The discourse that students read in its entirety is the fifth (586–618), entitled "Sur l'amour des dames vieilles et come aucunes l'aiment autant que les jeunes" ("On the Love of Old Ladies and How Some of Them Like It as Much as the Young"; my trans.). In a work that students immediately identify as wanting to be risqué, this last title is provocative for several reasons. With it, Brantôme proposes to focus on a subject heretofore unexplored: the old lady as positively erotically desiring and desirable. It stands as unexplored because, with his title, Brantôme immediately parts ways with the commonly accepted wisdom and images inherited from his forebears and contemporaries.

The old woman figured as a physical and mental catastrophe—feeble, sickly, and repulsive—appears in all centuries, and the sixteenth is no exception. As students in this course have already witnessed before reading Brantôme's discourse on old women, even writers of serious treatises seem incapable of curbing their vituperative outpourings of revulsion when the subject arises. In *Traité du ris*, for instance, Joubert speaks of how a "deception à la vue" ("disappointment in seeing") can trigger laughter.[2] As an example, he gives the case of our eagerness when a promise is made to us to show us "une fort belle et jeune femme" ("a very beautiful and young woman"; 25). The letdown occurs the moment we find ourselves tricked and confronted with just the opposite. If Joubert had chosen to construct the sentence announcing the unexpected surprise in parallel fashion, he would have written "une fort laide et vieille femme" ("a very ugly and old woman"), composed of an adverb, two adjectives, and a noun. Instead, even in a serious medical text the author seems unable to resist the temptation of engaging in an activity similar to that of the poets of the *contreblason* tradition, which students saw in full operative mode in Marot's *contreblason* on the ugly breast. In this case, instead of limiting himself to two adjectives (which sufficed to describe the pleasant surprise), Joubert heaps together close to twenty to describe this repulsive hag: "une vielhe ridee, barbuë, veluë, frisee, borgne, chassieuse, enasee, punaise, puante, morveuse, baveuse, rogneuse, poulheuse, orde et sale, bossuë, tortuë, ecropionnee, & plus difforme que la mesme laideur" (25–26). Even translators pull out all the stops with this passage: "with one eye, a runny nose, a thick and kinky beard and under-slung buttocks, dirty, smelly, drooling, toothless, flat-nosed, bandy-legged, humpy, bumpy, stinking, twisted, filthy, knotty, full of lice, and more deformed than ugliness itself" (Rocher 39). In finishing off his description with a comparison ("plus difforme que la mesme laideur"), Joubert wants his readers to go beyond the vast compendium of adjectives describing the old woman by asking them to imagine a hag so ugly that she even surpasses in ugliness the category of ugly.

Since students by this point have a thorough grounding in the tradition within which Brantôme embeds himself, they can better appreciate the creative challenges facing him. From the outset Brantôme sets out to prove his point by proclaiming that the libidinal force of an old woman can surpass by far that of her younger counterparts. To convince us, his opening words home in on precisely that part of the woman, be she young or old, that is the most provocative: her genitals. The lower part of the body thus becomes the focal point through the words Brantôme claims he heard pronounced in the Spanish court by a woman who was very honorable and beautiful but still a bit advanced in age ("mais pourtant un peu aagée"; 586), who announced in full confidence the following: "nulles belles femmes, ou au moins peu, se font vieilles de la ceinture en bas" ("No beautiful ladies, or very few, age from the waist down"; 587). When Brantôme asks her to explain what she means, the woman assures him that this youthfulness below—"d'en bas"—characterizes the physical appearance as well as the sexual desire that never diminishes there. In his treatise on laughter, Joubert states that it is ugly and indecent to uncover the "parties honteuses"—the "shameful parts" (16). For Brantôme, this venereal underworld becomes the star of the spectacle, but in such an unexpected way that it will have the desired effect, namely to inspire laughter.

What was found below the belt is not a new subject for French Renaissance writers. An acceptable subject for the anatomical *blason*, a woman's private parts gave rise to a host of opportunities for male poetic contests of one-upmanship, each poem offering an accumulation of detailed images of every aspect of the woman's fetishized body. While poets sang the praises of the maidenhead, addressing it with gentility in sweet diminutive terms ("Con, mon mignon, ma petite fossette, / Con rebondi en forme de bossette, / Con revêtu d'une riche toison / De fin poil d'or en sa vraie saison" ("Twat, my sweetie, my little dimple, twat rounded in the shape of a little hump, twat dressed in a rich fleece of fine golden hair in its true season"; "Con" 152–53), the private parts of the old woman gave birth to a torrent of venomous verses. Perhaps the most virulent in the sixteenth century were those of Rémy Belleau, a member of the Pléiade poets and secretary to the chamber of Henry III during the same time period that Brantôme frequented the royal court. Presented in my class in a student's oral presentation, Belleau's "Jean qui ne peult" ("John who can't") describes the punishment merited by a young man who finds himself physically impotent in the throes of passion with a young woman: specifically, the punishment involves a sexual encounter with an old woman whose private parts Belleau describes as follows: "béantes, baveuses, pourries, ulcérées, décorées de quelques épars cheveux gris qui ressemblent aux toiles d'araignées" ("gaping, runny, rotted, ulcerated, set off by some sparse graying hairs that resemble spider webs"; Kuin and Prescott 5). These images of grotesque otherness inspire Brantôme, but in an ingeniously different way. In the topsy-turvy world he creates, where the woman is on top in every sense, we can discern a variation of the male fantasy of the sexual capacities of women—what I call Venus envy—capacities that are impervious to the passage of time.

Continuing to quote the words of the Spanish lady, the text reads as follows:

> Or est-il que toute belle femme s'estant une fois essayée au jeu d'amour ne le desapprend jamais, et la continuë luy est toujours très-agreable et douce; ny plus ny moins que, quand l'on a accoustumé une bonne viande, on se fasche fort de la laisser; et tant plus on va sur l'aage, tant est-elle meilleure pour la personne . . . aussi tant la femme va sur l'aage, tant plus est friande d'une bonne chair qu'elle a accoustumé; et si sa bouche d'en haut y prend de la saveur, sa bouche d'en bas aussi en prend bien autant; et la friandise ne s'en oublie jamais ny ne se lasse par la charge des ans. . . . (587)

> So it is that every beautiful woman having tried the game of love once never unlearns it, and to continue in it is always very agreeable and sweet; akin to once having tasted a good piece of meat, one frets about having to do without it, and the older one gets, all the better the meat is for the person . . . ; similarly, as a woman gets older, she becomes that much more fond of a good meat to which she has become accustomed; and if her upper mouth savors it, her mouth down below savors it as much; and the tidbits are never forgotten nor does one tire of it by the weight of years. . . .

Through the totalizing statements he makes in this passage ("*never* unlearns"; "*always* very agreeable"; "*never* forgotten") Brantôme suggests that, once initiated, the woman retains this connoisseur's knowledge forever. Furthermore, he compares the pleasure that she derives from it to eating a particularly tasty morsel of meat that one wants to have always available and to delight in. So that nothing remains ambiguous in his pronouncements, Brantôme divides the woman into two symmetrical parts and thus develops the image that introduced his treatise on old women, where the Spanish woman distinguishes what's above the belt and what we find below it. More specifically, Brantôme focuses on these two mouths — that found above in relation to that found below. Thus in Brantôme's work the woman possesses two active mouths—the visible one and the invisible one that he begins to unveil bit by bit through his use of gastronomical metaphors. In short, the old woman craves all that gives pleasure to her two palates.

In contrast to other writers, Brantôme depicts this craving for savory morsels in a positive rather than a repulsive light. Abandoning Galen's notion that a woman's womb acts like a hungry animal, Brantôme develops instead the image of a discerning palate. So that the meat be transformed into something savory, one needs the ingredients only the woman can provide. Instead of being figured as a passive receptacle, the woman brings essential elements to transform this meat into an irresistible pièce de résistance. Once again, in his description of erotic coupling with the older woman, Brantôme underlines the aesthetic dimension of the act, all through culinary metaphors. He emphasizes the importance of what the old woman brings to the table by intercalating an Italian maxim *Que una galina vechbia fà miglior brodo ch'un'altra* ("that an old hen makes a better broth than a young one; 589).

The additional detail that Brantôme provides about woman's ardor when it comes to physical pleasure—and his statement that a woman remains always ready and available for it—gives rise to a remark filled with envy. For Brantôme, what he refers to as "[l'exercice] de Venus" ("the work of Venus"; 587), always pleasant and easy for the woman, underlines the physiological differences between the sexes. Brantôme admits that physical force diminishes with age, a hard reality to face given his belief that only the man is subject to this sexual waning. Woman can continue to receive and thus savor sexual pleasure "en quelque aage qu'elle soit" ("whatever her age"; 588), while this amorous work is described as a difficult burden given the impotence to which an old man, but not a woman, is subject. The woman who receives "comme une fournaise, tout feu et toute matière" ("like a furnace, all fire and all matter"; 588) evokes the image of the life force, the élan vital that stays with her forever, while the old man finds himself in the winter of his life, incapable of acting on his desires, even if he still feels what Montaigne describes as "quelques tiedes restes de cette ardeur passée" ("a few lukewarm embers of the former fire"; "Sur des vers" 849). In a stereotypical misogynistic vision, physiology defines woman as a passive receptacle. In Brantôme's work, however, this physiology is reshaped into a generative motor of vital energy that remains consistently strong for as long as she lives.

This lower realm is also miraculously exempt from the physical ravages of time. Unlike the old women in misogynistic texts, who when they scan their lower body lament the decrepitude of something that used to be so beautiful, in Brantôme's universe old women become ecstatic when they look at their private parts. What they see confirms that they have remained sexually desirable, and their partners concur once they look at the site of everlasting perfection that the woman reveals to them. As proof, Brantôme provides the example of a great lady "très-belle et bien adonnée à l'amour" ("very beautiful and devoted to love") whose lover returns after an absence of four years. Seeing the effects of the passage of time on the woman's face, he is "si fort desgousté et reffroidy" ("so strongly repulsed and chilled"; 597) that he does not want, and is probably unable, to resume his sexual relations with her. Brantôme's women do not deny that time can destroy the seductive powers of the visible face. However, in this fantasy universe they retain an invincible weapon to prevent the total rejection of their body: all they need to do is find or invent an occasion where they can uncover and display to the desired lover what lies below. Thus, feigning sickness, the great lady receives her former lover in her bed, in broad daylight. Here is what she says and does:

> "Monsieur, je sçay bien que vous me desdaignez à cause de mon visage changé par mon aage; mais tenez, voyez (et sur ce elle luy descouvrit toute la moitié du corps nud en bas) s'il y a rien de changé là. Si mon visage vous a trompé, cela ne vous trompe pas." Le Gentilhomme la contemplant, et la trouvant par là aussi belle et nette que jamais, entra aussi tost en appetit, et mangea de la chair qu'il pensoit estre pourrie et gastée. "Et voylà (dit la Dame), Monsieur, voilà comme vous autres estes trompés! Une autre fois, n'adjoustez plus de foy aux menteries de nos faux visages; car le reste de nos corps ne les ressemble pas tousjours. Je vous apprens cela." (597–98)

> "I know very well that you disdain me because of my face changed by time" (and at this point she uncovered the lower part of her body) "but come look and see if there is anything changed there. If my face has fooled you, this does not." Contemplating it and finding it as beautiful and sound as ever, the gentleman immediately developed an appetite and partook of the meat that he had thought rotten and spoiled. "So there," said the woman, "here is how you others are hoodwinked! The next time, don't be fooled by the lies of our false faces; because the rest of our bodies doesn't always resemble them. I am teaching you this."

Unlike the typical old woman who is horrified by the physical changes she sees and is so mentally slow-witted that she is incapable of reigniting a cool lover, Brantôme's old woman undertakes an educational campaign of enlightenment ("Je vous apprens cela"), where the recalcitrant, formerly ardent lover becomes the pupil. The woman in this manner demonstrates her superior knowledge of her own body, as well as the art of love, similar to Brantôme's depiction of the Italian courtesan as master of the art and her client as an ignorant student in need of an amatory education (Polachek, "Recherche" 240–42). The lesson makes us laugh because of the contrast between the formality of the distancing "vous" that she uses and the scandalously private nature of what she displays to her pupil. In opposition to the old woman we find dissected by the male poets in the *contre-blasons anatomiques*, the better to disgust the reader by her objectification, this woman chooses to present herself divided in two in order to assert her status as desiring subject. Once lured back into the intimate space of the woman's bed, the initially reluctant man undergoes an intellectual conversion as the woman initiates him to secrets and pleasures unknown to other unenlightened men.

Standing on its head the familiar image of the mirror as a *vanitas* reminder of the ephemerality of physical beauty, Brantôme chooses to use this trope in another manner. An older woman's face can only reflect back to her where she stands in the inexorable marching on of time. Here is a modus vivendi that another woman adopts: instead of subjecting herself to the painful reality of what she will see mirrored back to her, she refuses to look at her face, has her servants attend to her coiffure, and repositions the mirror so it makes visible to her her private parts: "par recompense, se miroit et s'arregardait par les parties d'en bas, y prenant autant de delectation comme elle avait fait par le visage autrefois" ("to compensate, took a mirror to her lower parts, taking as much pleasure in that sight as she used to when in earlier days she gazed at her face"; 598). Thus a subject that could have easily turned into a typical female lament on aging and loss of sexual desirability is transformed into a comic tale, amusing because of the bizarre solution found by the old woman as well as by the unexpected praise of a part of the old female body traditionally figured as repulsive but now transformed into a visual delight.

Given the angle of approach that Brantôme chooses to examine female erotic desire, it is easy to understand why no easy consensus exists on what he wants to accomplish in his description of the sexual mores of women of the Valois court. In which camp, for example, do we place Brantôme in the famous *querelle des femmes*? One male critic accuses Brantôme of giving voice to a "deep and salacious misogyny" (Muchembled 54), while a female critic claims that "he takes the side of women and defends their right to sexual liberty" (Lazard, *Pierre de Bourdeille* 229). These diametrically opposed views open up the possibility of lively topics of debate in the classroom, in which students offer textual evidence that can easily support one viewpoint or the other. Complicating ideological categorization even further is what often is forgotten when approaching this text: its prime goal is to entertain. As students see, subversion of expectations lies at the heart of Brantôme's comic game and results in a new model of female desirability.

In a volume devoted to women's writing, the subject I foreground in my title may seem surprising. After all, shouldn't all contributions focus on female-authored texts? The course I have described is predicated on the belief that women's literary production incorporates as well as transforms male models of representation of femininity. This may seem obvious to us as scholars, but in the typical undergraduate French literature course, this "given" is not part of the basic knowledge that our students bring with them. In a course I teach on French women writers and the dynamics of desire, a case in point involved a student's reaction to the first-person narrator of Hélisenne de Crenne's *Les angoisses douloureuses qui procèdent d'amour* proclaiming that her singularly beautiful body made her the constant source of public admiration. But since her beautiful face was not as outstanding as her body, people remarked on the disparity of these two parts (*Angoisses* [2005] 34). Why so much emphasis on her body instead of her mind? the student asked. And if she has a beautiful body as well as a beautiful face, what difference does it make if her face is not quite as outstanding as her body? Had I begun the course with how male authors present women, the student may have been better able to understand how common these tropes were and how even women who dared to enter into the perilous realm of literary production designed for publication and dissemination followed certain male conventions when creating fictional characters. By the same token, only by situating Louise Labé within a tradition that contextualizes her within a larger writing community can students get a full grasp of how a woman reworks the powerful Petrarchan tradition to assert herself as a speaking, desiring subject. In other words, by reversing the roles stipulated in the male model, Labé transforms the male into the object of a female desiring gaze. If in my course Brantôme's text is the lynchpin of the upending of traditional tropes, it is precisely because his comic text presents us with a world transformed. (How women writers of comic works respond in turn to male-authored transformations would be the logical course to develop after the one I have described here but is out of the purview of what I am focusing on in this essay.) We laugh at Brantôme's reversal of stereotypes, at his fantastic creation of a world where the aging *dame galante* becomes a speaking subject whose verbal wit and self-assured command of language as well as of her body become inextricably linked to her erotic physical attractiveness. As we have seen, she too is dissected into two symmetrical parts, but instead of leaving us with a fragmented, dissected corpse, Brantôme pieces her back together and demonstrates that the speaking mouth above functions in complete harmony with the one below—a far cry from the *blasonneurs* and carpe diem conventions that inform his comic send-up.

Notes

1. I have modified Bair's translation.
2. All translations are mine unless otherwise indicated.

Ann Rosalind Jones

Pernette Du Guillet among the *Néoplatoniciennes* of Her Time: Private Conversation Meant to Be Overheard

At first reading, Pernette Du Guillet seems to be a difficult poet because of the dense courtly-love and Neoplatonic vocabulary she uses to represent her intimate conversation with the man she loves. But this impression of an impenetrable private code oversimplifies the *Rymes*. A more complex picture emerges through a focus on the wider world she draws into many of her poems, in which the acts of speaking and writing for a public, persuading its members to join her, are persistent rhetorical strategies.

Du Guillet resembles other women writers of her time in this ongoing courtship of an audience. The one-to-one love relationship that she represents in the short epigrams and longer chansons of her *Rymes* links her to other writers of her time and to the larger audience on whom she calls for admiration and sympathy. Although the solitude *à deux* she depicts in her poems appears to arise from her initial claim for the unequaled perfection of her beloved, this idealization, in one form or another, was the basis for many Renaissance lyric sequences. So even as her admiration for the beloved man positions the two of them in a refined spiritual *entretien* transcending worldly love, she can maintain this distinction only by reference to less enlightened lovers and to readers populating both her textual world and the less ideal world outside it.

Du Guillet was the daughter of a Lyonnais nobleman, who, though he married her off at an early age, evidently allowed her to study (she knew Italian and Spanish as well as French) and to compose poems and songs to perform in meetings of the academies and salons in her city. Dying very young, she was eulogized for her impressive intellect and her pure heart: an unnamed poet prefaced her *Rymes* with praise for the "affection sainte / De chaste amour" ("holy affection / of chaste love") that was its topic (35), even though this love had been for a man who was not her husband.[1] This formula—"the holy affection of chaste love"—is close in meaning to Du Guillet's "parfaicte amour": "perfect love," purified of erotic desire but strengthened by the spiritual bond toward which the lovers have ascended. Du Guillet's poems produce this impression of love free of erotic impropriety in many ways, particularly in their various forms of address.

At the beginning of her *Rymes*, in the first epigram Du Guillet sets up a private mise-en-scène by defining the mystical intensity of her first meeting with the man destined for her and no one else, whom she recognized at once as the fulfillment of her particular destiny:

> Le haut pouvoir des Astres à permis
> (Quand je nasquis) d'estre heureuse et servie:
> Dont congnoissant celuy, qui m'est promis,
> Restée suis sans sentiment de vie. (36)
>
> The high power of the stars allowed me,
> at my birth, to be fortunate and served.
> So at the moment I recognized the man promised to me,
> I lost any sense of life.

She insists again in epigram 2 on the exclusive nature of this awakening, a transformation the man made possible for her alone: "Celuy, qui feit *pour moy* ce Jour au Monde" ("He who created *for me* this light in the world"; 38; my italics).

Yet in both poems she also envisions communication beyond the pair of lovers as an immediate effect of their meeting. In the sixth line of this first poem, she uses the verb *regraver*, to "re-etch," a term from printing, as Christian Barataud and Danielle Trudeau point out (36–37n6): "Fors le sentir du mal, qui me convie / A regraver ma dure impression / D'amour cruelle" ("except the sensation of pain, which summons me / to etch again into myself this deep, hard impression / Of cruel love"). Because *regraver* means to reincise a steel or copper plate, it is a reference to the process used by engravers to produce multiple copies—an example of which we are looking at here at the beginning of the book.

Du Guillet compares the forceful effort she must make to articulate the sudden effect of her first encounter with her beloved to the vigorous process by which an etcher cuts into a metal plate before it can be inked and covered with paper in the press. To produce a printed text, compositors, whose professional title offers a telling analogy to composers of verse and prose, aligned many small, separate letter blocks into words and then into lines. For pictorial woodcuts, a frame was constructed of four decorated or lettered panels aligned to form a rectangle around the image. *Regraver* thus works on two levels as a map of the structure of *Les rymes* to come. The poet combines many small poems into a public love story that invites a reading from beginning to end. But like a visual image, a *recueil* of lyrics also permits a multidirectional reading, freeing readers to move backward and sideways as does the viewer of a pictorial print. This metaphor of publication immediately establishes Du Guillet's attention to a public composed of readers whom she persuades to join her.

It is striking that Du Guillet begins her first poem with a metaphor from printing; only in her second does she turn to the kind of immediate voice we associate with lyric poetry. While epigram 1 emphasizes fierce effort, the second epigram represents a spontaneous, direct consequence of the speaker's *innamoramento*: Du Guillet recalls that her first meeting with the man she would call her "Jour" ("Sun," "Daylight") led her immediately to declare his brilliance to the world with a verbal ease very different from the strenuous physical effort described in the previous dizain. Toward the end of the poem Du Guillet writes, "Je . . . commençay louer a voix haultaine" ("I began to praise in a loud and lofty voice"; 38). The contrast between the two poems suggests that the writerly effort of sharpening the memory to recall and reinscribe love precedes but is more difficult than vocally celebrating the newly encountered beloved to the world.

This shift from private struggle to movement outward and upward is the central tenet of the Neoplatonic theory running through Du Guillet's poems and connecting them to earlier and contemporary writers. In the initiating text, Plato's *Symposium*, composed in Athens sometime after 385 BCE, the first speaker recalls a dialogue among his teacher Socrates and six other speakers defining love as the process of moving through an ascending order. The discussion moves from an older man's love for a younger man's physical beauty to the lover's recognition of individual beauty as one instance of perfect human beauty. From there, freed from the turbulence of carnal passion, the lover comes to recognize the beauty of abstract ideas and social institutions and of love as the organizing force of the physical universe; finally, transcending earthly experience, he comes to understand beauty as an ideal, eternal form drawing him on to a mystical union with the divine.[2]

Marsilio Ficino, writing in Florence in the late fifteenth century, drew on this view of love to compose an enormously influential Latin text in which he combined parts of the *Symposium* with Greek, Roman, and medieval Christian writings on love; he translated this synthesis into Italian under the title *Sopra lo amore* ("On Love"), published in 1544.[3] The book was not a scholarly commentary (it omitted a good deal of Plato's dialogue); rather, it belonged to a tradition of treatises on love set in dialogue form, not only among men, as in Plato, but among men and women.

These later treatises were usually less intellectually demanding than Ficino's; rather, they were written in the local vernacular for courtly and urban audiences, for whom they became a guide to polite, fashionable behavior.[4] Pietro Bembo's *Gli Asolani* ("The Conversations at Asolo" [1505]), set in a queen's court, represents three men discussing platonic love as experienced by a man and a woman.[5] Increasing Bembo's prestige, Baldassare Castiglione depicted Bembo as a character in his widely read *Il cortegiano* ("The Courtier" [1528]), which ends with an authoritative oration on platonic love, in which the mature courtier lays out the process by which an older man is both the lover who rises to communion with the divine and the teacher of a younger woman.[6]

The revision of classical and earlier Renaissance sources centralized heterosexual rather than homoerotic passion and dialogue, and it was soon given a strong Christian dimension in Leone Ebreo's three massive dialogues, *Dialoghi d'amore* (1535), led by the character Filone, a young philosopher and lover who discusses love with a curious, sharp-witted woman, Sofia.[7] Ebreo thus transformed the role played by Socrates toward the young Athenians of the *Symposium* into a pedagogical dialogue that represented a woman as a participant. This regendering of love dialogues drew on another element of Ebreo's argument. Following Plato in his view that enlightened love begins in the longing of a lover for a superior, Ebreo reversed and de-eroticized the master-disciple relationship by defining it as the love of a superior for the possibility of transformation in his disciple, her capacity to grow in beauty toward the intellectual beauty of her master. Like God toward his creation, the master anticipates seeing himself mirrored more and more perfectly in the growing understanding of the disciple.

In an era deeply suspicious of bonds between men and women outside marriage, such a relationship could easily be translated, without scandal, into a master's regard for a female disciple. Though Ebreo's Filone courts Sofia, his role as suitor is not mainly seductive. The basic premise Filone explains to her is that in ideal love the souls of the two lovers merge—impossible in bodily intercourse—resulting in their union of two into one and also into four, each soul enclosing the spirit of the other. The intellectual parallel to this process is not Filone's attempt to win Sofia's physical love but his attempt to elicit her intellectual potential for merging with him in complete understanding of his teaching. Using Sofia to counter prevailing assumptions of female inferiority, including women's inability to control their sexual appetites, Ebreo provides a model for safe and dignified rapport between the sexes: both men and women would understand love better by moving past its carnal demands to rest in the contentment ensuing from their rational, moderate experience of it. He was known in France, where Latin and Italian were widely read by intellectuals, before his dialogue was translated into French in Lyon in 1551 by the poet-philosopher Pontus de Tyard, a close associate of Maurice Scève.[8]

Who was Maurice Scève to Pernette Du Guillet? It is certain that he moved in the same Lyonnais intellectual circles that she did, but the clearest evidence of their acquaintance is textual more than historical.[9] In his massive collection of dizains, *Délie* (1544), he analyzes an intense, painful love that cycles between hope and despair, in which terror and paralysis battle against pleasure and hope; he associates Délie, a sometimes sinister beloved, with the moon in its various phases and with Hecate, the goddess of the underworld. In contrast, Du Guillet focuses on a perfectly enlightened love that she represents herself attaining with her Jour, and she responds to Scève's poems by offering alternatives to his pessimism. When Scève writes of being imprisoned by the ring Délie has given him (*Délie* 347), Du Guillet replies that he should recognize its circularity as a sign of her infinite fidelity (epigram 10); two dizains later Scève accepts the meaning she assigns to the gift (349).[10] In another interchange of poems, he writes of the power of desire and his hope that they will experience love's "doulx mourir" ("its sweet dying," with the simultaneous meaning of orgasm) as long as they breathe (136); in contrast, she reasserts the Neoplatonic ideal, emphasizing the duty the lovers share and the stable spiritual happiness to be expected as its outcome: "En noz espritz contentement durable" ("Lasting contentment in our souls"; 57–58, epigram 14). The repetition of *nous* and *nostre* in both sequences dramatizes an ongoing dialogue, but the details that distinguish even the most apparently similar poems invite the reader to recognize the dialogue as one between poets who sometimes disagree about the nature of love.

At times Du Guillet opens up the tête-à-tête of the Neoplatonic couple by using *nous* to point beyond herself and her Jour. With this plural pronoun, she positions herself among other imperfect lovers, as in epigram 49, which begins, "Point ne se fault sur Amour excuser" ("No one should ever use Love as an excuse"; 145). From her abstract warning here, she moves to another one directly addressed to her readers as much as to herself: it is not the power of love but "nostre folle plaisance" ("our reckless vanity") that disposes lovers "se laisse[r] vaincre" ("to let ourselves be conquered"). The focus of this opening makes it clear that Du Guillet envisions a double role for herself as writer of the *Rymes*: she is both a disciple, indebted to her Jour, and the teacher, in her turn, of lovers less enlightened by "parfaicte amytié" ("perfect love," transcending sexual desire and finding completion in the lovers' calm contentment).

Du Guillet's acknowledgment of shared foolishness here, however, is less common in her poems than her correction of such imperfection from a position of superiority outside it. In epigram 12, Du Guillet addresses teacherly advice to a reader about how to follow the precepts of her Jour: "Mais si tu veulx son pouvoir consommer" ("But if you want to experience his/Love's power to the full"; 53). In epigram 18 she addresses similar advice to a plural audience: "si vous voulez congnoistre clerement" ("if you want to understand clearly"; 65). She adopts the pedagogical role again in chanson 9 by contrasting the erotic pleasures other lovers have at night to "nostre amytié," the "noble affection" she shares with her Jour. Distinguishing this privileged relationship from the behavior of typical lovers, Du Guillet appropriates the didactic role occupied by her Jour in earlier poems. The disciple may criticize her readers, but she also needs them: they allow her to become a master herself.

Du Guillet spells out the value of a pedagogical relationship in epigram 53, moving from criticizing foolish lovers who can learn nothing from each other to celebrating the kind of Neoplatonic disciple-to-master unity defined in Ebreo's dialogues. She writes:

> Toute personne assés Jeune, et moins docte, . . .
> Par un monde et ignorant, et sotte
> Vouldra tousjours son pareil frequenter:

> Mais un cueur hault taschera de hanter,
> Ou il verra sa perfection pleine.
>
> Every person, rather young and less educated, . . .
> in an ignorant and stupid world
> will always want to be near an equal:
> but a lofty heart will seek to stay where
> it sees its own potential perfection. (169)

One can see the advantages of this rhetorical position by comparing Du Guillet's vision of love with a similar attitude toward love evinced by a woman poet writing in the early 1600s in a different place and language: the English noblewoman Mary Wroth, a participant in a large circle of relatives and writers in London and at King James's court. Highly placed at first in that court, Wroth retired to a more private life after her husband died in debt and her liaison with her cousin, William Pembroke, with whom she had two children, became known. Some critics have suggested that she intended her writing, which combines Neoplatonic and Christian (specifically Protestant) vocabularies, to rebuild her reputation.[11] Toward the end of *Pamphilia to Amphilanthus*, a sequence of over 103 poems published in 1621, Wroth composed a corona: fourteen sonnets, each beginning with the final line of the preceding one. This virtuoso form, like Du Guillet's longer chansons (e.g., 8), dramatizes the poet's ability to organize her thoughts rationally and lay them out elegantly. The corona is meant to impress a discerning public.

Likewise, Wroth assumes a pedagogical role similar to Du Guillet's. In the ninth sonnet of her corona, she makes the same distinction between virtuous and merely carnal love as does Du Guillet in the opening of epigram 49: "If lust be counted love 'tis falsely named / By wickedness a fairer gloss to set / Upon that vice, which else makes men ashamed" (Wroth 132; poem 85).[12] She also defines genuine love, as Du Guillet does, as illumination leading to mutuality and stable contentment. Early in the sequence she addresses the stars as ideal spectators:

> Clear, bright and shining as you are, is this
> Light of my joy, fixt steadfast nor will move
> His light from me . . .
> His sight gives life unto my love-ruled eyes
> My love content because in his, love lies.
> (111; poem 41)

Like Du Guillet, Wroth contrasts her love to the "outward showes" of other lovers, "poore fooles" given to exaggerated "sighs, or teares" (110; poem 40). In the corona she takes up a clearly didactic position: her choice of the path that "strait leads unto the souls content" authorizes her to offer advice to other lovers willing to be taught by Cupid, whom she has revised into the figure of a seer and teacher: "He may our profit, and our Tutor prove" (130; poem 82). She defines love as "the shining star of blessings' light . . . the root of peace"; she recommends to other lovers, "Shine in the eyes of faith, and constancy" (129). Indeed, her didacticism is more marked than that of Du Guillet, who, at least in her early poems, assigns the teacherly role to her Jour.

In the final sonnet of *Pamphilia to Amphilanthus*, speaking as a detached expert, Wroth defines the end of her writing as a move into wise retirement (134; poem 90). Unlike Du Guillet with her Jour, Wroth's Pamphilia loves a mostly absent man, but she uses this separation as further proof of her constancy. We see this theme persisting into this closing poem. Addressing herself, but also shaping her readers' final impression of the sequence, she writes:

> Leave the discource of Venus . . .
> To young beginners . . .
> And thus leave off, what's past showes you can love,
> Now let your constancy your honor prove.
> (142; poem 103)

Wroth's sequence, like Du Guillet's, builds up and calls readers' attention to the authority that Neoplatonism provided to women writers appropriating the tradition in which a male master led a less-experienced female lover to knowledge.

The tone of the debate in Du Guillet's *Rymes*, however, sometimes departs from the high seriousness of her pedagogical poems. Du Guillet can write epigrams criticizing her Jour as well as lesser lovers, poems that are amusing in their directness and common sense. A good example is epigram 24, in which she poses the question, "A qui plus est un Amant obligé / ou a Amour, ou vrayement a sa Dame?" ("To whom does a lover owe more, Love or more truly to his lady?"; 73). After a complex comparison privileging women as the source of moral knowledge, she concludes in a direct, pithy *pointe*: "C'est que sans Dame Amour ne seroit point" ("The fact is that without a lady, love would not exist at all"; 74). She opens epigram 26 with another logician's move, establishing the proposition on which she bases her argument for the indissoluble loyalty two lovers owe each other: "Prenez le cas que, comme suis vostre / (Et estre veulx), vous soyez tout a moy" ("Begin with the premise that because I belong to you (and want to do so), you should belong entirely to me"; 79). The wit of the poem consists in Du Guillet's command of dialectical reasoning, very far from the language of mystical mutuality in which one Neoplatonic lover unites so totally with the other that speech comes to seem unnecessary.[13]

This self-definition through playful debate can be clearly seen in prose dialogues written by sixteenth-century women, who make the argumentative process the explicit topic of their texts. Janet Smarr points out the intellectual esteem women won by taking part in dialogues in mixed-sex academies and salons: "Friendly dialogue with an educated man—or with a learned woman—becomes the university that is open to women . . . an alternate educational institution" (15–16). Because the liveliest dialogue depends on opposition between two or more parties, the written form centralized the articulate energy not only of the men but of the women who took part in it.

A case in point is the dialogue *Della infinità d'amore* (*On the infinity of Love* [Venice, 1547]), in which Tullia d'Aragona represents herself debating the nature of love with a well-known man of letters, Benedetto Varchi. She was a courtesan who spent her public life in academies and salons, and this polished dialogue reveals how, even from a much-less-respected social status, she constructed a rhetorical position for herself similar to Du Guillet's.[14] More than Du Guillet, in fact, Aragona consistently calls attention to the argumentative practices she is using. Toward the end of her dialogue she exclaims, "This logic is truly manna from heaven!" (74). In her disputation with Varchi, she insists on illustrative specificity by forcing him to offer examples of his general propositions: "Give me some examples that are easy to follow" (*Dialogue* 64). She exposes contradictions in her opponent's arguments: he has claimed that "love" and "to love" are the same in meaning but then defined the noun "love" as more noble than the verb (67). She refutes false oppositions: the soul may be nobler than the body, but each depends on the other (65). She also calls attention to her wit through ad hominem mockery: "I know the tricks you are up to" (58); "This snare . . . won't help you unless you are willing to dance around like a wooden puppet and show the double face of Janus" (77). The ease with which Aragona manipulates dialectic invites discerning readers to appreciate and to enjoy her mastery of Varchi, the better-known disputant.

Reading Du Guillet in relation to Aragona raises an interesting formal question: Are the knowledge and humor the Italian writer demonstrates to her readers as a character in a dramatic prose dialogue more or less challenging to reveal than in short, dense lyrics? Do the poetic forms Du Guillet uses communicate her intelligence and wit as much as the ways she constructs her arguments? Either way, like her calls to other lovers, her stylistic virtuosity is intended to engage more readers than her Jour alone.

An important kind of rhetorical performance in Du Guillet's later poems is her most clearly audience-directed one: not only praise but blame for her beloved, which she carries out along the lines of an epideictic oration. At the beginning of her *Rymes*, she imagines an exchange of public encomiums between her Jour and herself. She concludes epigram 5 with a request: "Preste moy donc ton eloquent sçavoir / Pour te louer ainsi, que tu me loues" ("Lend me then your skill in eloquence, / So I may praise you as you praise me"; 44). (Tullia d'Aragona, in her *Rime*, writes a similar request to the poet Benedetto Arrighi; she hopes that heaven will allow "that I may rightly praise you as much / as you do me"; *Sweet Fire* 80). Du Guillet turns to a larger audience in epigram 17. Instead of addressing her beloved, she addresses her readers as an audience for his "vertu" (his brilliance as thinker and poet) and for his praise of her: "sa grace et faconde / Me font cuyder la premiere du monde" ("his desire to please and his eloquence / make me thought the first and best of all women in the world"; 62). At the end of elegy 2, she imagines having the power to free him from serving only herself to write in a way that will bring pleasure to the larger world: "tout le Monde, / Lequel un jour par ses escritz s'attend / D'estre avec moy et heureux, et content" ("the whole world, / which through his writing some day expects / To be, along with me, both blessed and content"; 115).

But Du Guillet also works to turn her audience against her Jour. In her surprisingly malicious jealousy poems, she writes to raise hostile public opinion against him for his infidelity. A first instance of this appeal to outsiders appears in epigram 37, in which she addresses a mutual friend who has ended his relationship with her Jour. She does this to affirm to her other readers that this man shares her contempt for the choice her straying beloved has made: "Quand j'apperçoy vostre amytié desjoindre / Prenant sur luy . . . congnoissance / Qu'il me delaisse, encor une moindre" ("When I see your friendship with him withdrawn / Because you are coming to realize / That he's abandoning me, and what's more, for a lesser woman"; 119).

In her next two poems, she declares that other people share her scorn for this rival, which is also scorn for the man who has made such a foolish choice. In epigram 38, she adduces public opinion as support for her disdain for her rival: "la cognoissant a l'oeil / Comme chascun, non plus belle, que bonne" ("realizing at the sight of her, / like everyone else, that she is no more beautiful than good"; 120). In epigram 39 she criticizes both her beloved and the woman he is courting:

> Car de ses rayz a toutes faict lumiere,
> Veu qu'elles ont d'ignorance la nuict:
> Mais il y est, comme au feu la fumiere,
> Plus elle est noire, et plus fort il reluict.
>
> For with his rays he brings light to all women,
> given that they are in the night of ignorance.
> But among them he is like fire in smoke:
> the darker it/she is, the more brightly he shines.
> (122–23)

These final lines contain two negative implications: her rival is immoral and ignorant, and her Jour impresses onlookers now only because he looks brilliant seen against that woman's physical and mental ugliness.

Du Guillet rejects the role of a woeful, melancholy woman mourning the loss of her beloved (in contrast to Wroth, who takes exactly this position). Instead, her response is to expose her unfaithful lover to public disdain along with the woman he has chosen. She does not appeal to him to return. Instead, she builds up a shaming strategy to persuade readers outside the love triangle into agreement with her judgment of the couple who is betraying her.

Exposing the faithlessness of a lover in order to make it into public property is also an act of literary revenge in a massive lyric sequence that presents striking parallels to Du Guillet's: Gaspara Stampa's *Rime* (Venice, 1554). Stampa was a virtuosa, a professional composer and performer of songs for the intellectual circles of Padua and Venice. Like Du Guillet, she opens her canzoniere by praising her beloved, whom she identifies as Count Collatino di Collalto, a nobleman far more elevated in social status than she was. Despite this difference in rank, she writes jealousy poems that resemble Du Guillet's in their appeal to readers outside the couple.[15]

Stampa's lover is at first a source of illumination, as in sonnet 5: "Often enough, I'll liken my lord to the sky. / His handsome face is the sun, his eyes/ the stars, and the sound of his voice sheer / harmonies made by only Apollo."[16] Like Du Guillet, Stampa celebrates the beloved man's enlivening power: "And all the joy and love I have in my heart, / show themselves then in my features, / like a field of grass that the sun paints in day's / fullness during the desiring May" (Stampa 74; sonnet 18). Like Du Guillet's Jour, this sun inspires and elevates her writing: "Hour after hour I go about describing / you—your beauty and uncommon wit, / and merits worthy of a better style than mine" (94; sonnet 45).

But jealousy of her sun plays an important role in Stampa's later poems. The first time Stampa raises the issue, she nimbly links her complaint to love with a compliment to her sun:

> Would you like to talk to me a little, Love,
> about my dealings with your two sisters,
> Fear and Jealousy?

To Love she attributes the reply:

> "Indeed," he says, "there are a thousand others
> to whom they could be sent; but none
> of them has such great grounds for dread as you."
> (170; sonnet 125)

In the next sonnet Stampa expands this theme of suffering for an elusive lover to claim that, whatever happens, she will remain faithful to him. Though she begins, "So I'm pacified: content to fear, / happy to live in embittered jealousy," she invites her readers to recognize her as a heroine of love by concluding, "[S]uffering on his account is sweeter / Than joy with any other man would be" (98; sonnet 126). "And I, immersed in suffering so painful / find myself changed . . . / whenever his bright lights come before me" (170–72; sonnet 126).

Du Guillet can dismiss her rival contemptuously, but Stampa faces a more serious threat: her beloved is considering marriage to a woman of higher rank. In her next poem on jealousy, sonnet 213, she speaks first to him and then to herself from outside, using the shift to second-person perspective to dramatize the process of loss. She opens with a description of her silent despair: "Watching the heart, little by little, / being stolen away, and not to complain." But in the lines immediately following, she appeals to an audience who, like her, can see the man's infidelity and her fidelity as he cannot: "Seeing how clearly [his] flame is kindled / by another's eyes." She concludes, "these are the reasons I fear that my life / will slowly be drowned in a sea of tears" (246).

Instead of accepting such loss meekly, however, Stampa responds as Du Guillet does. She warns her beloved of how her readers will judge his betrayal: through her writing, not the count, she will win their sympathy. Explicitly in sonnet 305, she asks him, "Do you know what people will say, / where the force of love is never felt? / "Oh what a count—so cruel! / Oh what a lady—so faithful!" (344). As Wroth does in one of her sonnets ("Looke on mee"), Stampa demands attention for herself, ensuring that her readers, the onlookers in the fiction of the sequence, will understand better than her oblivious beloved the "sad disasters" (Wroth 111; poem 42) she so openly displays.

Because both Du Guillet's and Stampa's collections were published after their deaths, critics have hesitated to claim that the printed versions correspond to what their writers intended. But one thing is clear from these poems: each poet wrote them considering their effect on her readers. Wroth, too, creates a persona who deserves respect for the purity of her love. All three writers demonstrate that love poetry, however esoteric the vocabulary its writer employs, however closed the love relationship may seem, is always more than private; it is written to be read. Moreover, the processes of self-analysis and of instructing readers in love took preexistent, recognizable forms as part of the shared poetic language of Renaissance culture. By using such conventions, women writers interpellated their readers as admirers of their savoir faire.[17]

We have seen that all four of these writers manipulate the common vocabulary of Neoplatonism. But if we use this theory of love as a basis for comparison, we can also make it possible to recognize what is particular to each poet—above all, Du Guillet's exemplary alliance with her Jour, whose infidelity she presents as a temporary lapse of judgment rather than willed absence or deliberate cruelty. Even so, the darker shading of all these texts, as they call on readers for critical and hostile reactions to the men presented in them, suggests what a complex precedent Du Guillet set in her ambivalence toward her Jour.

"Prenez le cas" that women poets of the Renaissance all mistrusted to some extent the idealism on which the schools and courts of their time based their adherence to Neoplatonic love. How might this be accounted for? Were the advantages male poets derived from this discourse clearer and less troubled? Did women, lacking men's social power, need Neoplatonism to construct literary identities that could satisfy their readers' expectations of chaste propriety and at the same time draw them into complicity against unfaithful lovers who are also betrayers of Neoplatonic principles? Are there other women writers in whose work this provocative private-public dialectic can be identified? Locating Du Guillet in her international philosophical and poetic context leads to a broader and more nuanced investigation of the ways in which Renaissance women's gendered social situations shaped their self-representations, their techniques of using literary models to create sympathetic readers, and possibly even the kinds of appeal they make to us today.

Notes

1. Citations to Du Guillet are from *Rymes* (2006). This edition summarizes Du Guillet's life in rich detail, identifying the relevant sources (7–20). Translations are my own unless otherwise noted. For a recent verse translation, see James and Finch.

2. For an accessible edition with useful explanatory notes, see Gill's translation of Plato, *The Symposium.*

3. For an English translation of Ficino and a useful introduction, see Sears's *Commentary on Plato's* Symposium.

4. Jayne discusses the generic status of Ficino's dialogue (2–3).

5. A wide-ranging discussion of the dialogue in the Italian Renaissance is Cox. Another useful study is Snyder, especially chapter 3. For the French dialogue, see Kushner; Winn, *Dialogue.*

6. For a clear, accessible translation of *Il Cortegiano,* by Charles Singleton, see Castiglione, *Book of the Courtier.*

7. For an Italian edition of Ebreo (Judah Abravanel) see *Dialoghi d'amore.* An English translation with a useful introduction is The Philosophy of Love / Dialoghi d'amore *by Leone Ebreo.*

8. For a modern edition and introduction in English of Pontus de Tyard's French translation, see Dialogues. An early study of Neoplatonism is Robb.

9. On the cultural context of Lyon, drawing on French sources, see Kennedy 156–60.

10. On these poems, dizains 347 and 349, see Delaney.

11. For Wroth's biography, see Wroth, *The Poems of Lady Mary Wroth* 3–40; for a later version drawing on recent work including research by Margaret Hannay, see Lewalski 243–51.

12. I have modernized *j* and *v* in my spelling of the seventeenth-century text.

13. For a comment on the "para-judicial" vocabulary of this epigram, see Du Guillet, *Rymes* 79n4.

14. For a biography, see Tullia d'Aragona, *Dialogue* 21–27. Citations to Aragona's dialogue are from this edition.

15. For a biography of Stampa, see Bassanese. A recent study placing Stampa in her Petrarchan context is Braden, "Gaspara Stampa and the Gender of Petrarchism."

16. My quotations are from *Complete Poems*, which I occasionally revise in a more literal direction. To allow comparison, my page numbers refer to the Italian text, given first in Tower and Tylus's translation; the English version is set on the following page.

17. I take the term *interpellation* from Louis Althusser, who uses it to mean "hailing," that is, calling another person (in the case of this essay, a reader) into a preexisting system in which she or he is assigned to occupy a designated role. See "Ideology and Ideological State Apparatuses."

Part II

Authors, Works, Genres

Zeina Hakim

Louise Labé's *Elegies*; or, The Assuming of a Borrowed Voice

When I teach Louise Labé's poems to my undergraduate students, I often begin with the larger question of the status of the woman writer of the Renaissance. Given the ethical, political, and social position of the sixteenth-century woman, a woman's proper place was in the domestic sphere, and writing would only distract her from her duties. For moral and economic reasons, then, women were in large part excluded from a humanist education and discouraged from writing.

Despite this, I try to show my students that sixteenth-century women exchanged poems and correspondence and even engaged in controversy. Throughout Europe there were a small number of females who could and did write works of poetry, prose, and drama. Louise Labé was only one of a number of young women whose poetry and prose asserted women's right to an education and examined love, folly, and male-female relations. Her collected works were published by Jean de Tournes, also the publisher of Marguerite de Navarre's *Suyte des Marguerites*. Historians remind us, moreover, that the European Renaissance that granted easier access to the world of culture to certain privileged classes, aristocratic or bourgeois, was also a time of recognition for women—more accurately, a *certain* recognition for *certain* women. In this context, I also remind my students that toward the middle of the sixteenth century, Lyon was one of the centers of humanism in Renaissance Europe. There, women were asserting their right to display their literary merits.

However, it must be recognized that if women of the sixteenth century took part in poetic dialogue, rare were those who are still read today. Labé is one of those rare women, and that is why it is especially interesting to teach her works. Not only did she have the courage, in 1550, to defend her right to write, but she even managed to have her works published during her lifetime (in 1555), by one of the most celebrated publishers of Lyon, Jean de Tournes. I share these facts with my students as a starting point for study. Among the questions that come to mind are, How did Labé, a woman of somewhat common origins, manage to make a name for herself? For what reason did her works enjoy such recognition compared with the works of other women poets of her time?

It is important to notice that it was not by her choice of themes or motifs that Labé distinguished herself. On the contrary, paradoxically (as students become aware after reading her poems), she found her distinctive style by adopting a technique much used by men that was central to all serious literary creation of the time: *imitatio.* In other words, Labé made her mark by restatement, repetition, and imitation that subtly modified the original statement thus transposed. As soon as she starts reworking a statement, subtle personal touches can be detected, and Labé demonstrates her mastery of the subject at the same time as she seems, superficially, to limit herself to restatement. It is thus fascinating to study the ways in which Labé adapted male forms of expression to articulate her own thoughts.

During the class meetings we devote to Labé, I attempt to analyze with my students the signs of what might be considered feminine that appear, for example, in her *Elegies.* In this work she uses Petrarch's *Canzoniere* as a model, but she uses it to her own ends, modifying the terms of conventional exchange. The Petrarchan lyric, that is, the verse form and subject matter popularized by Francesco Petrarch (1304–74), was extremely popular throughout the European Renaissance; conventionally, it expressed the emotional vicissitudes of a suffering male subject whose consuming love was either unrequited or painfully difficult to articulate. The beloved female object was the premise for the speaker's emergence into language. Labé, who engaged the Petrarchan paradigm, profoundly altered the gender roles of speaker and beloved, claiming for herself an emotive agency that was untraditional for women.

It is important to point out to students, as did François Rigolot in his pioneering work *Louise Labé Lyonnaise ou la Renaissance au feminin*, that if Labé was able to claim as her own—as we shall see—the elegy, which let women speak for themselves when abandoned by their suitors, she added to this traditional form her distinctive mark, that of numerous references to important and well-known women figures.

Labé's poetic works are scant: six hundred and sixty-two lines contained in three elegies and twenty-four sonnets. I emphasize to my students that in choosing to write elegies, Labé had chosen a genre whose form had only recently been redefined and that still gave rise to a certain confusion as far as terminology was concerned. Labé was able to exploit the possibilities opened up by this lack of firm definition. In this context, we should remember that the elegy had just been introduced in France by Clément Marot, who, in 1534, published twenty-two short works bearing the title "elegies" in his *Suite de l'adolescence Clémentine*. For the Greeks, the elegy, at least in early examples, was not necessarily a song of mourning and sadness, but the Roman tradition represented by Catullus, Tibullus, Propertius, and Ovid conceived the elegy as a piece expressing the torments of love. The definitions of the elegy prevalent in the sixteenth century came especially from Horace and Ovid (among these the idea of a song of lamentation or weeping as opposed to the more grandiloquent style of the tragedy).

My students are quick to notice that Labé organized her collected poems by genre as Marot had done in 1532 in his *L'adolescence Clémentine*. We can be quite sure she did so by deliberate choice, for Petrarch's *Canzoniere* interspersed various kinds of pieces with sonnets. Labé chose to give her elegies a strategic place in her volume, signifying the beginning of her truly poetic work, grouped together to form a coherent body.

From the very first reading we identify the subject of the three elegies: the demonstration of the power of love, which will inevitably prevail over the will of the individual. But we might ask why, in the light of the universality of her theme, Labé limits her audience to the ladies of Lyon, as she states in her dedicatory letter. For it is obvious that elegies 1 and 3 address themselves emphatically to that body of women readers, and this idea is echoed by the very clear way in which the author presents herself, in the title to her *Works*, as "Louise Labé, the Lyonaise." In the same way, the dedicatory letter "To M.C.D.B.L." is signed "Louise Labé" and dated ("from Lyon, July 24th 1555"), and the debate is entitled "Debate between Folly and Love, by Louise Labé, the Lyonaise."

It would therefore seem, as the students quickly realize, that these texts give a leading role not only to the woman in love but also, and more important, to a representation of the woman writer. That Labé claims her status as a woman writer at different points in her work is hardly an accident. The central place granted to the writer and her position in society, moreover, reminds us throughout the work that one of the underlying themes of the elegies is the problem of *writing by women* and the status of such writing. Indeed, the lady readers to whom the elegies are addressed had already been indirectly solicited in the letter "To M.C.D.B.L.": "Je ne puis faire autre chose que prier les vertueuses Dames d'eslever un peu leurs esprits par-dessus leurs quenoilles et fuseaus" ("I can do no more than urge virtuous ladies to raise their minds a bit above their distaffs and spindles"; 42; 43).[1] By trading the distaff for the pen, Labé is asking that women drastically alter their ways of seeing themselves.

If ladies are solicited in elegies 1 and 3, this is not only because they might, like the woman courted by an ardent suitor, succumb to the arrows of love but also, and above all, because the woman in love might one day, by her example, encourage other women to make their voices heard:

> . . . Dames, qui les lirez,
> De mes regrets avec moy soupirez.
> Possible, un jour je feray le semblable,
> Et ayderay votre voix pitoyable
> A vos travaus et peines raconter,
> Au tems perdu vainement lamenter. (154 [elegy 1])
>
> . . . Oh, Women who read these words,
> Come sigh with me, for the sorrows you have heard!
> And maybe one day I'll do the same for you,
> helping your pitiful voices to sound more true
> as you tell about your pain and your sad trial,
> lamenting in vain for times gone this long while. (155)

It is indeed a matter of helping women readers to "tell about [their] pain" or to "lament" just as Labé, in dedicating her *Works* to Clémence de Bourges, encouraged Clémence to do even better than she had done:

> Et pource que les femmes ne se montrent volontiers en publiq seules, je vous ay choisie pour me servir de guide, vous dediant ce petit euvre, que ne vous envoye à autre fin que pour vous acertener du bon vouloir

> lequel de long tems je vous porte, et vous inciter et faire venir envie en voyant ce mien euvre rude et mal bati, d'en mettre en lumiere un autre qui soit mieus limé et de meilleure grace. (44)
>
> And because women are reluctant to appear in public alone, I have chosen you as my guide and dedicate this little book to you. I send it with no other goal than to assure you of the good will that I have long had toward you, and to instill in you, after seeing this crude and badly constructed work of mine, the desire to produce another that may be more polished and more elegant. (45)

Whatever else she says in this same letter, Labé is indeed desirous of serving as an example, and it is precisely this desire that she expresses in her *Elegies*. Her call for women who read her work to react favorably to it demonstrates she knew what was at stake. When she invites the ladies to "sigh" with her ("Oh, Women who read these words / Come sigh with me, for the sorrows you have heard!"; 155 [elegy 1]), she hopes they will empathize with her sufficiently to consider her texts a model, thereby justifying her wish to encourage writing by women.

My students thus become aware that, while establishing in her *Works* a poetic fiction that appears to be autobiographical, the *Elegies* allows Labé to go back, by mirror image, to the theme of encouraging women to write, which she had alluded to at the outset in her dedicatory letter. The gender of the author of love poems becomes an important parameter in the conception of the work since women *took over and transposed* existing models conceived by men. The *Elegies* suggests the possibility of a literary destiny for women. Labé seems to be saying that it is up to the ladies of Lyon to make their answer known. She urges all females to take advantage of any opportunity they are permitted to pursue an education and exercise the privilege of writing.

Thus I try to demonstrate in class how she chooses to use the elegy. For example, I point to her references to Ovid's *Heroides*, a text whose translation in 1500 by Octavien de Saint-Gelais greatly influenced the first elegies to appear in France. It is obvious that Labé made use of a form that presented, for her, certain advantages. In Ovid's work we hear *feminine voices*, those of deserted women or wives who address their complaints to their absent lovers or husbands. Ovid's heroines are, with the exception of Sappho (the sole historical character), famous figures from mythology. Similarly, Labé gives voice to a deserted woman taken from fable. By using the genre of the elegy, she links her poetic fiction to one aspect of the problem she was confronted with as a woman author: how to borrow from existing models created by men for their own purposes.

To illustrate this point we might take the following example, which is particularly meaningful to students: the reference to Ovid's Sappho in elegy 1.

> Encor Phebus, amis des Lauriers vers,
> N'avait permis que je fisse des vers:
> Mais meintenant que sa fureur divine
> Remplit d'ardeur ma hardie poitrine,
> Chanter me fait, non le bruians tonnerres
> De Jupiter, ou les cruelles guerres,
> Dont trouble Mars, quand il veut, l'Univers.
> Il m'a donné la lyre, qui les vers
> Souloit chanter de l'amour Lesbienne. . . (152)

> Phoebus, the friend of laureled poetry,
> had not yet allowed my verse to come to me.
> But now that his divine furor has filled
> my valiant breast, I feel my ardor build
> and it makes me sing — though not of the bruising thunder
> of Zeus, nor of the wars we suffer under
> at the will of Mars, when he moves the universe.
> The lyre he gave me once chanted the verse
> of love on Lesbos. . . . (153)

As we can see, the woman in love doesn't hesitate to boast her relationship with the divine patron of poets. Furthermore, one can infer that when women take to writing poetry, represented here in the language of the fable, they gain access to the rank of the heroines celebrated in fable.

Poetic endeavor, for Labé, consists not of epic tales but rather of "love on Lesbos." Aware of her vocation as a lyric poet and her place in the tradition, she turns to Sappho, a woman and a poet, for support and reiterates Sappho's refusal to follow the epic tradition.

Aside from Sappho, symbol of the woman poet, another woman appears as an emblematic figure: Queen Semiramis, a second case that I study with my students and that I discuss here, before concluding. Emanating from her portrait is the image of a sovereign whose virility surpassed that of most men. The account of her adventures can be divided into two parts, indicated by the passage from the third to the second person. After having addressed her account to ladies to whom she calls out, the woman in love directly berates the queen of Babylon:

. . . Royne de Babylonne,
Ou es ton coeur qui es combaz resonne?
Qu'est devenu ce fer et cet escu,
Dont tu rendois le plus brave veincu?
Ou as tu mis la Marciale creste,
Qui obombroit le blond or de ta teste?
Ou est l'espee, ou est cette cuirasse,
Dont tu rompois des ennemis l'audace?
Ou sont fuiz tes coursiers furieus,
Lesquels trainoient ton char victorieus?
T'a pù si tot un foible ennemi rompre?
(156)

. . . Oh Babylon's Queen, in state,
where is *your* heart, which war made resonate?
What has become of the great spear and shield
with which you made even the bravest yield?
Where have you laid your helmet, with its bold
and martial crest shadowing your head's blonde gold?
Where is your cuirass; where is the slim blade
that struck your boldest enemies afraid?
Where are the furious coursers who drew you on
in your chariot of victory? So soon
have you been broken, and by so feeble a foe! (157)

This change in Semiramis's behavior coincides with the evolution of a disturbing misfortune that distracted the queen from her military occupations:

Ne meritoit sa Royalle grandeur
Au moins avoir un moins facheus malheur
Qu'aymer son fils? . . . (156)

Didn't her royal grandeur at least deserve
a love less maddened than to make her serve
her son in love? . . . (157)

The importance of the story of Semiramis is contained in her taking her women readers to witness. The queen's disturbing misfortune turns out to be the guiltiest of passions and can only give rise to unanimous disapproval: the queen of the "haughty heart" (155) was a warlike sovereign of virile courage whose ambition made her cruel. However, an incestuous love for her son will transform her. No longer will "the pleasures of arms" move her. She will be shorn of her prestige and made to "languish." In a word, she is no longer herself. Her passion has deprived her of her masculine courage, which made her a heroine comparable to those of *Orlando furioso*, leaving her, paradoxically, a simple woman.

The image of Semiramis becomes frightening, and I point out to my students that her strange nature is already suggested in the theme of the woman warrior. The warlike attributes of Semiramis, especially the "branc" ("her furious sword's clean shining blade"; 154; 155) or "l'espee" ("the slim blade"; 156; 157) are undeniably the opposite of feminine attributes such as the "quenoilles et fuseaus" ("the distaffs and spindles"; 42; 43) mentioned in the letter "To M.C.D.B.L." Indeed, from the beginning of the account, Semiramis's warlike valor is associated with ambiguous images that tend to be confused with bloodthirsty passion.

> Semiramis, Royne tant renommee
> Qui mit en route avecques son armee
> Les noirs squadrons des Ethiopiens,
> En en montrant louable exemple aus siens
> Faisoit couler de son furieus branc
> Des ennemis les plus braves le sang,
> Ayant encor envie de conquerre
> Tous ses voisins, ou leur mener la guerre,
> Trouva Amour, qui si fort la pressa,
> Qu'armes et loix veincue elle laissa. (154–56)
>
> Even mighty Semiramis, a queen so proud
> she led her powerful army to put to rout
> the dark squadrons of the Ethiopians
> (and as an example to her troops, made run
> along her furious sword's clean shining blade
> her bravest enemies' congealing blood),
> and then desired to go conquer still more,
> bringing all of her neighbors out to war —
> even her Love pressed too hard, until she saw
> that she was vanquished, and gave up war and law.
> (155–57)

The image of Semiramis, victim of love, with which a woman in love can identify, goes against a long tradition, and, if Labé chose this legendary figure, it was in order to serve her purpose. Love has rightly punished excessive ambition, at the same time demonstrating its power. However, responding to excessiveness with excessiveness, love's punishment redeems

Semiramis's fault but makes her the victim of an incestuous love, which perhaps a woman of her stature didn't deserve.

Speaking directly to Semiramis, the woman in love engages in a certain strategy: having taken women readers to witness by her question concerning the disturbing misfortune of the queen of Babylon, she urges them to be indulgent toward a person suffering from the trials of love. Toward those women whom love has led astray, Labé recommends pity and compassion, unlike male poets of the sixteenth century, who, speaking of the revenge wrought on guilty heroines by Venus, adopted an ironic tone. Even Semiramis, whose misfortune might be considered to have redeemed her fault, becomes an example of the unfortunate woman in love, which could be presented to other women in order to make them feel what the fatality of love, common to all mortals, might do to them.

If Labé places her texts in the tradition of the elegy and the *heroide*, she also adds her personal touch to that tradition, making numerous references to feminine figures of times gone by, which she weaves into her poetic discourse. Labé calls on those who have preceded her, and she has recourse to models bequeathed by tradition, which she uses to give new life to literary fiction of the past.

Thus, placed at the center of the volume of her *Works*, the *Elegies* suggests that the adventure of love is complemented by another adventure when the writer is a woman who publishes her work—even more so if that woman, coming from a modest background of craftsmen, nonetheless dreamed of greatness. The volume of her *Works* sports the name of its author as if to underscore the fact that the writer was ready to assume its publication. By doing so, Labé dared claim the entire responsibility for her own works, hoping that one day her voice would find an echo among the women who read them.

Notes

This essay was translated by Amy Laborde.

1. All translations are from Labé, *Complete Poetry and Prose.*

Danielle Trudeau

A Case Study in Close Reading: Pernette Du Guillet's Chanson 7

Renaissance poetry is often presented as the imitation or rewriting of classical sources to the point that modern readers may have the impression that invention had no part in it. Certainly, allusions to classical myths, tragedies, and characters are familiar in Renaissance aesthetics, but they do not always indicate unconditional admiration for Greek and Latin cultures. Indeed, Renaissance poetry would be better described as the art of rewording and reshaping rather than slavish imitation of classical literature. In sixteenth-century France in particular, poetry was the genre through which women explored new questions and ideals regarding love relationships and shaped new models after or against classical ones. In order to understand the meaning this poetry may have had for contemporary readers, we must not only read it closely but also relate its forms and contents to the cultural environment to which it belongs and on which it attempted to leave its mark. The following analysis of chanson 7, by Pernette Du Guillet, may serve as an example of such contextualized close reading.

> Qui dira ma robe fourrée
> De la belle pluye doree,
> Qui Daphnes enclose esbranla:
> Je ne sçay rien moins, que celà.

Qui dira, qu'a plusieurs je tens
Pour en avoir mon passetemps,
Prenant mon plaisir çà & là:
Je ne sçay rien moins, que celà.

Qui dira, que t'ay revelé
Le feu long temps en moy celé
Pour en toy veoir si force il a:
Je ne sçay rien moins, que celà.

Qui dira que d'ardeur commune,
Qui les Jeunes gentz importune,
De toy je veulx, & puis holà:
Je ne sçay rien moins, que celà.

Mais qui dira, que la Vertu,
Dont tu es richement vestu,
En ton amour m'estincella:
Je ne sçay rien mieulx, que celà.

Mais qui dira, que d'amour saincte
Chastement au cueur suis attaincte,
Qui mon honneur onc ne foula:
Je ne sçay rien mieulx, que celà.
(*Rymes* [2006] 109–10)

If someone says I line my gown
With the golden rain that showered down
Inside Danaë's tower wall,
I don't acknowledge that at all.

If someone says my loves are many
That I don't say no to any,
Taking my pleasures where they fall,
I don't acknowledge that at all.

If someone says I showed to you
A fire I'd long concealed inside,
To see if I could conquer you,
I don't acknowledge that at all.

If someone says my goal with you
Is to raise the passion young men share
And then to tell you, "Oh, no, no"—
I don't acknowledge that at all.

But if it's said that Virtue's worth,
Which has clothed you since your birth,
Sparks your power to enthrall,
That's the truth on which I call.

But if it's said my heart is charmed
By a pure love that never harmed
My honor or my soul at all,
That's the truth on which I call.
(Jones, "Pernette" 229)[1]

In the 1546 edition of Pernette Du Guillet's *Rithmes,* published in Paris by Jeanne de Marnef, the above poem and seven others are labeled "CHANSON" or "CHANT" (Jones, "Pernette"). This makes them stand out in a collection otherwise largely composed of epigrams unidentified by the name of their form. Neither the original 1545 edition nor the later 1552 reprint distinguish the chansons from the other poems. The fact that they received special attention in the Parisian edition may be significant. Indeed, the publication of song collections was very active in Paris in the 1540s, but in 1543 Clément Marot, in a poem dedicated to the ladies of France, had called for a kind of "chanson" that would be more appropriate for them than the voluptuous love songs so popular at the time. Given the power of love over women, Marot said, there was room for the promotion of a Christian concept of love that brings contentment instead of unhappiness. Marot's program was to be fulfilled by the two major French women poets of the decade, Marguerite de Navarre and Pernette Du Guillet, in different yet complementary directions. While the king's sister composed religious poems or modern psalms that would be named "chansons spirituelles" ("spiritual songs"), Du Guillet's chansons only spoke of human love and celebrated the Neoplatonic ideal of love we find at the time in Maurice Scève and Antoine Héroët. We will here examine one of the chansons to see how Du Guillet used the form to promote an alternative to "folle amour" (foolish love).

The Form

In his study on Du Guillet, Verdun-Louis Saulnier found four forms of poems in the 1545 and 1552 editions of the *Rymes*: sixty epigrams, ten chansons, two epistles (satires), and five elegies. This diversity, for a long time considered a weakness of the collection, is more often viewed today as a preference for an aesthetics of *varietas* in response to the opposite aesthetics of uniformity of Scève's *Délie* (Rieu 35; Galand-Hallyn). With ten poems the chanson is the second most numerous form in the *Rymes*. According to Thomas Sébillet, for whom the French chanson was the equivalent of the Greek ode, the form did not follow specific rules and was relatively free compared with the other fixed forms. The chansons in the *Rymes* vary in rhythmic and rhyme structure and in length, but not in theme, which is always human love. Even chanson 10, entitled "Conde claros de Adonis," tells the story of the "folle amour" that drove a wild boar to want to kiss Adonis and caused the death of the young boy.

From a rhythmic point of view, *chants* and chansons introduce a slower pace compared with the far more numerous epigrams, which are tense and concise with their one or two sentences running through eight to twelve lines. The chansons also contrast with the epigrams and the elegies by their division into stanzas and by the use of repetitive devices such as refrains and anaphors. While elegies are linear homophonic narratives, the chansons divide their subject in parts that can be recited or sung by two or more performers. Finally, while the epigrams convey tension, the elegies introspection, the chansons, with their repetitive character, are suitable to the representation of obsessions and fantasies. In chanson 7, the speaker examines the various kinds of loves she won't indulge in. After dismissing them one by one, she comes to define the "holy love" that her Friend has inspired in her.

At first sight, the chansons seem to appear at random in the collection, an impression reinforced by a remark from Antoine Du Moulin, the editor of the book, who wrote that Du Guillet left her poems scattered among other papers in a draft state ("brouillars"). Until recently, Du Moulin's statement promoted the perception that the *Rymes* were composed after Du Guillet's death mainly by the publishers, Du Moulin and Jean de Tournes. This view has been considerably softened by recent critics (Charpentier, "Projet poétique" 145; Barataud and Trudeau 11) who have pointed out the existence of sequences or chapters within the collection. Chanson 7, for instance, takes place in a "chapter" of the collection devoted to the celebration of "perfect friendship" ("parfaicte amytié") and the "perfect friend." If we look at the poems that precede and follow it, we can find that chanson 7 forms a triptych with chanson 6 and epigram 34, and this group appears in turn to be inserted between two elegies. This sequence is composed of symmetrical forms: it opens and closes with two elegies surrounding two chansons—actually a *chant* and a chanson, according to the 1546 edition—which in turn surround epigram 34. All four pieces gravitate toward the epigram, which begins with the eulogy of the Friend and ends with that of the poet herself, claiming she is most able, intellectually speaking, to benefit from the Friend's "golden words" ("Tes mots dorez"; 108). Epigram 34 therefore constitutes the core of our sequence. Like triptychs, or altarpieces (*retables*), whose panels display episodes of a saint's life, the sequence unfolds around epigram 34. Yet one significant difference with the triptych is that the central piece of the poem is not bigger than the surrounding ones but is the shortest. The motif of the "enclosure"—frequent in the allegorical tradition—is at play at different levels of the sequence, especially in chanson 7.

Chanson 7 is composed of six stanzas of four eight-syllable lines—a frequent type of line in the *Rymes.* The rhymes are flat, *aabb*, *b* being the same two-letter syllable, *-la*, in all stanzas. Masculine and feminine rhymes are present, but they do not systematically alternate. This is normal for the period, although Du Guillet was one of the few who applied the principle of alternation in some of her poems before the Pléiade poets set it as a standard. The poem features techniques borrowed from folklore, court poetry, and classical material (e.g., *The Greek Anthology*). Typical of traditional folk songs are repetitions, or anaphors. Each stanza begins with or includes the phrase "Qui dira" (literally, "Whoever says," translated by Jones as, "If someone says") and ends with the sentence "Je ne sçay rien moins que cela" (literally, "I know nothing less than that"), with only one word variation in the fifth and sixth stanzas, where *moins* becomes *mieulx,* while the rest of the sentence remains identical. These constraints are just the most apparent ones that the poet imposed on herself, while the chanson, as noted above, did not have to follow any specific pattern. A network of rules regarding the choice of words, their form, and their meaning runs across chanson 7.

The general vocabulary contains only a few concrete words, some of which are used figuratively (*robe*, *fourree*, *pluye*, *doree*, *Jeunes gentz*, *vestu*, *estincella*), and most rhymes are based on notions (ideas) rather than objects (*je tens / passetemps*; *il a / cela*; *çà & là / celà*; *holà / cela*). Instead of similarities, the rhymes often present contrasts: *revelé / celé*; *attaincte / saincte*—even though some associations of ideas are also created: *ardeur commune / importune*; *Vertu / vestu.*

Since the first line of each stanza must include "Qui dira," and the last line is almost similar in each, there are only two and a half lines left to develop the new situation required by the change of stanza. Constraints are present in these lines also. The third and fourth lines must rhyme in

-*la* and with a word as abstract as *cela*. A rule has been applied here: the first, fifth, and sixth stanzas—which thematically are opposed views of the world—show parallel structures such as action verbs at the rhyme: *esbranla*, *estincella*, *foula*, while in the enclosed stanzas the rhymes are abstract and based on adverbs, the verb *avoir* and an interjection: *çà & là*, *il a*, *holà*. This alternation coincides with syntactic variations in the third line of each stanza: in the first stanza, the third line brings a relative clause—an explanation; in the second and third stanzas, the third lines are complements or circumstances of the main action or verb; in the fourth and fifth stanzas, the third lines contain a type of clause not yet encountered, direct-object clauses; finally, in the last stanza, we have a relative clause that thematically opposes the relative clause in the first stanza. The enclosing structure of the sequence appears once again within the poem in which three stanzas are framed by the first and last two ones and marked by variations: *Je* and *Tu* appear, here as subject, there as object, here under the guise of a possessive—*mon, ton*—there under that of an indirect pronoun—*me*, *te*. The first-person singular is the most visible in the three stanzas, but its action is always directed toward the second person, *tu* or *toi* ("you").

Thus the difference among the stanzas rests in their first two lines. Since the first one has to begin with "Qui dira," twenty-one syllables remain to develop a new idea in each stanza. The challenge was to produce a new, rich meaning by combining a few words.

These formal constraints remind us how much Du Guillet owed to the "Rhétoriqueurs." In chanson 7 the constraint of repeating the same phrases in the first and last lines is tempered—or rather balanced—by variation between, in the vocabulary, the characters' signifiers, the rhymes, the syntax, and the ideas.

The Stanzas

In each of the first four stanzas the variation consists of representing forms of love that the speaker then dismisses: the first stanza brings up greed, the second selfishness, the third vanity, the fourth deceitfulness. In the last two stanzas the speaker presents another form of love, this time acknowledging it as hers. This is "holy love," a relationship based on mutual admiration and exempt of eroticism.

In the first stanza, the speaker alludes to the story of Danaë, and, for a moment, we may believe that the chanson will continue comparisons with mythological figures, like those of which the Pléiade poets—Pierre de Ronsard for example—will be fond. Yet in this respect Du Guillet radically opposes the Pléiade. When she mentions a myth, it is most of the time to denounce it as an example of "error"—something to avoid. In her poetics, myths always signal illusion or, to use her own words, the "night" of ignorance that she could escape thanks to her Friend, whom she calls "her Day" ("mon Jour"). If myths are exemplary, it is always as counter-examples. The mythological poem called "Conde claros de Adonis," a tale on the death of Adonis, is an antimythological and anti-Petrarchan piece. Mythology and astrology share the same negative status in her poetics and ideology. Mythology, therefore, is not very prominent in the *Rymes*, and, when it does appear, it is mostly to contrast with her values and a truth she acknowledges as hers.

Yet mythology is part of Du Guillet's strategy to lure in the reader. In chanson 7, the Danaë story is alluded to in the first stanza as bait for the reader, then dismissed: "I don't acknowledge that at all." In the Christian moral tradition, the story of Danaë being seduced by Zeus in the form of a rain of gold received a symbolic interpretation and became an icon of venal love, perhaps already by Saint Augustine's time, since he uses the story to illustrate the shallowness of mythology in the *Confessions*. It is not by chance that Du Guillet picked that same story in order to illustrate a cause for "love" that should be rejected. One may note that the story and the characters are domesticated, Danaë and the speaker forming one persona dressed in a "robe fourrée" *d'or*, the kind of gold-laced dress a sixteenth-century Lyonnese lady would wear. Mythology is not the object of the poem as it will become in Ronsard's *Amours*, but it can nevertheless serve many purposes. Consistent with her models—Marot, Héroët, and Scève—Du Guillet aimed at elevating poetry by infusing it with the higher moral values to which she adhered. From her perspective, mythological characters and stories were shells that could be filled with a richer moral substance.

Placing the mythological figure of Danaë in the first stanza served the purpose of luring in the readers in a way similar to the "silene boxes" described by Rabelais in the prologue of *Gargantua*: the hidden truth ends up being administrated, like a medicine, and subverts the myth or illusion by taking its place. The chanson does not simply dismiss the myth; it also represents another bedazzlement story caused by another form of gold. In the last two stanzas, the speaker will emerge as a new Danaë spiritually impregnated by the Friend's virtue. The motif of the golden rain appears to be a development of the previous poem, epigram 34, which ended on the image of the "golden words" that the speaker said she was more capable of appreciating for their right value than anyone else. The motif of enclosure, which is a feature of the Danaë's story, characterizes the sequence and is the organizing principle of chanson 7. The first and last two stanzas, both thematically linked to the Danaë's story, surround the three central stanzas, which can be viewed as enclosed by two different Danaës, the venal against the virtuous, engrossed by true love.

It is usually assumed that chanson 7 was written in reaction to slander and that Du Guillet took up the pen to defend herself. Further evidence of that may be seen in similar allusions to malicious rumors in Scève's *Délie*. Actual calumny may have been the initial raison d'être of the chanson, but one can't help remembering the allegorical tradition, which had a strong influence on Du Guillet's poetics and in which slander, under the name of Bad Mouth (Male bouche), was a dangerous adversary of lovers. Also, as we have seen, the myth of Danaë is conjured up only to be sublimated and turned into a spiritual adventure, as if the speaker were not only being accused of greed by others but also accusing herself of possible greed. What if the chanson expressed fantasies of vices that may have tempted her but to which she would never succumb? She, at any rate, shows her awareness of these vices in other pieces of the collection. For example, the second stanza of chanson 7 contains a paradoxical eulogy of selfishness similar to that developed in chanson 5 and reminiscent of Bertrand de La Borderie's *L'amie de court*. The third and fourth stanzas of chanson 7, respectively devoted to vanity and deceitfulness, anticipate elegy 2, the poem that follows and closes the sequence. In the elegy the speaker fancies herself naked in a fountain, singing a song of praise to her lover to make him interested in her (20–21), and imagines that she provokes his sexual desire only to splash him with cold water if he dares try to touch her. Thus, what we have in these three central stanzas is more than just a reaction to slander. It is a variation on fantasies expressed in chanson 5 and a prelude to those that will blossom in elegy 2.

The three central stanzas introduce the same desire to seduce that will be the subject of elegy 2, dividing this theme into the components of selfishness, vanity, and deceitfulness. We can see a progression in the imagery evoked in each stanza, from flirtation for fun (2) to the intention of arousing love (3) to explicit sexual provocation (4). In the second stanza, the speaker describes what could happen if she were like any other young girl, since flirtation is a pleasure of life. The third stanza pushes the fantasy a little further on the erotic side, imagining that she might have declared her love just to see if her friend would reciprocate. This implies that she has real love not for him but mostly for herself. When this fantasy returns in elegy 2, it ends by imagining how her vanity could prevent her lover from accomplishing his poetic mission in the world. In the same way vanity and selfishness will be more developed in elegy 2, so will the erotic fantasy, which will take the form of a nude scene in the fountain, accompanied by song and music, where the speaker represents herself as some sort of siren. In chanson 7, the erotic allusion is clear, almost blunt in the fourth stanza: the "passion young men share" that embarrasses them ("qui les Jeunes genz importune") is an erection. As in elegy 2, the speaker imagines she could enjoy provoking sexual desire without having the intention of giving herself, just to exercise power over her friend.

Conversion

A simple interjection—"holà!"—both signals the moment when the young woman pushes away the man she seduced and indicates the end, within the chanson, of the series of fantasies. Similar stops occur abruptly in other poems of the collection that deal with fantasies. In elegy 2 this happens when the speaker compares herself to Diana and imagines she would turn her lover into a stag; in elegy 3, "La nuict" ("The Night") laughter wakes up the speaker from her bad dream. Both elegies end with the idea that the higher ideal the speaker has set for herself will bring her "contentment" instead of the constant, vain agitation attached to the pursuit of earthly values. Similarly, in chanson 7, a simple interjection, "holà!," serves several functions: it interrupts the sexual fantasy in progress, it closes the series of seduction imagery, and it signals a change of direction within the song.

The chansons in the *Rymes* often represent a change occurring within the speaker or the topic of the poems, a feature that characterized other medieval lyric forms such as rondeau and ballade, as well as folk songs in general. It was and still is one of the challenges of the genre to communicate this sense of change with an economy of means and through the repetition of a few musical and lexical patterns. Du Guillet cultivated the chanson in the traditional way, but she devoted the form mostly to represent positive, moral transformations: in the course of her chansons sorrow, frustration, or error change into acceptance and contentment. These metamorphoses will occur either suddenly or progressively, and they are achieved through slight stylistic differences. In chanson 7, the routine established by the repetition of the first two words "Qui dira" is broken by "*Mais* qui dira" in the last two stanzas. Also in the same stanzas, one word, "mieulx," replacing "moins" in the last line, completely transforms the statement that concluded the first four stanzas. Meanwhile, the relationship between the speaker and her Friend has also undergone a reversal: the Friend has become the seducer instead of being seduced, the speaker admits her passive role, and "chaste love" has replaced "foolish love." In Du Guillet, metamorphoses in the classical sense are kept under close watch, while another sort of metamorphosis, moral and positive, affects the speaker. The poems illustrate the process through which one reaches contentment.

Richer in vocabulary than the central stanzas, the last two borrow metaphors from the mythical story of Danaë: gold, clothes, sparks. Here, however, they represent something totally different from the rape of a woman by a god: they signify the spiritual transportation of one human being by another whose "virtue" and nothing else incites emulation. All of a sudden, the slanders and sensual imagery become vague rumors in the background and make way for the dazzling effect virtue has caused on the speaker: " . . . la Vertu, / Dont tu es richement vestu, / En ton amour m'estincella" ("But if it's said that Virtue's worth, / Which has clothed you since your birth, / Sparks your power to enthrall"). The classical story of Danaë is retold with the opposite meaning. It is no longer the story of a rape but that of a spiritual illumination. The chanson parodies the idea of the golden rain by sprinkling the lines with the keywords of the *Rymes*: "Vertu" ("virtue" or "worthiness"), "amour" ("love"), "saincte" ("holy"), "chastement" ("chastly"), "honneur" ("honor").

Conversion, sometimes achieved through rhetorical palinode, occurs in several of the *Rymes*, and most of the time in the chansons. In chanson 5, for instance, after advising women to be unfaithful, the speaker unexpectedly voices hope that men will finally become faithful: "Amour nous vengera / Quand foy les rengera" ("Love will relieve us / Once lovers believe us"; 99); the chanson did not seriously disparage faithfulness, it only pretended to do so in order to reaffirm it as a higher value for women. A more explicit palinode ends elegy 2, when the speaker completely surrenders herself to the Muses and gives up her dream of enslaving her Friend: "Laissez le aller les neuf Muses servir / Sans se vouloir dessoubz moy asservir, / Soubz moy qui suis sans grace, & sans merite" ("Let him go to serve the nine Muses, / I must not insist on enslaving him to me / to me, who lacks both grace and merit"; 114). Chanson 7 also brings a conversion from false representations of love to true, holy love and leaves us not so much with the story of Danaë in mind as with that of the Annunciation. Indeed, the ravishment represented in the last part of chanson 7 is tantamount to the great Christian mystery. Like the Christian discourse that turned upside down the pagan myth to reinterpret Danaë as a figure of Mary, chanson 7 dismissed the errors contained in the original myth and replaced them with the pursuit of a higher ideal in which both lovers find contentment.

Joachim Du Bellay, in the *Deffence,* quoted the first words of Du Guillet's most famous chanson, "Conde claros de Adonis," as a "chanson vulgaire" that modern poets should not imitate. His contention was that the French chanson was not the equivalent of the Greek ode, as Sébillet had written. We don't know whether Du Bellay knew that Du Guillet was the author of the Adonis poem, but in the light of our analysis of chanson 7 it is clear that the purpose of the chanson in Du Guillet, as well as that of mythology, were miles away from what they would be in the Pléiade's poetics. Du Guillet practiced poetry as a moral genre whose purpose was to lead the reader, and mostly the female reader, to contentment. Her chansons, like the *Rymes* in general, tell stories of error transformed into its opposite. In Du Guillet's vision of the world, unhappiness is a curable disease, the Christian doctrine is the remedy, and poetry is the vehicle of its message. In this respect, Du Guillet's chansons, and her *Rymes* in general, take place within Marot's and Marguerite de Navarre's project of spiritual poetry: they dismiss the notion of human love as eternal cause of discontent and make it a figure at the secular level of the Christian concept of love.

Note

1. The translations of chanson 5 and elegy 2 quoted in this essay are also from Jones, "Pernette" 228–30.

Jane Couchman

Gender and Genres: Teaching Women and the Epistolary Genre

Research on French Renaissance and the Reformation women's letters has been stimulated by our ongoing search for neglected texts written by women and by recent attention to the epistolary genre in general. Women wrote letters for publication, offering examples of polished and sometimes polemical epistolary rhetoric. The *Epistres familieres et invectives* (1539) of Hélisenne de Crenne was the very first collection of humanist letters published in French. Women exchanged *lettres missives* with the intention of having an impact on family and political life. Less literary and more practical, these letters illustrate women's awareness of epistolary conventions (even when bending or subverting them), and they too communicate women's textual voices. It has become practical to teach epistolary texts in the undergraduate classroom, now that several are available in accessible French editions and English translations. Women's letters can be taught in courses dealing with literary genres or with other works written by the same woman and to illustrate the range and variety of texts produced by women. Interesting for textual analysis in the literature class, they can equally contribute to courses in history and in women's studies. In looking at ways of integrating women's letters into classroom teaching, I begin with letters published during the women's lifetimes and then discuss *lettres missives*, focusing on letters and correspondences that are available in recent editions. Colleagues who become interested in women's use of epistolary rhetoric may enjoy seeking out other examples to include in their courses or may assign detective work to their students.

In what follows I list a few of the growing number of historical and critical works dealing with women's epistolary texts, with the epistolary genre, and with women's literacy more generally. The best resource for contextualizing women's letters is still Évelyne Berriot-Salvadore's *Les femmes dans la société française de la Renaissance*. The online dictionary of the Société Internationale d'Études des Femmes de l'Ancien Régime (www.siefar.org) contains short, generally up-to-date biographies and bibliographies by leading scholars. The introductions to Elizabeth C. Goldsmith and Colette H. Winn's *Lettres de femmes* and Jane Couchman and Ann Crabb's *Women's Letters across Europe* offer useful information about women letter writers and the epistolary genre. Luc Vaillancourt's *La lettre familière au XVIe siècle* and the first section of Claude La Charité's *La rhétorique épistolaire de Rabelais* are recent general studies of epistolary form in the Renaissance. Elizabeth Goldsmith's *Writing the Female Voice*, especially her chapter "Authority, Authenticity, and the Publication of Letters by Women," and Janet Gurkin Altman's "Women's Letters in the Public Sphere" introduce the study of women's published letters. For women's *lettres missives*, see Couchman, "What Is 'Personal' about Sixteenth-Century French Women's 'Personal' Writings?" The modern editions and translations cited here for individual authors include valuable introductions covering the authors' lives, the composition of their works, guidance for analysis of the letters, and footnotes rich in references to the contexts of the works and to recent criticism.

Language is always an issue in teaching texts from the Renaissance and the Reformation. Most recent French-language editions of women's letters respect the original spelling and vocabulary; glossaries are usually provided. Bilingual editions also tend to use the original text in French, with the English translation set on facing pages. My experience has been that, with a brief introduction to Renaissance orthography and syntax, and when texts assigned are not too long, students can decipher, enjoy, and analyze these texts.

Published Letters

Humanist and Sociable Letters

Hélisenne de Crenne (the pseudonym for Marguerite Briet) is the author of the first-ever letter collection published in French. The most accessible edition of her *Epistres familieres et invectives* (1539), with modernized spelling, has been prepared by Jean-Philippe Beaulieu (see *Epîtres*). Critical editions have been edited by Jean-Philippe Beaulieu and Hannah S. Fournier (*Epistres* [1995]) and by Jerry Nash (1996). There is an English translation: *A Renaissance Woman: Hélisenne's Personal and Invective Letters*. The *Epistres* were published one year after Hélisenne's novel, *Les angoysses douloureuses qui procedent d'amours* (1538). Many of the letters relate to the themes and actions in the novel, while the novel incorporates letters into its structure. Teaching the letters with the novel makes sense in both thematic and rhetorical terms. Given the author's complex use of her pseudonym, the two works open up an interesting discussion about authorial voice.

The *Epistres* was very successful, appearing in six editions between 1539 and 1560. Crenne's language (sometimes excessively *latinisant* in syntax and in vocabulary) and her multiple examples from Greek and Latin sources mark her as a humanist, for whom the epistolary form is a privileged means of communicating knowledge and opinions. Both the *dispositio* and the *inventio* of Crenne's work reflect humanist principles (see Beaulieu, "*Dispositio*"; Beaulieu and Desrosiers-Bonin, "Allégorie"). The *Epistres familieres* illustrates several standard epistolary forms: thanks for hospitality; polite refusal of an invitation; advice to a friend; condolences; confession of amorous passion; an encomium on friendship. The first, third, and fourth *lettres invectives* form a forceful defense of women. The author defends the publication of her novel and argues for the rights of women to be educated and to express themselves. The second *lettre invective*, written by Crenne in the voice of her husband, offers a brilliant restatement of the misogynist position in the *querelle des femmes*.

The translation of the *Epistre consolatoire de Messire Jean Boccace envoyee au Signeur Pino de Rossi*, by Marguerite de Cambis, is a fascinating text that illustrates Cambis's mastery of two central aspects of humanist erudition, the rhetoric of the familiar letter and learned translation. The *Epistre consolatoire* conforms perfectly to the model for a humanist letter of consolation, which Cambis's translation only enhances. Well aware of contemporary theories of translation, she did not hesitate to embellish and amplify the *texte de départ* to make her version more elegant. This text is relevant to humanism in general and to women's education and participation in the *translatio studii* of humanist thinking from Italy into France.

With Anne Larsen's three-volume edition of the *Œuvres* of Madeleine and Catherine Des Roches, this extraordinary mother-daughter pair have come into their own. Larsen's partly bilingual selection of their works, *From Mother to Daughter*, makes it even more practical to include their published letters in undergraduate courses, whether on their own or with other works such as Catherine's poetry or her double dialogue on the education of women. The *Missives* (1586, 1999) is a collection of polished versions of letters written by the two women in the context of their salon. The letters represent the *style mondain*, a courtly or sociable style of familiar letter that gradually replaced the humanist familiar letter toward the end of the sixteenth century. They illustrate the skill of the Des Roches not only in creating "rhetorical markers of class" (Larsen, Introduction 244), that is, in establishing and maintaining their networks and in offering elegant compliments, but also in discussing illness and other familiar topics. The letters exchanged between Madeleine and Catherine give us glimpses of their life together and their encouragement of each other's education and writing. There are more than a hundred letters in the *Missives*; happily, Larsen has made a careful selection for her English-language collection, illustrating the variety and rhetorical skill of the Dames Des Roches. Depending on the language of instruction, we can use her translations or refer to the original versions in Larsen's 1999 edition.

Religious and Polemical Letters

In 1539, Marie Dentière published her *Epistre tresutile faicte et composée par une femme Chrestienne de Tornay. Envoyée à la royne de Navarre seur du roy de France. Contre les Turcz, Iuifz, infideles, faulx Chrestiens, Anabaptistes, et Lutheriens.* The title and the clandestine publication alert us to the polemical nature of this text, written by a former nun who converted to Calvinism. This work will be available in the *Œuvres de Marie d'Ennetières*, edited by Diane Desrosiers-Bonin, William Kemp, and Isabelle C. Denommé (forthcoming). The *Epistle to Marguerite de Navarre*, edited and translated by Mary B. McKinley, offers an excellent introduction and translation. The short, introductory section of the *Epistle* in which Dentière defends the rights and responsibilities of women to speak out on matters of faith and doctrine should be included in any study of women's contributions to the *querelle des femmes.* For the body of the *Epistle*, McKinley's identification of the specific controversies to which Dentière was responding is extremely useful. Discussions of the nature of the Mass and the Lord's Supper, the relative importance of faith, works, and grace to salvation, and the implications of the doctrine of election and grace echo debates among reformers as well as between the Reformed and the Catholic Churches. McKinley's marginal notes reveal how seamlessly Dentière echoes biblical passages with which she was thoroughly familiar. Dentière's *Epistre* is an excellent resource for studying the polemical rhetoric of the Reformation in the voice of a woman.

The anonymous *Epistre d'une damoiselle françoise à une sienne amie dame estrangere, sur la mort d'excellente et vertueuse Dame, Leonor de Roye, Princesse de Condé* was published in the same year in English (1564) as *The Translation of a Letter Written by a French Gentilwoman to an Other Gentilwoman Straunger, Her Frind* [sic], *upon the Death of the Most Excellent and Vertuous Ladye, Elenor of Roye, Princess of Conde.* The *Epistre* has been edited by Colette H. Winn, with a very useful introduction situating Éléonore de Roye and placing the *Epistre* in its rhetorical context as a didactic work, an encomium on an edifying death, and a work of consolation. The English version has not been reedited but is available in microfilm (see Couchman, "Vertu"). Évelyne Berriot-Salvadore describes this eulogy of one of the great noblewomen of the Reformation as the closest we have to a manual for the education of the Huguenot gentlewoman (*Femmes* 63). Éléonore is presented as a devoted wife, an affectionate mother, and a faithful believer in the Reformed faith who shows remarkable patience during her last painful illness. She speaks at length of her faith and offers prayers for herself and for others. The *Epistre* can be read with students as an epistolary encomium and as an account of the beliefs and values of a noble and well-educated woman. It can be read in conjunction with the English translation in the context of the relations between French and English Protestants in the early years of the reign of Elizabeth I.

Several other highly placed women used the epistolary format in pamphlets published during the Wars of Religion. For example, Jeanne d'Albret defended her position as leader of the Huguenot cause in publications such as the *Lettre d'un cardinal . . . à la royne de Navarre* (1564), the *Lettres de . . . Jane, royne de Navarre* (1568), and the *Lettres de la royne de Navarre au Roy* (1569); Catherine de Médicis also had letters published; however, none of these is available in a modern edition.

Dedications in Epistolary Form

Prefaces were often written in the form of letters designed to recommend the work to the dedicatee or the intended audience and to guide the reader's interpretation of the text. One of the most celebrated is the humanist-feminist prefatory letter to the *Euvres* (1555) of Louise Labé (to Mademoiselle Clémence de Bourges). This text is available in French in François Rigolot's edition of Labé's *Œuvres complètes* (41–43) and in English in the superb bilingual edition of Labé's *Complete Poetry and Prose*, prepared by Annie Finch and Deborah Lesko Baker (42–44). The *Œuvres* of the humanist Marie de Gournay included numerous dedications in epistolary form; her dedicatory letter of "Le promenoir" to her "adopted father," Michel de Montaigne, is particularly interesting; Gournay establishes her privileged relationship to Montaigne by comparing the two of them to the legendary friends Damon and Pythias and echoing a poem by Étienne de la Boétie (Apology 29–32; *Œuvres* 1282–87). In her dedication of her *Sonets, prieres et devises en forme de pasquins pour l'assemblée de messieurs les prelats et docteurs, tenue à Poissy* (1562) to Charles de Guise, Cardinal de Lorraine, Anne de Marquets interrupts an extended humility topos to declare that "la defence de la foy, en avoit esté le seul argument & sujet" ("the defence of the [Catholic] faith was its sole argument and subject" [1566; a2v] Gendre 322). Similarly, Marie de Fortia uses the dedication of her edition of Anne de Marquets's *Sonets spirituels* (1605), to Anne de Beauvilliers, the wife of Pierre de Fresne, to signal the piety of the work, the holiness of the author, and the worthiness of the dedicatee. In their address to the "Dames devotieuses" who will read the *Œuvres chrétiennes* of their mother, Gabrielle de Coignard, Jane and Catherine de Mansencal insist that Gabrielle "n'avoit desiré d'estre une grande clergesse" ("did not want to be a great scholaress"), for "elle disoit que c'estoit savoir tout que n'ignorer point les moyens de son salut" ("she said that not to be ignorant of the means to one's salvation was to know everything"; 130). In 1587, Charlotte de Minut, abbess of the Poor Clares in Toulouse, published editions of two works by her late brother, Gabriel de Minut. For each work, she wrote a dedicatory letter, expressing her strong views about the devastation suffered by her convent sisters and the citizens of Toulouse during the Wars of Religion, asking for compensation, and urging that the conflict be brought to an end. She chose dedicatees who were in a position to take action, addressing "Nostre Sainct Pere le Pape sixte cinquiesme de ce nom" in her edition of Gabriel Minut's *Morbi gallos* and prefacing her brother's *De la beauté* with an "Epistre à la royne [Catherine de Médicis]." While Minut's works have not been reedited, Susan Broomhall's analysis of them, " 'In My Opinion': Charlotte de Minut and Female Political Discussion in Print," includes interesting extracts and places them in the context of women's public voices during our period.

Verse Epistles

The word *épître* can also designate a poetic form that was popular during the Renaissance (for example, the "épîtres" of Clément Marot). Like prose epistles, verse epistles were addressed to a specific person and used variants of epistolary rhetoric. Louise of Savoy, Marguerite de Navarre, and Francis I exchanged verse epistles (see Champollion-Figeac), as did Marguerite de Navarre and Jeanne d'Albret (see Albret and Marguerite de Navarre). A bilingual edition of Marguerite de Navarre, *Selected Writings*, edited and translated by Rouben Cholakian and Mary Skemp, contains some of the verse epistles composed by Marguerite in exchanges with her mother, her brother, and her daughter.

On a very different level, Catherine d'Amboise chose "*espiltres*" to communicate her pious requests to Christ and to the Virgin Mary (*Poésies* 52); she is rewarded with a response from Christ, also transcribed as a verse epistle. Catherine M. Müller's edition of Amboise's manuscript, *Poésies*, includes the illuminations that show an angel delivering Catherine's letters to Christ and to the Virgin Mary and receiving Christ's response to bring back to her.

Lettres Missives

Women wrote letters to family members, friends, clients, and superiors for many reasons still familiar today: to extend and consolidate their networks; to keep in touch from a distance; to share news of births, children, marriages, injuries, illnesses, deaths; to manage property and carry on lawsuits; to request favors for themselves and for others; to advance their own political positions or those of family members and clients; to pass on letters they had received. Many of these correspondences can still only be consulted in archives. Some have been edited according to late-nineteenth- and early-twentieth-century standards, with spelling and syntax modernized, and sometimes with considerable editorial intervention: Catherine de Médicis, Jeanne d'Albret, Éléonore de Roye (included in Delaborde's biography), and Catherine de Bourbon. Elizabeth McCartney transcribes extracts from the letters of Catherine de Médicis (in the original French and in McCartney's English translation) that are extensive enough to enable students to get some sense of her epistolary rhetoric. A few collections of *lettres missives* are accessible in recent editions, and it is to these that I will principally refer here.

Royal Women

For a fuller discussion of ways to use the letters of Marguerite de Navarre in the classroom, see Colette H. Winn's *Approaches to Teaching Marguerite de Navarre's* Heptameron. Marguerite's *Correspondance, 1521–1524, avec Guillaume Briçonnet* is generally accessible, as are the first two chapters of Robert D. Cottrell's *Grammar of Silence* in which two of Marguerite's letters and one of Briçonnet's are cited in full in French and in English. These are particularly useful in the context of Marguerite's Evangelical faith and her interest in the dialogue form; the fact that Marguerite had the letters copied into a single manuscript indicates that she saw them as a coherent and important document (see Beaulieu, "Postures"). Patricia Francis Cholakian and Rouben C. Cholakian have edited a selection of fifteen letters from Marguerite to Francis I (Marguerite, "Letters"), chosen to illustrate the various aspects of their relationship as well as Marguerite's epistolary rhetoric in the context of the multiple readers of these letters.

Diane of Poitiers, mistress of Henry II, followed the models for women of power offered by Christine de Pisan. She participated in the royal council and formed alternating alliances with the Montmorency and the Guise factions to maintain the balance of power at court. The 1970 Slatkine reprint of the 1866 edition of her letters is reasonably accessible. This can be supplemented with the English translation of twelve of Diane's letters by Sandra Sider. Diane wrote to her relatives, clients, and allies, sending advice, encouragement, and condolences and instructing them about marriage alliances, clerical benefices, foreign embassies, and even the conduct of war. She was deeply involved in the upbringing of Henry and Catherine de Médicis's children, writing frequently to Jean de Humières, tutor to the Dauphin Francis, and his wife, governess of Henry's younger children, about their health, their food, their education.

Éliane Viennot has brought together nearly five hundred letters in a critical edition of the *Correspondance, 1569–1614* of Margaret of Valois. If anyone still accepts the depiction of *la reine Margot* offered by Alexandre Dumas, this collection should correct that error. The letters reveal Margaret as an active participant in political life, a discerning patron of the arts, a strong proponent of the Counter-Reformation, and an accomplished letter writer. Her interlocutors include the French royal family (her mother, her brothers, her husband), the principal rulers of Europe, great French families, politicians and diplomats, her friends and her lovers. Through her letters we can observe, among other things, Margaret's astute negotiations with Henry IV and his ministers about the royal "*démariage*" and the strategy that allowed her to return to Paris after twenty years of exile and to live there comfortably as a patron of art and literature and as a friend and ally of Marie de Médicis. Marguerite's letters can be read in conjunction with her equally fascinating *Mémoires.*

Huguenot Women

John Calvin himself encouraged Huguenot women's *lettres missives.* One of his most effective strategies for establishing the Reformed faith in France was to write to Huguenot noblewomen, encouraging them to persuade their husbands and other family members to convert. Calvin was thus authorizing the women to speak and write with authority about matters of religious and political importance, an invitation that many of them accepted; my general study of this phenomenon is forthcoming ("Models"). Their correspondences demonstrate women's nuanced use of epistolary rhetoric in weaving together everything from pregnancy and children's toys to matters of urgent political and confessional significance.

The correspondences of several of these women, or biographies that include letters, were published in the late nineteenth and early twentieth century; some have been reprinted, but many are not easily available. For example, the letters of Jeanne d'Albret were published in at least two books and several periodical articles between 1854 and 1928. Many of Éléonore de Roye's letters are reproduced in Jules Delaborde's *Éléonore de Roye, princesse de Condé.* Letters written by Charlotte Arbaleste de Mornay and by Catherine de Parthenay, duchesse de Rohan, were published in *Mémoires et correspondance* (1571–1623) of Philippe Duplessis-Mornay.

Happily, some Huguenot women's letters appear in recent editions, including those of several women of the Orange-Nassau family: William of Orange's third and fourth wives, Charlotte de Bourbon and Louise de Coligny, and his daughters, Louise-Julienne, Elisabeth, and Amélie de Nassau. See Jules Delaborde's biography of Charlotte de Bourbon for extensive extracts from her letters in French and my translation of a selection of letters in English with commentary on the correspondence rhetoric. For Louise de Coligny's letters in French, see Coligny's "Lettres" and

Correspondance; and, for her epistolary rhetoric, see Couchman, "Give Birth." Broomhall has contributed "Lettres de Louise-Julienne, d'Elisabeth et d'Amélie de Nassau à Charlotte-Brabantine de Nassau (1595–1601)," and Eugénie Pascal offers lively insights into the correspondence of Elisabeth de Nassau in "La lectrice devenue scriptrice."

"Ordinary" Women's Letters

It is not surprising that we have letters written by educated women writers and powerful noblewomen. The few letters we have from less-educated women, from merchant women, and even from poor women encourage us to continue the search for other women's epistolary voices. In 1569, Gaspard de Saillans published letters exchanged with members of the family of his future wife Louise de Bourges, including three written by his wife. Although Louise protests that she is "nullement experimentée à escrire lettres" ("had no experience writing letters"; Louise de Bourges 73), her writing is fluent and conversational, and the letters offer a rare view of family and connubial relations. In *Les femmes dans la société française de la Renaissance*, Évelyne Berriot-Salvadore includes a selection of letters exchanged by the parents and children of the La Trémoïlle family (481–502), as well as women's letters from the correspondence of Guyot de Masso (502–10), among other documents relating to women. Broomhall's "Burdened with Small Children" is a study, not an edition, of letters in which women of Tours in 1573–74 requested poor relief; however, Broomhall provides lengthy extracts from archival texts in the original French with her own English translations. This collection gives us a rare glimpse of the personae these women created, usually with the help of a scribe, in the hopes of convincing the members of the poor relief council that they were worthy of assistance.

Women's letters are available for nearly all ranks of French society, from women with limited education to erudite humanists, from energetic defenders of both the Catholic and the Protestant causes. These letters illustrate many aspects of epistolary form and rhetoric, offer a variety of women's voices, and suggest how women responded to and attempted to shape their world.

Carla Zecher

Georgette de Montenay's *Emblemes, ou devises chrestiennes*: Material Object, Digital Subject

The new availability on the Internet of digitized facsimiles of three very different versions of Georgette de Montenay's book of emblems makes it possible for students to explore this important textual and pictorial work in innovative ways. Montenay's *Emblemes, ou devises chrestiennes* was the first emblem book by a woman writer, the first emblem book devoted entirely to Christian imagery, the first French emblem book to use engraved copperplate instead of woodcut illustrations, and a book that attracted wide attention in Protestant Europe in the late-sixteenth and early-seventeenth centuries. The original French version was printed twice in Lyons, in 1567 and 1571. A Latin adaptation, *Emblematum christianorum centuria*, was published in Zurich in 1584 and reissued in Heidelberg in 1602. A polyglot edition, the *Livre d'armoiries*, appeared in Frankfurt in 1619, including translations into Latin (both the 1584 version and a new one), Spanish, Italian, German, English, and Dutch. Finally, the French version of 1571 was reissued in 1620 in La Rochelle, attesting to continuing interest in the book in Huguenot circles. Montenay's French epigrams were retained in the Latin edition of 1584 and polyglot edition of 1619, as were the original engravings by the artist Pierre Woeiriot, which indicates that the copperplates must have been transported from Lyon to Zurich and then Frankfurt (Adams, Rawles, and Saunders 2: 177–91). Presumably Jean Marcorelle, who printed the book in 1571, took them with him when he fled from Lyon to Geneva after the Saint Bartholomew's Day Massacre (Adams, *Webs* 15).

Montenay's popular book, then, was issued in many print forms in the early modern period. Today, an equally bewildering array of editions are available in print and on the Internet. A print facsimile of the 1571 publication was edited by Christopher Smith in 1973. Recently, copies of the 1571 book have also been digitized for *Gallica*, the digital collection of the Bibliothèque Nationale de France, and for the University of Virginia's Renaissance in Print project. Additionally, facsimiles and transcriptions of both the 1571 book and the 1584 Latin translation are found on the site *French Emblems at Glasgow*. The Virginia and Glasgow digital facsimiles are of much better visual quality than the one prepared for *Gallica*, and both university sites provide an interpretive framework, although the Glasgow commentary is more copious, incorporating some of the recent research of Alison Adams. As the least mediated version and because of its simplicity of navigation, the Virginia facsimile might be the best choice for the main class text, allowing students to approach the book most nearly as a material object. Students could then later make a foray to the Glasgow site to find more background information, to use the various search functions, and to view the Latin version. This site provides English translations for all the French and Latin mottos and poems. Finally, students can see the 1619 polyglot edition on *Gallica*, where a print facsimile initially published in 1987 has now been digitized as well.

Montenay's book is admirably suited to helping students think about print history, about books as objects, about the interaction of visual and verbal imagery in religious books, and about female authorship of emblem books. Just one copy of the 1567 printing has survived, in the Royal Library in Copenhagen. One might explain to students that Adams has examined that copy and reports that the prefatory material includes an epistle to the reader (dropped from the book in 1571), which indicates that Montenay finished writing the epigrams in 1561 but that the engravings were only completed in 1565 or later, in part because of the presence of the plague in Lyon in 1564–65 (Adams, Rawles, and Saunders 2: 179–80). In the 1571 book students will find, immediately following the title page, an excerpt from a privilege that was issued in 1566 for five years to the Lyonese printer Philippe de Castellas, who must have subsequently turned it over to Marcorelle, who brought the book out again just before the privilege would have expired. One might remind students that between 1567 and 1571 France was beset by the second and third wars of religion. The privilege also indicates that the book's title originally began with "Cent emblems," an element that would be reinstated in the Latin edition of 1584, and—unusually—the privilege identifies the engraver. Students might be interested to hear that in this period, book illustrators often worked anonymously. Even if the Virginia facsimile is serving as the class's main text, one might want to ask the students to look at the title page of the 1571 copy digitized for the Glasgow site, where an anonymous hand added "Huguenote" below Montenay's name, thereby—at some unidentified point in time—explicitly linking its author with the Protestant cause.

Students will find that, after the privilege, the 1571 front matter consists of a dedicatory verse epistle to Jeanne d'Albret, queen of Navarre; a verse epistle to readers; and a poem addressed to Montenay. In the back of the book they will find a series of sonnets and other miscellaneous verses. Assuming that the class is taking the Virginia copy as a starting point, the students will see that the title page is preceded by an engraved portrait of Montenay, also by Woeiriot. If they go to the Glasgow and *Gallica* sites, however, they will discover that in those two copies of the 1571 book the portrait is missing. One might tell them that the copy in the collections of the Newberry Library in Chicago, otherwise in excellent condition, also lacks the portrait. It reappears in the copy of the 1584 Latin edition digitized for Glasgow, but this time inserted after the other prefatory material rather than before. It was apparently omitted from the copy of the 1619 edition that was used to prepare the 1987 facsimile that has been digitized on *Gallica*, because the editors of that print edition had it reproduced at the very beginning of that book, before their own prefatory material. It does appear, however, in the 1619 copy preserved in the collections of the Folger Shakespeare Library in Washington, DC. In short, this vanishing portrait is something of a mystery, and students might be asked to reflect on the possible reasons, practical or political, why it was omitted from some copies of the book. One might want to remind them of the many moments in the process of production of a book at which decisions may be made as to the inclusion or exclusion of various items, as well as the fact that in this time period purchasers typically bought a book as a set of loosely wrapped leaves and then had it bound themselves.

The Montenay portrait invites comparison with other author portraits of the time. It depicts her seated at her writing table, quill in hand, surrounded by tools useful to poetic production: an inkwell, a lute, and two open music books (1571 ed., image 13). The date of first printing is engraved on the underside of the pegbox of the lute. If students compare this portrait with other author portraits, they will find that the Montenay portrait is unusual in that it depicts her body down to the waist and shows her engaged in writing. The more typical author portrait recalls the medallion tradition, presenting an isolated head or bust. Indeed, Woeiriot also engraved a portrait of Louise Labé, which conforms more closely to tradition, and one might ask students to think about the differences between Montenay's lute, dedicated to glorifying God, and Labé's lute, featured in several sonnets in her *Euvres* (1555) that are highly secular expressions of female desire (Perrier, Introduction). The Montenay portrait functions like an emblem itself, for, just like the emblems in the book, there are textual elements in the portrait and a huitain printed below it. To draw out all of the implications requires moving back and forth between the image and the text. In the portrait the phrase that the poet has already inscribed on the sheet of paper in front of her, "Ô plume en la main non vaine" ("O quill in the hand not prideful/useless") reappears as the fifth verse of the poem that follows, while the motto that forms the last verse, "Gage d'or tot ne te meine" ("Let not the promise of gold guide/seduce you") is an anagram of her name: Georgette de Montenai.

Students could next be asked to think about the layout of the emblems within the body of the book. Unlike the paratextual material, the emblems are printed on only one side of the page. This is not the norm for emblem books of this period. Even those with engraved rather than woodcut images are typically printed on both sides of the page. The blank versos in the Montenay book were necessitated by the choice of a fairly translucent paper, which allows for a heavy show-through. The visual effect of this layout is that each page spread embraces an emblem as a self-contained element, promoting (albeit passively) the idea of the value of the individual emblem. The reader fully views only one emblem at a time (along with a hint of the previous one and sometimes even of the next one). The blank versos make the book look more like a personal album than most other printed emblem books of the period, and they would have allowed for manuscript use by readers, who might have added favorite quotations or personal reflections on the material presented in the emblems (Perrier, Introduction). The same is true for the 1619 edition, where there is a blank verso after each set of translations. Many such books—a unique mixture of print and personal manuscript culture—survive from the early modern period. Indeed, working with printouts from the digital editions, students could assemble groups of favorite emblems and add manuscript pages that gloss them, thereby creating their own personal albums.

Students may be surprised to see that although Montenay's epigrams are in French, the emblems' mottos are in Latin. Many of them are taken from the Vulgate Bible with which Montenay would have been familiar. She must have supplied them to Woeiriot, either directly or through the printer, for they are incorporated into the engravings, usually in cartouches, rather than being printed above the images as is common in earlier emblem books.

As a way to begin thinking about the innovativeness of Montenay's book in the religious context of the 1560s and early 1570s, students might be asked to consider Protestant injunctions against the use of imagery. Wouldn't it be inappropriate for a Protestant writer to design a book in which illustrations play such a key role? But if that is the case, then how might we account for the recurring editions and translations—for its evident popularity in Protestant circles? In this regard Simone Perrier points out that pictorial images were considered acceptable in cultivated Huguenot circles because they were not religious in themselves and because they were not intended for use in explicitly devotional contexts ("Corps" 55, 59). Indeed Montenay herself, following the example of earlier emblem writers, recommends her emblems for such purposes as household decoration in her dedicatory epistle to Jeanne d'Albret. Further, there is no reason to think that Montenay (or her printer, who surely hoped to make a profit on sales of the book) would initially have targeted an exclusively Protestant audience; it was only later that the book became explicitly labeled "Protestant." Some readers, of the French version at least, may well have been Catholic, for most of the emblems are generically Christian. Montenay married a Catholic nobleman, Guyon de Gout, in 1561 (probably), which makes it all the more likely that when she first wrote her epigrams, in the somewhat more open religious climate of the early 1560s, she did not intend them to be perceived as strongly partisan. Indeed, the language adopted in her dedicatory epistle casts a wide net, targeting all manner of slothful and dissolute readers:

> Ces cent pourtraitz serviront d'aguillons
> Pour reveiller la dure lascheté
> Des endormis en leur lasciveté.
>
> (1571 ed.)

These hundred portraits will serve as needles
to awaken the hard cowardice
of those who sleep in their lascivity.
(my trans.)

With regard to the emblems themselves, we see that Montenay refers to them here as "portraits," and it would make sense to encourage students to dip in and out of the book, treating it as a gathering of vignettes rather than plowing straight through. This is what would have been expected of the book's early modern readers, who would likely have used it as a starting point for reflection and meditation, rather than something to be consumed cover to cover. In this regard, it would be helpful also to remind students—especially given that they will be encountering the book on the Internet, where it is always tempting to click away after only a few minutes—that readers would have spent a lot of time with the book. It would have been an object of value to acquire and retain for a lifetime.

Adams has identified fifteen thematic sequences within Montenay's book, and a list of these could be given to the students as an aid to their own study of individual emblems: "Salvation through Christ alone" (emblems 2–5), "Faith not works" (6–13), "Warnings" (14–24), and so on (*Webs* 29–74).[1] Students may find it easiest to grasp the implications of the handful of overtly political emblems found in the book. Numbers 21 and 84 attack the papacy, while numbers 7, 25, and 34 associate evil with representations of Catholicism (Adams, *Webs* 9). Many other emblems will seem more opaque, because they assume a thorough knowledge of the Bible. In this regard the Glasgow site will be invaluable, since its critical apparatus provides biblical references for the emblems.

The two emblems that frame the collection could be examined together. The first emblem, the one that immediately follows the portrait of Montenay in the Virginia copy, depicts another woman at work: it shows Jeanne d'Albret as a bricklayer, building the house of God.[2] Adams proposes that the book's final emblem, which has usually been interpreted as referring to Montenay herself, may be alluding to Albret. While it is possible that the marriage bed cradling branches of thorns depicted in the illustration is Montenay's own, it seems more likely that it is Albret's, for the accompanying verses gloss the motto "Patientia vincit omnia" ("Patience conquers all"), a paraphrase of "Amor vincit omnia," and although Montenay's own marriage must have been a very recent occurrence, 1561 was a year of crisis in Albret's relations with her husband, Antoine de

Bourbon, who was unfaithful to her personally and who was increasingly shifting his support toward the Catholic cause (Adams, *Webs* 27).

Students might also be asked to select a favorite emblem and then check to see how it was reinterpreted in the different translations in the 1619 edition, as Adams has done with emblem 8 (*Webs* 11–24). There may well be students in a given class who can read the Spanish and Italian epigrams. Knowledge of Latin, German, and Dutch may be harder to come by, but students could be dispatched to obtain assistance with these languages. If someone could be found to translate the Dutch, that would be ideal. According to Adams the German is expendable in that the renderings amount virtually to doggerel, but she notes that the Dutch translations are characteristically more sophisticated and inventive than any of the others (*Webs* 23). Students will find that the translations are loose to the point that one may call them rewritings and that they therefore invite study.

My own favorite, emblem 20 in all the editions, bears the single-word motto of "Cane" ("Play") and is a good candidate for comparison across editions and through the years, since its implications hinge on a pun that is particular to French. In the engraving, an elderly king sits under a rough tent, while a man with a stag's head brings him a trumpet, which the king orders him to sound (image 68 [1571 ed.]). The epigram criticizes the king for his blind reliance on his advisers, by punning on the words *cerf* ("stag") and *serf* ("servant"). This monarch is the *cerf* of his *serfs*, the *servant* ("stag") of his *servants*, merely the trumpeter of his council rather than its head. Early modern readers would likely have recognized in this idea a parody of the title adopted by the popes, *Servus servorum Dei*. Readers also, with their knowledge of Latin, would have realized that *Cane*, the emblem's motto, is an adjective denoting "old, white-haired," as well as the imperative of *cano* ("to sound or play an instrument"). The French equivalent for the verb *cano* is *tromper*, which denotes both "to play the trumpet" and "to dupe" someone. The emblem thus alludes to the danger in which this monarch places himself; by trusting too much in his advisers, he risks being duped by them. Perhaps Montenay was thinking specifically of the pope's subservience to his cardinals or even, closer to home, of the French king's deference to the Guises. In the later editions of the book, translators were unable to retain the pun on *cerf* and *serf*. The 1584 Latin edition characterizes the "prince" in the image as being a leader "unfit to impose laws on his people," because he rules them by reputation instead of reason. In the polyglot edition the German translator describes the

Oberkeit ("governing authorities") as wearing donkey ears, while the English translation simply states that the monarch featured in the emblem is a "brute, / Which hes a trompet, and cannot flutte" (Montenay, *Livre* 110).

The "Cane" emblem thus demonstrates the limitations of translation and adaptation. One would want to carry out the same exercise with other emblems as well, for in some instances looking at the translations (rewritings) might yield information about the intellectual world of the individual translators or of the Protestant community in Zurich in the 1580s or in Frankfurt after the turn of the century. To draw out that kind of information from the emblems would require a large study, perhaps beyond the scope of an undergraduate course, but it might still be useful to ask students to consider the extent to which translation is very creative work and that a translation may tell us as much about the translator's world as about that of the author's.

Finally, students might be encouraged to compare some of Montenay's emblems with earlier emblems that treat similar themes. There are many examples to be found in the seminal collection of emblems by Andrea Alciato, which Montenay credits in her dedicatory epistle with having inspired her to compose her own emblems. On the Virginia and Glasgow Internet sites students will find digital facsimiles of several French editions of Alciato's emblem book with which Montenay might have been familiar. Themes and topics may easily be searched on the Glasgow site by choosing a particular emblem by Montenay and then using the site's "Iconclass" function to find similar imagery in emblems by earlier writers. Comparisons could be carried out with a view to identifying which elements of Montenay's emblems reflect Christian, as opposed to straightforwardly moralizing, thinking; Reformed, as contrasted with Catholic, thinking; or gendered thinking.

Ultimately, my hope is that all of the activities suggested here will enable students to provide nuanced answers to a series of very basic questions. Why were emblem books such a popular form of literature in early modern Europe? What was their appeal? What is special about Montenay's book in contrast with others of the time? What sort of intellectual, social, and religious world does it represent?

Notes

1. The emblem numbers are the same in all editions of the book.

2. On the University of Virginia's Gordon Collection site hosting the 1571 edition, emblem 1 appears as image 30.

Edith Joyce Benkov

The Pasquin and Political Commentary: The Case of Anne de Marquets

To introduce students to the complexities of French politics and religion during the second half of the sixteenth century, the Colloquy of Poissy provides a propitious starting point. As a gathering of high-ranking clerics and members of the nobility, the Colloquy of Poissy is a unique event in the French Renaissance. Motivating forces behind the colloquy held in 1561 are many and varied: the traditional French disdain for the authority of the papacy; a means of sidestepping the soon-to-be-reconvened Council of Trent; a desire to establish France as an equal to Spain; the rank of many Protestant nobles; Catherine de Médicis's attempt to consolidate the power of her regency; the prospect of a civil war—to name simply a few of the most commonly cited (see Nugent). It also marks a collaborative effort organized by the Chancellor Michel de l'Hôpital, the cardinal of Lorraine, and Catherine de Médicis to resolve the impending religious crisis in terms of a diplomatic solution. When representatives of the Catholic Church, the French monarchy, and a contingent from Calvin's Geneva came together at Poissy, the framing context was that of negotiating a treaty. Some on the French-Catholic side, especially the cardinal of Lorraine, hoped, perhaps naively, to lead the errant lambs back into the fold through the eloquence of their arguments; others, such as Claude d'Espence looked toward a reconciliation of doctrine; Catherine de Médicis orchestrated the negotiations, waiting for the conflict to be resolved in terms of a national agreement to avoid the destruction of her fragile realm.

Although the colloquy failed to achieve its ends, it did bring to the fore Anne de Marquets (1533–88), who as a member of the Dominican nuns residing at the convent, had been relegated to the role of observer on the sidelines. During the colloquy, epigrams composed by Marquets circulated in manuscript form. These texts fell into the hands of one of the Calvinists' supporters—perhaps even Théodore de Bèze himself, and elicited an anonymous reply: "Response aux Pasquins tirez de la Saincte Escripture et destournez de leur vray sens par une nonain de Poissy, en faveur des preslats de France" ("Response to the Pasquinades Taken from Holy Scripture and Altered from Their True Meaning to Be in Favor of the Prelates of France by a Nun from Poissy"; Gendre 348–49; my trans.). The forty-eight-line "Response" thrust Anne de Marquets into the limelight. An unknown nun who had spent over half of her life in the convent at Poissy was suddenly at the center of a political and literary scandal. In 1562, Marquets undertook the publication of the Poissy-related texts to prevent any further abuse of her works. When she entitled this collection *Sonets, prieres et devises en forme de pasquins, pour l'assemblée de messieurs les prelats et docteurs, tenue à Poissy, M.D.LXI* ("Sonnets, Prayers, and Devices in the Form of Pasquinades for the Assembly of Prelates and Doctors Held in Poissy, 1561"), she reitereated that a portion of her works were pasquinades, a popular genre, recognized for its satiric content. Although Marquets's political writings are less well known than those of her contemporary Pierre de Ronsard, they open up a space for considering questions of gender and genre at the beginning of the *troubles* that reigned in France for four decades.

Introducing Marquets's "prieres et devises en forme de pasquins" into the classroom poses some possibly problematic elements, not the least of which is access. The 1566 edition in PDF format is available online through the Bibliothèque Nationale de France site *Gallica*, an edition of the 1562 version of the text appears in an article by André Gendre, and a transcription of the 1566 edition resides online through San Diego State University. And, at this time, no English translation of the work exists. Students reading Marquets's work will have to cope with Latin as well as Renaissance French; they will encounter a work deeply steeped in the politics and history of the period; and they will need to set aside their modern understanding of Catholic-Protestant relations. With these caveats in mind, Marquets's choice of the pasquinade makes her work of particular interest for the study of political-religious writings during the Reformation. Nonetheless, in my experience students have overcome these obstacles with success and enthusiasm.

The pasquinade derives its name from *Pasquino*, a statue located in Rome, not far from the Piazza Navona. While the origins of the statue's name are unclear, the statue itself is associated with Cardinal Oliviero Carafa, reputed to have inaugurated the first official *Pasquino* celebration, in the early sixteenth century, after a series of anonymous Latin verses making satirical comments on the Borgia pope were posted on the statue. The lampoons, once posted, often circulated in manuscript form. As the practice became institutionalized and the popularity of the *pasquinate* spread, printed collections began appearing in Rome as early as 1509 (Reynolds 181). These pasquinades focused primarily on political issues as well as the pope and members of the College of Cardinals, whose adherence to doctrine, morality, and political motivations were criticized. The authors themselves, although ostensibly anonymous, clearly had close ties to the papal court or to the university. Pietro Aretino is cited among the more well-known contributors to the corpus of *pasquinate*. Strong language and sexual explicitness are not lacking in these texts, although the principle characteristic of the genre is its biting satire. The edition *Pasquinate romane del cinquecento* ("Sixteenth-Century Roman Pasquinades") is a particulary useful collection.

Given the antipapal nature of the pasquinade, the first major collection, *Pasquillorum Tomi Duo (Pasquinades in Two Volumes),* including works in Latin, Italian, and German, was published not in Rome but in Basel, in 1544. Although not named in the text, the editor has been identified as Celio Secundo Curione, an Italian humanist reformer, persecuted by the Inquisition and later exiled. Not surprisingly either, the genre found favor with other reformers. Indeed, Ulrich von Hutten may well have had a hand in some of the pasquinades published in the *Pasquillorum.* Later that year, Curione brought out a second volume under his own name, *Pasquillus Ecstaticus et Marphorius.* This work, although thematically related to the pasquinade, greatly expands on the typical length of a pasquinade and presents a dialogue between Pasquillus and Marforius (another person depicted by one of Rome's "talking statues") concerning the veracity of the Catholic version of the afterlife. Pasquillus recounts a vision in which he is led by an angel to see the false heaven (the pope's) and the true heaven (Christ's). Pasquillus's role in this dialogue is to lead

Marforius to the truths of Protestantism. The *Pasquillus Ecstaticus* was translated into French, German, and English, assuring that the text would have broad readership across Europe.

With this background, it is easy to see that by the time of the Colloquy of Poissy, the pasquinade and *Pasquino* had became fully integrated into the polemical battles between Protestants and Catholics. Thus, when Anne de Marquets decided to adopt the form for her own purposes, the pasquinade had acquired a distinctly Protestant tone. A clear area with which to begin classroom discussion then deals with the problematic nature of the pasquinade. How can this seemingly inappropriate genre, when placed in the hands of a devout Catholic, comment on a gathering of Protestants and Catholics? Might the choice of the witty Italian genre at the same time be a reminder that the (unofficial) ruling power in France was indeed an Italian? Yet just as the Italian who ruled France had perhaps broken with her homeland and, implicitly, with the directives of the pope through her intent to launch a new, national strategy, so too Anne de Marquets made such a break, altering the recognized thematics of the genre: satire of the pope and Catholicism is absent.

Further, an echo reverberates outside the textual limits of Marquets's pasquins sequence that seems to blatantly engage Curione's text. The *Sonets* portion of the volume that Marquets brought out after the colloquy consists of a sonnet sequence, recounting a prophetic dream. In a vision she is led by an angel who shows her how Catholicism will ultimately triumph over Protestantism. Marquets's vision overlays that of Pasquillus in *Pasquillus Ecstaticus.*

The pasquins sequence in Marquets's collection is relatively short, consisting of twenty-six poems "prieres, sentences, et devises" of varying lengths (generally 3–4 lines), each preceded by an epigraph in Latin culled from scripture and addressed to a specific person or group. Marquets's addressees include those attending the colloquy, among them the cardinals, the members of the assembly, the nuns, as well as an exterior audience, the people of France. In all, Marquets cites thirty-one different biblical texts: eleven of which are Old Testament sources, seventeen from the New Testament, and three from the Apocrypha. A series of contradictions pervades the pasquins. These contradictions reflect the ambiguous position of Marquets in relation to the colloquy, to writing, and to the genre she chose. Yet that she chose this moment to write signals her unwillingness to being relegated to the sidelines. She was not content to remain no more than an observer. Taking up the pen counteracts the imposed silence, allowing her to self-position as an engaged poet, commentating on the debate and its participants while appropriating and reconfiguring a genre noted for its anti-Catholic sentiment.

An examination of how Anne de Marquets structures these poems and of the choices of the biblical texts used as epigraphs in the pasquin sequence raises a number of questions that highlight some of the central issues of the Reformation. The Council of Trent in 1546 had reaffirmed the Augustinian canon, including the Apocrypha among the accepted texts. This decision was not uniformly accepted by the various Protestant contingents. While it is not then surprising that Marquets, a Catholic, would not hesitate to use the Apocrypha, her inclusion of these disputed texts marks a stance that clearly negates their rejection by the Protestants. Contextually, the clash over what constituted the canon and other questions of doctrine were being played out at the Colloquy of Poissy. Thus, Marquets's choices in these instances underscore the deep theological divisions dividing the Protestants and Catholics at Poissy.

Marquets also uses a significant number of Old Testament references (just over a third of her epigraphs). How might one interpret the selection of these texts in the framework of Protestant emphasis on the Old Testament? Could this be seen as a gesture of reconciliation or, on the contrary, a studied affront? To complicate matters here, it must be noted that most of the Old Testament sources are from Psalms (7 of 11). Marquets's mustering of the Psalms to further her viewpoints can be read as an aggressive act toward the Calvinists. By citing in Latin, she implicitly rejects the project of the Genevan Psalter, a collaborative effort to translate Psalms into the vernacular. Begun by Clément Marot, the psalter was completed in 1562, by Théodore de Bèze, who attended the colloquy. The fact the psalms in the vernacular are an integral part of the Calvinist liturgy also makes the choice more confrontational. Although the Latin of Marquets's text poses problems for many students, undergraduates and graduates alike, its very challenges underline how Marquets approached the pasquinade. Early pasquinades were written in Latin; as the genre grew in popularity, pasquinades were translated into the vernacular and writing in the vernacular became common as well. Juxtaposing Latin and French, in her *pasquins*, Marquets recalls the origins of the genre and its contemporary status.

Yet another line of discussion in relation to Marquets's preference for Psalms coincides with vision of the poet espoused by the Pléiade and with the voice of the poet, David, within Psalms. Through her contact with Ronsard, who contributed a poem to the *Sonets, prieres et devises*, Marquets would have been exposed to the Pléiade's poetic ideals, and the importance of the divine inspiration of the poet. David's voice in the Psalms reflects the voice of the individual poet. That Marquets would echo this rhetorical position in her texts is not at all surprising. Yet David's voice was also interpreted as a parallel to Christ's voice as he spoke to his heavenly father. How does gender interact here with Marquets's calling up of David's voice? The intersections of gender, theology, poetic theory and the reactions to Marquets's pasquins can lead students to broaden their vision of reading works in the framework of the religious struggles of the period.

Marquets's discursive and authorial strategies reflect a complex layering. She takes the classic pasquinade and transforms it into something else: a hybrid of biblical discourse and gloss. Both for praise and criticism but without satirical overtones, it gives voice to an individual who would have been expected to avoid engaging in poetic and religious confrontation. A close examination of the interplay between biblical citation and Marquets's gloss reveals a multifaceted and daring rhetorical strategy. The original context of the citations, rather than the words cited by themselves, give full meaning to each of her pasquins. These fully articulated readings, by their insistence on the error of the Protestants' ways, clearly could undermine the irenic goal for which the colloquy had been convened.

Marquets establishes a dialogue between the citations and her short poetic gloss. Thus each pasquin becomes a hybrid text, depending on what Michel de Montaigne called a "sufficient reader" to understand the two parts as a whole. The discovery of how this dialogue functions to create meaning in each of the pasquins can be a fruitful assignment. And it is through this dialogic relationship that Anne de Marquets affects a shift in the temporal structure of the pasquinade's original function as a satiric genre, by melding the historic immediacy of satire with divine truths.

How this strategy works is clear if we again take up the notion of the "sufficient reader" and return to the question of Marquets's intended audience. In her introductory "Letter to the Reader," Marquets claims the poems were produced for private rather than public reading. Within the convent, or circulating among the cardinals and other church officials, Marquets would have had readers sufficiently schooled in chapter and verse to recognize the biblical citation, its context, and the relation to the gloss. While the overarching voice of the pasquins is laudatory, its strong criticism of the Protestants is not truly masked. Further, in terms of the distribution of the poems, only two of the pasquins directly address the

Protestants. This seeming negligence may indicate Marquets's (mistaken) confidence that they would indeed be rendered harmless to the Catholic faith by the end of the colloquy.

The very obvious dialogue between biblical text and Marquets's gloss in her pasquins may help us understand the reaction these texts did elicit when they finally became public. A brief examination of three of the texts clearly demonstrates Marquets's textual practices and provides a model for using the pasquins in a classroom setting. The opening *pasquin* has no named addressee (although the vocative "O Dieu" ["O Lord"] leaves little doubt about it); the pasquin serves a general commentary, setting the tone and establishing the overarching context for the other twenty-five, that is, the colloquy itself. Marquets juxtaposes two psalms, 73 and 89, to implore God to remember his congregation and to look upon his servants: "Memor esto Domine congregationis tuae" ("Remember [o Lord] thy congregation"; Ps. 73.2); "Et respice in servos tuos" ("Look upon your servants"; D1r; Ps. 89.16).[1] Psalm 73 invokes God to go forth against his enemies and concludes with the warning: "Forget not the voices of thine enemies: the tumult of those that rise up against thee increaseth continually" (Ps. 74.23 [KJV]). For Anne de Marquets's audiences at the Colloquy of Poissy, the voices of the enemies can only be read as those of the Calvinists, as they expose their doctrine while the Catholics in attendance embody the congregation. The second citation, from the so-called prayer of Moses, a reflection on God's omnipotence poses the question: "Who knoweth the power of thine anger?" (Ps. 90.11 [KJV]). The "sufficient reader" would have no trouble understanding the combined meaning: the Catholics are besieged, but God's mercy will prevail for them and his and their enemies will be defeated. In her gloss, Marquets establishes a parallel break between the groups in attendance at the colloquy:

O Dieu seul autheur de tous biens,
Regarde d'un œil favorable
Cette compaignie honorable,
Et qu'il te souveinne des tiens,
Leur faisant protecter & croire,
Ce qui est conforme à ta gloire.
(B3r)

Lord, unique creator of all good,
Look with a favorable eye
Upon this honorable group
And may you remember your own

And make them protect and believe
Everything for your glory.
(my trans.)

While less obviously belligerent than the enemies of Psalm 73, the gloss still clearly marks the we-they position that sets the tone for the entire sequence of pasquinades.

The two of the pasquins indirectly (although obviously) addressed to the Calvinists, "A ceux qui errent en la foy" ("To those who err in their faith") and "A ceux qui veulent demeurer obstinez en leurs erreurs" ("To those who want to remain steadfast in their errors"), precede the final pasquin of the sequence. By their position, they place the Calvinists the furthest from the congregation referred to in the first pasquin. Moreover, unlike the other pasquins, those implicitly addressed to the Calvinists criticize rather than praise or counsel. "A ceux qui errent en la foy" begins with an epigraph combining two citations from the Old Testament: "Revertimini a viis vestris pesimis" ("Turn ye from your evil ways"; 2 Kings 17.13, qtd. in Marquets D3r) and "Et convertimini ad Dominum Deum vestrum, quia benignus et misericors est" ("And turn unto the Lord your God for he is gracious and merciful"; Joel 2.13). Read together, as is obvious, they offer an unequivocal command to the Calvinists at the colloquy. The citations combine two Old Testament texts, 2 Kings and Joel. Kings tells specifically of the errors committed by the people of Israel, how they erred in their faith. Joel calls for the errant to return to the merciful God and to call an assembly to acknowledge "the name of the Lord [and be] saved" (Joel 2.22). Thus the broader scenario created by replacing the citations in context mimics the hopes for the colloquy. Further, by drawing on Old Testament sources Marquets once again uses texts that inform Protestant theology. However, while the epigraphs create a somewhat neutral backdrop, Marquets's gloss is scathingly direct: "Laissez pauvres errants le chemin vicieux / Que liberte de chair vous a fait entreprendre" ("Forsake the path of vice that unrestraint of the flesh had lead you to take"). Marquets alludes to the Protestant practice of allowing pastors to marry. Thus the sin of the flesh expands on the meaning of those who have strayed from the path, their errors based in carnal desire.

The pasquin that immediately follows, addressed to those "who want to remain steadfast in their errors," establishes a contrast between those who will return to the fold and those who refuse to do so. The relatively lengthy epigraph comes from the New Testament: "So do these also resist the truth: men of corrupt minds, reprobate concerning the faith but they shall proceed no further: for their folly shall be manifest unto all men, as their's also was" (2 Tim. 3.8–9). The letter from Paul to Timothy denounces blasphemers as unthankful and unholy, but, more important, the specific verse concerns Jannes and Jambres, two disbelievers of Moses who appear only in the New Testament. Thus the "sufficient reader" will understand the context and see that Marquets indeed attempts to confound the "men of corrupt minds" through a reference that creates a parallel between the supposed Egyptian magicians and the Calvinists. Marquets's paraphrase of this verse: "Truly soon will their sway end / for their folly will be shown to all" (C3v) echoes the assertion in her vision that the Catholics would triumph. Thus as the pasquins come to a close, the position that Marquets espouses is evident: only by returning to the true faith will the Protestants rid their hearts of vice and imperfection. For Marquets, the debates at the colloquy will make their error manifest to all.

If I have dealt with these examples at some length, it is to suggest possible models for reading the pasquins that highlight the immediacy and the impact of these texts for the Colloquy of Poissy. The anonymous attack on Anne de Marquets highlights the dangerous territory into which she had entered, one in which she was likely to be viewed as a trespasser and transgressor, since she has clearly appropriated scripture for her own purposes. Had the texts remained confined to Marquets's circle of like-minded individuals, perhaps she would have had little cause for concern. But the ensuing controversy and the failure of the Colloquy of Poissy shed an unfavorable light on the convent and on its now-famous inhabitant.

Anne de Marquets retuned the pasquinade into a vehicle of praise for the Catholics and criticism of the Protestants. In the pasquins she exploits the immediacy associated with the genre as satire and mediates it through the eternal truths of scripture, achieving a balance that is at once present and everlasting. Statues that talk, women who write—is there really so great a difference between the two in the Renaissance? For what was the pasquinade but a forum to give voice to those who would otherwise be silenced? In the context of the Renaissance woman writer, might not Anne de Marquets's appropriation of the pasquin signal a desire to break out of the silence imposed on the nuns of Poissy during the colloquy and create a forum in which her voice and that of others like her could be heard?

Note

1. I here use the numbering of and cite the 1562 edition of *Sonets*, available also in a reprint by Gendre. Translations are mine.

Jean-Philippe Beaulieu

Feminine Authorial Ethos: The Use of Marie de Gournay's *Discours sur ce livre* as an Introduction to Her Collected Works

Despite the fact that Marie le Jars de Gournay's stature as a cultural and literary figure of the late Renaissance has been recently acknowledged by the publication of several critical editions and monographs, her writings are still seldom read and studied, with the exception of the well-known "proto-feminist" texts (*Égalité des hommes et des femmes* and *Grief des dames*). Because of its abundance and complexity, Gournay's textual production as a whole is difficult to grasp, especially in a teaching environment where it is generally impossible to take into account the numerous political, didactic, moral, and poetic texts that Gournay assembled in *L'ombre de la damoiselle de Gournay*, a compendium of *meslanges* (or "miscellanies") published first in 1626 and again in 1634 and 1641 under the new title *Les advis, ou, Les presens de la Demoiselle de Gournay*. In fact, it is not an easy task to give an overall faithful image of this corpus, whose multiple parts are interwoven and thus require the kind of exhaustive reading that is not always feasible in a classroom. The specific course taught will obviously dictate the choice of Gournay's texts that will be studied within the modest scope of a semester-long program. For instance, in the context of a course on women and translation, the *Lettre à Mgr de Gelas sur la version de deux Oraisons Latines* and *De la façon d'escrire de Messieurs l'Eminentissime Cardinal Du Perron et*

Bertaut would obviously be studied. But if our desire is to create a reader of Gournay's overall literary output, I suggest that, no matter which texts of the *Advis* we teach, students really ought to read the *Discours sur ce livre*, which is the first work printed in the collected works in the last two versions of 1634 and 1641. In this substantial but rarely discussed preamble (in her extensive study of the collection's history, Franchetti [37] writes just a few words on it), Gournay presents the various texts that make up the two "livres" of her work, explaining their nature and content. More important, in so doing, she fashions the persona of a female author of considerable intellectual ambitions, partly masked by the rhetoric of modesty. As the introduction to a book that gives constant and tangible presence to the authorial figure, *Discours sur ce livre* is most interesting and useful in showing how Gournay brings us into her *meslanges* through the authorial ethos she constructs, that is, through the rhetorical dimension of a speaker's attempt to construct a self-representation (Galand-Hallyn 45–49). If one considers the difficulties Renaissance women faced in becoming recognized public figures, the study of their rhetorical ethos seems an appropriate way to give students an understanding of the issues pertaining to their writing. In Gournay's case, as I argue in this essay, the necessity of so doing is even more striking, since the *Discours*, as the opening text of the collected works, manifests the articulation of an ethical stance that ushers readers into one of the most substantial and ambitious collections of women's writing in the first half of the seventeenth century. In the following pages, I go through the *Discours* to underline some elements that could be used to study the way this text projects a strong authorial figure that gives unity and meaning to the whole collection.

In the publication's history, the *Discours sur ce livre* only appears in 1634, since the prefatory material of the 1626 edition consists of a brief *Advis au lecteur*, which continues to appear after the *Discours* in later editions with the title *Au lecteur*. This development may underscore Gournay's wish to replace the generalized address at the beginning of her publication with a personalized dedication, addressed to a female figure somewhat preciously named Sophrosine and seeming to mask an intimate acquaintance of Gournay—possibly Marie de Bruneau, dame Des Loges, dedicatee of the *Deffence de la poësie* (Franchetti 33). Interposed between author and reader, the allegorical Sophrosine must be considered the ideal reader, favorable to the author and, more generally, to the "interests du sexe," that is, to women (1: 553).[1] Given Michel de Montaigne's intellectual ascendance over Gournay, which is emphasized by many scholars, one may be surprised she did not call on her *père d'alliance* to fill this role of privileged reader as she had in the title of her first published text, *Le proumenoir de Monsieur de Montaigne* (1595). This issue is not a simple one to deal with and requires a discussion on the nature and limits of his undeniable yet probably overstated influence, as I have suggested elsewhere (Beaulieu, "Relire" 81–82), especially since, from one edition to another, she tends to diminish her references to him. In the *Discours* itself, the 1641 edition dispenses with an entire passage treating Montaigne as a peerless model (Beaulieu, "Marie de Gournay" 32). Moreover, given the protofeminist positions associated with Gournay and the number of female dedicatees throughout the collection (Beaulieu and Fournier, "'Les interests'" 50–51), it is hardly surprising that Gournay claims allegiance to a community of women, communicating an ethos entirely different from *Au lecteur*, which is addressed to the general reader whom she treats with less respect and warmth.

Two attitudes are thus discernible in the *Discours* and *Au lecteur*, both resulting from Gournay's concern, as a female author, for how her texts were likely to be received. As early as 1626, an increasingly antagonistic relationship with part of her readership is detectable, to which Gournay's authorial persona often brings attention and which some critics have described as pugnacious rambling (Schiff 24–25). It seems to me, however, one should broach this question in the light of Gournay's intellectual ambitions, which, formed by Renaissance humanism, had become unseemly for a woman in the first half of the following century, governed as it was by an urbane cultural ideal proscribing any show of erudition (Timmermans 52). This at least partly explains the awkwardness that seems to characterize Gournay's literary undertaking when her first collection was published. This circumstance necessitated increasing her authorial presence in the 1634 peritext by means of a defense of her work specifically requested by her dedicatee. Suggesting moderation and mental resolve, the name Sophrosine remains abstract, emphasizing the symbolic nature of the connection with a figure distinct from the mass of anonymous readers. A kind of triangular relationship is therefore established between Gournay's "I," Sophrosine's "You," and the "He" of the reader. However, toward the end of the *Discours* (1: 567), this relationship shifts toward the public reader, whom Gournay finally addresses, thus ensuring a transition to the following *Au lecteur*.

At the very start of *Discours sur ce livre*, a singular connection between the two women leads Gournay to undertake an examination of her own work, despite the difficulty of judging the fruit of one's labor. Throughout this reader's guide to the collection, Gournay builds an image of herself as author. This self-referentiality, expressed through a commentary on her text, demonstrates a desire to influence the reader's thoughts about it and thus about her. The overview that Gournay proposes may thus be interpreted as a guide or map of her authorial process, an intellectual topography in which she attempts to impose, somewhat defiantly, the image of a woman writer whose ambitions and whose identification with her work are both considerable. Even though Gournay's assertions should not always be taken at face value, their study in class is most useful in delineating what the author finds necessary to point out and comment on in what she designates as a "*guide generale*" (1: 554).

The first group of considerations in the *Discours* concerns language and style. Note that Gournay brings attention to particularities in her usage, especially with respect to capitalization and italics. In referring to revisions made to previous versions: "Quant au stile, j'advoue qu'en ma premiere impression j'avois laissé couler quelques obscuritez, dont à mon advis j'ay corrigé desormais la plus-part" ("I admit that in my first impression I let slip a few obscurities, which, to my mind, I have for the most part corrected"; 1: 556), Gournay reveals a way of assuming authorial responsibility that includes attention to even the minutest details of writing. The author shows herself to be a wordsmith, sensitive to the construction of texts and ready to justify her idiosyncrasies by acknowledging an awareness of common practice. As demonstrated by the space—one and a half pages—she devotes to explanations of textual detail, her position is clear: at a time when language is too often "regraté" and "refripé" ("cheapened" and "overwrought"; 1: 555), her stylistic choices are thoroughly considered and well thought out.

This way of affirming her peculiarities despite current fashion is clearly expressed in the main criterion she advocates as a guide to the reading: originality. Originality, even partial (since no book, she says, can be entirely original), is what Gournay claims for herself in the following pages for judging the kind of text she favors—the *discours de raison.* Sensitive to gender-related aspects of the act of speaking publicly, Gournay issues a challenge that speaks volumes about the obstacles that women writers have had to deal with throughout history:

> Il sera bon de voir après, quel Labeur de femme vainqueur de la malice des temps et des hommes, sera capable d'effacer le mien: je dy vainqueur

> de la malice des temps et des hommes: car quels ravages n'ont-ils point fait de cette part sur les Corinnes, les Saphons, les Hypathies, les Aretes et autres? (1: 558)

> It may be good to see afterward what woman's Labor, overcoming the malice of time and men, will be capable of eclipsing my own: I say the malice of time and men, for what ravages have they not wrought on the Korinnas, the Sapphos, the Hypathias, and others?

Not finding substantial productions by women in the past, she posits her own work (despite men's ill will) as a kind of enduring monument—not a modest ambition, especially considering the negative reception Gournay expects because she is a woman.

As to the homogeneity of the collection, Gournay claims that it contains enough high-caliber pieces to ensure the quality of the whole. Confronted by the spitefulness of some, Gournay opposes a fraternity of texts united by their common mother, "the weakest writing being the strongest's sibling" ("le plus foible n'est point indigne d'estre frere du plus fort"; 1: 559). This familial metaphor is a discretely recurring one in the *Discours* and in some other texts—Anna Lia Franchetti (55) notes the presence of similar images in *Deffence de la poësie*'s dedication to Madame Des Loges—and it assimilates authorial responsibility with that of a mother, which explains the protection Gournay seeks to provide her collection against its critics. Creating a family network of sorts, with Sophrosine as its godmother, Gournay assumes the appearance of a mother having a hard time letting her children face the potential threat of adversaries.

As insignificant as it might be, she humbly says, her work is her own and testifies to her assimilation of materials. Authorial responsibility is wholly assumed here, and, in the framework of the *Discours*, goes well beyond simply describing the texts in the collection. Gournay says that she does not care that others might deem her conceptions of poetry "ill assorted" and "outdated" ("heteroclites, & peu cogneues en nostre siecle"; 1: 561). This dismissal of certain readers' judgment constitutes a kind of challenge that places us at the very heart of Gournay's ethical process. Her self-affirmation consists in submitting her text to the reader's judgment in order to take it back and provide a suitable interpretation. In the tradition of *captatio benevolentiae*, Gournay shows herself attentive to readers' suggestions and to their advice to amend her writings "if need be" (1: 562); but her confidence in the reader is entirely rhetorical, clearly belied by other statements regarding the problematic status of a woman's text.

The affirmation of her dual condition as woman and author is manifest in the association she makes in the *Discours* between the self-referential text *Apologie pour celle qui escrit* and the "feminist" treatise *Égalité des hommes et des femmes* (1: 562–63). Gournay dwells on both these texts, devoting a paragraph to each, when she had dealt summarily with more substantial pieces. A close connection is made between them, although they are not even adjacent in the collection. Their order is even reversed, since, in the 1641 edition, *Égalité* occupies pages 292 through 310, while the *Apologie* closes the first book (590–633). How can one then not see in this association a shift from the personal to the collective, from one woman's experience to a statement in favor of all women, reminding us that the movement of meaning in the *Discours* never occurs outside gender issues.

Referring to the second book of *Advis*, Gournay suggests a new criterion, namely consistency. Assumed here is a correlation between her translatological considerations in *Lettre à Mgr de Gelas* and the quality of her own translation: "Il est requis d'observer . . . si je suy les reigles que je prescrits moy-mesme" ("One must observe . . . whether I follow my own rules"; 1: 563). Inviting the reader to compare her versions with those of known translators, she eventually expresses the modest though significant wish that she gain a hearing among such trusted peers. And to show how little she fears comparison, she declares that she included fragments of translations of the *Aeneid* by Jacques Davy Du Perron and Jean Bertaut, which she either extended in her own words (in the first instance) or set beside her own renditions (in the second). With fairly typical defensiveness, Gournay denies allegations of having chosen the worst samples to set her own in a better light.

Here, as elsewhere, the author seems unwilling to trust the reader's good judgment; she explains and justifies herself while anticipating prior or potential future criticisms. In the closing remarks of her overview, where she discusses the *Bouquet de Pinde* (her collection of poems), particularly "Pincture de mœurs," she qualifies the evaluative criteria to prepare the reader not for beautiful poetry but for well-rounded poems having no gaping weaknesses, no padding, and no holes ("sans baaillement de feiblesse . . . sans bourre, et sans cheutes"; 1: 565). "Pincture de mœurs" occasions a return to Sophrosine, with a suggestion of familiarity and intimacy that allows the author to present herself as the mother of her book: "passez, s'il vous plaist, de l'examen du Livre à celuy de la foy de sa mere" ("please turn from an examination of the Book to one of its mother"; 1: 565). Retrospectively, the metaphor explains Gournay's attitude, which I suggested earlier is that of a mother defending her offspring; whatever their merits, the various editions of her collection, referred to as brothers, are in some sense mirrors or extensions of their mother.

A discussion of the history of the title of the collection further indicates how attached the author is to her writings. Gournay regrets that her publisher, to please certain critics, pressed her to change the original title—*L'ombre de la Damoiselle de Gournay*—which marked the book as "the image of [her] mind, the principal part of [her] being" ("l'image de mon esprit, maistresse pièce de mon estre"; 1: 566). This close, identifying relationship seems so crucial that the author engages in a diatribe against those minds so incapable of grasping the subtleties of such titles that her publisher was forced to adopt a title that eschews the identifying connection between text and author.

More than a little agitated by the issue, Gournay ends her *Discours* with heated remarks on her quarrel with the Malherbian reformists, remarks that foreshadow the often polemical tone of *Advis.* All this reminds us, if it wasn't clear already, that the work could not be published without safeguards, perhaps because of a fundamental mistrust expressed at the very end of the *Discours* and of which Sophrosine becomes the guarantor, since she is the one who asked for a clarification of Gournay's defense (1: 567). Such justifications are a necessity, says Gournay, and must be revisited throughout the collection, whenever she is forced to bring certain explanations back onto the table. The defensive tone is thus set and justified by the bond of friendship between women. This setup is significant, since it foreshadows the complicity established between female dedicatees in the collection, opposing them against an indistinct and rarely named mass of critics and detractors.

The text ends on an almost aggressive note, when Gournay shifts her attention away from Sophrosine to address the reader, whom she enjoins to consider that she is particularly set upon by bad writers. Sophrosine gives way to the less sympathetic and less competent reader that Gournay confronts with scant deference in the defensive, polemical *Au lecteur*—a revised version of the preface published in 1608, in *La bienvenue de Monsieur le Duc d'Anjou*—clearly addressed to an unreceptive audience. The reader is thus interrogated and admonished in a curious mixture of rhetorical modesty and self-affirmation. The suggestion, articulated at the beginning of the text, that she should have kept quiet and spent her time sleeping instead of writing is belied by the book's very existence, engendering a confrontational dialectic between reader and author that leads, in the end, to a parting of the ways: "sentant que ton humeur est pointilleuse en chois d'Escrits, et la mienne en chois de Lecteurs; j'ai creu qu'on ne nous pouvoit mieux accorder qu'en nous separant" ("sensing the scrupulousness in your choice of readings, and mine in my choice of readers, I felt we could not agree better than by separating"; 1: 568). A strange way of addressing one's readers to declare a kind of incompatibility between oneself and them! Rash and a killjoy ("*raba-joye*"), the text proclaims its own singularity. Forgoing all hope of being received by a favorable ear, it puts the reader truly to the test. Gournay's criticism of the fashionable set is severe; her era, she suggests, is incapable of appreciating a woman who has striven to achieve such "excès" that is, a "bon Ouvrage de la façon des Muses" ("a good Work worthy of the Muses"; 1: 570).

Constantly on the brink of breaking relations with its reader—displaying what Franchetti describes, in another text, as an "anti-*captatio benevolentiae*" (59)—this preface demonstrates, as early as 1626, that Gournay felt she was out of step with the expectations and practices of her time; she speaks of her book's "sentiments," or sensibilities, being "moulez à l'air d'un autre Siecle" ("modeled on another century"; 1: 568). The author adopts—convincingly, since it is of her own making—the rhetorically antagonistic position of affirming oneself *against* something. She seems, however, to have softened the stance with the addition of the *Discours sur ce livre* in 1634, which, by means of a special connection with a sympathetic female figure, manifests an authorial *ethos* less geared toward confrontation. The polemical stance is felt here too, of course, but is ballasted by the attempt firmly though politely to steer the reader toward the desired interpretation.

This contradicts a current notion that suggests Gournay strengthened her confrontational stance as she grew older. While this may not be seen as entirely incorrect (when one examines what she changed and added in the 1634 and 1641 editions), one should refrain from giving these texts an essentially psychological reading, as does Michèle Fogel in her well-documented biography of Gournay. We are here in the domain of ethos, that is, of a rhetorical construction that has connection to the author's personality but cannot be entirely assimilated with it. From this perspective, it is noteworthy that the rhetoric used to open the collection from 1634 on situates Gournay in a more supple ethical position, which may show her to be unappreciated by some but certainly understood by others—perhaps mostly, though not exclusively, women—of whom Sophrosine becomes the emblematic figure.

Gournay never allowed herself to withdraw into a defensive position that would cut her off from the world; she claimed she was too concerned about being equal, original, consistent—to use the terms given in *Discours sur ce livre*—not to be concerned about her readership. Her authorial persona, however, always resisted entirely giving in to the latter, as evinced by the presence at the end of the collection of an admonishment that says a lot about the confrontational attitude with the reader that one feels in *Discours* and *Au lecteur*. That same persona also emphasized her willingness to fully assume responsibility, now and forever, for the fruit of her labor, regardless of qualitative criteria: "Si ce Livre me survit, je deffends à toute personne, telle qu'elle soit, d'y adjouster, diminuer, ny changer jamais aucune chose, soit aux mots ou en la substance" ("If this Book should survive me, I forbid anyone, whoever they may be, from adding, diminishing, or changing anything within it, either in word or substance"; 2: 1864). Can one find a stronger affirmation of an antagonistic relationship with the world, a relationship revealed throughout the "reasoned discourses" of *Advis* and heralded in the introductory pieces?

The way Gournay describes herself in *Apologie pour celle qui escrit* and "Pincture de mœurs" confirms she is assuming complete responsibility for the texts, for the better or the worse. Therefore, as I suggest in this brief survey of the *Discours sur ce livre*, it would be most unwise for any student of Gournay's works to read *Advis* without taking into account the ethos put in place in this preamble. By reason of its wholly genuine and radical character, this authorial stance, associated with a type of writing largely beyond the domain attributed to women in the Renaissance, probably makes Gournay one of the first women writers in the modern sense. To explain Gournay's uniqueness in the light of the appropriate cultural parameters, our teaching should ultimately aim at having her distinctive voice be heard. And I hope I have shown the necessity of a careful reading of *Discours sur ce livre* to commence the journey through what Gournay ironically calls her "griffonneries" (1: 567).

Note

1. All citations to Gournay come from *Œuvres complètes*, which reproduces the 1641 edition. Translations are my own.

Part III

Critical Concerns

Approaches and Methodologies

Leslie Zarker Morgan

Louise Labé and Italian in Sixteenth-Century Lyon

As an Italianist teaching a French Renaissance women writers course at the 300 level (advanced literature) to undergraduates, I seek to acquaint students with the poet and time in which she lived (historical and literary). Louise Labé lends herself particularly well to this approach, for she appeals to students both because of her purportedly scandalous life and for her relatively short texts. Lyon is also a fascinating city and serves well to introduce students to life outside Paris, frequently the primary (if not only) area in the hexagon with which they are familiar. I use the influence of Italian language, literature, and culture as a framework of the course to help link the three primary authors we read, Christine de Pisan, Louise Labé, and Marguerite de Navarre. The course is included in the gender studies minor, medieval/Renaissance studies minor, and French major and minor, further interests that form the course.

We complete reading Christine de Pisan's *Cité des dames* in the first part of the course, so students become familiar with certain medieval literary concepts (e.g., the *querelle des femmes*, allegory) and the names of Boccaccio and Petrarch. Thus historical and cultural changes between the end of the Hundred Years' War and the concept of Renaissance initiate the four-week Labé portion of the course. Students are assigned Joan Kelly-Gadol's essay, "Did Women Have a Renaissance?," before the first class dedicated to Labé. I ask them while reading to draw up a list of what they associate with the Renaissance in contrast to the Middle Ages, which we discuss in class and use to explore what they expect to be different from Christine de Pisan's works in Labé's. While the essay is older, it is a seminal piece from which to begin, and it helps formulate cultural and literary expectations of what is to come.

In addition to a discussion of the reading and an outlining of the debate about how to define the Renaissance, the geography and border position of Lyon in the sixteenth century are part of my point of departure for the first class session dedicated to Labé. Using historical maps (such as those on the Web site *History of Europe*, which has maps in French and Italian) we review the political situation of France in the sixteenth century and note the position of Lyon, on the border with Savoy, as well as the location of the major Italian city-states: Florence, the Papal States, Ferrara, and Venice. Other points worth recalling are the following: Charles VIII (d. 1498) left Lyon on 22 August 1494, to retake Naples, via Rome, in 1495. The sister of his successor, Louis XII (who ruled from 1498 to 1515), Renée, married Ercole II of Ferrara (reigned 1534–58). Ercole's brother, Ippolito, was appointed archbishop of Lyon in 1539 by Francis I and came to Lyon in 1540 to be invested with the post that he finally resigned in 1551. Francis I, of course, attempted to recoup French lands in Italy and was captured at Pavia in 1525. Connections between France and the Italian peninsula are also well illustrated by marital ties: Francis I's son Henry II (b. 1519; ruled 1547–49) married Catherine de Médicis in 1533, and the length of her life (she died in 1589) allowed her to rule as regent and exert considerable influence over the court. The Médicis family's influence continued into the next generation, when Marie de Médicis married Henry IV, who died in 1610. When Italian governors ruled Lyon, they continued joining Italian families; in 1562, Jacques of Savoy, Duke of Nemours, married Anna d'Este, daughter of Renée (and thus granddaughter of Lucrezia Borgia). The French royal family stayed in Lyon at numerous points during the sixteenth century; Henry II put in two particularly festive appearances, one in 1542 and another in 1548, occasion of an illustrated book published by Rouillé in Lyon. During these classroom discussions, I give all versions of the names: French, English, and Italian.

To deepen the students' understanding of the city's importance, I assign a film about the history of Lyon (it includes all eras, not just the Renaissance) that gives an excellent overview of the city's favorable position

(*Lyon, Site Historique. Patrimoine Mondial*). Students view the film outside the class after the first meeting (exercises to go with the film are included in app. 1); the volumes *Vivre à Lyon au XVIe siècle* (Boucher) and *Guide de Lyon: Renaissance, âge classique* (Gutton) contain excellent photographs of the Italian section, the *quartiers* of Saint Jean and Saint Paul with the *galeries* such as the Philibert Delorme in rue Juiverie and the so-called house of Henri IV (Gutton 49). These, together with a personal collection of photographs, including some Italian examples (e.g., the Palazzo Davanzati in Florence, built around a courtyard and now reopened as a museum of daily life, has similar interior porticos and color), demonstrate architectural relations with Italy.

At the conjunction of the Rhône and Saone Rivers, Lyon was a natural center for merchants. Its population and culture in the sixteenth century were high: the population of Lyon was 60,000 to 65,000, including permanent inhabitants (based on city documents) and the foreigners also present (according to the registers of the Hôtel Dieu, preserved from 1529 on). During the first half of the century, Lyon may have held from 50,000 to 55,000 residents, which returned to between 30,000 and 35,000 by the end of the century (these figures from Boucher, *Vivre* 67). We can compare this with Paris, which had about 200,000 inhabitants (*Ville de Paris*). The estimates from other sources are similar, though some contend that Lyon rivaled Paris. An exact census of Italians in Lyon during the sixteenth century is impossible, especially since upper-class immigrants brought with them servants and attendants (Boucher, *Présence* 12–22). The role of Italian bankers is evident from not only the names and work of Italian families but also documents such as a loan from the Strozzis to Henri II (Boucher, *Vivre* 59–62). It is clear that the Italian population there was so extensive that a number of printers published just for the Italian population, as it is also clear that many of the printers were Italian or of Italian origin; from 1529 to 1563, of thirty-eight printers documented, five were from Piedmont and Savoy, three from Venice (Gascon qtd. in Boucher, *Vivre* 9). The first edition of Petrarch's *Rime sparse* published outside Italy came from the Tournes Press of Lyon in 1545 (Rigolot, "Louise Labé and the climat lyonnois" 407). Petrarch's text was declaimed at the Fourvières Club, which was not really a formal academy in the Italian sense with rules and regulations but rather a meeting place for local poets (Boucher, *Vivre* 112; *Présence* 138). Henri-Louis Baudrier's *Bibliographie lyonnaise* lists Dante's *Inferno* and *Commedia* nine times, from 1503 through 1575, with the majority (five) of editions by Guillaume Rouillé based on a Venice edition, with two each by other publishers. Petrarch's name appears twenty-five times from 1501 to 1579, again predominantly by Guillaume Rouillé (with twelve editions), seven references of which are to the *Trionfi* or *De remediis utriusque fortunae*. Ludovico Ariosto's *Orlando furioso* appears in nineteen editions, which include publications of individual excerpted tales from the work such as Isabella and Zerbino or the *Cinque canti*, between 1544 and 1583; some of these are also translations into Spanish or French. Here, too, Rouillé is important, with eight of the editions (which includes a shared edition in Spanish). The history of printing in Lyon is illustrated in the first part of the compact disc produced by the Musée de l'Imprimerie de Lyon (*Impressions*).[1] Further information can be provided with inventories and reproductions of publications either on the Web (*Virtual Museum*; *Musée*) or in printed version (Johnson, "Books"; *French . . . Printing*). In Lyon, Labé was appreciated not only for her company but also for her "bibliothèque fournie de livres latin, français et italien" ("library full of Latin, French and Italian books"; Bourgeois 78). Thus the first class prepares students to examine the poetry of the era in Lyon.

The historical situation of Labé's era is well covered in *Renaissance and Reformation France* (Holt), from which we discuss the introduction and chapters 1–4 during the course segment dedicated to Labé to help reinforce the points raised in class. (I occasionally use selections from *Histoire de Lyon en bande desinée* [Pelletier and Bayard 83–96] to lighten the mood.) Hannelore Sachs also contains mainly delightful discussions of cultural details about the French infatuation with Italian culture that occurred at all levels of society during the sixteenth century. The culture of Italian courts was a model for towns (Sachs 15). This included the use of soap and perfumes—Isabella d'Este was known for her concoctions that she sent even to France. In general, Italian makeup (Sachs 32) and even clothing styles were prized; Francis I asked Isabella d'Este for a doll dressed like herself, "with the upper and undergarments and the sleeves—as these were often attached only loosely with ribbons—and with her coiffure, so that the ladies at his court could adorn themselves in the same manner" (Sachs 32). Isabella d'Este seems in particular to correspond about fashions with those outside Mantua (see Croizat's fascinating discussion of the prestige of Italian fashion at the French court in the sixteenth century as documented in fashion dolls and letters about them). In the more historically oriented Mark P. Holt, the chapter "Gender and the Family" (99–118) offers a wider view of women's legal position. Students read this as part of the assignment for the second class, which leads to questioning the position of Labé, a married bourgeoise not present at a court (unlike Christine de Pisan). For the second part of their assignment, I ask students to do a Web search for "Louise Labé" to find out what they can about her life. Finding that she "dit-on, s'habilla parfois en garçon, fit des tournois et même la guerre, et ce qui est mieux, fit l'amour avec délectation et le chanta avec ferveur" ("it was said, sometimes dressed like a boy, participated in tournaments and even in battle, and what is even better, made love with delight and sang about it with fervor"; Brisson), that she studied horseback riding and fencing with her brothers, that she "aurait pris part, en habits masculins, au siège de Perpignan sous le nom de 'capitaine Loys'" ("supposedly took part, dressed in men's clothes, in the siege of Perpignan under the name of 'Captain Louis'"; *Vie*; my trans.), not to mention that she held a salon frequented by the big names of the day and that "rumeurs à propos des mœurs" ("rumors about her morals"; *Rumeurs*; my trans.) were flying, they are ready to read all about it from her own pen.[2]

But before moving directly to Labé, during the second and third classes students read selections from Petrarch's *Canzoniere* and other Italian poets. In 2004, a bilingual edition (used in the *aggrégation*) was published. We look at the first and last poems (to construct the context and idea of a collection) as well as a sample of other poems—the sonnets in closer detail—including a flight from others (35, "Solo e pensoso i più deserti campi" ["I walk alone and troubled, desert places"]), an anniversary poem (61, "Benedetto sia il giorno, e 'l mese, et l'anno" ["Now blessed be the day, the month, the year"]), arguably the most famous *canzone* (126, "Chiare, fresche et dolci acque" ["Clear, fresh, and pleasant water"]), and a nationalist piece (128, "Italia mia" ["O Italy, my land"]) for a total of six—three sonnets and three *canzoni*, to give an idea of Petrarch's breadth and main topics as well as the structure of the *Canzoniere.*[3] I also provide one sample each from four Italian women poets of the sixteenth century, which we look at in class, to demonstrate the importance of the Petrarchan model for women poets, together with a brief informatory background of the "salon" tradition in Italy: the poem "Mentre da vaghi e giovenil pensieri" ("When I was nourished by sweet youthful thoughts"), by Veronica Gambara (1485–1550), is comparable to Petrarch's first sonnet of the *Canzoniere*; the poem by Vittoria Colonna (1492–1547), "Provo tra duri scogli e fiero vento" ("Between harsh rocks and violent wind I feel"), for its navigational and stormy imagery and to acquaint students with her name and personality[4] (the publication of her *Rime* at Padua in 1538 marks a watershed, the beginning of the period of most important publishing of women's works in Italy, a period that lasted through 1623 [*Feminist Encyclopedia* 292]); Gaspara Stampa (1523–54), "Voi ch'ascoltate in queste meste rime" ("O you who listen to these mournful verses"), "Mesta e pentita de' miei gravi errori" ("Sad and repenting of my grievous errors") (*Selected Poems* 2–3, 218–19);[5] and Veronica Franco (1546–91), letter 22, "A Warning to a Mother Considering Turning Her Daughter into a Courtesan" (37–40).[6] Of course biographical details of these authors are also fascinating, from Vittoria Colonna's connections with Renée of France in Ferrara to Gaspara Stampa's career parallels with Labé (Blanc). Other Italian women poets provide interesting object lessons—for example, about who published the women's poetry. Stampa's was published after her death by her sister (see Zancan on Stampa's editions); Colonna's work has never been satisfactorily published—editors have changed the order and misattributed works. One interesting anecdote is that of Tullia d'Aragona's (c. 1510–56) tomb: she and her child were buried in Sant'Agostino in Rome, but the tombs were "lost" in a later restoration (see Marino 37 for a description of the burial). If there were more time, we would look further at Stampa, since there is both a French translation available (1992) and a separate bilingual English-Italian edition (*Selected Poems*) and since her reputation and career in many ways parallel those of Labé and she is of the same generation (Blanc). Stortoni and Lillie's *Women Poets* as well as the *Feminist Encyclopedia* are useful points of departure with basic bibliography and biography for background information in general, both for these authors and others. The tribulations of these women and the complicated traditions of their works help prepare for our study of Labé, whose work even in 2006 has been called a fabrication (Huchon). The Italian women's situations and fate provide a sobering glance at what it was to be a woman in the sixteenth-century Mediterranean and demonstrate the links between cultures from Rome and Venice to Lyon. If there were more time or an instructor wished to provide further background, the film *Dangerous Beauty*, about Veronica Franco, offers the possibility to discuss anachronisms and the modern desire to see oneself in Renaissance works. (For a chronological contrast of Italian and French women writers, together with the French and Ferrarese rulers of the time, see app. 2.)

For the fourth class students read an introduction to humanism in Europe (Mann) to place Petrarch and the importance of textual analysis in the Renaissance. I also mention the importance of Petrarch to

France and to the monarchy, given Petrarch's time in France, and Maurice Scève's purported discovery of Laura's tomb in Avignon (1533) that led to Francis I's coming in person to give homage at the tomb (Pellegrini 8). Together with the background on humanism, students read Labé's first five sonnets. I ask them to consider themes that we have already seen in earlier poems. In class, we examine issues of the significance of where sonnets fall in the series and their form at the level of the collection and of the individual poems (since Petrarch uses both *canzoni* and sonnets). Labé's first poem is of course in Italian. We compare the subject matter and key words with those of Petrarch's initial sonnet, as well as her interests and preoccupations with those of Christine de Pisan and the Italian women's poems that we have read (on Ulysses, see Moore, 108–09). After our analysis together of these poems (our class times are one hour and fifteen minutes two times a week), for the next two weeks we read the rest of the poems, with students taking the analysis of selected individual sonnets; they also write an *explication de texte* on one as their written assignment for the section. When we arrive at the final twenty-fourth sonnet, we again discuss and compare this sonnet with Petrarch's, but here this last with his first, examining the role of repentance (for what?) and religion (which?) in the sonnet and the book of sonnets. If there is time, we also look at *Discours V* (or a selection from it) for Louise's famous quote, "Brief, le plus grand plaisir qui soit apres amour, c'est d'en parler" ("In short, the greatest pleasure that exists after love itself, is to talk about it"; *Œuvres* [1986] 76).

Since many of our students take only one advanced literature course, it is wise to also introduce them to the "canonical" poets of the same era in France. For that reason we also spend one day looking at two samples each of Pierre de Ronsard and Joachim Du Bellay. I give the students copies of the poems, chosen for their relation to Labé's poems—for example, "Malheureux l'an, le mois, le jour, l'heure et le point" ("Unhappy the year, the month, the day, the hour and the minute"; *Œuvres* 51; my trans.);[7] "O fleuve heureux" ("O happy river"; Du Bellay, *Olive* 316; sonnet 77; my trans.); "Ciel, air et ventes, plains et monts découverts" ("Sky, air and winds, plains and bare mountains"; Ronsard, *Amours* [1963] 43; sonnet 67; my trans.); and "Quand vous serez bien vieille, au soir à la chandelle" ("When you are very old, in the evening, by the fire"; Ronsard, *Amours* [1963] 431; sonnet 24 of *Sonnets pour Hélène*; my trans.). I ask one student to look up Ronsard and another Du Bellay in order to provide us with a short background; one student prepares each of the poems, comparing subject, form, and voice to those that we have read by Labé and other writers, especially Petrarch.

Through Labé and Lyon, in parallel with the Italian works of Petrarch and Italian women Petrarchists of the sixteenth century, students can see specific examples of the role of Italian culture in the formation of French Renaissance taste in their historical and geographic context. The course also touches on women's mediation and interpretation of culture—not univocal but varying according to personal situation and interests, from noble to bourgeoise, from profession to avocation—and women's integration or reinterpretation of borrowings. At the conclusion of the Louise Labé segment, students have an appreciation for the cultural roles of women in France and Italy in the sixteenth century, an understanding of the arrival of humanism in France, and a basic knowledge about Lyon and the political situation of France in the mid–sixteenth century. The final portion of the course, Marguerite de Navarre's *Heptameron*, introduces them to the questions of religion and international relations, for which the knowledge of Lyon—second city of France at the time—Labé's concerns about love, and an appreciation of social values for women and literature have prepared them.

The course French Women Writers of the Renaissance is a pleasure to teach. Since many of our students are female, reading the works of women in earlier centuries appeals to them, though they may not characterize themselves as feminists, and in fact many refuse that label. Italy's fascination has made our study-abroad program in Rome one of the most sought after in the panoply offered here, and of course French majors and minors who study in France visit Italy during their time abroad. One of the students at the end of one semester in which I taught the course noted, "I didn't even know that there were any women writers in the Renaissance!"—highlighting the way in which the Renaissance is still taught in many history and literary survey courses and the contribution this sort of course or unit can make.

Notes

1. For reviews of the compact disc, see Ramunni; Vial. Note that to use the CD under *Windows XP* one needs to tinker with the settings: one must manually add virtual memory to over 3,000 MB and run the program in *Windows 95* mode. For more information about the editions of Petrarch in France, see also Tarugi for the number of editions of each text and dates (245–47).

2. The historical reading and gender discussions also set up the final portion of the course, dedicated to Marguerite de Navarre, as Holt's volume continues for

four more chapters (5–8) dedicated to the Wars of Religion and the Reformation (119–228).

3. Translations are from Nichols's translation.

4. Both the text and translation are available in Stortoni and Lillie's edition.

5. These poems by Stampa are also available in *Rime* 18–19 and 116–17.

6. This letter is also excerpted in Stortoni and Lillie 174–79; see also Jones, "City Women" for a closer comparison with Labé.

7. The French has been normalized to modern spelling from Du Bellay. This is Sonnet 25 of *Les regrets.*

Appendix I

Lyon: Ville mondiale (film)

Complétez les exercises sur une autre feuille de papier, s'il vous plaît!

1. Où se trouve Lyon en France?
2. Qui fonda la ville et quand?
3. Nommez les différentes parties de la ville de Lyon et dites quelles parties étaient particulièrement importantes au Moyen Âge et à la Renaissance.
4. Nommez quelques édifices importants et dites à quoi ils servent à l'époque actuelle.
5. À en juger par le film, quels liens existe-t-il entre les différentes époques de la ville de Lyon?
6. Quels monuments ou objets artistiques trouvons-nous aujourd'hui à Lyon?
7. Quelles découvertes (relatives au commerce, etc.) proviennent de Lyon?
8. Pour quelles professions la ville est-elle renommée aujourd'hui?
9. Nommez quelques artistes importants qui ont travaillé à Lyon.
10. La religion a toujours joué un rôle important à Lyon. Donnez quelques exemples de figures bien connues dans le domaine religieux et expliquez ce qui leur vaut cette renommée.

Appendix 2
Writers and Rulers in Italy, France, and Ferrara[†]

Italian Women Writers	French Women Writers	French Rulers	Ferrarese Rulers	Italian Male Writers of the Renaissance (Selected)
				Pulci (1432–92)
				Boiardo (1441–94)
				Machiavelli (1469–1527)
Veronica Gambara (1485–1550)		Charles VIII (1483–98)	Ercole I (1471–1505)	Ariosto (1474–1533)
Vittoria Colonna (1490/92–1547)	Marguerite de Navarre (1492–1549)	Louis XII (1498–1515)	Alfonso I (1505–34)	Castiglione (1478–1529)
Tullia d'Aragona (c. 1510–56)				
Chiara Matraini (1515–1604?)		Francis I (1515–47)		
Laura Bacio Terracina (1519–c. 1577)				
Isabella di Morra (1520–46)	Pernette Du Guillet (1520–45)			
Gaspara Stampa (1523–54)	Louise Labé (1522?–1566)			
			Ercole II (1534–59)	
Veronica Franco (1546–91)		Henry II (1547–59)		Tasso (1544–95)
Moderata Fonte (1555–92)		Francis II (1559–60)	Alfonso II (1559–97)	
		Charles IX (1560–74)		
		Henri III (1574–89)		
		Henri IV (1589–1610)		

[†] Birth and death dates (when known) are provided for writers, and dates of reign for rulers.

Carla Freccero

Reading the *Heptameron*: Feminist and Queer Approaches

At first glance, it is tempting to enlist Marguerite de Navarre's *Heptameron* for feminism, and, indeed, during the 1980s, this is exactly what happened in United States institutions of higher education, when academic feminist-literary criticism was in its heyday (Gallop). After all, the *Heptameron* explicitly declares itself to be a revision of Boccaccio's *Decameron*, a text that playfully stages the *querelle des femmes*, that medieval version of the battle of the sexes. Marguerite's text further encourages a feminist reading in that it equalizes the number of men and women in the group of storytellers and thematically focalizes through its female characters. Biographical elements also come into play; literary historical studies in the seventies and eighties in the United States were devoted to the "uncovering" of women "hidden from history" and to the gender and race equalization of the literary canon in many of the disciplines. Marguerite, long acknowledged in French literary studies as a "minor" writer in the prose tradition, began to feature prominently in sixteenth-century survey courses dedicated to representing the achievements of female writers and writers from the colonies.[1] Typical of this period of rediscovery was the effort to understand early modern writers and poets through the lens of modern feminist concerns as articulating a female specificity of both desire and the project of writing. Ann Rosalind Jones's 1981 comment about two sixteenth-century female poets, Pernette Du Guillet and Louise Labé, is telling in this regard:

> Speaking out of silence, entering the terrain of male discourse from the margins, Pernette and Labé take over its central position as speakers and appropriate its rituals for their own ends. Their women's voices do more than modify poetic style. They rewrite the rules of the game. ("Assimilation" 153)[2]

A difficulty arises then when, in reading a woman's text of the past, feminists do not "hear" a voice that echoes their own, finding instead a world where the women desire to occupy traditional places in society. While it has not seemed anachronistic, in Marguerite's case, to seek a gender-specific discourse (most literary scholars do so in her case, and not always in a feminist vein), recovering a feminist message has proved somewhat more intractable.[3] Marguerite has often been represented as an author who praises women, but only in those traditional and traditionally self-sacrificing roles that have been assigned to them by male Renaissance treatise writers. Thus she is said to assign women the roles of moral and spiritual guardians of society, the preservers of the institution of marriage against the fickle and anarchic waywardness of men. The authors of *Histoire du féminisme français* go so far as to attempt to recuperate her for the feminist cause by remarking: "Peu importe que nous pensions aujourd'hui que le mariage n'est plus libérateur. Il l'était, semble-t-il, en 1540" ("Little does it matter that today we no longer regard marriage as liberating. In 1540, it seems that it was" [Albistur and Armogathe 156; my trans.]). Finally, if feminism is understood to be secular, egalitarian, collective, and democratic in its political impulses (for the liberal feminism of the academy this is indeed the case), then what is a reader to make of Marguerite's evangelical Christianity and her royalism, not to mention the easy dispensability of servants in the prologue to the *Heptameron* and elsewhere?

If feminist readings of the *Heptameron* are challenged, if not fatally compromised, by the disparities between feminism as it is understood in the modern West and whatever female empowerment might be attributable to this female-authored text from the sixteenth century, then the challenges posed to a queer theoretical reading may seem insurmountable. After all, as historians of sexuality have amply demonstrated, the binary division between heterosexual and homosexual as categories of sexual orientation did not exist as such (Foucault; Goldberg; Halperin; Sedgwick). Furthermore,

Marguerite, a devout Christian and sister to the king of France, certainly would not have thematized the sin that is not to be named ("sodomy"), although her compatriot, Pierre de Bourdeille, seigneur de Brantôme, did not hesitate to impute such practices to the court and especially to ladies of the court. Even if queer theory is understood in the sense of a critique of heteronormativity, it would seem strange to apply its insights to a text that seems precisely to defend heterosexual institutions such as marriage against prior, more orthodox Catholic understandings of celibacy as normative ideal (Lochrie).

Nevertheless, once historical specificities are taken into account, the *Heptameron* is a text that can be said to lend itself both to an analysis of gender and sexuality (desire) in literature (and thus, perhaps, to an understanding of sixteenth-century feminism) and to an analysis of the way a literary text challenges—but also importantly and simultaneously bolsters—some of the reigning normativities of its day. To approach this text from feminist and queer perspectives, then, is not necessarily to find in it unambiguously feminist and antinormative messages; it is, rather, to examine its ambivalent and historically specific contributions to the analysis of gender, sexuality, and ideology through the lens of modern categories of analysis.

Marguerite de Navarre's *Heptameron* is a social text, an act of indirect intervention into matters of state by means of the conceit of both "fiction" and "*veritable histoire*," or "true history." Margaret Ferguson notes that, like Baldassare Castiglione, who also "rewrites" Boccaccio and stages a battle of the sexes conducted by discussants in a *locus amoenus*, Marguerite "gives us the portrait of the author as courtier—someone who needs exquisite skills of persuasion as she attempts to play one of the most difficult of the roles Castiglione's male interlocutors discuss: the role of the courtier not only as 'ornament,' but as educator of the prince" ("Recreating" 178).

Thus, for example, in story 42, Parlamente (whose name is an explicit political reference and who is the presumed author-figure) recounts a pedagogical tale involving a young prince whose advances are repeatedly refused by an exemplarily virtuous but poor young woman named Françoise. Unlike so many of the plots of the *Heptameron*'s novellas, where the woman in question would have been taken by force, this story results in the prince's being educated into virtuous and chaste conduct by his namesake (François/Françoise) and, it is suggested, his nation ("*françoise*") through the figure of a young woman. As if to underline the national allegory at work in the tale, Oisille suggests that Françoise would have more aptly served as founding exemplar of virtue than Lucretia, the Roman heroine whose rape and suicide precipitate the Roman republic:

> Je ne voy que ung mal, . . . que les actes vertueux de ceste fille n'ont esté du temps des historiens, car ceulx qui ont tant loué leur Lucresse l'eussent laissé au bout de la plume, pour escripre bien au long les vertuz de ceste-cy. (498–99)
>
> "There is only one thing I would regret," said Oisille, "and that is that the virtuous actions of this young girl didn't take place in the time of the great [Roman] historians. The writers who praised Lucretia so much would have left her story aside, so that they could describe at length the virtue of the heroine of your story." (389)[4]

Here a certain French nationalism (as against Roman exemplarity) articulates itself, while the feminized figure of France educates its monarch into virtuous conduct, thus becoming herself a historical actor in the development of the French nation-state. In this particular tale, then, fiction and "*verité*" collude in the production of an indirect intervention in matters of state rule: the fashioning of its sovereign as a chaste and virtuous prince.[5]

In the sixteenth century, state politics are very deeply and indistinguishably a matter of family relations; sovereignty is a legal, metaphysical, and blood concept that binds together state, God, and family. As Sarah Hanley notes, "Early modern monarchies were characterized politically by intertwined private-public (family-state) relations" ("Family and State" 54). Marriage served as one of the primary state-making instruments. On the one hand, the control of marital arrangements meant the control of property and its transmission through inheritance; on the other, marriage (reproduction) was the primary means by which sovereignty (and the sovereign) achieved self-replication. Marriage was thus, unsurprisingly, a focus of contestation in the early modern nation-state, in part because it was a peculiar arrangement, subject to both canon and civil law, and thus the site of a convergence of potentially conflicting interests between church and state but also among people.

As with the monarchy, the ruling class's interest in marriage involved inheritance: in the sixteenth century there emerged, through the system of venality—whereby political positions became inheritable goods and could also, therefore, be bought and sold—a class of professional lawyers, the *noblesse de robe,* who staffed administrative and judicial offices in the kingdom. A system was therefore instituted whereby political offices could be hereditarily transmitted to the next generation as family property. This particular interweaving of family and state interests created an incentive—realized over the course of the sixteenth century in France—to increase the power of constitutional and civil law over that of ecclesiastical or canon law and to bring marriage, the key to state making as well as to the hereditary transmission of property and goods, under the control of secular law and thus of family and state.

From Gratian's twelfth-century *Concordia discordantium canonum*, which summarized case law and opinion, until the mid–sixteenth century in France, consent of the parties involved was the sine qua non of a legal marriage, which came under the jurisdiction of canon law and the ecclesiastical courts.[6] Until the sixteenth century, it was also theoretically possible for people to marry without the consent of their families, an event referred to as clandestine marriage and repeatedly targeted for regulation throughout the century. The *Parlement* of Paris in 1556 promulgated an edict against clandestine marriages, and in 1557 the king, Henri II, also issued an edict against them, which was to be the subject of a treatise by Jean Coras, the man who would later be one of the judges in the trial of Martin Guerre (also a story about clandestine marriage).[7] Natalie Zemon Davis argues that, until 1564, when the last session of the Council of Trent established specific guidelines to ascertain the validity of a marriage, consent of the partners alone continued to constitute a valid union even in the absence of a priest and witnesses. "People," she argues, "used [clandestine marriage] for reasons of their own: they were minors and their parents were opposed to the marriage; they were marrying within a prohibited degree of kinship and could not get a dispensation; they wanted to have intercourse and this was the only way to do it; one of the partners was already married to a person in another place" (*Return* 46–47).[8] In practice, of course, families exercised the maximum control possible in contracting alliances and thus, over the course of the Middle Ages, "a contest developed between two institutions [family and church] for control over the connubial fate of children" (Hanley, "Family and State" 55).

Queen Marguerite de Navarre, sister to King François I, was involved in an international diplomatic tug of war between her brother and her husband (Henri de Navarre) over the marriage of her daughter, Jeanne. The archives reveal her caught between kin (her brother the king) and lineage (her husband), ultimately acting as the obedient subject who effects the king's will on both her husband and her daughter. Jeanne—best known historically as a Protestant leader and the mother of the future King

Henri IV—seems to have protested her mother's and the king's choice of the husband she eventually married, a marriage that was later annulled on the grounds of nonconsent. Marguerite's fiction at several points articulates a female subject's protests before a female monarch specifically on the issue of consent in the choice of a marriage partner (see stories 21 and 40). In her fiction, then, Marguerite de Navarre seems to confront the question of the daughter's agency and to "resolve" the conflict of wills in the best interests of both the queen and her subject. Marguerite demonstrates, both textually and in the documented archives of her life, an active investment in questions of family-state rule and the place of the (sovereign) woman within them, reinvesting the maternal sovereign, in her fiction, with the authority to fashion the state.[9]

In the early 1500s, legists and scholars schooled in the humanist techniques of philology and historical research proved the fraudulence of what was called the French Salic law that was supposed to exclude women from succession to monarchic office in the kingdom. As a result, the exclusion of women from rule was no longer a constitutional matter (Hanley, "Monarchic State"; "Loi salique"). Elsewhere in Europe queens ruled, while in sixteenth-century France, foreign brides for kings were the rule rather than the exception. Some of them—most notoriously Catherine de Médicis—were installed as queen regents, while kings regularly failed to generate successors: only two of the five Valois kings, for example, had legal marital progeny. In reactive response, Hanley argues, legists and members of the parliaments developed a French law canon "which secured legal foundations for the male right to govern along the lines of a Marital Regime in law" ("Monarchic State" 109). This law canon—defined as the articulation, compilation, and deployment of public law (patterns of laws and case precedents condensed into a series of political maxims) and as the production of political rituals—also gave shape to the French nation as a state, for it provided an "indigenous French body of laws . . . able to contend with the law codes cited . . . by other European states and the papacy" (109).

Over the course of the sixteenth century, then, these legists and members of the parliaments developed a body of laws—what Hanley characterizes as a marital-regime government—securing secular legal foundations for a male right to govern and to transmit property and definitively excluding women from the political sphere. This French legal canon encompassed public law (which addressed the constitutional foundations of the state encapsulated in the marital maxim, "The king is the husband and political spouse of the kingdom"); civil law (which governed the family and marriage); and natural law (which established the natural superiority of males over females and the priority of male seminal transmission in matters of succession). Thus the king was the husband of the kingdom; the inalienable dowry brought to him from the kingdom was his territory; and his royal sons were the political progeny born to him of this union: "They are children of the French people and the kingdom." This interweaving of political and marital relations produced an intimate linkage between "family formation and state building by contractually uniting king and kingdom in a political state marriage likened legally to that of husband and wife in a social civil marriage" (Hanley, "Monarchic State" 110). Finally, natural law also worked to ensure that the king alone could produce heirs to the throne: the coupling of king and kingdom amounted to an "autogenetic male generative act" (111). Based in arguments from Aristotelian reproductive science that male seed was formative while the female contributed only matter, political theorists developed a biogenetic seminal theory of authority, whereby husbands produce heirs and kings produce successors through seminal creation. Even though, as Lorraine Daston and Katharine Park have argued ("Hermaphrodite"; *Wonders*), there were at the time competing scientific theories of reproduction, notably from Galen, this is the one that seems to have predominated as a political maxim in part no doubt to prevent succession to the crown from unions involving French queens and foreign husbands. It also effectively excluded women from rule, since only men born of the seed of kings could inherit the throne. This theory finds its culmination in the shift in monarchic public policy in the 1570s regarding the principles of succession from a policy that designated peers of France (the king and his barons) to one that specified Princes of the Blood (direct descendants of the king and his cadet lines) (Jackson). Blood and semen here are also used interchangeably, further demonstrating the tacit coarticulation of racial and sexual theories and policies in early modern French nation-state formation: at one and the same time, French "nation-ness" is defined as "male" and "not foreign," the familiar configuration associated with nationalism here articulated as a set of concrete and discrete elements of political theory and social practice.[10]

I want to turn now to a story in Marguerite de Navarre's *Heptameron* that may be seen to respond to the "queerness" in this fantasy of nation building by exposing sixteenth-century monarchic strategy as incestuous and homosocial even as it aspires to a corresponding fantasy of maternal rule. In exposing that patriarchal strategy, while nevertheless substituting for it an equally autocratic maternal one, Marguerite de Navarre's text also reaffirms a racial homogeneity for the state and ultimately endorses its heteronormativity, even as it rejects male domination.

Story 30 is about a very young and wealthy widow with a son, who decides not to remarry, "tant pour le regret qu'elle avoit de son mary que pour l'amour de son enfant" ("whether out of sorrow at the loss of her husband or whether out of her love for her child"; 402; 317).[11] Thus already there appears the double bind that Christiane Klapisch-Zuber has named "the cruel mother" syndrome: on the one hand, it is the widow's duty (to her family of birth) to remarry and thus to place back into circulation the wealth she has inherited through her husband's death; on the other, it is a sign of her devotion to her family of marriage that she does not, retaining the wealth for the male heir of that family (her son).[12] The delicate and sometimes aporetic positioning between kin and marriage (or lineage), between endogamy and exogamy, both crucially defines "woman" as currency and gift (between and among groups of men) and specifically brings the particular difficulties of Marguerite's position between these two lines into relief. In Marguerite's case, of course, loyalty to the family of birth was also loyalty to the king of France. Thus positioned, the widow of story 30 decides to withdraw from the social order altogether. Klapisch-Zuber, it is interesting to note, remarks that when women in early modern Italy chose to remain within the family of marriage—thus ensuring the financial solvency of their husband's heirs—they were said to become both a father and a mother to their dead husband's children (128).

Marguerite's widow finds a holy man to serve as the son's "maistre d'escolle" ("schoolmaster or tutor"), while she herself has a "damoiselle," a young lady who sleeps in her room. At fourteen or fifteen, when the son reaches puberty, he begins to pursue the lady-in-waiting, at which point she complains to her mistress. The widow does not believe her but hatches a plan to trade places with the *damoiselle* and wait to see if the young man goes to her bed. If he does, she decides to "chastier si bien son filz, qu'il ne coucheroit jamais avecq femme qu'il ne luy en souvynt" ("give her son such a chastising that he would never in the whole of his life get in bed with a woman without remembering it"; 404; 318). One wonders at this point whether the maternal intention is not already to produce an incestuous mother-son relation, given that the goal is for the son to think about his mother whenever he has sex with a woman.[13] He does, of course, and the mother, incredulous, waits so long with him in the bed that "elle convertit sa collere en ung plaisir trop abominable, obliant le nom de mere" ("her anger turned to pleasure, a pleasure so abominable, that she forgot she was a mother"; 404; 318). She becomes pregnant; the narrator remarks, "en ceste nuict là, engrossa de celluy, lequel elle vouloit garder d'engrossir les autres" ("that night she became pregnant by the very one whom she desired to prevent getting others with child"; 404; 318). She then sends her son off to war to hide her shame and gets her brother to collude in the concealment of the birth of a beautiful daughter, who is immediately sent out to wet nurse and to live with a faraway relative. The son, back from the wars in Italy, begs his mother to permit him to return home, whereupon she refuses to see him until he has married a woman he loves very much.

The son meets and marries the widow's daughter—his own daughter and sister—much to the mother's horror and dismay. She consults with the theologians as to what course of action to take, whereupon they advise the following:

> Que la dame ne debvoit jamais rien dire de ceste affaire à ses enffans, car, quant à eulx, veu l'ignorance, ilz n'avoient point peché, mais qu'elle en debvoit toute sa vie faire penitence, sans leur en faire ung seul semblant. (407–08)
>
> The lady should never say anything of this affair to her children, for they had acted in ignorance and consequently had not sinned. But she, their mother, was to do penance for the rest of her life without giving the slightest indication of it to them. (321)

The two live extraordinarily happily ever after: "s'entre-aymoient si fort que jamais mary ny femme n'eurent plus d'amitié et semblance, car elle estoit sa fille, sa seur et sa femme, et luy à elle, son pere, frere et mary" ("never was there such love between husband and wife, never were a husband and wife so close. For she was his daughter, his sister, his wife. And he was her father, brother, and husband"; 408; 321).[14] Not only, then, do they desire each other, but they also accomplish that "grande amitié," or friendship, that Marguerite's platonic theory of conjugal reciprocity holds up as the highest ideal of the marriage relation. The mother devotes the rest of her life to doing penance. One editor of an early edition of the *Heptameron* includes in his notes epitaphs found in churches that pose the riddle of kin relations in this fashion: "here lies the child, the parent, the sister, the brother, the wife and the husband, but there are only two people here" or again, "here lies the son, here lies the mother, here lies the daughter with the father, here lies the sister, here lies the brother, here lie the wife and the husband, but there are only three bodies here." The editor also includes contemporary compilations of the Oedipus and Jocasta story (475n526; my trans.).

But the differences between this tale and Oedipus are striking. In the Oedipus story, son and mother marry unbeknownst to each other, and tragedy ensues, with Oedipus blinding himself and Jocasta committing suicide. In this tale, on the other hand, the incestuous marriage is between father/son and daughter/sister. Marguerite's story is not a tragedy. No one dies, the young couple's love is confirmed, and their marriage remains intact. Indeed, they are the perfect couple. Further, the perspective of the tale is the mother's, not the son's or the father's. Thus, while the tragedy of Oedipus chronicles the destruction of the city through endogamous (or incestuous) kinship relations, and others as monstrous the maternal figure, this tale affirms as utterly harmonious the "friendship" and "resemblance" of the product of incestuous unions. In order for this to be achieved, the mother must, of course, be condemned and excluded from the reproductive cycle she sets in motion, which was what she had planned for herself all along. Nevertheless, she remains—autogenetically and parthenogenetically, as it were—the source and origin of a bloodline.

This fictional fantasy of maternal sovereignty seems then to intervene into matters of state making in early modern France, to comment on masculine and sovereign autogenetic theory with an equally autonomous feminine and maternal theory. Claude Lévi-Strauss's remark about this aspect of incest, a social incest that, for him, includes marriage, is telling: "l'inceste, entendu au sens le plus large, consiste à obtenir par soi-même, et pour soi-même, au lieu d'obtenir par autrui, et pour autrui" ("incest, in the broadest sense of the word, consists in obtaining by oneself, and for oneself, instead of by another, and for another"; 561; 489). This fantasy also resembles the fantasy, articulated in story 42, of twin sovereign subjects of the nation distinguished only by the masculine and feminine forms of the proper name (of the nation): François and Françoise.

Finally, and also unlike Oedipus, the incest in this story is doubled: mother/son and daughter/sister with father/brother. The result is that every kinship position in the family has its heterosexual erotic counterpart. In the beginning of the story, the mother and son each have a same-sex double: the son a holy man who serves as his tutor, the mother a *damoiselle* who sleeps in her room. The story details the son's departure from his tutor to submit to the secret tutelage of nature and lessons other than the one the schoolmaster teaches (heterosexual desire); it also details the mother's substitution of her person for the person of the *damoiselle*. Gayle

Rubin has suggested that before or simultaneous with the incest taboo (the purportedly universal rule that, according to Lévi-Strauss, inaugurates culture, whereby opposite-sex family members are prohibited from sexual union), there must also be a taboo on homosexual desire, one that is, or comes to be, suppressed as a rule.[15] Marguerite's text also figures this movement from a homosocial and perhaps homoerotic space to the place where sexual difference sets the incest in motion. Thus even as the text reaffirms its commitment to heterosexuality—however nonnormative that heterosexuality may be—it also renders legible the traces of another order that is left in its wake. It would seem then that, in story 30, the fantasy of female autogenesis here works to compensate for the loss occasioned by exogamic heterosexual exchange, an exchange that is, Lévi-Strauss argues, necessary to the movement from family to group or family to society and, finally, family to nation.

Judith Butler argues that melancholia determines the modern Western heterosexual subject (*Bodies*). Melancholia is the result of loss, a loss at the origin of subject formation that, she argues, is foreclosed or refused as a loss. She names that loss as the loss of the same-sex object of love. The normative or usual response to this loss, in her rewriting of Sigmund Freud's theory of sexed subjectivity, is to identify with (rather than desire) the same-sex object of love, to incorporate it and thus to become gendered and heterosexually desiring. In this text, the fantasy of incest partly preserves the lost object of love as an object of desire, for the marital union of brother/father and daughter/sister produces perfect friendship and perfect "semblance," desire *and* identification seamlessly joined in the platonic androgyne. This is the "dream" of incest that Lévi-Strauss identifies as "saisir et . . . fixer cet instant fugitif où il fut permis de croire qu'on pouvait ruser avec la loi d'échange, gagner sans perdre, jouir sans partager" ("seizing and fixing that fleeting moment when it was permissible to believe that the law of exchange could be evaded, that one could gain without losing, enjoy without sharing"; 569; 497). And indeed, this is also the dream of the widow, whose refusal to reenter an economy of exchange—to remarry—amounts to just such an evasion of the renunciation and sacrifice required of "the traffic in women" (Rubin). Thus the maternal sovereign produces the beginning of a line of succession that cannot be alienated from her domain.

By focalizing the narrative through the maternal figure, that is, by adopting the widow's point of view, Marguerite restores the subjectivity absent—as Luce Irigaray has so acerbically noted—from Lévi-Strauss's account of woman as gift in the economy of exogamic kinship.[16] The fantasy of a lineage produced through incest also indirectly comments on the fantasy of French nationalism as the foreclosed (simultaneously legislated and refused) homoerotic and incestuous desire to obtain "by oneself, and for oneself"; the sweetness ("*la douceur*," Lévi-Strauss calls it) "d'un monde où l'on pourrait vivre *entre soi*" ("of a world in which one might *keep to oneself*"; 570; 497. This is a fantasy that inextricably joins race, sex, and gender in its exclusions.

Lévi-Strauss comments:

> Les satisfactions symboliques dans lesquelles s'épanche, selon Freud, le regret de l'inceste, ne constituent donc pas la commémoration d'un événement. Elles sont autre chose, et plus que cela: l'expression permanente d'un désir de désordre, ou plutôt de contre-ordre. (563)
>
> Symbolic gratifications in which the incest urge finds its expression, according to Freud, do not therefore commemorate an actual event. They are something else, and more, the permanent expression of a desire for disorder, or rather counter-order. (491)[17]

The counterorder that the fantasy of maternal autogenetic creation sets up in this story is precisely the gynocracy railed against in French legists' tracts justifying the exclusion of female rule and succession through the female line; it is, in other words, a will to power articulated in the very terms set forth by the French state. In exposing those terms as incestuous, Marguerite's text thus also exposes—as an incestuous autogenesis unmediated by heterosexual reproduction—the queerness of a fantasy of nation building based on direct father-to-son seminal transmission and on the effacement of woman from matters of reproduction. And yet this counterorder nevertheless affirms the self-replicating principle on which the state it criticizes is based, for although "women" are now included in the polis, "foreigners" are not.[18]

Butler has argued that another figure of incest—Antigone—allegorizes a crisis of kinship in and of the state; she asks, "What in her [Antigone's] act is fatal for heterosexuality in its normative sense? And to what other ways of organizing sexuality might a consideration of that fatality give rise?" (*Antigone's Claim* 72). She points out that Antigone "fails to produce heterosexual closure" for the oedipal drama, seeming rather to "deinstitute heterosexuality by refusing to do what is necessary . . . by refusing to become a mother and wife" and ultimately by choosing the tomb over the bridal chamber (76). Marguerite de Navarre's ambiguous heroine also finds herself entombed, consigned to perpetual silence. Her withdrawal, however, does not bring closure; on the contrary she sets in motion the possibility of a reproductive lineage. One cannot help thinking of Marguerite's other, "archival," sovereign strategy, the one that positioned her daughter to become the mother of a king (Henri IV) and thus a royal line. If, in the history of patriarchal feminine exemplarity (albeit in its "negative" or "destructive" form), Antigone represents the Greek version of Roman Lucretia as exemplar, then perhaps in this "matriarchal" scene, the widow is story 30's version of Françoise, a less shattered feminine heroine, agent and catalyst of the nation.[19]

If story 30, with its theme of incest, is a response to the state's strategic policy of reproductive homosocial incest—a form of gender endogamy—then it posits a utopian (and thus imaginary) solution to a problem that as yet (in the period) has no means of redress. This is not because of any historical prematurity with respect to political intervention in state policy but because, in part, nonmonarchical solutions to the problem are neither imaginable nor, for the royalist Marguerite de Navarre, desirable. Further, for this particular sister of a king, imagining the place of the monarch as feminine requires identification (with the male monarch)—another possible meaning of incest—rather than substitution or replacement. However, this fantasy of maternal sovereignty—protofeminist and protonationalist in appearance—may have had its practical uses in at least one instance of female sovereignty. Maureen Quilligan argues that the figure of incest and the "fantasized incestuous genealogies" generated elsewhere by Marguerite de Navarre provided the enabling terms of a form of female authority in the Renaissance, a form of authority that culminated in another figure of incest—one who lived to speak and rule—Elizabeth I, who adopts Marguerite's metaphor of incest in her translation of Marguerite's *Mirror of the Sinful Soul* and uses it as "an action that brings about a most spectacularly scandalous halt in the traffic in women" ("Incest" 214). Married to and mother of her people, Elizabeth, the virgin queen and also prince, remetaphorizes the incest whose literality undoes both Antigone and Marguerite's widow, abstracting kinship into the terms of the body politic. Her nonreproductivity, however, a seemingly necessary condition for this abstraction, points to the place where kinship and the state remain joined, where succession and lineage continue to converge in a politics of family and state.

Elizabeth, in any case, is hardly any more exemplary than Antigone or Marguerite's widow. Her self-production illustrates what would persist as a conundrum of liberal feminist political theory in the modern state and civil society: that women may be either embodied or abstracted sovereign subjects, but they cannot be both simultaneously.[20] Further, the nationalism achieved through metaphorical incest confirms the exclusionary racial politics of the nation. Nevertheless, the detachment of kinship from blood that Elizabeth's symbolics of sovereignty performs suggests possible ways that kinship—including the same-sex kinship of domestic partnership and adoption and the kinship of political affiliations—would be opened up, in time, to enabling and "transformative articulation[s]" that do not finally consign their subjects to silence or death.[21] In all these cases of exceptional women—a character in political myth (Antigone); a female ruler (Elizabeth); and a female author and her active, desiring, fictional mothers and daughters (Marguerite)—we can read a critical approach to patriarchal power and a kind of female autonomy and agency, coupled with a critique of normative sexual arrangements that could be called queer. This is the kind of reading that is enabled by feminist and queer literary criticism and theory; above all, it yields an understanding of some of the contradictions involved in literary representation in its encounter with modern identitarian movements for social change.

Notes

1. See Jones and Vickers for a discussion of the canonization of French women writers, Marguerite among them.

2. In subsequent essays and books, Jones—like many feminist literary critics—continues to modify her position; see "City Women," "Surprising Fame," and *Currency of Eros.*

3. See Polachek, *Heroic Virtue*, for interesting discussions of this question of Marguerite, female authorship, and feminism.

4. Citations from the *Heptameron* come from the 1967 Michel François edition. English translations are from Chilton.

5. For a discussion of nationalism in story 42, see Freccero, "Practicing Queer Philology." For the relation between nationalism and literature in sixteenth-century France and in Marguerite de Navarre's *Heptameron*, see Hampton.

6. Cited in Hanley, "Family and State" 54. See also Gottlieb; Donahue; Noonan.

7. Coras, it should also be mentioned, later became chancellor of Toulouse for the Protestant queen of Navarre, Marguerite de Navarre's daughter, Jeanne.

8. Ruggiero documents similar informal marital practices in early modern Venice.

9. For a lengthier discussion of these circumstances, see Freccero, "Marguerite de Navarre," "1527: Margaret of Navarre," and "Archives."

10. For the coarticulation of nation and sex more generally, see Mosse, and Parker, Russo, Sommer, and Yaeger.

11. For a reading of story 30 that focuses on its subtexts—which are numerous and include Masuccio Salernitano, Matteo Bandello, and Martin Luther—as

well as its religious and moral content, see Cazauran. On incest in the period and in narrative fiction, see Archibald, who discusses story 30 briefly and also discusses its departures from Bandello and Luther (140–44); see also Boehrer.

12. See ch. 6 (117–31).

13. Similar dynamics are at work in story 10.

14. Here the French is more pointed, featuring the reciprocal form of the verb that also suggests its reflexivity, while marking what they have between them as friendship and "resemblance."

15. For a critique of Lévi-Strauss's discussion of the nature-culture divide, see Derrida; also Butler, *Antigone's Claim*, esp. 15–20.

16. Irigaray criticizes Lévi-Strauss's discussion of the exchange of women as currency in establishing ties between groups for his failure to account for women's own agency in these exchanges.

17. Note that the French says "le regret de l'inceste" rather than "the incest urge." Thus Lévi-Strauss is noting symbolic (rather than actual) situations where the incest "urge" is a nostalgic fantasy.

18. Indeed, in *Antigone's Claim*, Butler suggests that, in addition to the prohibition on incest, a "miscegenation prohibition" would need to be theorized in Lévi-Strauss's discussion of how "cultures maintain an internal coherence precisely through rules that guarantee their reproduction," or "self-replication," one of the "social" dimensions of incest that persists through exogamic exchange or marriage: "Moreover, one can see in the work of Lévi-Strauss the implicit slide between his discussion of kinship groups, referred to as clans, and his subsequent writing on race and history in which the laws that govern the reproduction of a 'race' become indissociable from the reproduction of the nation. . . . [H]e implies that cultures maintain an internal coherence precisely through rules that guarantee their reproduction, and though he does not consider the prohibition of miscegenation, it seems to be presupposed in his description of self-replicating cultures" (74).

19. Butler details the ways Antigone has been taken up as example or representative, by Georg Wilhelm Friedrich Hegel, by Luce Irigaray, and by Jacques Lacan, among others. The early part of *Antigone's Claim* focuses, in part, on a refutation of the specific ways Antigone is made to signify representatively by these thinkers. In chapter one she writes, "Antigone represents not kinship in its ideal form but its deformation and displacement, one that puts the reigning regimes of representation into crisis and raises the question of what the conditions of intelligibility could have been that would have made her life possible?" (24). Near the end of the book, Butler also writes, "Although not quite a queer heroine, Antigone does emblematize a certain heterosexual fatality that remains to be read" (72). It is in this sense, then, that I say Butler makes of Antigone a "negative" example, an example of a certain negativity that, in bringing heterosexuality to crisis, has the potential to "raise questions" and "open up" other conditions of possibility.

20. For an exploration of the problem, in political theory, of women as citizens, on the one hand, and as sexual subjects, on the other, see Kaplan's discussion of Mary Wollstonecraft, especially 31–56. See also the debates in Hirsch and Keller.

21. The phrase "transformative articulation" is Butler's; see *Antigone's Claim* 21.

Nancy Frelick

Reading Hélisenne with Transference

In his study on the early modern psychological novel in France, *Le roman sentimental avant l'*Astrée, Gustave Reynier describes *Les angoysses douloureuses qui procèdent d'amours* as the first autobiographical book, "le premier livre français qui puisse s'appeler 'le journal d'une femme' " ("the first French book that could be called 'a woman's journal' "; 118; my trans.). Even though he acknowledges Giovanni Boccaccio's *Fiammetta* as an important source for much of the text, Reynier identifies Hélisenne, the heroine and narrator of the story, with the author of the work and speculates that her tale must come from real life. He expresses a clear preference for the first part of the novel, which he calls a "véritable roman sentimental" ("a real sentimental novel"; 112; my trans.) because it appears to conform to his modernist criteria of realism, originality, sincerity, and passion and, no doubt, because it provides the best fit with his description of the early modern psychological novel. Notwithstanding the contradictions in his own arguments, he is dismissive of the second and third parts of the *Angoysses*, which he sees as lacking in coherence, and pronounces his outright rejection of the epilogue, Quézinstra's "ample narration," which gives a mythical account of the lovers' death and apotheosis, as well as the book's fabulous translation into print, thanks to the intercession of the Greco-Roman pantheon, calling it "purement païenne et tout à fait inutile" ("purely pagan and completely useless"; 121–22; my trans.).

Some other early critics, such as Louis Loviot, who wanted to establish the "real" identity of "Hélisenne de Crenne," blur the distinctions between details in the life of the supposed author, Marguerite Briet, according to archival data, and elements of Hélisenne's story, making statements that confuse fiction with biography: "Marguerite Briet, ainsi se nommait donc Hélisenne" ("Marguerite Briet, for that was Hélisenne's name"); and "le mari d'Hélisenne, je veux dire le mari de Marguerite Briet . . . s'appelait Philippe Fournet [or Fournel, according to Saulnier], écuyer, seigneur de Cresne" ("Hélisenne's husband, I mean Marguerite Briet's husband . . . was called Philippe Fournet [or Fournel, according to Saulnier in "Quelques"], Equerry, and Lord of Cresne"; Loviot 139; my trans.). Despite obvious problems posed by the text (including Hélisenne's death before the end of the work, the changes in genre and narration at various points in the book, the use of deus ex machina in the epilogue, and other elements that defy verisimilitude), a number of subsequent critics perpetuated the identification between author, narrator, and character, continuing at times to use the names of Marguerite and Hélisenne somewhat interchangeably.

It is interesting to discuss these issues with students, for there are clear illustrations that these sorts of readings limit the scope of the text and lead to procrustean measures to ensure the text fits with the interpretative grid. For supporting evidence, one can just list the number of articles that examine only the first part of the novel and show students the first two modern editions (both from 1968) that seem to follow Reynier's advice, truncating the text and publishing only part 1 of the *Angoysses* (see the editions by Demats and by Vercruysse). Indeed, as Martine Debaisieux ("'Des dames'" 28–29) points out, both editions are disappointing in their disparaging treatment of the author's use of language (see Vercruysse's edition) and sources (Demats italicizes all borrowings from Boccaccio and Caviceo). Even as they promote or disseminate various works by early modern women, these approaches help perpetuate several fundamental myths or underlying assumptions about women's writing: that it must be autobiographical, that it is derivative, and that it is always second-rate. They also tend to put the critic or editor in a position of superiority or dominance with respect to both the text and the author, as if such readers possessed greater lucidity or insight than literary works or their creators. Needless to say, this sort of perspective has often been especially detrimental to women writers of the French Renaissance, owing, no doubt, to lingering prejudices regarding women's inferiority to men, especially with respect to rational or intellectual abilities, not to mention creative genius, which for centuries was portrayed as available only to men in medical and philosophical discourses on the subject. As we have seen, sometimes even champions of works by early women writers (critics and editors such as Reynier, Vercruysse, and Demats, whose significant contributions helped bring the *Angoysses* back to light) appear to struggle with contradictory ideas and opinions with respect to gender norms and modernist aesthetics that find expression in ambivalent statements about authors or texts. Moreover, although there has been a proliferation of outstanding books and articles on women writers of the French Renaissance in recent decades—work focusing on close textual readings that puts universalizing notions into question—it is interesting to note that readings that bespeak (sometimes unstated and perhaps even unconscious) negative assumptions about sixteenth-century women writers continue to appear. Notable examples that may elicit great discussions in class are studies suggesting that some works attributed to women were written by men. For example, Mireille Huchon's recent book on Louise Labé emits the problematic hypothesis that Labé's works were written by men as a lark,[1] giving credence to Labé's most virulent detractors, treating their defamatory comments as historical fact, and concluding therefore that Labé and Pernette Du Guillet were not writers but vulgar prostitutes. These affirmations are not backed by archival data but remain purely hypothetical and rely on questionable citations taken out of context; erudition functions as a screen to give these arguments authority, despite the lack of evidence. The unstated (and perhaps unconscious) logic subtending such affirmations seems to rely on the problematic assumption that (unlike men) women could not have both a sexed body and a literary mind. Labé is thus relegated to being no more than a sexual body, an object of exchange in the male economy of letters and of desire, rather than a full-fledged author who strove to establish her own corpus, persona, and value through her writing, opening up a new space for herself, her work, and her readers through her carefully crafted creations.[2] Along somewhat different lines (with significant differences owing to the use of a pseudonym and long-standing questions around Hélisenne's "real" identity, for example), Huchon's student, Anne Réach-Ngô, has written a thesis on early modern editorial practices in which she suggests that Hélisenne de Crenne's works were written by male editors as a kind of literary diversion. Students enjoy debating the potential merits and possible motivations for such hypotheses, along with questions about whether there can be an essentially masculine or feminine "écriture"

(Cixous) that can be used to determine the sex of an author or whether gender is always performative (see Butler, *Gender Trouble*). Yet it may ultimately be more fruitful for them to focus on discerning the various discourses that permeate critical and literary texts, as well as utterances of all kinds, paying attention to the ways in which patriarchal or misogynist discourses, among others, may be unconsciously internalized and perpetuated. This is especially valuable for students who sometimes reproach early modern women writers or their characters for not being feminist enough. Careful examination of the discursive aspects of texts can also help students appreciate the ways in which various discourses or rhetorical strategies may be used in women's writing to subtly *show* rather than *tell* complex truths about women's experience that could not be voiced overtly or to mimic and subvert patriarchal discourses through techniques Robert Cottrell likens to montage and masquerade ("Female Subjectivity" 13–16). Such readings ultimately encourage awareness about the dialogic dimension (the "heteroglossia," as Bakhtin puts it) in texts and speech acts of all sorts, helping us reflect on the discourses that shape us from without as well as from within: on the one hand, our identities as subjects are, in many ways, imposed on us by positions ascribed to us within preexisting linguistic and symbolic structures (according to a name, race, gender, ethnicity, nationality, etc.); on the other hand, as we saw earlier, we unconsciously internalize all kinds of discourses that influence us and that we unwittingly repeat and externalize in various ways.

One way to help students put these ideas in perspective with respect to textual analysis is to explore a transferential model inspired by Lacanian psychoanalysis. Unlike so-called classic psychoanalytic readings of the type performed by Marie Bonaparte that rely on the problematic assumption that creativity stems from pathology and that illustrate a kind of transference (Freud would have called it countertransference) with respect to the author, Lacanian theory stays away from biographical criticism and aims instead to read the logic of desire inscribed in the discourses of both the text and the interpreter.[3] As Shoshana Felman suggests, the advantages of such a model are not only its emphasis on detailed textual analysis (indeed many techniques in psychoanalysis come from linguistic and literary analysis) but also its recognition that literary texts contain elements that destabilize notions about reading and interpretation and therefore undermine traditional assumptions about the relationship between text and critic. Indeed, just as the functioning of the unconscious subverts the Cartesian cogito and the Hegelian notion of absolute knowledge, the Lacanian theory of transference destabilizes the traditional opposition between analyst and patient or teacher and student, seeing both as equally subject to transference and to the workings of the unconscious (Felman, *Jacques Lacan* 69–97). Similarly, it deconstructs traditional notions about the role of the reader with respect to the text: it does not assume that literature is simply to be analyzed through an interpretative grid seen as a "masterly discourse of competence" that the text or author do not have. On the contrary, it is the text that has authority:

> . . . the very type of authority by which Jacques Lacan indeed defines the role of the psychoanalyst in the structure of the transference. Like the psychoanalyst viewed by the patient, the text is viewed . . . as a 'subject presumed to know'—as the very place where meaning and *knowledge* of meaning reside. With respect to the text, the literary critic occupies thus at once the place of the psychoanalyst (in the relation of interpretation) and the place of the patient (in the relation of transference). (Felman, "To Open" 7)

The analyst does not therefore look upon the text (or author) as a "mere object of interpretation" to which a theory is *applied* from a position of rationalism and superiority but sees literature and psychology as mutually *implicated* in a dialogic relation (Felman, "To Open" 8–9) and recognizes that in some sense there is no way to judge the text from the outside (there is no metalanguage), that there is no end to the process of interpretation (there is no terminus, no cure in analysis), and that the text itself draws in and affects readers in profound ways. Far from being a passive (or wholly conscious) exercise, reading is therefore seen as a kind of interaction in which both reader and text are implicated in a kind of mutual and self-reflexive process of interpretation that involves various unconscious operations. Readers must therefore be willing to take up the challenge not only of undertaking detailed textual analyses in order to uncover deep structures that may not be readily apparent, but they must also be willing to analyze themselves, to explore areas of discomfort and ambiguity in order to map out the dynamic of their own transferential relations to texts by examining their own (conscious and unconscious) discourses and responses to texts and authors, to knowledge and authority. This challenge can be especially difficult, since both texts of jouissance (as Barthes names them in *Le plaisir du texte*) and psychoanalytic theories can elicit great resistances in readers, resistances that are already indicators of the kind of affective charge one finds in transference. As we can see with Hélisenne's *Angoysses*, and as critics like Reynier must have felt, the reader is not in a position of mastery, for the text undermines the fantasy of such mastery and, as we saw earlier, critics wanting to assert their authority over the text sometimes resort to measures (such as truncating the text or discrediting the author) that deliberately ignore important elements in the work that seem to resist interpretation. Indeed, as I ultimately suggest, part of what such critics apparently failed to see in the *Angoysses* is, ironically, that the text stages some of the very problems related to the dialogic and unconscious processes involved in reading, writing, and interpretation that are continually played out in its reception.

To encourage students to focus on the text and to avoid the temptations and perils of biographical criticism (and the kinds of transference it generates), it may be useful to begin with an exploration of questions related to what Michel Foucault called the "author function," which (as he points out) was quite different in the early modern world when anonymity was common and "texts which we now call 'literary' (stories, folk tales, epics, and tragedies) were accepted, circulated, and valorized without any question about the identity of their author," no doubt in part because, unlike scientific discourses, which required an authority (often from antiquity) as a guarantee of reliability, the truth-value of fictional discourses was moot ("What Is an Author?" 125). Foucault also reminds us that the "author-function" is a construct and that all "realistic" dimensions assigned to "an individual . . . we designate as an author . . . are projections, in terms more or less psychological, of our way of handling texts" ("What Is an Author?" 127). It is useful for students to realize that in our exploration of the "author-function" in Hélisenne's text, we can thus choose, on the one hand, to focus on the constructions of critics (a study of the reception of the text according to the kinds of imaginary projections we saw in the biographical approaches mentioned above, for example) and, on the other hand, to examine the ways in which the self-conscious fictional narrator and authorial persona named Hélisenne is constructed in the text. It is to this textual dimension that I now turn. Indeed, when considering the construct that is Hélisenne, it is useful to bear in mind that this name is essentially a signifier that points to other signifiers rather than to a single stable signified. The signifier Hélisenne cannot be strictly identified with any extratextual referent as such, though it may suggest a number of intertextual references, including, among others, Elisenne, the mother of Amadis of Gaul; Dido, otherwise known as Elissa or Helisa; as well as Helen of Troy, Iseult, and other ill-fated heroines named in the work as *exempla*, which instead of converging on a single signified or referent, point to a multiplicity of indeterminate signifiers.[4] Indeed the signifier *Hélisenne* is an effect of language, "un effet de signifiant" as Lacan puts it (*Mon enseignement* 100); it is part of a complex of subject positions designated by various shifters (pronouns, verbs, and adverbs) that suggest action in a time and space and that exist only on the printed page. Moreover, as both Foucault and Lacan suggest (following Freud and structuralist linguists such as Jakobson and Benvéniste), there is always a split in the speaking subject. In his translation of Freud's enigmatic "Wo es war, soll Ich werden," Lacan stresses the nonidentity of the speaking subject ("le sujet de l'énonciation") with the subject of discourse ("le sujet de l'énoncé") or, to put it another way, he highlights the spatiotemporal distance between the self who experiences feelings or events in a first instance and the subject who then reflects back on these experiences, analyzing and describing them retrospectively through language. He uses the split between *moi* and *je* to illustrate this distinction in French (*Mon enseignement* 105). This split can be seen in the distance and difference between the persona of the fictional narrator-author (or speaking subject in the text) and the heroine of the tale in Hélisenne's *Angoysses*. The authorial persona is not identical with the character, even though they share the same name, Hélisenne, because they operate in different times and places. Moreover, as Jean-Philippe Beaulieu points out, their relationship to language is different; the wretched heroine is often speechless or aphasic, whereas the narrator-author is effusive and erudite ("Erudition and Aphasia"). And neither is identical to the real author, who lived in an entirely different dimension from her textual constructs and whom critics now generally identify by a different name: Marguerite Briet. As we find out at the end of part 1 of the *Angoysses*, the fictional narrator-author Hélisenne is composing her work from the tower in the castle named Cabasus, in which she is imprisoned. At the beginning of the text she is thus describing herself retrospectively and looking back on the succession of events that caused her present predicament. After the first part, the narration becomes even more complex as other layers are added and the storytelling is mediated through the gazes and voices of the male characters, Guénélic and his companion Quézinstra. To complicate matters further, we are told that the second and third parts (from which the heroine is mostly absent) are "composed by Lady Hélisenne, speaking in the person of her beloved Guénélic."[5] Furthermore, it is difficult to tell whether the change from a confessional mode in the first section of the book (see Krause, "Confessions") to a chivalric mode in parts 2 and 3 (see Beaulieu, "Données chevaleresques") is supposed to represent a continuation in time and space of the story in part 1 or whether these later segments are meant, as Tom Conley suggests, to convey another sort of shift, one to a kind of sublimation on the part of the authorial persona, who can be pictured sitting in her prison, creating purely imaginary diversionary tales in which the lover, Guénélic, who had seemed far from worthy in the first section, is idealized as a knightly hero and given the requisite male companion to help in the search and rescue of the Lady Hélisenne (328). The epilogue, Quézinstra's "ample narration," represents another change in narration and poses other problems, not least because of the shift to what we might call a Vergilian textual universe (possibly prefiguring the author's translation of the *Aeneid*).[6] Mercury appears upon the death of the lovers to give Quézinstra a tour of the underworld and assure him (and readers) that the lovers end up in the heavenly "champs Hélisiens" (rather than the *bolgia*, to which the adulterous Francesca and Paolo are consigned in Dante's canto 5 of *Inferno*—an image that may well have been in readers' minds, an intertext, one might add, that would have supported Hélisenne's claim that her story was to be read as a negative exemplum had it been included). In the end, Quézinstra decides to retire from the world and tend to a temple he is erecting to the memory of the lovers. In the meantime, Mercury carries the book found at Hélisenne's side to the gods on Mount Olympus, where Pallas and Venus enter into a bitter dispute about which goddess it should properly belong to (thereby continuing and personifying the debate in *Les angoysses* between love or folly and reason and foreshadowing elements in the later work, *Le songe*).[7] Jupiter settles the dispute by deciding Hélisenne's book should be disseminated and read by all; he gives Mercury the task of taking the volume for publication to the city of Paris (which is praised by the gods), thus flattering Parisian readers and giving the book mythic origins.

One can see from the aspects discussed so far that Reynier's modernist criteria of realism and sincerity are not applicable to this work when taken as a whole. Moreover, one can also begin to see not only that the desire to establish a strict identification between the heroine of the novel and an actual extratextual author is a psychological projection (as Foucault suggested) but also that biographical and modernist paradigms (their attachment to so-called reality, as well as their emphasis on the referent or on the signified rather than on the signifier) often rely on unverifiable hypotheses, unquestioned assumptions, and (intentional, affective and other) fallacies that suggest they rest on a kind of fantasy regarding language, truth, and meaning as well as the self-identity and unity of subjects, about whom in any case we know very little when it comes to early modern writers.[8] Indeed, while it may be tempting to pass over elements in texts that initially seem to resist interpretation, psychoanalytic techniques teach us that these points of resistance in texts and in ourselves (if we hold on to the belief that literature is mimetic and that language should be clear and transparent, for example) may be precisely the points that yield the greatest riches, if we can learn to discern the kinds of logic that subtend them at the level of the signifier. Moreover, our reactions to signifiers that resist easy interpretation can also be meaningful: by self-critically examining our own reactions to certain aspects of the text, along with our expectations or assumptions, we become aware of the role of readers in the construction of meaning. Students need to see how important it is to engage with these complex questions instead of dismissing or avoiding points of resistance, as early critics and editors had done with the *Angoysses.* Indeed, as a number of recent readers have shown, the complexities of the work that seemed to pose insurmountable problems for modernist readers like Reynier are a great point of entry into the text. One way to appreciate all parts of the novel is to focus on reading it discursively by considering the dialogic role of various intertexts and exempla and discussing whether the contradictory points of view given by Hélisenne are indications of an unreliable narrator or whether they might be seen to evoke and put into question larger issues—for example, the difficulties of interpretation, the performative dimensions of reading, and the transformative, seductive, or even subversive aspects of narrative (see my "Contagions of Love").

Indeed, one might say that refusing to deal with the work at this level (at the level of the signifier rather than the referent or the signified) expresses a desire to remain in what Lacan terms the imaginary, to be entranced by the fictional unity of the text and the seductive intimacy formed in the illusory dyad between author and reader (a desire we can liken to wishing to read the work as a "readerly" text of pleasure, rather than the more disruptive jouissance of "writerly" texts Roland Barthes describes in *Le plaisir du texte*). Remaining in the imaginary (always associated with misprision, misreading, or *méconnaissance* in Lacanian theory and with the illusions of ideology in Althusserian thought, because such discourses mask their artificiality and inherent contradictions even as they claim to *be* reality) implies a negation of the symbolic dimensions of texts.

Both the imaginary and symbolic coexist in texts, which make use of these dimensions on the paradigmatic and syntagmatic axes (respectively) to represent, or rather construct, "realities" (not to be confused with the real, which cannot truly be grasped or represented, though it is often suggested obliquely as what is ineffable, traumatic, or hallucinatory). Reading from the imaginary (without taking into account the symbolic dimension) means eliding the *constructedness*, the artificiality of these representations. From this imaginary perspective (which is blind to its own assumptions or ideologies), texts are read as if they are faithful representations, or accurate reflections of a "reality" taken as true and unproblematic or self-evident. When taking into account the symbolic dimension (which in any case structures the imaginary), one can see that "reality" itself is an imaginary and linguistic construct shaped in part by various conscious or unconscious desires and interests and that the real as such must remain inaccessible, owing to the mediation of the imaginary and symbolic dimensions that structure human psychology and therefore our sense of reality. When we pay attention to the constructions, contradictions, and complexities of the symbolic we become aware of the artificial nature of many concepts: the illusory oneness of the subject and the fantasy of unity of the confessional narrative in Hélisenne's text, for example. In some ways one might say that our resistances to dealing with these elements are suggestive of the heroine's own struggles in the realms of the imaginary, symbolic, and real. It is almost as if the author has tended us a kind of textual mirror (see Buzon, "Miroirs"), in which we are invited to contemplate ourselves and which we must study carefully in order not to be deceived, enthralled, or captivated (as is the heroine) by images or fantasies, by what we think we see. Indeed, the *Angoysses* can be said to dramatize transference on different levels. If we use the distinction from narratology between *story* and *discourse*, for example, we could say that both levels in the text stage and problematize different aspects of transference. At the risk of oversimplifying, we might say that, on the one hand, the story of the heroine's capture by the gaze of the other in the *innamoramento* (Winn, "Symbolique" and "Perception") and her passion for a youth on whom she projects qualities, power, and knowledge he does not possess but that confuse him with the other can be seen to illustrate the imaginary, metaphoric dimension of transference, expressed through the paradigm of love (and the symptoms of lovesickness), which Lacan describes as a "specular mirage" (*Four Fundamental Concepts* 268).[9] On the other hand, the ambivalent relationship between the fictional narrator-author and her intertexts, or exempla, which she is staged as reading and rewriting in problematic ways in the *Angoysses* and *Epistres* (see Buzon, "Roman"), serves as a kind of *mise en abyme* of the transferential relation between readers, authors, and texts at the discursive level, dramatizing the difficulties of interpretation and illustrating the complexities of the symbolic order, which figures the metonymic dimensions of desire—its insistence, repetitions, and displacements—and the infinite slippage in the relational logic of subjects and signifiers in the signifying chain.

Far from being an incoherent, second-rate autobiographical or psychological novel with outdated aesthetics whose value is in the passion and sincerity of the confession of a "true" story, as some early critics seemed to think, the text, on close scrutiny (instead of a reading based on naive attachment to univocal signification or to extratextual referents), indicates that Hélisenne's *Angoysses douloureuses qui procèdent d'amours* can be read as a sophisticated study of the subtle and intricate layers of internal and external discourses that constitute and structure human psychology. Reading with an awareness of transference thus enables us to see that the *Angoysses* is indeed a psychological novel, though one that is not limited by the constraints of biography, revealing instead greater truths through the structure of fiction by allowing us to examine not only the structural dynamics of love and transference but also different dimensions of desire implicated in reading, writing, and interpretation, which also imply a relation of passion (with shadings of love, hate, and ignorance) with respect to texts and their authors.[10]

Notes

1. Éliane Viennot has posted the critical debate spawned by Huchon's controversial book on the SIEFAR Web site, on a page titled "Louise attaquée!"

2. For more on Labé's self-fashioning, as opposed to constructions by various readers, see my "Images captivantes: Louise Labé Amazone."

3. The assumption that creativity stems from pathology can be traced back to medical discourses linking melancholy and genius: see, for example, the study of the (pseudo-)Aristotelian *Problemata* in Klibansky, Panofsky, and Saxl's *Saturn and Melancholy.* To examine more on the differences between the readings of Edgar Allan Poe by Bonaparte and Lacan, see Felman, *Jacques Lacan* 35–51. *The Purloined Poe: Lacan, Derrida and Psychoanalytic Reading*, edited by Müller and Richardson, is a very useful resource since it contains important readings, including Poe's text, Bonaparte's article, Lacan's interpretation, and Felman's critique, among others.

4. For discussions of the onomastics behind the name Hélisenne, see Buzon's introduction to her edition of the *Angoysses;* Debaisieux, "Subtilitez féminines"; Wood, *Hélisenne de Crenne: At the Crossroads*; and Nash, "Constructing Hélisenne."

5. All references to the French text are to the 2005 edition, *Angoisses*; all English translations of the text are from *The Torments of Love.*

6. For more on this translation, see Wood, *Hélisenne de Crenne: At the Crossroads* 135–51.

7. See Cottrell's "Hélisenne de Crenne's *Le Songe*" for a reading of that text.

8. See Wimsatt and Beardsley regarding "intentional" and "affective" fallacies.

9. See my "Lacan, Courtly Love, and Anamorphosis" for a discussion of Lacan's use of courtly love to illustrate transference.

10. Clearly influenced by Buddhist teachings, Lacan names the three passions love, hate, and ignorance, which he locates at the junctions among imaginary, symbolic, and real (see Evans, *Introductory Dictionary* 6).

Cécile Alduy

The Anatomy of Gender: Decoding Petrarchan Lyrics (Labé, Scève, Ronsard)

There is something uncanny about reflecting on how to teach Louise Labé as a woman writer at the very time when she has been denied the authorship of the *Euvres* so far associated with her name. In her controversial book *Louise Labé: Une créature de papier*, Mireille Huchon replaces Labé in the author's role with a group of male practical jokers led by Maurice Scève and Claude de Taillemont. However contentious—and arguably unfounded—this hypothesis might be, it echoes serious theoretical, textual, and methodological questions that never fail to arise when discussing Labé's work in the classroom: What could a woman write and publish in 1555 France? Was there a legitimate space for feminine writing in the context of a rhetorical order ruled by men and designed for them? And, How do we interpret the rewriting of commonplaces and texts past in Renaissance love lyric—as parody, imitation, or subversion?

Huchon's two main arguments, namely that a bourgeoise like Labé could not have written such poems and that the Lyonnais poets revolving around Jean de Tournes were on the contrary already masters in Petrarchan rhetoric and familiar with other hoaxes, can be looked at as debatable answers to real questions. What Huchon shows implicitly is the importance of preexisting social and literary norms that, according to her, would exclude preemptively a woman like Labé from writing. But which competing definitions of gender, literary, social, philosophical, medical, or other, were women writers actually submitting or reacting to?

Decoding the entanglement of social and literary codes framing women's lyrics in the sixteenth century is indispensable when approaching Labé. If there was only one key notion I would like students to take away from our discussions, it would be that of codes: how gender is a complex cultural construction rather than a universal, biological fact, and how literature, and particularly Renaissance poetry, cannot be understood without a grasp of its own set of rules. It is essential to read Labé in context: not only with and, better, after the poets she is responding to but also within a larger cosmological understanding of gender influenced by the Bible, Greek philosophy, astronomy, and medical theories. What, then, was the definition of *the feminine* in the Renaissance? Students don't have to be aware of Huchon's theory to be puzzled by the sexual identity of the lyric voice in the *Euvres de Louise Labé Lyonnaise*. A remarkable trait of Labé's poetry is indeed its propensity to alter our stable notions of gender polarities. But is this a consequence of the Petrarchan code she adopts, of a cultural context different from ours, or of an idiosyncrasy? These questions are enclosed in the more straightforward question, Was it acceptable for women to speak like this? that students are prone to ask. My goal is to help them unfold the conceptual ramifications of their original puzzlement and to introduce them to the historical and rhetorical context they need in order to assess whether Labé's poems were transgressing, subverting, or complying with the literary canon.

In graduate seminars, the *Blasons anatomiques du corps féminin* and selected poems from Maurice Scève's *Délie*, Pierre de Ronsard's *Amours*, and Joachim Du Bellay's *Olive* are read before Labé.[1] In undergraduate survey courses, students first explore the Pléiade and ponder the place of the body as signifier and agent of subversion in Rabelais's *Gargantua*. All are soon aware that Renaissance texts are embedded within a complex network of literary allusions, codes, and polemics. What is more, reading Scève and Ronsard before Labé helps deromanticize Renaissance poetry: once students notice that each poet writes within a genre, the Petrarchan collection, and reworks a common set of images, devices, and myths, the temptation to conflate the lyric voice and the poems' pathos with the authors' feelings gives way to a genuine interest in the writing process and the challenges of interpretation.

Teaching French Petrarchan poetry implies indeed having to make the vexing admission that, however beautiful, these love poems probably were not written under the spell of a heartfelt romantic passion but instead answered specific writing codes based on imitation and commonplaces. Only within these conventions could the artistic singularity of an author be asserted and recognized. Yet inhabiting this framework had different implications for women writers in a cultural context where writing and, worse, publishing were praised for men but dismissed for women as a defaming show of promiscuity (Jones, *Currency*). Furthermore, the Petrarchan idiom, forged for a masculine voice, presupposed a set of gender roles that seems to forbid women to speak. The lyric *I* might lament the lady's cruelty, but unrequited love is what prompts the poet to write endless sonnets: the silence of the lady is the condition of the writer's prolixity. This is the conclusion of recent feminist studies, and one to which students readily come after reading Scève or Ronsard. But if we want to address their next set of questions and define whether Labé's lyrics express a genuinely different view of desire and the other than those of her male counterparts, we have to go one step further in the anatomy of gender construction.

A key issue is to determine what was encoded as "feminine" physically, socially, and figuratively in the cultural unconscious. It is not enough to state, as Nancy Vickers did, that the canonical Petrarchan collection voices a man's homage to a silenced woman and dissects her physical beauty in disjointed body parts. What if, as Lawrence Kritzman, Edwin Duval, and Kathryn Banks have suggested, the very position of service of the lover and the pathology of love he endures (the weeping, the aphasia, the alienation) were deemed female in other, potentially dominant discourses, such as etiquette books, medical treatises, or pedagogical compendia? And what if, in Ronsard or Scève's works, the poet's creative process was represented in an inverted sexual imagery as the fecundity and receptivity of a female matrix (Kritzman)? The fascination with women's sexuality—the ultimate goal of the seduction game underlying Petrarchan discourse—is often sublimated only to resurface as a figurative investment in female symbols of passivity and procreation, for instance in Ronsard's *Amours*, sonnet 6, where the poet is inseminated by Cupid, nests for nine months, and sees hundreds of birdlike "Amoureaux" hatch thanks to his careful brooding. How, then, was a woman writer to situate herself not only within a set of commonplaces designed primarily for men but also within a code, Petrarchan poetry, that featured a representation of gender fraught with ambiguities and at odds with other dominant models?

My method is interdisciplinary and interactive: the students' questions, not mine, provide the starting point for our discussion. In each course, they either post on a collective blog or send me ahead of time questions that arose during their reading. Not only is this an effective way to gauge the class's grasp of text and context, but it forces students to be inquisitive readers from the start. Putting their reactions in print, they naturally start to elaborate on their initial musings. From, Who was Labé writing for? to, Is there hope for reciprocity in Labé's love? their genuine questions usually go right to the point. They then discover that there is no simple answer: what they thought was ingenuity or ignorance on their part is a legitimate interpretative issue. We can then rephrase their questions to establish useful theoretical distinctions, for instance between historical and biological definitions of gender on the one hand and textual representations on the other: Is gender encoded in the text or in the author?

When we read Labé, are we dealing with *a* woman's writings (potentially in a male diction), with "feminine writing" or *écriture féminine* (a gendered *text*, the poetics of which is inherently different), or with a female voice (which male authors could not only fake but codify)? Is Labé writing *as* a woman, or *like* a woman? In asserting she writes as a woman, we assume that the author's biological gender and her intentions to speak up as a representative of it are essential to the text's modus operandi. In contending she writes like a woman, we are looking for what would have been recognized as a woman's "voice" and presume gender could be read in the choice of words, metaphors, or syntax—in the *body* of the text rather than in that of its historical author. It is worth letting students ponder what a complex, almost intractable concept "woman" is before they engage with the poems. As uncomfortable as this temporary suspension of interpretation might be, they are excited to be confronted with the very question of literature and its interpretation. Voice, self, author, gender roles, or biological identity—what are we looking for when we try to determine how "feminine" a *text* is?

A multidisciplinary approach that presents students with a variety of discursive and iconographic representations of women is a winning strategy for engaging students in a deeper reflection on the fluctuating definitions of gender in literature and history. Focusing on the body as a privileged place of gender identification is particularly effective: when given the opportunity to compare images and texts from poetry and medicine, students become fascinated by the representation of creation and procreation from the 1540s to the 1550s. An effective approach is not only to contrast Labé's poems with the rhetoric of desire and myths of creation of her male counterparts but also to connect the gendered representation of creativity in poetry to the early modern material culture of birthing and to medical illustrations of the womb. I designed the Renaissance Body Project Web site to facilitate such a comparison. Alongside a discussion forum and bibliographic resources, it provides a database of medical plates, woodcuts, architectural drawings, and paintings of women. From Andreas Vesalius's *De Humani Corporis Fabrica* to Charles Estienne's *De Dissectione Partium Corporis Humani* and the *Blasons anatomiques du corps féminin* (1543), anatomical sketches offer a peek into not only women's most secret parts but also the mind-set of the time and its imagining of gender difference.

For instance, the elaborate staging of the female reproductive system in Estienne's dissection plates highlights how medical books situated female identity exclusively in the womb. The female body is represented only in relation to gestation, and the underlying assumption of the other etchings detailing skeleton, muscles, and nervous system is that male anatomy is otherwise a universal template from which women do not differ. The reproductive organs themselves are depicted as smaller, weaker, inverted versions of man's. What room for a different sense of self and desire was there for women in this worldview? The fascination with female reproductive organs is also apparent in the title page of Vesalius's *De Fabrica*: at the optical center of the picture lies the opened belly of a female corpse, where the gaze of the staged audience converges with that of the reader. Students are keen to comment on the institution of the theater of anatomy itself and connect the mise en scène of a woman dissected for a male-only audience to the scopic drive of French Petrarchan collections (*Délie* starts with "L'Œil") and their evocation of fragmented female body parts.

Men's desire to see is compounded by the interdiction to show for women: they have to be modest and virtuous, in poetry and in medicine, or else have to be dismembered into pieces of anatomy to be seen (Vickers; Sawday). The only time a woman is represented in full in the Vesalius corpus is overshadowed by strong moral connotations: in his translation of Vesalius's opus, Jacques Grévin—a Petrarchan poet himself—inserts a slightly revised version of the plate from Vesalius's *Epitome* (1543), which stages Man and Woman in full size as Adam and Eve; between them rises now a snake, wrapped around a skull instead of a forbidden fruit (*Portraicts anatomiques* 28). In a typical double bind, woman is defined as the origin of life and death, sin and punishment, her sexuality an object of eroticization and condemnation. The "scientific" project gives way to a mythological archetype; a moralizing agenda dictates the prudish pose of an intrinsically immodest creature, here covering her sex with her hand, whereas surgeon, crowd, and reader were gazing between her legs on the dissection table and in the other plates of the book.

French Renaissance poets were often versed in medicine, when they were not doctors themselves like Jacques Grévin or Nicolas Ellain. Moreover, French Petrarchists drew heavily from the doctor and humanist Marsilio Ficino and his interpretation of Plato: they inherited a philosophy of love that was at once a pathology and physiology of lovesickness. Scève's and Ronsard's repetitive imagery of the eye, the heart, and the migrating "spirit" belongs to this holistic medical and cosmological system (Hunkeler). Their poetry is no less concerned than the medical discourse of the time with a description of symptoms, with physiological imbalance, and with the feminine mystery hidden to the sight but intensely feared and desired. In this context, how does Labé represent and publish her own desiring body? As a poet, does she submit her beloved to the same visual scrutiny and dismemberment, or is she exploring other modes of representation? Short exercises can yield interesting conclusions: a simple listing of all the body parts evoked in her poems reveals that "cœur" ("heart") has replaced the overpowering "œil" ("eye") of Scève and Ronsard as the most frequently used anatomical word.

If woman existed only as a matrix in medical books, we have to remind our students how this view had wide-ranging implications for a definition of gender that was at once cosmological and physiological: procreation was conceived not as the meeting of male and female reproductive cells but as the insemination of life-giving semen into a fundamentally passive receptacle, the womb, that provided only matter, nutrition, and protection rather than life or soul to the new being. As a cosmological principle of masculinity, semen is active, "chaud sec conceptif / Donateur de la vie" ("hot dry creative, life-giving"; Scève, *Microcosme* 219 [bk. 3, line 253]).[2] In other words, only man was creative in procreation. Galenic medicine and Aristotelian philosophy converged here to draw gender lines along the opposition between form and matter, agency and passivity, outward and inner qualities, life giving and life bearing, and these divisions extended to every realm of social life. In anatomical plates, male écorchés are usually represented in action and in the open, a cityscape in the distance alluding to their engagement in civic life. By contrast, Estienne's women are confined to their rooms, leaning in languid poses of sweet surrender among equivocal drapes: passive, inert, and receptive.

With this in mind, the typical Petrarchan lover appears more feminine than masculine in some respects. Transfixed by Love, he is in a perpetual state of passivity and paralysis in front of the lady: *she* has the power to give him life or death. In addition, the typical Petrarchan antitheses found in Labé's sonnet 8 ("Je vis, je meurs . . . , J'ay chaut estreme en endurant froidure" ["I lie, I die . . . I'm utterly hot and all I feel is cold"]) or in Ronsard extend beyond a list of alternating affects to express metaphorically the fundamental instability of gender in Petrarchan poetry.[3] When we remember that the medical theory of humors ascribed a specific balance between the four elements for each sex and defined male and female bodies as respectively hot, dry, and light on the one hand; and as cold, wet, and heavy on the other, the "icy fire" felt by the lover and so well described by Leonard Wilson Forster becomes more than a physical impossibility: it depicts a sexual conundrum, what the surgeon Ambroise Paré exposed under the category of the hermaphrodite.

By contrast, Labé's persona is all about power, force, agency, expansion: outspoken and strong willed, she reclaims the public sphere in her preface, advocating for self-expression and publication. She takes the initiative in love and in the arts, becoming a creative, active—shall we say, masculine—force that gives (immortal) life to herself and others. Such is the image conveyed by the very last section of her book, an homage to Labé that concludes her *Œuvres* with the praise of her male counterparts. The first poem of that section, a sonnet "Aus poetes de Louize Labé," attributed to the Lyonnais Jacques Peletier du Mans, could not be more explicit:

> Elle des dons des Muses cultivez,
> *S*'est pour *soy-mesme* et pour autrui saisie:
> Tant qu'en louant sa dine poésie
> Mieux que par vous *par elle vous vivez* . . .
> Trop plus *se* fait *par sa* plume estimer.
> Et *de soymesme* elle *se* faisant croire
> A ses loueurs *est cause* de leur gloire.
> (*Œuvres complètes* 141)

> The gifts cultivated by the Muses she seized for herself and for others: so that when you sing her praiseworthy verses, you live thanks to her more than thanks to yourself. . . . She made herself so esteemed by her pen only. Being the source of her own fame, she is the cause of her appraisers' glory.

Students only have to notice the abundance of reflexive verbs or the recurrence of "vouloir" and "pouvoir" in Labé's poetry to consider how she is her own creation. Amour rages against her *because* she is a strong warrior "pour plus fort contre les fors paroitre" ("He'll look stronger, among the strong"; 123 [sonnet 4, line 14]); and if he is a formidable adversary, she is readily on top when she assails her lover ("Tant emploiray de mes yeus le *pouvoir*, / Pour *dessus lui* plus de credit avoir / Qu'en peu de tems feray grande *conqueste*" ["So well will I use the power of my eyes / to increase my credit over him / that in a short time I will have made a great conquest"]; 124 [sonnet 6, lines 12–14]). This contrasts starkly with Scève's definition of male and female principles in the cosmos: "Et autant que de masle accreut le femenin, / *Sexe de soy suget, & foible*" ("And as much as the male [principle] has augmented the feminine, / a sex in itself weak and subservient"; *Microcosme* 166 [bk. 1, lines 645–46]).

Yet students are often perplexed by the shifting nature of Labé's sexual identifications: she speaks in the name of the "sexe faible" in her preface; calls upon Venus, goddess of beauty and fertility, as a protector (123 [sonnet 5]); describes herself as a "Nymphe" (131 [sonnet 19]) or a passionate "femmelle" (122 [sonnet 2]). But she also invokes such ambiguous models as Sappho, who sings "l'Amours Lesbienne" (107 [line 15]); Semiramis and her "cœur *viril*" (108 [elegy 1]); Diana, the virgin hunter (131 [sonnet 19]), and compares her fate to that of Jason (117 [elegy 3]), Jupiter, or Phoebus (133 [sonnet 22]). As she identifies with "masculine" heroines in the elegies only to adopt the feminized persona of the weeping Petrarchan lover in the sonnets, Labé revels in switching guises and gender. If anything, she resembles Ronsard's androgynous Beloved, for whom "on ne sçait (tant bien elle desguise / Son chef doubteux) s'elle est fille ou garçon?" ("one cannot tell whether she is a girl or a boy, so ingeniously does her beauty disguise itself as both"; Ronsard, *Selected Poems* 11 [sonnet 90, lines 13–14].[4]

This unstable identity can be traced to a new narrative of love that brings about a redefinition of self, gender, and the place of pleasure in erotic poetry. Twice in her poems, Labé equates falling in love with a profound alteration of sexual identity. First, Semiramis surrenders her masculinity when struck by Love:

> Tu as laissé les aigreurs Marciales,
> Pour recouvrer les douceurs geniales.
> Ainsi Amour *de toy t'a estrangee*,
> Qu'on te diroit *en une autre changee*.
> (109 [elegy 1, lines 87–91]; my italics)

> You have left behind Mars' bitter ways
> To recover Love's voluptuous pleasures
> And thus by Love you're from yourself estranged / Love has estranged you from yourself

> So one might think you're to another changed. / so that it seems that you're to another changed

The topos of love as alienation ("estrangee"; "en une autre changee") is rephrased as an explicit transgendering. Similarly, Labé used to favor masculine activities such as riding, fighting, and learning (elegy 3) but abandoned these manly exercises to reciprocate her lover's passion and imitate *his* feminine persona: "Puis le voyant aymer fatalement, / Pitié je pris de sa triste aventure: / Et tellement *je forçay ma nature*, / Qu'autant que lui aymay ardentement" ("Then when his fatal passion I could see, / I was shaken to pity by his sad adventure, / And I struggled so, my nature to foreswear, / that soon I loved as ardently as he"; 132 [sonnet 20, lines 5–8]; my italics). While the Petrarchan lover does not underline the gender shift he undergoes as he is transformed from an active, masculine, free agent to a weeping, passive, feminized figure, Labé exposes the implications of this model and details a new narrative: she rewrites the *innamoramento* as an act of will against her own nature ("je forçay ma nature" ["my nature to foreswear"]) that will transform her into a woman. Long before Simone de Beauvoir, Labé states that "on ne naît pas femme: on le devient" ("one is not born a woman: one becomes one").

However, the typical alienation of the Petrarchan lover is itself transcended by a later shift from the aphasic, mute, hence dispossessed, female *amante* to the now eloquent voice of the poetess, endowed by Apollo with the power to sing lesbian songs: "Encore lors je n'avois la puissance / De lamenter ma peine et ma souffrance . . . Mais meintenant . . . Il m'a donné la lyre" ("I did not at that time have the strength / to sing out my pain and suffering . . . But now [he gave me] the lyre"; 107 [elegy 1]). The then/now divide characteristic of Petrarchan temporality is rewritten to coincide with a new split of the self: after the conversion of the unguarded, unloving heart into a forever-suffering lover that one finds in Scève or Ronsard, a second stage in Labé's poetry goes from alienation on the level of the fiction to poetic mastery on the level of expression. In thus rewriting the split, Labé stages herself as both poet and lover, active and passive, power and surrender, forceful and defeated, outer and inner—"fille *et* garcon" ("girl and boy"; Ronsard, *Selected Poems* 11; my italics).

What is more, she displaces the locus of identity beyond the confines of a single body. The recurring motif of her extravagance (etymologically, "vaguer hors": "ayant *erré* maint tour . . . Il me convient *hors* de moymesme vivre" ["wandering further . . . I have to live outside myself"]; 131; sonnet 17) and outrageous behavior points to a need to transcend individual boundaries and dominant norms: "Et ne *me* puis donner contentement, / Si *hors de moy* ne fay quelque saillie" ("And I cannot give myself contentment / without some place outside myself to move"; 137 [sonnet 18, lines 13–14]; my italics). She seeks erotic union as a path to self-fulfillment: "Lors double vie à chacun en suivra. / Chacun en soy et son ami vivra" ("And we'll each have two loving lives to tend / one in our single self, one in our friend"; 137 [lines 9–10]).[5] Pleasure and will, self and other, inclusiveness and alterity, mind and body—Labé refuses the expected limits of a biological definition of the self to integrate the masculine and the feminine within a complete fusion with her lover (sonnets 7, 9, and 13).

This drive to come out of oneself and shift gender roles points out in return the difficulty for Labé to fit in either set of commonplaces, Petrarchan code or woman's role. Labé bitterly denounces the descriptive fallacy of Petrarchism in sonnets 2 and 23 as she quotes empty metaphors students might recognize from Scève or Du Bellay: "Las! que me sert, que si parfaitement / Louas jadis et ma tresse doree / Et de mes yeus la beauté comparee / A deus soleils" ("What good is it how well, alas, you sang / those long-ago praises to my rich gold hair, / or told me that my gorgeous eyes compared / to suns from which Love's brightest arrows sprang"; 134). Worse, the literary code of descriptive poetry explodes when she tries it out for her beloved. Apart from the ambiguous sonnet 2, "Ô beaux yeux bruns" ("Ah handsome brown eyes"; 122) (but who speaks, and of whom?), Labé's "ami" is hardly described—*et pour cause.* In fact, the possibility of representation is explicitly put into question: "Quelle grandeur rend l'homme venerable? / Quelle grosseur? quel poil?" ("Which height makes a man earn the most admiration? / Which weight? Which hair?"; 132 [sonnet 21]). The rhetoric of praise falls apart in this curiously unpoetic sonnet because there exists no such thing as a canon of masculine beauty in Petrarchan poetry. Labé subverts gender role not only by her sulfurous admission of carnal desires but also by pointing out the rhetorical void left for the lady to reciprocate as a poet. The notion of a woman writer is indeed a theoretical oxymoron in the context of Petrarchan poetics, as the first Greek ode of the *Escritz de divers poètes à la louange de Louize Labé* confirms: the anonymous (and presumably male) author wonders at this "écrivain nouveau et féminin" ("novel and feminine writer"; 142): more precisely, "nouveau" because "féminin."

Labé takes up this challenge by reclaiming another kind of erotic poetry, or rather the eroticism of poetry itself. If joy and reciprocity cannot be found in the Petrarchan template, a woman can still give herself pleasure and autonomy with erotic fantasies—in the form of dreams (sonnet 9) or, better, poems, the fictions Labé imagines speak of her power to create and thus bypass narrow gender definitions. As she insists in the preface on the pleasures she draws from reading her own work, Labé short-circuits any biological determinism that would limit her identity to that of her body: for her, "conception" is in the brain, not the womb:

> . . . quand il avient que nous mettons par escrit nos *concepcions*, combien que puis apres notre cerveau coure par une infinité d'afaires . . . , si est ce que long temps après, reprenans nos escrits, nous revenons . . . à la mesme disposicion où nous estions. Lors nous redouble notre aise, car nous retrouvons le plaisir passé qu'avons ù en la matière dont escrivions. . . . Et outre ce, le jugement que font nos secondes concepcions des premieres, nous rend un singulier contentement. (95; my italics)
>
> But we happen to put our thoughts down in writing—even though afterward our mind races through endless distractions . . .—by going back much later to what we wrote, we can still recapture the moment and state of mind we were in before. Then we experience twice the enjoyment, for we rediscover the pleasure we had in the past . . . in the subject we were writing about. . . . And beyond this, the judgment that our second impressions allow us to make of our earlier ones repays us with an unparalleled satisfaction.

Ultimately, the "double vie" of erotic fusion first sought in love is found in the self-eroticism of the poetic act ("re*double* notre aise"), a self-sufficient and self-defining undertaking by which Labé becomes both writer and reader, object and subject, voice and audience. The "saillie" "hors de soi" without which she could not "[se] donner contentement" (literally, "to give herself contentment") is in the end the writing life itself (131 [sonnet 18]). If men's laws forbid her to wander outside, the depth of time lived and relived through imagination will offer a wide enough field to explore. Labé recasts the private space where women are confined as a place for interiority and self-possession. She defines a new territory of feminine sovereignty: not only a new rhetorical space, but an inner world created by the pleasurable activity of the mind.

An interdisciplinary approach that compares images of women in medicine and poetry helps students decipher how Labé navigates a multiplicity of codes while tracing her own path. It might even lead them to wonder at the instability of gender in Petrarchan poetry and to ponder the notion of literature as a space of creative exploration that wanders outside norms of conduct that are otherwise prevalent in society. Against this background, the *Euvres de Louise Labé Lyonnoise*, whatever the gender and number of its author(s), are rewriting the boundaries of self, gender, and desire.

Notes

1. For editions of the *Blasons*, see the 1550 and 1866 editions of *S'ensuivent les Blasons.*

2. Translations are mine unless otherwise noted.

3. Quoted from *Œuvres complètes* [1986] 125. All further citations to Labé are from this edition. Translations from Labé's poems are mine, or freely adapted from both *Complete Works* and *Complete Poetry and Prose* unless otherwise noted. Translations from Labé's prose is from *Complete Poetry and Prose.*

4. Translation is from *Selected Poems*, a dual-language edition.

5. This and all subsequent translations from Labé's poems are from *Complete Poetry and Prose.*

Claude La Charité

How Should Sixteenth-Century Feminine Poetry Be Taught? The Exemplary Case of Marie de Romieu

Undergraduates' idea of poetry is often strongly influenced by Romanticism, which poses something of a problem in how undergraduates read and interpret the feminine poetry of the Renaissance. This preconceived idea of poetry assumes that the lyrical subject or *I* in the poems and the author who wields the pen are necessarily the same. Students are naturally tempted to see an autobiographical element in all poetry. This expectation is reinforced, notably, in the famous dedication to Clémence de Bourges that Louise Labé placed at the head of her 1555 collection and that appears to evoke a highly personal journey, namely, the struggle of a sixteenth-century woman to practice literature.

Unfortunately, in the case of Marie de Romieu, this expectation inevitably disappoints, for most of the poems in her only collection, *Les premières œuvres poétiques* (1581), are enunciated by a masculine *I* or give no indication of gender. But this was also true for a good number of women poets of the period, so much so in fact that Louise Labé seems to be an exception rather than an emblematic figure.

Faced with such a paradox, students often wonder how the anomaly can be explained. At this point I ask them to reread the collection of poems by Marie de Romieu while focusing particular attention on the reading protocol that defines it, especially when the issue is the poetic practices of contemporary women in the long opening poem, the "Brief discours que l'excellence de la femme surpasse celle de l'homme."

The simple awareness of a poetic practice founded on the aesthetics of imitation makes it possible, then, to expand the concept of androgynous writing privileged by many women writers and, more broadly, the principles of ventriloquism and transvestism that underpin the poetic virtuosity of the Ancien Régime.

The Impasse of the Romantic Illusion of Autobiographical Poetry

The nineteenth century was significant in awakening the public to a phenomenon characteristic of the Renaissance—access by a large number of women to both literary culture and practice. In *Les femmes poètes du XVIe siècle*, Léon Feugère listed over sixty women writers for France alone, infinitely more than during the Middle Ages. The emergence of this new field of study was informed by the methodology prevalent in literary studies at the time, consisting, on one hand, of the conception imposed by the Romanticism of an autobiographical poetry where poet and lyrical subject coincide and, on the other, of literary history in the manner of Gustave Lanson, who tended to read all literary work in the light of the author's biography.

In such a context, it comes as no surprise that a canon of French Renaissance women writers was formed to which Louise Labé contributed the lion's share of works. Since her poems may be read as one of the very first literary evocations of love experienced passionately by a feminine conscience, it was believed that the intimate struggles in this poetry reflected a woman's sincere and authentic expression of existential experience and erotic desire. Using the poetic works, critics contrived to put together an improbable biography while seeking to identify the person to whom the love poems were addressed (Olivier de Magny, Henry II, etc.) and attributing to the poetess a love life as tumultuous as it was conjectural.

Thanks to Prosper Blanchemain, who was responsible for the first modern re-edition of her collection in 1878, Marie de Romieu did not escape this effort to resurrect the women poets of the Renaissance, and, as with Labé, critics then fashioned an imaginary biography based on the rare, seemingly autobiographical details concealed in her work. Accordingly, they supposed that the poet was married since her letter to her brother mentions the care of her "mesnage" ("household"; 4) and that she was mother to a son owing to the poem entitled "A son fils" ("To Her Son"; 95–96).[1] From her collection, tradition retained the opening poem, the "Brief discours," because of its apologetic and militant nature, which lends itself marvellously well to a reading within the larger framework of the women's quarrel (Richardson), and because it seems to hint at the allusive mode of the obstacles Marie de Romieu herself, following Labé, ran up against in her effort to practice literature.

This interpretative bias involves folding the poetic text over the biography and lends itself well to analyzing a poem like the "Brief discours," where the *I* is clearly feminine and demonstrates a solidarity with all women:

> Quant à moy, je sçay bien qu'entre nous femmelettes
> On peut humainement trouver des fauteletes. (12)
>
> As for me, I well know that among us little women
> One can humanly find little faults.

One might even suppose that the poetic voice of the poem, confused with that of Marie de Romieu, defends the higher interests of her sex based on her experience as a woman.

Despite its limitations, this autobiographical approach to the poetry of Marie de Romieu enjoyed great success. In 1901, for example, Émile Bourras was writing, "As we enter more deeply into the study of the works of Marie de Romieu, we observe that her most beautiful verses are inspired by the intense analysis of her own personality" (460). Her poetry, therefore, was seen to be personal, introspective, and autobiographical.

A good number of the poet's love poems use a masculine or genderless *I,* which becomes quite an obstacle when we search this poetry for the relation of an intimate experience lived by the poet. This seeming incoherence in the psychological unity of the poetic subject would, moreover, lead certain critics to postulate either that Marie de Romieu never existed (Le Sourd) or that the work published under her name had in fact been written by her brother Jacques de Romieu (Winn, "Femmes et culture"). In 1985, Voichita Sasu, refusing to relinquish either the autobiographical and introspective model or the existence of Marie de Romieu, sought to explain the presence of masculine lyrical subjects by the poetess's modesty, making it possible to preserve the authenticity of the poems' erotic experience: "Marie de Romieu finds undeniable grace and modern accents to sing the power of love. . . . However, an excess of modesty prevents her from speaking about herself and motivates her to entrust her words to the lover" (170).

Even this ingenious hypothesis, however, cannot account for the complexity and diversity of the lyrical subjects in the poetry of Marie de Romieu. Not only do we find the masculine *I* in love poems intended for women (La Charité, "Ce male vers enfant"), but we also find a good number of poems where sexual identity is never revealed; we are confronted, furthermore, with pieces written for third parties and even a hymn that evokes a love relationship between two women. Obviously, the tradition of interpretation inherited from Romanticism and Lansonian literary history is powerless to account for this type of poetic practice.

The "Brief discours" as Reading Protocol for the *Premières œuvres poétiques*

After thus proposing a kind of intuitive reading itinerary for students founded on our present-day a prioris, I suggest they read the collection of poems by Marie de Romieu with an eye to the clues that will allow them to apprehend the competencies and references of the Renaissance reader, in keeping with the method recommended by Hans Robert Jauss for reconstructing the first readership's horizon of expectations.

One finds the collection's main hermeneutical clue in the major French Renaissance authors given in the "Brief discours," which lists ten sixteenth-century women in a manner reminiscent of the "top ten" great poets or orators of antiquity: Catherine de Clermont, Antoinette de Loynes, Madeleine Chemeraut, Hélisenne de Crenne, Madeleine and Catherine Des Roches, Margaret of Valois, Madame de Chastellier, Marguerite de Navarre and Catherine de Médicis. This group includes *salonnières*, writers, and patrons of the arts (La Charité, "Décade").

This passage may be considered a veritable reading program, valid for the collection as a whole. The praise of Catherine de Clermont, Countess of Retz, is particularly rich in information:

> Ma comtesse de Retz, vien, que tu sois escrite
> La premiere en mes vers . . .
> S'il faut feindre un souspir d'un amant miserable,
> S'il faut chanter encor un hymne venerable,
> Tu ravis les esprits des hommes mieux disans. (20–21)

My countess of Retz, come, that you may be written
First in my verses . . .
If one must feign the sigh of a wretched lover,
If one must sing moreover a venerable hymn,
You captivate the souls of the most eloquent men.

The passage spells out the three conditions that inform all practice of feminine poetry in the Renaissance—imitation, borrowed roles, and emulation. The use of the verb "feindre" ("to feign") is a good indication of the fictional and conventional nature of this poetry, conceived as the rhetorical exercise of the *ethopoea*, where the lyrical subject seeks to write as a character completely different from the poet, as in Ovid's *Heroides*, in which the characters of mythology write letters. Here the borrowed role is indisputable; the Countess of Retz seeks not to put an intimate erotic experience into verse but to assume instead the borrowed role, masculine, of an "amant miserable" ("wretched lover"), not of a weeping mistress. The Marie de Romieu reader automatically thinks of poem 8 of her collection, "Eclogue d'un amant desespéré, sa dame se monstrant courroucee à l'encontre de luy, avec la complainte qui s'ensuit" ("Eclogue of a Desperate Lover, His Lady Manifesting Anger toward Him, with the Ensuing Complaint"). Finally, the allusion to the will to surpass the "hommes mieux disans" ("most eloquent men") supposes, in the genre of the ode, a practice of emulation where the poet seeks to beat men in their own playing field by borrowing for her own use the conventions of the poetry of the Pléiade and the modern Pindar, "ce divin Ronsard, la gloire des François" ("this divine Ronsard, the glory of the French"; 99).

In the sigh of the wretched lover, we recognize a Petrarchan poetics that was very common in the salon of the Countess of Retz, to judge by the manuscript album of poetry that has come down to us. The authorship of the pieces in this album poses a problem. The only two poems we ordinarily associate with Catherine de Clermont, poems 168 and 170, are attributed to her based on data that are—again—biographical (Retz 10n7). Since poem 168 depicts a widow mourning her deceased husband, critics sought to view it as the countess's homage to Jean d'Annebaut, dead in 1562, or Albert de Gondi, dead in 1602. Likewise, since poem 170 contains an invocation to the lute, it is attributed to the Countess of Retz because she played this instrument. A closer look, however, shows that nothing in this poem indicates the gender identity of the lyrical subject. In fact, judging by Catherine de Clermont's skill in feigning a wretched lover's sigh, the vast majority of pieces in her album could just as well be attributed to her. What is essential here is that a woman writing love poems as a masculine subject is presented as the norm rather than the exception.

This game of sexual transvestism, where a woman writes in the manner of a man or seeks to represent herself as the other sex, was also a common practice in the work of at least three women writers included in the list of the "Brief discours": Hélisenne de Crenne, Marguerite de Navarre, and Margaret of Valois. In familiar letter 13 of her *Epistres familieres et invectives* ("Personal and Invective Letters") (1539), the character of Hélisenne changes into a man to avow her love to the recipient in what, in prose, most closely approaches a love poem (Beaulieu, "Lettre de femme"). The two other cases involve royal princesses who, to better exercise the political authority reserved for men, often tended to represent themselves with masculine characteristics. Thus Marguerite de Navarre, in a letter addressed to Francis I from Dax, in March 1544, writes, "c'est le desir que j'ay heu toute ma vie de vous pouvoir fere service non coume seur, mais coume frere" ("it's been my life's desire to be able to serve you as brother, not sister"; "Lettres" 30). Finally, in her *Mémoires*, written after Marie de Romieu's collection, Margaret of Valois multiplies the effects of masculine self-representation by using *exempla* of famous men from antiquity such as Themosticles and Alexander when speaking of her early childhood.

Even if the motivations for the princesses' sexual transvestism may appear to differ from those of writers such as Catherine de Clermont or Hélisenne de Crenne, the fact remains that literary practice and political power were male prerogatives under the Ancien Régime and that, far from looking to cultivate their sexual difference, women who aspired to such prerogatives sought, rather, to enter into a relationship of emulation with men, where this difference was most often disguised or unmentioned.

Even when their feminine identity is affirmed, as in Marie de Romieu's "Brief discours," it is far from a subjectivity in the modern sense—that is, the poet's civil and social identity—and is closer to a rhetorical ethos, the construction of a speaking subject within and by the discourse, whose final aim is persuasion rather than self-expression. And this is even more so insofar as the "Brief discours" is the rewriting of an Ortensio Lando paradox, a rewriting that once more demonstrates an effort of imitation and emulation to reverse the paradox of feminine superiority, and where only the display of a feminine ethos can produce an effect of this nature (Larsen, "Paradox and the Praise"; La Charité, "'Brief discours'").

Transvestism, Ventriloquism, Androgyny, and Poetic Virtuosity in Marie de Romieu

Renaissance poetry, whether written by men or women, proceeded in essence from imitation; the bases for imitation could be not only contemporary models such as Petrarchan poetry or the poetry of Ronsard or Philippe Desportes but also, and perhaps especially, the models from antiquity. There was unanimous agreement that the precept of Aristotle's *Poetics*, rediscovered around the middle of the sixteenth century, was aesthetic truth: "The poet must in fact speak as little as possible in his own name, since when he does this, he does not imitate" (Aristotle 125).[2]

In the comparisons critics attempted to establish between Marie de Romieu and Louise Labé—for example, Blanchemain insists on the shared vocation of the two women poets and the proximity of their native soil: "sur le bord du même fleuve et presque dans le même pays" ("on the banks of the same river and almost in the same region"; Romieu, *Premieres œuvres* [1878] vi)—the problem is not so much that any analogy is imperfect as that the premises with which we read Labé, seeing in her the expression of a modern feminine subjectivity nourished by existential experience, are erroneous. Recent work by Mireille Huchon has successfully shown to what extent Louise Labé's poetry was indebted to the great models of antiquity, whether the poetry of Sappho, rediscovered in 1554, or even the poems from the *Greek Anthology*.[3]

Thus the enigmatic poem 2, "Hymne de la rose à M. Françoise de la Rose" ("Hymn of the Rose to Mrs. Françoise de la Rose"), by Marie de Romieu, who celebrates the love of one woman for another, becomes clear in the light of the imitation of Sappho:

> Celle qui gist icy sous ceste froide cendre,
> Toute sa vie aima la Rose fresche et tendre,
> Et l'aima tellement qu'apres que le trespas,
> L'eut poussée à son gré aux ondes de là bas,
> Voulut que son cercueil fut entouré de Roses
> Comme ce qu'ell'aimoit par dessus toutes choses. (35)

> She who lies here under this cold ash,
> All her life loved the fresh and tender Rose,
> And loved it so well that after death,
> Pushed her as she wished to the drowsy depths,
> Wanted her coffin to be surrounded by Roses
> Which she loved above all things.

One of the exemplary women of antiquity, the poet of Lesbos very naturally found her place in the "Brief discours":

> Saphe trouva les vers
> Qui depuis, de son nom, furent nommez Saphiques,
> Estimez hautement des hommes prophetiques. (19)

> Sappho found the verses
> Which since then, from her name, were named Sapphic,
> Esteemed highly by prophetic men.

Among the imitations of contemporary authors by Marie de Romieu, the following poems stand out: poem 12, "Pour estrenes à Monseigneur le Mareschal de Retz et à Madame sa femme: Rien I.D.L.D.I.P." ("For a Christmas Present to My Lord the Marshal of Retz and Madame His Wife: Nothing I.D.L.D.I.P."), where the initials should be understood to stand for "imité du latin de Jean Passerat" ("imitated from the Latin by Jean Passerat"); poem 32, "Imitation d'un sonet de Petrarque" ("Imitation of a Sonnet by Petrarch") (in this circumstance, the famous "Pace non trovo"); and poem 48, which ends the collection: "Complainte de la mort de nostre sauveur Jesus Christ" ("Lament on the Death of Our Lord Jesus Christ"), imitating the "Lamentatio de morte Christi Domini," by Jacopo Sannazaro.

It happens, moreover, that Marie de Romieu's imitation does not attach itself to any particular figure but stems more generally from the lyrical tradition as a whole, where the lyrical subject is unobtrusive, abstract, or universal. Of the forty-eight pieces that make up the collection, twenty-nine—or over sixty percent—use a lyrical *I* of indeterminate gender.

As Nathalie Dauvois showed so well, the lyrical enterprise of the Renaissance aimed not so much for an autobiographical outline as for the systematic exploitation of all possibilities of expression while multiplying the enunciating authorities within the same poem or from one poem to another, with the poet contriving to invent different borrowed roles. Some of Marie de Romieu's pieces give way, moreover, to a complex arrangement where the poet adopts a succession of different masks, as is the case for poem 3, "Hymne de Charles de Lorraine, Prince de Chevreuse" ("Hymn of Charles de Lorraine, Prince of Chevreuse"), in which the poet's indeterminate *I*, Europe personified, and Jupiter take turns speaking.

> Charles qui portez le nom
> Et surnom
> Du grand Charles de Lorraine,

De qui tousjours l'univers
    Par les vers
Va cornant la gloir' hautaine.

Recevez ce que j'appens
    (Aux despens
De la douce Calliope)
A voz pieds. Aidez-moy, Sœurs,
    Mes douceurs,
A le chanter par l'Europe.

"Ha, ne fault que j'aye soin,
    Car plus loin
Vostre nom se doit estendre,
L'Asie vous veut avoir,
    Et vous voir
Sa large terre deffendre."
. . . .

Jupiter entend soudain,
    En sa main
Qui tient le tonant tonnerre,
Les discordantes humeurs
    Et rumeurs,
Qui lors estoient sur la terre.

"Qu'est cecy? dit il, cessez
    Et laissez
Ceste fascheuse querelle.
Je vous soullageray tous
    Pere doux
Par ma santence nouvelle." (36–37 [stanzas 1–3, 6–7])

Charles who bears the name
    And surname
Of the great Charles de Lorraine,
About whom the universe always
    Through verses
Trumpets the exalted glory.

Receive what I place
    (At the expense
Of sweet Calliope)
At your feet. Help me, sweet Sisters,
    To sing
Him throughout Europe.

"Ha, I must not take care,
    For farther on,
Your name must be heard,
Asia wishes to have you,
    And to see you
Defend her vast earth."
. . . .

Jupiter suddenly hears,
    Who in his hand,
Holds the thundering thunder,
The discordant moods
    And rumours,
Which were then on earth.

"What is this, he says, desist
    And cease
This irritating quarrel.
I will comfort you all,
    Sweet Father,
With my new judgement."

In this multiplication of borrowed roles, where virtuosity is measured by the effects of transvestism and ventriloquism, as well as by the gap between the lyrical subject and the conscience of the poetess, one observes at least seven poems written for third parties, where the poetess serves as a kind of "public writer":

Poem 9: "Elegie en faveur, et personne du Seigneur Gratian Meissonnier mon cousin passionné de l'amour chaste et honeste de Lucresse avec le sonet cy apres mis" ("Elegy in Favor, and the Person of Lord Gratian Meissonier, My Cousin Passionate about the Chaste and Honest Love of Lucretia, with the Sonnet Given Afterward")
Poem 10: "Je ne suis point ce Tarquin impudique" ("I Am Not This Shameless Tarquin")
Poem 19: "A Damoiselle Agnes Langlat sur l'anagramme du Sieur Jacques Miliard qui depuis a esté marié avec elle, luy parle" ("To Damoiselle Agnes Langlat, concerning the Anagram of Lord Jacques Miliard, Who Has Since Married Her, Speaks to Her")
Poem 27: "En faveur du sieur Charles Chalverot" ("In Favor of Lord Charles Chalverot")

Poem 28: "Sonet fait en la personne d'un jeune Seigneur pour presenter à M.M.B." ("Sonnet Made in the Person of a Young Lord to Present to M.M.B.")
Poem 31: "Sonet sur l'anagramme de deux noms" ("Sonnet on the Anagram of Two Names")
Poem 37: "Pour le sieur Garinot" ("For Lord Garinot")

Of the forty-eight poems, only three reveal a feminine lyrical subject: the opening "Brief discours"; poem 2, "Hymne de la rose à M. Françoise de la Rose"; and poem 22, "A un mal disant" ("To One Who Speaks Ill"), all the others being either masculine or of indeterminate gender. From the perspective of gender studies, such an observation may seem disappointing, leaving the impression that Marie de Romieu was timid, modest, conservative, even nonexistent. However, by the yardstick of the practices of her time, this aptitude for multiplying the enunciating authorities and assuming borrowed roles no doubt appeared as the clear sign of obvious poetic virtuosity.

In truth, the poetry of Marie de Romieu—and this is what I strive to show in my teaching—displays no feature specific to feminine writing; it demonstrates, rather, the clear will to invent an androgynous writing that is neither completely masculine nor completely feminine but that seeks, as in the platonic myth, to reconstruct the original wholeness of our humanity and, in so doing, to aim for the universal (La Charité, "Marie de Romieu et l'écriture androgyne").

This myth of androgynous writing, put forward by the Dames Des Roches in the poem "Agnodice," from their *Œuvres* (1579), would serve to legitimize feminine writing throughout the Ancien Régime, right up to the preface of the *Rhétorique françoise à l'usage des jeunes demoiselles* ("French Rhetoric for Young Ladies"), by Gabriel-Henri Gaillard in the mid–eighteenth century, where, without naming his source, the rhetorician paraphrases the poem by the Poitevine ladies (v). The introductory pieces in Marie de Romieu's collection repeat over and over that she is a kind of virago, a woman who, through her mastery of writing, reveals herself worthy enough to be a man. Jean-Édouard Du Monin goes so far as to write that her "mâle vers, enfant de [s]a verve femelle" ("male verse, child of her female verve") inspires the desire in him to become a "nouvel Androgyne" ("new androgyne"; 7).

If we modern readers, inheritors of the rights acquired by the women's movement and fiercely insisting on sexual equality, find it shocking that the greatest praise for a woman writer in the Renaissance was to be considered equal to a man, it remains nonetheless true that confronting the radical otherness of the past holds a fascination and is potentially able to undermine our certainties, particularly because of the belief shared by Renaissance men and women that literary culture was capable of humanizing us, regardless of our sex, origins, or background. Marie de Romieu, born the daughter of bakers and considered a "demoiselle" (La Croix du Maine, *Premier volume*, sig. Ccv v) of the nobility by La Croix du Maine, thanks to her literary work, no doubt firmly believed in this utopia.

Notes

This essay was translated by Eugenia Drolet.

1. All references in this essay to *Les premières œuvres poétiques*, by Marie de Romieu, refer to the 1972 André Winandy edition. Translations are provided by Drolet.

2. Translated from the French by Drolet.

3. I do not evoke here the issue of attributing the works of Labé to a group of poets, authors of the introductory pieces in her collection, notably Maurice Scève, Olivier de Magny, and Marc-Antoine Muret, although I feel that Huchon's demonstration is quite convincing.

Leah Chang

The Cross-Dressed Text: Reading Men Writing as Women in Sixteenth-Century France

Undergraduates typically enjoy analyzing texts by early modern French women writers, especially in courses that are dominated by male authors. When approaching female-authored texts, however, students often bring to the seminar table a set of assumptions about gender and gender difference during this period. Among these, one will likely find the following: that early modern women were usually illiterate; that women who were in fact educated and who, moreover, chose to write were defying an oppressive patriarchal culture; that publication for women was probably difficult and most likely considered scandalous; that women thus usually published anonymously if at all. Although there are foundations to some of these assumptions about women, writing, and publishing in the early modern period based on Pauline injunctions on women's chastity, silence, and obedience, it can be tricky to get students to think about women and gender in other aesthetic, stylistic, and theoretical ways, outside a historical framework of the oppressed against the oppressive, in which (they presume) the text represents the direct voice and experience of the historical female writer.

Frequently underpinning this student view of women and authorship is a difficulty in divorcing narrative voice from authorial voice and, moreover, in differentiating the protagonist from the author figure who is presented in the book as well as from the historical writer who composed the book. One way to encourage students to explore these differences, and consequently to think with greater nuance about gender and textual production in the early modern period, is to introduce a section on what I will call here the "cross-dressed" text; that is, texts written by men in the voice of a woman in a type of poetic ventriloquization, as well as texts in which a male author adopts the poetic rhetoric of an ostensibly female poet. In my course, the section centers largely, but not exclusively, on the figure of Sappho in both classical and early modern renditions. While the section can appeal to students interested in the concept of passing (with which many are already familiar through contemporary discussions of race and class), the concept of ventriloquization or cross-gendering also becomes a methodological tool to help students differentiate between the many voices—authorial, narrative, protagonist—operating in any given text. It also pushes students to question the ways in which gender inflects prevalent themes in early modern literature, particularly notions of love and desire. To male writers of the French early modern period, for example, what does female desire sound like? What is its vocabulary? Is there a difference in the ways in which women and men speak and write of love? Is there a gender to genre or a genre associated with gender? And what are male writers revealing about early modern French culture when they write in female voices? A contemporary interest in exploring the contours of female desire? An interest in imitating classical models? Or, alternatively, are they mocking the concept of women who speak and write about love?

Although it can be useful to introduce a few of these questions as a point of departure, many are raised by the students themselves as they read through the various texts. The course in which I have used this section focuses on questions of the body, gender, and difference in sixteenth-century France, but the section could also play a role in courses specifically dedicated to women writers or to representations of women. Since the texts I suggest here are also widely available in English translation, they could be integrated in a more broadly conceived, transnational course on early modern views of gender.

Sappho and Ovid

By the time we begin the section on female-voiced texts, students in my course have already been exposed to various poems from the Petrarchan tradition and are thus familiar with early modern vocabulary associated with male desire for a female beloved. The focus on female-voiced, male-authored texts begins with a turn to three texts from antiquity, Sappho's best-known fragments and Ovid's *Heroides*, poem 15, the letter from Sappho to her lover, Phaon. These texts—and especially Ovid's take on Sappho—were enormously influential in early modern France and provide a backdrop for later study of sixteenth-century texts. They also allow instructors to show students how early modern texts were consistently in dialogue with their classical predecessors and how those predecessors too aspired to rework previous textual models.

Although Renaissance readers were generally more familiar with the figure of Sappho through Ovid than from exposure to her fragments (which were just being rediscovered and reproduced for early modern audiences in the mid–sixteenth century) and although Ovid's own familiarity with the specifics of Sappho's corpus remains unclear, I find it useful to begin with a brief reading of Sappho's best-known fragments, 1 and 31, conventionally known as the "Ode to Aphrodite" and the "Ode to a Beloved Girl." The objective is not to set up a template for an evaluative comparison (to judge what Ovid got "wrong" about Sappho) but rather to establish a *champ lexical* for Sappho's dominant theme: incessant and unrequited female desire. This in turn prepares students for an analysis of how Ovid presents both female desire and the voice of a woman who writes about desire. Some students come to the course familiar with the figure of Sappho, including the identification of her beloved as female; others are encountering Sappho for the first time. Ovid's portrait is in fact one of many crafted during antiquity and the early modern period in an effort to establish a biographical face for a figure who, historically, remains largely mysterious. The lack of historical information on Sappho works to an advantage in the classroom, allowing instructors to draw students' attention away from Sappho's historical identity and, initially, from the identity or gender of the beloved to focus instead on how Sappho's narrator describes her passion. Students readily seize on the vocabulary of unrequited suffering and seemingly endless desire that, in the "Ode to Aphrodite," appears through prosopopoeia: "Whom should I persuade (now again)," Aphrodite asks, "to lead you back into her love? Who, O / Sappho, is wronging you?" (Sappho 3). In the "Ode to a Beloved Girl," the emphasis on the physicality of love, the use of metaphor to describe desire, and the image of a passion that renders the narrator virtually inarticulate also appeal to students: "no: tongue breaks and thin / fire is racing under skin / and in eyes no sight and drumming / fills ears" (Sappho 63).

Turning to Ovid's *Heroides*, poem 15, the gender identity of the beloved is a useful starting point to analyze how Ovid reworks preceding models, be they the Sapphic fragments or legends surrounding Sappho's persona. Students will see immediately that in Ovid's epistle the gendering of the love relation has changed. Sappho's passion is now directed not to a woman but to a young man: Phaon, the beautiful young boatman of Ovid's version, rejects the older Sappho, ultimately pushing Sappho to throw herself off the Leucadian cliff in the hope of quenching her passion. Nevertheless, Ovid retains some of the most poignant imagery of the fragments. Notably, he re-creates the image of burning passion: "I burn—as burns the fruitful acre when its harvests are ablaze, with untamed east-winds driving on the flame" (Heroides 181). So too does he appropriate Sappho's inability to articulate her passion (189). Whereas Sappho's narrator claims that "tongue breaks," the poetic powers of Ovid's Sappho are disabled; she claims no longer to be able to compose her famed lyrics (181, 195). The retention of this imagery suggests not only Ovid's familiarity with the hallmarks of the Sapphic corpus but also a deliberate, even ironic, twisting of Sappho's pathos that begins with a reworking of gender. Sappho's sublime lyrics and imagery are appropriated by Ovid to create a story of tragic female desire, a story marked not by an effort to capture poetically an essence of unending passion (for a woman) but by a narrative account of pathetic and hopeless love (for a young man) that can only end with the protagonist's anticipated death in the waves of the sea.

Ovid's attempts to "reauthor" Sappho can be discussed at another level if instructors invite students to consider how the Latin poet presents Sappho not just as a lover but as a poet. *Heroides*, poem 15, is the only one of the epistles voiced not simply by a female protagonist but by a female lyricist. Ovid's reworking, then, takes place not just in the regendering of a vocabulary of love but in what the female narrator says about her own writing of love. I have mentioned that Ovid's Sappho claims to have abandoned lyric in her love for Phaon. She goes on to say that the force of passion has compelled her to take up the elegiac model: "Perhaps too, you may ask why my verses alternate, when I am better suited to the lyric mode. I must weep, for my love—and elegy is the weeping strain; no lyre is suited to my tears" (Ovid 181). Ovid makes a shift in poetic composition part of the regendering of the love interest, insinuating, moreover, the power of heterosexual love, above and beyond that of same-sex desire. Sappho's desire for Phaon silences the lyric that Sappho's love for a woman produces and instead forces the poet to seek another type of verse—Ovid's (masculine) elegiac verse. Students can be invited to consider the implications of Ovid's appropriation: Does Ovid offer homage to a lore and vocabulary of female desire? Or does *Heroides*, poem 15, represent, as Elizabeth Harvey has argued, a violent appropriation, in which Ovid attempts to absorb and *master* Sappho—rescripting the gendering of her desire, changing poetic genre, and reshaping the very nature of her writing in this story of passion—in order to present his own preeminence as a (male) author?

Ronsard, Catullus, and Sappho

Turning to the sixteenth century, Pierre de Ronsard offers another opportunity to discuss through several texts intersecting notions of authorship, female narrative voice, and female desire and to consider how female desire was perceived and constructed in complex ways during the period. Ronsard works well in the section because most students bring to the reading some familiarity with his poetry. Students already associate Ronsard's love poetry with a distinctly Petrarchan rhetoric, one that may be characterized as poet centered and highly masculine and in which the poet and his search for poetic glory are as central in many of the poems as the narrator's ostensible desire for the beloved women.

Given this Petrarchan background, students are often surprised to learn that Ronsard also wrote what could be called a lesbian poem (one of several he composed), an elegy in a female voice. In "Pour vous monstrer que j'ay parfaite envie," Anne writes to her Diane, offering the lady her portrait in the name of "amitié" ("friendship" that can carry connotations of intimacy, even passionate love). The nature of the female-female relations depicted in this poem is ambiguous and thus ripe for discussion. There is no doubt that a female narrator addresses a female beloved directly and describes her ardent affection. But the exact sentiment underlying that affection is obscure. Whereas Ovid's Sappho explicitly describes her physical longing for Phaon, Ronsard's narrator consistently invokes the ambiguous "amitié" as the underlying pull behind her affection: "Et tellement vit en vostre amitié / Qu'autre que vous n'y a part ny moitié"; "Car l'amitié que je vous porte est telle / Qu'elle sera après mort immortelle"; "Nostre amitié qui sainctement je porte" ("And so [my soul] lives in your friendship / That it finds no part or other half in any other but you"; "For the friendship that I feel for you is such / That it will be immortal after death"; "Our friendship that I esteem as saintly"; Ronsard 2: 890).[1] The Neoplatonic notions of spiritual affection embedded in early modern notions of "amitié" are underscored here by a vocabulary approaching religious passion. If the narrator "burns," it is through a "saintly" flame that ignites her "faith" in her *amie*: "[le portrait] qui reluist tout ainsi / Que fait ma foy, qui purement s'enflame / De la claret de votre sainte flame" ("[the portrait] that shines / As does my faith, which is purely aglow / with the claret of your saintly flame"; Ronsard 2: 890). The passion of love, then, could be read here as purified, even sanctified, in the name of "amitié." At the same time, however, the narrator also consistently refers to the beloved as "Maitresse" ("Mistress"), suggesting the power she wields over the narrator, and invokes a Petrarchan—and Sapphic—image of dying for love for Diane, of spilling her own blood in "immortal service" for the beloved (Ronsard 2: 891). The narrator finishes by giving not only her portrait but her blood, heart, and life to the beloved: "C'est la raison pourquoy je vous dédie / Mon sang, mon Coeur, ma peinture, et ma vie" ("This is why I dedicate to you / My blood, my Heart, my portrait, and my life"; Ronsard 2: 892).

What kind of relation between women is Ronsard describing here? Asking students to probe the mythological models he uses underscores the ambivalence of the passion the poet seeks to develop. On the one hand, the narrator alludes to the "ardeur violente" that the Trojan soldier Coreobus felt for Cassandra (Ronsard 2: 890); on the other, she also refers to the bonds of friendship between two men, Orestes and Pylades. Obviously missing in the text is an exemplary model of either friendship or passionate love between two women—this is perhaps what Anne and Diane are meant to offer. Nevertheless, the ambiguous nature of the "love" between two women explored in this poem also invites questions about the availability of such a model to a male poet in mid–sixteenth-century France. Although grammatical qualifiers clearly identify both narrator and beloved as female, to what extent does the poem deliberately show its own masquerading? Does writing about female desire, in other words, simply mean transferring Petrarchan and Neoplatonic vocabulary typically associated with male-narrated poetry to the voice of a woman? Does the significance of such vocabulary change when a woman is perceived to use it? Or does the ambivalence of such a poem suggest that, because of the limits of sixteenth-century poetic vocabulary, Ronsard is effectively unable to write or speak of female passion "like a woman"? While the goal of these questions is to locate an evolving rhetoric of "female passion" in the period, they also encourage students to challenge essentialist notions of what that passion might be.

It is difficult to know whether Sappho was a model for Ronsard's elegy (although it has been proposed that John Donne likely knew Ronsard's poem when he composed his own lesbian text, "Sappho to Philaneis"). Yet another poem by Ronsard, however, showcases both the fate of Sappho in sixteenth-century France and a different version of textual cross-dressing and intertextuality, in which the male poet-narrator at least appears to mantle himself not in the voice of a woman but in the vocabulary of a woman poet, Sappho. In Ronsard's case, however, that vocabulary is appropriated, at least at first blush, to describe male love for a woman, rather than female love for a woman. In the courses I have taught, Ronsard's *chanson*, "Je suis un demy-dieu, quand, assis vis-à-vis" represents the last segment in the section on the cross-dressed text.

A discussion of this poem juxtaposes Sappho's fragment 31, the "Ode to a Beloved Girl," with imitations by Catullus and Ronsard, foregrounding the intersection between textual cross-dressing and *imitatio*. Like Rémy Belleau and Pontus de Tyard, who could also be introduced here as points of comparison, Ronsard appears to imitate Sappho's "Ode to a Beloved Girl," in which the female narrator appears to gaze on the female beloved, who sits next to another, male, suitor. The Sapphic fragment captures the envy, pathos, and longing of the narrator and the impossibility of requited passion, an impossibility defined both by physical distance—as the narrator appears to look upon the beloved from afar—and gender difference, since the rival suitor is male and the narrator is female: "He seems to me equal to gods that man / whoever he is who opposite you / sits and listens close / to your sweet speaking." The poem then shifts away from the beloved to focus on the inner turmoil of the narrator-lover, who, in a poetic paradox, sings of her own inability to speak and of the burning of her passion when she gazes at her beloved (Sappho 63).

However, since this Sapphic fragment (first published in 1556) was most likely unavailable to Ronsard when he published his poem (1555), Ronsard was probably imitating Catullus's *Carmen* 51, itself an imitation of Sappho's fragment 31 and widely available to early modern readers:

> To me he seems godlike, in my eyes even
> More than divine (if that's not sacrilegious),
> The man who sits beside you all day gazing,
>   Hearing all day
> Your musical laughter. Dazed by love, he loses
> The use of all his senses. Oh, the moment
> I see you, Lesbia, my voice, throat-strangled,
>   Withers away,
> My tongue lies paralysed, subtle sensations
> Of fire snake through my limbs, my ears are deafened

By their own noise, and, as for eyes, dense darkness
 Blindfolds them both.
Sloth is your enemy, your disease, Catullus;
You revel in it, crave it, and adore it.
By what else were great kings and flourishing cities
 Ruined but sloth?" (85)

Lesbia is an inflection of Sappho; she is Catullus's homage to the poet from Lesbos. But in transforming Lesbia into the beloved, Catullus, like Ovid before him, also rescripts Sappho, now a voiceless female beloved to Catullus's male poet-lover. Catullus, moreover, writes himself clearly into the poem in the final four lines of the poem, which he added in his imitation of the fragment; these same lines dismiss the sentiments of the first part of the poem—emotions, imagery, and vocabulary of interior passion introduced by Sappho—as the hyperbolic product of too much leisure. The poem, then, not only rescripts gender roles—woman's love for a woman becomes man's love for a woman—but also imposes a judgment on passionate, Sapphic interiority.

In Ronsard's imitation of Catullus's imitating Sappho, something quite different happens:

 Je suis un demi-dieu, quand, assis vis-à-vis
De toy, mon cher souci, j'escoute les devis,
Devis entre-rompus d'un gracieux sou-rire,
Sou-ris qui me retient le coeur emprisonné;
En contemplant tes yeux, je me pasme étonné,
Et de mes pauvres flancs un seul vent je ne tire.
 Ma langue s'engourdit, un petit feu me court
Frétillant sous la peau: je suis muet et sourd.
Et une obscure nuit dessus mes yeux demeure;
Mon sang devient glacé, le courage me faut,
Mon esprit s'évapore, et alors peu s'en faut
Que sans ame à tes pieds estendu je ne meure.
(Ronsard 1: 161)

 I am a demigod, when, sitting there next
To you, my dear care, I listen to your banter,
Banter interrupted by a graceful smile,
Smile that holds my heart imprisoned;
Contemplating your eyes, I swoon amazed,
And from my poor chest I cannot draw a single breath.
 My tongue swells, a little fire runs
Flittering beneath my skin: I cannot speak or hear.

And an obscure darkness passes before my eyes;
My blood turns icy, courage fails me,
My mind evaporates, and it takes only a little
For me, without my soul, to lie at your feet and die.

As students will immediately perceive, Ronsard has shifted the voice and focus of the poem—the "je" that speaks is no longer the alienated lover but rather the male suitor who sits beside the female beloved. Unlike Catullus, Ronsard does not write himself into the poem, but the interior focus of the poem provides ample opportunity to develop qualifiers and adjectives ("étonné," "muet," "sourd") that identify the speaker as male. Now the subject of the poem, the male narrator's desire is transformed into a Petrarchan suffering and a description of the beloved's power over the narrator, which implicitly leads to an unspoken moment: will the beloved capitulate to the lover and relieve his suffering? Likewise, one can question the power structure offered in the poem. While poems by Sappho and Catullus shift quickly away from a beloved who does not even seem to be aware of the narrator's presence, Ronsard's narrator appears to address the beloved directly; the physical passion he describes appears part of a calculated seduction. The discussion might thus center on the meaning of the first phrase: the narrator may be a "demi-dieu" in his ability to turn passionate suffering into a means of seduction. On a different level, the phrase may also allude to Ronsard's own mastery of the rhetoric of the poem, his ability to transform Catullus's imitation of a female-narrated poem into a different narrative of male passion that also highlights his own poetic glory.

There is, however, one other twist to this poem worth considering. In the light of the male-female love developed in the texts by Ovid and Catullus, were early modern poets aware that the beloved of Sapphic poetry is female? Given Ovid's *Heroides*, in which Sappho claims to have given up women for Phaon, it is possible that early modern poets knew but chose to ignore this gendering of the beloved when they imitated the fragment (albeit through Catullus). However, after carefully reading Ronsard's poem, students in my course have consistently noticed that while the male identity of the narrator is underscored, the gender identity of the beloved is decidedly lacking. One should perhaps assume this beloved is a woman, both because of Catullus's imitation and because of the conventions of French Renaissance male-authored poetry. Unlike Catullus, however, Ronsard does not write the name of the female beloved into the poem, thereby firmly establishing the male-female relation. Moreover, the second line of the poem leaves the gender identity of the beloved intriguingly ambiguous: "De toy, mon cher souci . . . . " While "souci" ("anxiety" or "care," here evidently an affectionate name for the beloved) is grammatically masculine in French, the grammatical gendering of the word also effectively masks the gender of the beloved, leading to the next question: Is it not possible that, within the context of this poem, the male narrator could be speaking to a man, as easily as he could be speaking to a woman? If so, has Ronsard not succeeded in regendering the relations of the poem, while still maintaining its same-sex emphasis, transforming Sappho's female-female love into male-male love? The impossibility of resolving this question definitively leads to lively discussion in the classroom. But it also forces students to read texts carefully for syntactic and grammatical cues and consequently to interrogate their own presumptions that automatically gender the beloved as female in a male-narrated (and -authored) poem and vice versa when reading early modern texts.

Male Writers, Female Authors

The emphasis on Sappho in this section provides a basis for other comparative approaches and texts. Alongside Ovid and Ronsard, instructors could add to the readings John Donne's "Sappho to Philaneis," written in the voice of Sappho to her beloved Philaneis, who like Sappho was known in antiquity as both a poet and a courtesan. Equally compelling, if not directly based on the legacy of Sappho, are portions of Giovanni Boccaccio's *Elegia di Madonna Fiammetta*, written in the voice of Fiammetta, who claims to warn readers to avoid being caught in the passions of love. The *Fiammetta* was an important source text for Hélisenne de Crenne's *Angoysses douloureuses* (1538), which purports to impart a similar didactic and sensual message and which engages in its own form of cross-dressing: in the second and third parts of the story, Hélisenne the narrator (who also poses as the author) claims to write in the voice of her beloved Guénélic. But Boccaccio also usefully enriches discussion about the ways in which writing in a female voice constitutes in itself a form of *imitatio*. Boccaccio's debt to the *Heroides* is clear in the text, inviting discussion of a provocative gendered paradox: that for Boccaccio the male poet to imitate, appropriate, and perhaps even surpass the *auctoritas* of his classical male predecessor, Ovid, it was necessary for him to write, like Ovid, in the voice of a woman.

In my course, the section on the cross-dressed text, with its attendant meanings of thematic and rhetorical appropriation as well as gendered ventriloquization, prepares students for a discussion of certain women authors of the French Renaissance, including those whose historical identity as writers has been questioned, especially in recent years. Beyond Hélisenne de Crenne, whose shift from female to male voice also highlights a provocative conflation of protagonist-narrator-author in her book, the recent controversy surrounding the attribution of *Les euvres de Louise Labé Lionnoise* (1555) can show students what may be the most extreme possibility of textual cross-dressing in the French Renaissance. A discussion of Mireille Huchon's hypothesis that the *Euvres* was in fact composed by men pushes students to interrogate the terms of authorship, voice, and gender that they bring to the study of early modern texts and to recognize the importance that textual cross-dressing may have played even in the material production of early modern books: it is one thing for a male writer to compose in the voice of a woman but publish the work in his name; it is quite another for male writers to print and publish as a woman. Whether one accepts Huchon's hypothesis, students are intrigued by the political ramifications of her argument: where do the *Euvres* stand, for example, in the canon of French female-authored texts in print? They are also interested to know that the controversy surrounding the *Euvres* centers on the very terms that we have analyzed thus far—attribution, authorship, voice, and imitation (particularly of Sappho and of the *Heroides*)—and that critics who have engaged in the debate define their stances in these terms. Thus Huchon claims that the male writers of the *Euvres* were imitating forms by other male writers of antiquity, notably Ovid. Deborah Lesko Baker, on the other hand, has argued that the unified female voice sustained throughout the *Euvres* casts doubt on the collaborative project that Huchon proposes and is likely the product of a female author with a sustained protofeminist interest. Despite the interest of the debate, instructors can ask students to move beyond ascribing value to the text only in terms of historical attribution by engaging in a close reading of various poems in the *Euvres* and by thinking through the intersection of female voice, thematics, and imitation and the ways in which the *Euvres* constructs its own gendered canon. Elegy 1, which seems to invoke Ovid's Sappho in the *Heroides*; sonnet 5, which in its opening lines may allude to Sappho's fragment 1; and the dedicatory epistle and sonnet 24, both of which invoke female readers who may one day also write love poetry, show how female passion is used thematically in the *Euvres* to create links that transcend chronological boundaries among ancient, early modern, and future female writers (Labé, *Complete Poetry and Prose* 42–44, 152,

180, 218). If only women can know passion in this form, then female passion, as it is construed in the *Euvres*, becomes a figure for imitation and a unique kind of authority shared only among women, in this case a cadre of female authors. Through the example of the *Euvres* students can consider how writing "like a woman" may center less on questions about the writer's historical identity than on the complex connections among gender, authorship, authority, and imitation with which early modern writers, male and female, consistently grappled.

Note

1. All translations of Ronsard are mine.

Comparative Contexts and Strategies

Anne R. Larsen

Teaching the Influence of Renaissance Women Writers on One Another: The Case of Catherine Des Roches

Courses on Renaissance women's literature increasingly emphasize the study of communities and networks of literary women. The notion that once prevailed in early feminist Renaissance studies of the lone woman prodigy writing in the isolation of her study, alienated from family, friends, community, and state, is not historically verifiable. While there may have been isolated cases, such as Isabella di Morra (b. c. 1515) in Italy, most early modern women writers were integrated in dynamic communities of like-minded intellectuals from whom they drew inspiration. Mothers and daughters, extended kinship relations, familial and intellectual alliances, close friends, convents, coteries, court circles, and separatist households—all provided essential forms of support.

Closely linked to the study of women's networks is the investigation of how women writers influenced one another (Robin; Smarr). In a course including Renaissance women writers, I consider briefly three important types of communities that supported women intellectuals: the transnational humanist Latinate community; the French Italianate court of Catherine de Médicis; and the familial and intellectual alliances between male and female writers and among women writers. I take as my test case Catherine Des Roches (1542–87), a writer largely educated by her learned mother,

Madeleine Des Roches (1520–87), with whom she headed an influential salon in Poitiers; a Latinist familiar with the works of transnational women who wrote in Latin, she was also an Italianist who translated poems by contemporary Italian poets. Several of her poems circulated in manuscript anthologies at the Valois court.

Des Roches's knowledge of contemporary women intellectuals is evident in two exceptional feminist dialogues of her *Secondes œuvres* (1583), the *Dialogue de Placide, et Severe* ("Dialogue between Placide and Severe") and the *Dialogue d'Iris, et Pasithée* ("Dialogue between Iris and Pasithée"). To strengthen her defense of women's education, she cites a significant number of modern women writers whom she describes as "sages sçavantes qui se font renommer de nostre tans" ("wise learned women who are famous in our own time"; Des Roches and Des Roches, *Secondes œuvres* 217; *From Mother* 227). They include the Italian Cassandra Fedele (1465–1558), Olympia Morata (1526/27–55), Laura Terracina (c. 1517–c. 1577), and Ippolita Torella (1499–1520); the Portuguese Luisa Sigea (1522–60); and the French legendary figure Clémence Isaure. Instead of limiting her list to the ancient exemplars of catalogs of illustrious women, most of which were connected to the *querelle des femmes* controversy, Des Roches names contemporary women writers who were models for her and gave her a sense of commonality and community. I explore how she might have encountered their writings and how these influenced her thinking.

Communities Supporting Women Intellectuals

The international Latinist humanist community included many women celebrated for their learning and writings. Four key features of this community empowered women intellectuals (Stevenson, "Female Authority"). First, national, political, and linguistic boundaries were not as significant to Latinist women as they were to vernacular women. Latinists benefited from writing in a universal language, which facilitated the circulation of manuscript and printed texts and ensured the widest diffusion possible. Second, women Latinists occupied the same authorial space as educated men; they wrote Latin, and sometimes Greek, prose and poetry, which was universally admired. Third, male patrons of Latinist women promoted them as unique and above their sex. They, on the other hand, preferred to see themselves as members of a group of talented peers. Finally, Latinist women knew other women writers: they knew their female predecessors,

Sappho, Proba, Corinna, and others from the ancient and Christian past, and they were aware of their contemporary female peers.

In the second half of the sixteenth and the early seventeenth century, women Latinists, and some writing in the vernacular like Catherine Des Roches, began to refer to one another's writings and promote a sense of commonality. Elizabeth Jane Weston (1581–1612) praised Olympia Morata and Camille de Morel (b. 1547) and her sisters, in part because of Weston's connections with the humanist pedagogue Charles Utenhove (b. 1536), who had translated Morata and taught the Morel girls (Hosington). The writer Marie de Romieu (c. 1556–98) mentions a dozen celebrated women who were active as court figures and as writers (Romieu, *Les premières œuvres poétiques* [1972] 20–21). The Dutch polymath Anna Maria van Schurman (1618–78) was at the center of an international female epistolary network and was writing in several languages (Schurman, Whether; Stevenson, *Women*).

In France, a transnational community supportive of learned women could be found in Italianate cities such as Lyon and at the court of Catherine de Médicis (Campbell). Franco-Italian nobles transmitted to the Valois court the cultural and literary practices of their native academies and salons. Italian noblewomen such as Vittoria Colonna (1492–1547) and Veronica Gambara (1485–1550), canonized for their "social prestige and moral capital" (Cox, "Women Writers" 20), became role models for French women. Marguerite de Navarre (1492–1549) corresponded with Colonna, and in Lyon the editor of Pernette Du Guillet's *Rymes* (1545) urged the "Dames Lyonnoises" to imitate their Italian female peers (Du Guillet, *Rymes* [2006] 112). Offshoots of Italian academic societies, such as the mixed Académie du Palais, connected with the court of Henry III, and the literary circles in Paris and Poitiers were highly influential. These emerged alongside the Italian academic model but with a crucial difference: women were at the helm, selecting and presiding over musical and dance entertainments, which coexisted with debates, readings, storytelling, conversation, plays, and the production of coterie literature. Women's growing sphere of influence in shaping manners, language, style, and taste and in creating new forms of literary discourse was nothing short of a "spectacular revolution" that would determine the civilizing process over the course of several centuries (Craveri 11). These communities or sites of sociability, education, and learning helped women writers rethink traditional gender roles.

Finally, literary partnerships, viewed in terms of family ties, were important to women writers. Male writers not only chose talented women of their own clan—Clément Marot (1530–63) had a *mère d'alliance* ("literary mother"; Isley 31), while Jacques de Romieu (1555–1632) collaborated with his sister Marie de Romieu—they also formed partnerships with unrelated women writers whom they viewed as their literary sisters or daughters. François Le Poulchre de La Motte-Messemé (1546–96) addressed Marie Le Gendre, dame de Rivery (dates unknown), as "ma fille" ("my daughter"; Le Gendre 113), and, in her *Dialogue des chastes amours d'Eros, et de Kalisti* (1596) ("Dialogue of the Chaste Loves of Eros and Kalisti"), Le Gendre signed the dedicatory epistle to La Motte-Messemé "vostre treshumble et obeissante fille d'alliance" ("your very humble and obedient literary daughter"; Le Gendre 116). Probably the most famous cross-sex intellectual and literary alliance was that between Marie de Gournay (1565–1645) and Montaigne. Other talented women turned to their families and female children to form with them intellectual partnerships that supported and inspired their writings. The Dames Des Roches collaborated with each other to create their own legitimizing community; Antoinette de Loynes (1505–68) and her daughters Camille, Diane, and Lucrèce de Morel composed letters and poems and performed together in compositions penned by well-known poets (Will); Catherine de Parthenay (1554–1631) wrote ballets for the court of Catherine de Bourbon (1559–1604), in which her daughters, Henriette, Catherine, and Anne, and her two sons performed (Parthenay).

Catherine Des Roches's Feminist Catalog

In what ways does Catherine Des Roches's feminist catalog depart from *querelle* catalogs? Early modern biographers of illustrious women either do not mention contemporary women at all, or they indicate at most two or three—Christine de Pisan (1365–c. 1430), Hélisenne de Crenne (born c. 1510), and Marguerite de Navarre are the three most frequently cited (Berriot-Salvadore, *Femmes* 355). Des Roches, on the other hand, draws attention to a number of women writers from her own century and times and, most crucially, focuses on their literary identity, not merely their exemplary virtue or piety. In most of the catalogs, illustrative women are praised for how well they embody social and moral expectations (Ajmar; Benson); they appear as well in profeminist and epideictic *querelle* lists as proof of their superiority over men or as a way to flatter a female patron (Berriot-Salvadore, *Femmes* 356).

Des Roches's appreciation of the literary merits of her exemplars' writings recalls the nationalistic trend in the second half of the century of glorifying the French state and its culture over the superiority of other nations. François de Billon, in his *Fort inexpugnable de l'honneur du sexe feminin* ("The Impregnable Bastion of the Honor of the Female Sex" [1555]), praises the writings of French women as evidence of the "Triomphe du royaume gallique" ("Triumph of the Gallic Kingdom"; Berriot-Salvadore, *Femmes* 359). He hails women writers of major regions and cities, giving to each pride of place. But Des Roches, although she states in the *Dialogue between Iris and Pasithée* that numerous French women writers would become known to posterity, indicating that she knew of or had read their works, mentions by name only one (legendary) French female patron of the arts—Clémence Isaure—and alludes to another, Diane de Morel (died. c. 1581 [Des Roches, *Secondes œuvres* 220; *From Mother* 228]). She assumes that her educated readers are familiar with the French women writers of her time, who were increasingly numerous in court circles and urban coteries. By naming women writers from Italy and Portugal, on the other hand, she conveys the universality of the learned woman writer and crosses borders to show how they, too, participate in a growing community of women writing.

Exemplars of Active Historical and Literary Engagement

How might Des Roches have known the writers whom she cites, and how did they influence her? Olympia Fulvia Morata, an outstanding Latin and Greek stylist, lived at the d'Este court where, in 1540, Renée of France, Duchess of Ferrara (1510–75), chose her as study companion (she was then fourteen) to her daughter Anna d'Este (1531–1607). When in 1548 Anna d'Este married François de Lorraine (1519–63), soon to be Duke of Guise, Morata lost her post. She may have been dismissed on account of a growing hostility at court to Reformist ideas to which her father adhered. Morata subsequently married a German Protestant physician and left for Germany, where, after harrowing adventures that she describes in her letters, she died at the age of twenty-nine. Her extant works were edited and published in Basel in 1558 by the humanist Celio Secondo Curione (1503–69). Three further, more complete editions appeared in 1562, 1570, and 1580.

Des Roches could have read any of those three editions. In the dedicatory letter to Elizabeth I of England, Curione defends women's intellectual capabilities, citing, in addition to standard exemplars such as Aspasia, Sappho, and Corinna, lesser-known women like Telesilla, Cleobulina, and the daughters of Stesichorus, and one modern woman only, Cassandra Fedele (Morata, *Complete Writings* 71). Des Roches mentions all these women in her works. Furthermore, in the "Dialogue between Placide and Severe," she draws specific attention to Ippolita Torella's Latin elegy to her husband, Baldassare Castiglione (Des Roches and Des Roches, *Secondes œuvres* 220; *From Mother* 227–28; this poem was, in fact, written by Castiglione in Torella's name). Torella's elegy is included at the end of Morata's edition, an added proof of Des Roches's direct knowledge of Morata's writings (Morata, *Orationes* 274–78).

Habitués of the Des Roches salon during the Grands Jours of Poitiers in 1579 could have recommended that she read Morata's works. Although Morata was held up early as a Protestant martyr, Protestants and Catholics alike enlisted her as an exemplar in the *querelle des femmes* (Morata, *Complete Writings* 33). Théodore-Agrippa d'Aubigné (1552–1630) and Guy du Faur de Pibrac (1529–84), both guests of the Des Roches coterie, highly admired Morata's erudition. Aubigné praised Morata in a letter to his daughters (Aubigné 853), while Pibrac had visited the court of Ferrara, where he conversed with Morata; he named his eldest daughter Olympia in Morata's memory (Cabos 30).

Included in Morata's works are two Latin dialogues, the first between Morata and her close friend Lavinia della Rovere Orsini (1521–1601) and the second between the characters Theophila ("She who loves God") and Philotima ("She who loves Honor"), stand-ins for Morata and Orsini. These dialogues, written by a woman and featuring female speakers, are striking because they are highly infrequent in the Renaissance. The way in which Morata models a conversation between contemporary female speakers could have inspired Des Roches's move away from the medieval allegorical genre of the *débat*, the form of her earlier dialogues, to the Ciceronian, humanist interchange between historicized characters. Janet Smarr notes that Morata was the first woman to compose Ciceronian Latin dialogues that feature real persons engaged in a lively intellectual conversation (Smarr 80, 232). In the first of Morata's dialogues, Lavinia praises Olympia for persevering in her studies while other women "waste [their time] on fixing their hair, getting dressed, or on other pleasures and the relaxation of mind and body" (Morata, *Complete Writings* 102). She especially admires her friend's resolve not to listen to "the urgings of silly women and the attacks of men" who claim that she would never find "a husband who would prefer you to be educated than to be rich" (Morata, *Complete Writings* 102). Such criticisms of women adorning their body rather than their mind and of the slanderous attacks on learned women are found in Des Roches's two feminist dialogues. Thus Morata's dialogues were influential in Des Roches's development as a dialogue writer.

Luisa Sigea, the Spanish preceptor of the Infanta Maria of Portugal (1521–77), also used female speakers in a lengthy Ciceronian Latin dialogue, *Duarum Virginum Colloquium de Vita Aulica et Privata* ("Dialogue between Two Young Women on Courtly and Private Life"), composed in 1552 in Lisbon. This dialogue features two young women, the spiritual Blesilla and the courtier Flaminia, who debate the merits and drawbacks of life at court. Blesilla tries to convince her friend that withdrawing from corrupt court influences and living a studious life would enable her to maintain a purer devotion to God. Flaminia remains unconvinced, believing that she can live a pure, chaste, prudent, and spiritual life while residing at court. Besides, she states, "[A] hidden and solitary life does not lead so directly to tranquility of life" (George 183). Des Roches would have agreed with Flaminia since she too maintains that an active life is preferable to a contemplative one (Des Roches and Des Roches, *Secondes œuvres* 249; *From Mother* 213).

Although Des Roches could not have known Sigea's Latin dialogue, which was not published until 1905, she may have read Guillaume Postel's praise of Sigea in his *Tres-merveilleuses victoires des femmes du Nouveau-Monde* ("Very Marvelous Victories of the Women of the New World"), published in Paris in 1553 (Postel 21). Des Roches mentions in her catalog Sigea's *Syntra*, a Latin elegy of 108 lines published posthumously in Paris in 1566. Sigea's father, the humanist preceptor Diego Sigeo (or Diogo Sigeu), a French native possibly from Nîmes, gave the manuscript poem to a fellow Nîmois, Jean Nicot, the French ambassador to Portugal, asking him to have it published in Paris (Sauvage; Matos 115). Sigea's speaker foretells in the poem a brilliant future for her royal pupil, the Infanta Maria, who was courted by Philip II of Spain at different intervals between 1545 and 1553. In the bucolic surroundings of the royal palace at Cintra, on the outskirts of Lisbon, a guardian water nymph introduces the poet to the assembly of the gods, who tell her that the Infanta will marry Philip. The conclusive lines suggest a happy future for Sigea as well: "Since I foresee these things being fulfilled in [the life of] my Princess, there will be for me [also] a place among the dwellers of heaven" (George 179).

This same sense of pride in belonging to the few in the sodality of Minerva marks Sigea's correspondence. Sigea wrote to Philip II, "Remember that she who asks this favor of you has (if I may say so) easily surpassed all other women of her age in the cultivation of the Muses" (George 181). Sigea was instrumental in the formation of the secular humanist woman and for this reason would have been an influential model for Des Roches.

Cassandra Fedele became the best-known female scholar in Europe and the first public professional of her sex in Italy. Like Morata and Sigea, she was a child prodigy in Latin and Greek. Like Morata, she delivered a public declamation at a young age and gained entrance into a network of leading humanists associated with the University of Padua. Des Roches learned of Fedele from a Latin letter by Angelo Poliziano (1454–94) to Fedele, in which he compares her to Vergil's Camilla, a warrior maiden famous for acts of heroism (Fedele 90–91). Poliziano mythologizes Fedele into "not woman" so as not to have to engage her as a real, historical agent; doing so would have entailed granting her "some active relation to power [that] could not be allowed to stand as woman's achievement" (Grafton and Jardine 48). Des Roches interprets Fedele's exemplarity in an altogether different way. In the "Dialogue between Iris and Pasithée" she displaces Fedele from an idealized, rarefied context into a real-life situation where she is shown as a model providing direction for (real) women's lives.

Des Roches was familiar with the poems of the Neapolitan poet Laura Terracina, the most prolific of the sixteenth-century Italian women poets writing in the Tuscan vernacular and a vocal defender of women's writing (Dersofi; Jaffe 163–86; Shemek). Unlike Morata and Fedele, Terracina came from the urban nobility and lacked a formal classical education. Undeterred, she actively sought fame through writing as a woman. Recognition came to her early, when she was admitted under the name Phebea into Naples's Academy of Incogniti ("The Unknowns") three years before the publication of her *Rime*, edited by Lodovico Domenichi for Gabriel Giolito in Venice (1548). Between 1548 and 1567, she published eight volumes of poetry. She also composed a ninth unpublished collection and a codex of more than two hundred poems. Her themes, echoed in Des Roches's writings, include a conscious bid for poetic fame, the praise of women's beauty and intellect, chastity as a strategy to legitimize the learned woman, the distrust of carnal love, the critique of the violence of the age, and the injustices women suffer in a world of male privilege. Like the Des Roches mother-daughter team affiliated with the urban upper-gentry and nobility of the robe, promonarchical and staunchly Catholic, Terracina was part of the urban elite and supported the Spanish monarch and the Counter-Reformation. Like Des Roches, Terracina was a career poet.

Des Roches could have read as well Terracina's immensely popular work *Discorso sopra il principio di tutti i primi canti di "Orlando furioso"* ("Discourse on the Beginning of All the First Cantos of *Orlando Furioso*"), comprising forty-six seven-octave cantos and reprinted fourteen times between 1549 and 1638. Terracina's revision of Ludovico Ariosto's *Orlando furioso* is inspired by the witty Italian *centone*, a genre popular in literary coteries and related to the genre of the Latin cento of late antiquity (Piéjus 80–81; Shemek 134). In the cento, a poet breaks apart the verse of a canonical poet, such as Homer, Ovid, or Vergil, to recombine it into a composition with a new meaning. This literary technique achieved its first notable success with the Vergilian cento of the fourth-century poet Faltonia Betitia Proba (c. 322–c. 370), who is included in Des Roches's catalog several lines below Terracina. Just as Proba rewrote portions of the Old and New Testaments by weaving together Vergilian verses, so Terracina rewrote the opening stanzas of all forty-six cantos of the *Orlando furioso* by inflecting their meaning to express her own feminist viewpoint on a range of issues. Terracina's bold advocacy of women's right to be "bramose / sovente in operar la penna et il foglio" ("eager / to use frequently pen and paper"; Jaffe 184) is readily expressed in Des Roches's works.

Catherine Des Roches and Clémence Isaure, the Legendary Patron of the Arts

Des Roches's catalog ends with Clémence Isaure, a legendary figure thought to have founded the Collège de Rhétorique et de Poésie Française, which was later subsumed under the Académie des Jeux Floraux ("Floral Games") of Toulouse (Couadau; Gelis; Luciani). The Floral Games originated from the Gay Sabor (or Gai Savoir), created by the troubadours in 1323 as a poetic competition in Occitan. In the sixteenth century, the games were held under the patronage of Isaure, who was credited with donating her entire fortune for the continuation of the Collège de Rhétorique. She was a type of mythical tutelary patron saint of Toulouse, in keeping with the tradition in Italian cities of choosing a leading patron (Couadau 49).

Toulousain poets and town officials played with Isaure's supposed historicity to the point of renaming, in the church Notre Dame la Daurade in Toulouse, a tomb and a funeral statue of a woman by the name of Bertrande Yzalguier (or Issalguier), from which the name Isaure was thought to derive. The statue was erected at the town hall in 1549. Poets who were winners of the games and known to the Dames Des Roches included Pierre de Ronsard and the lawyer Pierre Le Loyer and Guy du Faur de Pibrac, both habitués of their coterie. Winners were awarded floral bouquets along with monetary prizes.

Isaure's importance for learned women cannot be underestimated. Antoine Du Verdier lauded Isaure in the *Bibliothèque* for "sa liberalité, son intention et l'affection qu'elle a portée aux sciences pour inciter tous esprits à la vertu" ("her liberality, interest, and the affection which she bore for the sciences to incite all minds to virtue"; La Croix du Maine and Du Verdier 3: 395). In 1540, Pierre Trassebot, a Toulousain poet, argued before the Collège de Rhétorique that the women of Toulouse should have the right to participate in poetic public competitions according to the tradition founded by Isaure: "Madame Clémence, whom God pardons by his clemency, who gave the three flowers, long ago wished and ordained that whosoever would like to recite [could do so], without excepting women, and with a strongly liberal desire . . . including both males and females" (Broomhall, *Women and the Book Trade* 148). Finally, the *Œuvres chrétiennes* (1594) of the Toulousain poet Gabrielle de Coignard (c. 1550–86) contains a plausible dedicatory reference to Isaure, "venerable Dame mere de nos Prelatz et Gouverneurs, l'exemple et le vray miroir de toute devotion et vertu" ("venerable lady, mother of our prelates and governors, the example and true mirror of all devotion and virtue"; Coignard, *Œuvres* [1995] 130; *Spiritual Sonnets* 35). In short, the legendary Isaure created a public space for women's poetic voices through her patronage of the Collège de Rhétorique and a scholarly venue for "women sharing in civic life and literary culture" (Broomhall, *Women and the Book Trade* 148).

As this essay indicates, teaching Catherine Des Roches's feminist dialogues gives students a sense of the intellectual dynamism and international flavor of Renaissance women's writings. Three of the women writers whom Des Roches cites, as well as a selection of her own works, can now be read concurrently in The Other Voice series (Morata, Fedele, and, soon, Terracina). Reading these women writers across linguistic, geographic, and generic boundaries enables students to appreciate the cross-border literary and cultural connections among Renaissance women who were inspired by and influenced one another's writings.

Note

I am grateful to Charles Huttar for his helpful comments.

Gary Ferguson

Women's Writing, Anne de Marquets, and the Priory of Poissy

It is difficult to imagine that Anne de Marquets would be the primary focus of a university course, even at the graduate level. Nevertheless, given the diversity, originality, and quality of her poetic works, there is every reason to accord these a significant place in a course on women writers of the Protestant and Catholic Reformations, or even on French early modern religious writing in general. In addition, there are considerable benefits to including a selection of her works in a course dedicated to women writers of the Renaissance or one in which women's writing is a major topic of concern. Offering the most distinguished example of poetry in French by a nun, Marquets's verse can contribute significantly to the pedagogical goal of examining the full range of women's literary culture in the sixteenth century by means of a comparative discussion of the different social and literary contexts in which women were able to engage in writing and publishing and of the diversity of social and literary strategies they employed.

The convent, as a context within which many early modern women spent their lives, is likely to be relatively unfamiliar to twenty-first-century students, evoking perhaps, if anything, a vague sense of women enclosed against their will and subjected to multiple physical limitations. It is useful to bring the class to understand, then, that while convent life certainly imposed particular constraints, it might also have offered distinct advantages, both social and cultural or intellectual. Thus for some women, it might have been no less and indeed perhaps more attractive than marriage. Studying Anne de Marquets in conjunction with writers such as Marguerite de Navarre, Madeleine and Catherine Des Roches, Gabrielle de Coignard, Pernette Du Guillet, and Marie Dentière allows a comparison of the material conditions governing life in a convent with the situation of women at court and in the city. Since court, city, and convent together made up three distinct but overlapping contexts within which early modern women were able to pursue a literary career, students can explore, in relation to each, the opportunities women were able to forge or to exploit, the constraints they had to negotiate, and the kinds of fruitful associations and alliances they were able to create and maintain (patronage relationships, familial ties, schools, salons, etc.). Students can thus gain a more accurate perspective from which to examine and gauge the various interventions of each writer in the public debates of the day—not only the Reformation or Counter-Reformation but also, notably, the *querelle des femmes*—as well as to analyze and situate the similarities and differences in the articulations of each woman's literary voice and the rhetorical and/or poetical strategies she employs. In general, these issues interest students, who are often surprised by the degree of feminism they find in a writer like Marquets, who, as a nun, they may well have expected to be more or less uncontroversial. If, in addition to the writers named earlier, Louise Labé is also to be studied, then a discussion of the issues raised by Mireille Huchon (*Une créature de papier*) will, of necessity, take into consideration the same questions of poetic voice and of historical context and literary community.

Before broaching specific examples of Anne de Marquets's poetry, I generally begin by discussing with students the ideas they may have about convents and draw them to reflect on the ways in which these may or may not be appropriate to thinking about life in a large, wealthy community of noblewomen, like that of the Dominican priory of Poissy in the sixteenth century. In particular, we consider a number of aspects of the women's living conditions pertinent to their ability to write and to publish: the thriving school run by the sisters for the education of young girls, some but not all of whom would later become nuns themselves; the relatively relaxed nature of the sisters' observance of the religious rule and the high degree of contact they maintained with the outside world (especially with members of their families, the court, and so on); their ability to hold personal property, including money, books, and even in some cases private rooms. I describe the Colloquy of Poissy (1561), trying to convey both the importance of the ideological and political stakes involved in the meeting and the phenomenal physical event that it would have represented. I also introduce the figure of Christine de Pisan, who may be known to some students already, and note her ties with Poissy and the possibility of an imaginary link between the priory and the author's *Cité des dames.* In order to reinforce and develop an appreciation of the cultural life of the convent within which Marquets lived and wrote, I ask students to read sections of my introduction to her *Sonets spirituels* and/or my article "Rules for Writing."

The poems I assign for class discussion are taken from the *Sonets spirituels*, which to me represent Marquets's most significant and accomplished work, the richest both thematically and stylistically. It would be just as possible, however, to include poems from *Sonets, prieres et devises en forme de pasquins* (ed. Gendre), as examples of a rare, historically driven intervention by a woman writer into the domain of religious polemic, or even selections from *Les divines poesies de Marc Antoine Flaminius* (of which as yet, however, there exists no modern edition). The sonnets I generally select, some of which are available in English translation (Ferguson and Hampton), fall into three main groups. First, sonnets 32, 36, 49, 152, and 176 compose a series of poems associated with Christmas (and therefore thematically easily approached by students) that describe, and in some cases develop metaphorically, activities and experiences uniquely feminine (notably motherhood and the suckling of infants) or historically typical for many women (e.g., the care of children and the state of wifehood). These poems raise clearly the question of the gendering of the poetic voice of the writer, which in turn needs to be set in the context of what is frequently seen as a late-sixteenth-century "feminization" of devotional discourse, characteristic, though in varying ways and degrees, of many religious authors, not only female but also male (see Ferguson, "Feminisation"; cf. Fournier).

Sonnet 152, for example, establishes a parallel between God who protects the Christian who calls out to him amid life's vicissitudes and a nurse who responds to the cry of a child about to fall. In sonnet 176, the lyric *je* addresses Christ through the feminine persona of the wife; in poem 32, the Christian is urged to give birth spiritually to Jesus through faith, charity, and virtuous living and then to feed him from the two breasts of love of God and of neighbor. Students readily pick up on these feminine images, eager to see in them an inscription of the gender of the writer. If no one raises the point, I usually ask what difference it makes, if any, that Anne de Marquets was a woman who was neither a wife nor a mother. Discussion then shifts to the extensive metaphorical use Marquets makes of these tropes and what we are to make of such a literary procedure. Some students may discern a mark of solidarity between the poet and women of different walks of life outside the convent; others may see a desire to extend elements of feminine experience, on an imaginative plane, to the whole of humanity and even to God. Finally, the importance of these tropes as traditional metaphors for defining the life of religious women must be considered. Thus students can come to appreciate how the lyric *je* who speaks as a wife is at once a woman and everyone / the soul united to God/Christ and, at the same time, how that metaphor might have particular resonance for a religious woman as "bride of Christ." Similarly, the "mere spirituelle" ("spiritual mother"; 108; 216) of Jesus is an Every-wo-man, nonetheless likely to have held particular imaginary force for a woman who had renounced physical maternity for life in a community of sisters, comprising equally—depending on age, rank, and role—mothers and daughters.[1] In the context of the doctrinal disputes of the Reformation, the teaching propounded can also be seen to be distinctly Catholic in its emphasis on the importance not only of faith but also of charity: that is, on a love of God that translates into good works, virtuous living, and love of neighbor. In this way, students develop a multilayered understanding of Marquets's lyric voice, an understanding that appreciates the importance of its gendered aspects yet avoids reading these in terms of an uncritical essentialism. In order to reinforce this point, I might draw some comparisons to the works of other women writers perhaps figuring in the course, for example, the *Œuvres chrétiennes* of the laywoman Gabrielle de Coignard. While Coignard's poems were written around the same time as Marquets's, the lyric subjects of the two poets are very different. Marquets's poetic subject, in fact, is seldom an *I* (and sonnet 176 is something of an exception in this respect). Much more commonly, her verse favors third-person expressions such as "l'homme" ("man") and "celuy" ("he / the one"); when the subject is in the first person, it is usually in the form of the plural, communal "nous" ("we"). By contrast, Coignard's spiritual sonnets give vivid expression to a female poetic *je*, who is highly individualized: like Coignard herself, *je* is a widow and a mother who describes many aspects of her life, including the anxieties caused by her ill health and the burden of bringing up her daughters alone. When motherhood and widowhood are evoked by Coignard, that is, they usually figure not metaphorically but in quite literal ways that relate to the poet's all too real and pressing concerns (see sonnets 5, 11, 31, 46, 101, 103, 105, and 119; cf. Ferguson, "Feminisation"). If Marguerite de Navarre's *Miroir de l'âme pécheresse* is included in the course, a more complex comparative discussion can be broached, focusing on the shifting emergence of a feminine *je* in this work and on Marguerite's extensive use of relational metaphors that also draw on the figures of the wife and the mother, along with those of the daughter or son and the sister.

The second group of poems I read with students, concerning the Virgin Mary as well as other women saints, is formed by sonnets 372, 373, 396, 399, 441, and 442. As a number of critics have observed, Mary holds a place of particular importance in the *Sonets spirituels.* Having been prefigured by all the virtuous women who preceded her and serving as the principal example to all who come after her, Mary is presented as standing at the turning point of sacred history. By the same token, she is not only the first among women but the first among all human beings (see Fournier; Ferguson, Introduction 62–64; Yandell, *Carpe Corpus* 129–53). Indeed, the role played by this woman in the Christian story of humankind's redemption is everywhere stressed, frequently in highly striking and original ways. Sonnet 372, for the feast of the Annunciation, celebrates Mary's acceptance of God's will that she bear his son. The Virgin's famous declaration—"Behold the handmaid of the Lord; be it unto me according to thy word" (Luke 1.38 [KJV])—is interpreted in traditional terms as a sign of humility. Far from presenting Mary's action as one of obedient passivity, however, Marquets refers to the Old Testament books of 2 Samuel and Judges in order to compare Mary with the wise woman who saved her city by arranging the beheading of Sheba and with Jael, who killed Sisera by driving a tent peg through his head. Sonnet 396 describes Mary, at the conclusion of her son's life, as not only sharing the suffering of Jesus on the cross but also experiencing that pain as a second childbirth and longing to take him again to her breast as he cries out in thirst. If, for the Christian, Jesus's death marks his passage through the womb of the grave to new life in the resurrection, Anne de Marquets's vision stresses the active role of Mary in that process of rebirth, to which her labor is no less integral than it was to the incarnation. Similarly, a little further on, in sonnet 399, Mary is presented as the only human being who kept faith after Christ's crucifixion, when the apostles themselves had scattered in confusion. Mary's unwavering fidelity ("constante foy") thus made her, at this crucial moment, "de la foy la gardienne unique" ("the sole guardian of the faith"; 322; my trans.). Sonnet 373 can be situated in the tradition of the amorous lyric involving the topos of the *reverdie* or the return of spring. At the same time, Marquets is paraphrasing scripture in the form of the direct discourse of the lover to the beloved in the Song of Songs (or "of Solomon"), which, following traditional Catholic exegetical practice, she presents as words addressed by God to the Virgin. Such a lyric configuration again emphasizes the uniqueness of Mary; it also draws attention to the role of the poet who stages the dialogue in which the amorous speaker is none other than God himself. Sonnets 441 and 442, finally, celebrate the female saints that the Catholic Church recognizes as virgin martyrs and whom Marquets praises in traditional terms not only for their chastity and humility but also for their strength and courage. Victorious over themselves and the temptations of Satan, such women, for the poet, reveal that their female bodies contain a "manly" heart ("cœur viril"; 347; my trans.).

The third group of sonnets, comprising numbers 143, 190, and 193, are the most overtly feminist, in the sense of offering an explicit defense of women and their capacity for virtue and heroic action based on the roles women played in the Easter story of Christ's death and resurrection. The sonnets thus form a particularly rewarding and coherent series. Sonnet 143, inspired by Luke 23.27, describes the meeting of Jesus, as he carried his cross to Calvary, with some women of Jerusalem. In the sonnet's quatrains, Marquets sets up a stark contrast between the leaders of the Jews, filled with hatred and rage, and the women, who shed tears of pity and (like Mary in sonnet 396) identify with Jesus's suffering. The tercets describe the moment when Christ is nailed to the cross, introducing the traditional reference to Psalm 22 and concluding with the general observation that "we" (i.e., all people) are responsible for the torment he endures. The excoriation of the leaders of the Jews does not serve, then, to place blame solely on them; everyone, including the women of Jerusalem, stand in need of redemption. Nevertheless, the latter, to whom Marquets refers simply as "[l]es femmes" ("the women"), allow the poet to make the wide-reaching claim "Qu'à ce sexe convient une saincte amitié" ("That holy friendship befits this sex"; 173; 217). The expression is ambiguous, suggesting that women are both capable of showing and deserving of being offered holy friendship. The role played by women in the passion narrative is thus emphasized by Marquets to point out what is due to those of her sex in the light of their moral qualities. When we remember that much medieval and early modern misogynous discourse affirmed that the weakness of women's nature made them equally incapable and unworthy of friendship, we can appreciate the force of Marquets's counterclaim.

Similar ideas are taken up in sonnet 190, for Easter day, which describes the women who came to the tomb to anoint Jesus's body (see esp. Mark 16.1–2) and who, because of the strength of the love filling their noble hearts, were not afraid of the Roman sentries. Again, the constancy of the women's unwavering love is stressed, so that they become exemplars of the true friend (denoted by the masculine demonstrative "[c]eluy") who remains faithful in all circumstances. Again (as explicitly in sonnet 399 with reference to Mary), an implicit contrast is drawn between the courage, faith, and unfaltering love of the women and the confused fear of the dispersed apostles. Sonnet 192 also concerns a woman at Jesus's tomb, Mary Magdalene, who, on account of the strength of her love, was granted the honor of being the first to see the risen Christ. This leads into the remarkable sonnet 193, a scathing apostrophe addressed to "Hommes par trop ingrats et de cœur endurcy" ("You exceedingly ungrateful and hard-hearted men"; 202; 219).

Drawing on scriptural and liturgical texts (see Ferguson, "Biblical Exegesis"; Marquets, *Sonets spirituels* [1997] 59–62), sonnet 193 again stresses the vital role played by women in the events of Easter morning: the women to whom the risen Christ appears are sent to announce the good news to the disciples; in this way, they become, for Marquets, nothing less than apostles to the apostles. Most strikingly in this poem, an opposition is created between "nous"/"women" and "vous"/"men," the latter being figured as unjust and heartless detractors, who, in very concrete metaphorical language, are admonished: "Ne jettez plus sur nous d'injures si grands sommes" ("Stop heaping upon us such great burdens of insults"; 202; 219). The end of the poem repeats the same demand, using a highly significant choice of verb: "blasonner." In his *Dictionarie of the French and English Tongues (1611)*, Randle Cotgrave offers as possible translations of this term "to praise, extoll, commend," but "also (the contrarie) to reproove, dispraise, derogate, or detract from." Obviously, the negative meaning of "blasonner" is primary in sonnet 193; nevertheless, it is important to remember that the verb assumes its derogatory signification in relation to the *blason*, a poem in praise of a particular physical object, but that also, in a form sometimes known as the *contreblason*, turned to vituperation (cf., famously, Clément Marot's "Du beau tetin" ["On the Beautiful Breast"] and "Du layd tetin" ["On the Ugly Breast"]). In both cases, however, the *blason* effected a complete objectification of whatever it described—most frequently a part of the female body. The final admonition of sonnet 193 thus expresses a social demand, but one that also concerns in particular a specific male poetic tradition. After discussing these various aspects of this final Easter poem, I often ask (unless a student has raised the point already, though this is unusual) if there is any instance where the "nous"/"we" subject does not represent only women. Someone will then notice that the last line of the second quatrain, the structural center of the sonnet, reads: "Car d'une mesme chair environnez nous sommes" ("For we are all bound by the same flesh"; 202; 219). The argument of verses 3–8, which alleges the common creation of women and men, the fact that women as well as men can be virtuous but that no one of either sex is perfect, thus builds up to the affirmation that all people share the same "flesh," that is, the same fallen human nature. Even in this most explicitly critical of poems, then, Anne de Marquets looks for ways out of the gendered opposition whose oppressive effects on women she deplores by recalling the universal (flawed) humanity common to all.

By way of concluding study of Marquets's *Sonets spirituels*, I often have students look at the very first and two final poems of the collection, numbers 1, 379, and 380, in which the writer speaks directly in the first person of her poetic project (on this topic, see Ferguson, "Le chapelet"; Yandell, *Carpe Corpus*). Although variations on the humility topos are present, whatever reticence or sense of incapacity is described has nothing to do with being a woman but is the result of the inadequacy of any human being to speak worthily of things divine. Moreover, Marquets expresses her trust that her work will in fact be pleasing to God and a source of honor to herself, as well as her hope, finally, to be brought to sing God's praises with the angels. It is important to remember that the lyric subject is speaking here as a writer only and not as the person publishing the collected work, which was done after Marquets's death by a younger religious sister and former pupil. Even so, these opening and closing sonnets reveal a woman confident in her vocation—as a Christian, as a nun, and, in particular, as a poet.

Either before or after discussing Marquets's poetry, it could be fruitful to read with students Marie Dentière's *Epistre tres utile* (*Epistle to Marguerite de Navarre*), which, in its turn, can also be read along with (extracts from) Jeanne de Jussie's *Petite chronique* (on teaching the former, see McKinley, "Marie Dentière"; on teaching the latter, see Klaus, "Reading Jeanne de Jussie's *Short Chronicle*"). A very different view of female religious life is offered by Dentière, a woman who left the Augustinian convent in Tournai, where she was professed, for active ministry as a married Protestant laywoman, and who preached the Reformation to the community of Poor Clares in Geneva (of which Jussie's *Chronique* gives a brief description from the point of view of the nuns). In addition to feeding a consideration of the advantages and disadvantages of convent life for women, Dentière allows an expansion of the discussion to the question of the place accorded historically to women within Protestantism and Catholicism more generally. In comparison with Marquets, Dentière might be seen as articulating a more overtly feminist argument. In relation to Mary Magdalene and the women at Christ's tomb, for example (who offer Marquets material for her strongest criticism of men's treatment of women in sonnet 193), Dentière speaks of their being "commanded . . . to tell, *preach*, and declare" the resurrection "to others" (*Epistle* 55; my emphasis). At the same time, Protestant reformers, including Calvin, were often hostile to such an inclusive vision and scathing of Dentière personally when she tried to put it into practice. Reading Dentière in juxtaposition with Marquets also allows a historical connection to be made with Marguerite de Navarre, to whom the *Epistre tres utile* was addressed. If works by Marguerite and Gabrielle de Coignard are read in the same course, then these writers together represent not only the worlds of the court, the city, and the convent; they also reflect the entire spectrum of women's religious engagements—Catholic, Protestant, and Evangelical.

In introducing Marquets's works to students, I usually say a few words to prepare them for the uniquely Christian and more specifically Catholic subject matter of the poems, which, to one degree or another, may be part of the cultural heritage of some of them, but to others (at least outside the context of a Catholic institution) is likely to be quite unfamiliar. In general, my experience has been that students are willing to make whatever imaginary leap may be necessary to begin to appreciate some of the interest and originality of Marquets's work. Most, moreover, are intrigued to discover how a woman could write as such and in her own distinctive voice in a tradition in which they may well not have expected this to be possible.

Note

1. French quotations from *Sonets spirituels* cite Ferguson's edition; English translations cite *Sonets Spirituels*, trans. Ferguson and Hampton, unless otherwise noted. Some translations are modified.

Mary B. McKinley

Marie Dentière's *Epistle to Marguerite de Navarre* and the *Heptameron*

Marie Dentière's *Epistle* (1539) introduces students to a dedicated activist of the Protestant Reformation. Addressed to Marguerite de Navarre (1492–1549), the sister of King Francis I, the epistle brings together, if only in print, two women who played very different roles in that movement. Marguerite's public presence at the royal court has allowed us to know much about her life (Cholakian and Cholakian; Reid). Dentière's life (1494–1561), however, has yielded its details much more sparingly and only to painstaking research (Kemp and Desrosiers-Bonin; Graesslé, "Vie"; McKinley, Introduction). Dentière left her Augustinian convent and her family, named Dentière or d'Ennetières, in the early 1520s and joined French Reformers at a safe haven in Strasbourg. From there she went with her husband, a former Catholic priest, to Switzerland, where the couple preached the new religion together with Guillaume Farel, a leader of the French Reformers. Widowed with children, she married again and, with her husband Antoine Froment and Farel, took part in the Protestant takeover of Geneva in 1535–36, shortly before John Calvin arrived there. She reappears fleetingly in the Reformed Church's history up to the year of her death.

In 1539 Marguerite de Navarre was already recognized as a protector of the French reform movement known as *évangélique*, from the French word for *gospel*, *évangile*. That group hoped to reform the Catholic Church from within, returning to the spirit of the church described in the New Testament. In 1533 Marguerite's poem *The Mirror of the Sinful Soul* had been attacked by the theologians of the University of Paris, the faculty known as the Sorbonne. Marguerite had welcomed the young John Calvin to her castle in Nérac and sheltered Jacques Lefèvre d'Étaples, the father of the French *évangéliques*, until he died there in 1536 (Farge; Heller). The poet Clément Marot had sought refuge with her after the Placards affair in October 1534. That event, when broadsheets blaspheming the Catholic Mass were posted throughout Paris and in other French towns, had led to a crackdown (Marcourt). Harsh persecution pursued the French Reformers as never before. Several dissenters and suspected heretics were executed. Shaken by the affront to his authority, Francis withdrew his support from the Reformers. With that change in royal attitude, the Sorbonne and the French parliament, which had often been frustrated by Francis in their efforts to suppress the evangelical Reformers, regained power and influence, becoming Francis's ally in the effort to restore order. The Placards affair ushered in a long period of persecution, exile, prison, and death for many advocates of evangelical reform (Knecht, *Renaissance Warrior* 313–21). It became much more difficult for Marguerite to intervene and protect them.

With a diverse group of students, I cannot take for granted that everyone knows even the basic facts about the history of Christianity. Before discussing how the books we are reading reflect that history, I ask a general question of the class: What names or ideas do you associate with the Protestant Reformation? Usually a few students will volunteer Luther and Calvin. Some might mention marriage for the clergy and challenging the pope's authority. I write brief headings on the board as others volunteer and make sure that the list includes the words *faith and works*, *Bible*, and *Eucharist*. I refer students to basic reference works: *A Catholic Dictionary of Theology*, *The Oxford Dictionary of the Christian Church*, and *The Oxford Encyclopedia of the Reformation*, and I assign a few key terms to groups of students, asking them to report on their research when those words come up in our readings.

The first published work of Reformed theology by a woman written in French, the *Epistle* appeared in Geneva. It carried a false printer's name and address in Antwerp, but authorities recognized the product of Jean Girard, a well-known printer in Geneva. After internal disagreements, Geneva's Council of Two Hundred had expelled Calvin and Farel. Dentière's husband, Antoine Froment, reported that the Queen of Navarre had written to his wife and asked her to explain what had occurred. Dentière apparently sent a copy of the *Epistle*, perhaps in manuscript, to Marguerite. There is no evidence that she answered. Although the *Epistle* predates the *Heptameron*, composed in the 1540s, I introduce it after students have read Marguerite's book. The *Heptameron* provides a context for the *Epistle*. Most of its stories are set in the early sixteenth century, and many of them portray situations, such as abusive clergy and superstitious faithful, that led to criticism of the Catholic Church. Its framing discussions often comment on those situations from a Reformer's point of view (Thysell). Students can find in the *Epistle* attacks on beliefs and practices of the Catholic Church that the *Heptameron* criticizes through fiction. I begin our study of Dentière by assigning my introduction to *Epistle to Marguerite de Navarre* (1–30) and the opening sections of the *Epistle*: the dedicatory address (51–54) and the "Defense of Women" (51–56).[1] I point out that the nineteenth-century editor, A.-L. Herminjard, omitted the "Defense" in his selections from the *Epistre* (McKinley, "Absent Ellipsis"). Albert Rilliet, editor of the *Guerre et deslivrance* (74–76), a work sometimes attributed to Dentière, and, more recently, Backus ("Marie Dentière" 184–85), have included the complete "Defense" in French.

When introducing students to sixteenth-century literature, I always emphasize rhetoric. Rhetoric, the art of persuasion, was one of the seven liberal arts, the basis of the medieval curriculum. Rhetoric, along with grammar and dialectic (or logic), made up the trivium, the language arts. Rhetoric taught young men to strive for eloquence, a quality essential in public life. Since women were excluded from public life and silence rather than eloquence was the ideal that society set for them, rhetoric was not usually part of a woman's education. Women writers, however, needed to persuade just as much as men did, so I ask students to look for the rhetorical strategies that Dentière uses in her *Epistle* to engage Marguerite and her wider audience. Dentière begins by addressing Marguerite:

> Tout ainsi, ma tres honnorée Dame, que lés vrays amateurs de verité desirent sçavoir & entendre comment ilz doibvent vivre à ce temps si dangereux: aussi nous femmes, debvons fuyr & eviter toutes erreurs, heresies, & faulses doctrines: . . . comme desia assez par vos escriptz est demonstré. (*Epistre* a2; "M[arie] D[entière]" 295–96)

> My most honored Lady, just as the genuine lovers of truth desire to know and understand how they should live in these very dangerous

> times, so we women should know how to flee and avoid all errors, heresies, and false doctrines, whether from false Christians, Turks, infidels, or from others suspect in doctrine, as your writings have already sufficiently shown. (*Epistle* 51)

That first sentence functions rhetorically to create a bond between Dentière and Marguerite. Its opening words are a formula of respect shown to someone of a higher social position. However, the words "we women" quickly bring the two together by stressing what they have in common simply as women. By acknowledging Marguerite's writings, Dentière suggests another affinity between the two women. With the *Epistle*, Dentière becomes a fellow writer. She uses Marguerite's example to authorize her as a woman writing on religious matters. Those rhetorical strategies put her in a stronger position to ask for Marguerite's help:

> Et pourtant ma tres honnorée Dame, vous ay bien voulu escrire, non pas pour vous enseigner, mais affin que puissiez prendre peine envers le Roy vostre frere, pour obvier à toutes cés divisions, qui sont regnantes és lieux, places, et peoples, sur lesquelz Dieu l'a commis pour regir et gouverner. (*Epistre* a3; "M[arie] D[entière]" 297)
>
> However, my most honored Lady, I wanted to write you, not to teach you, but so that you might take pains with the King, your brother, to obviate all these divisions which reign in the places and among the people over whom God commissioned him to rule and govern. (*Epistle* 52–53)

Dentière urges Marguerite to exercise her political power and declare her faith openly: "Ce que Dieu vous a donné, et à nous femmes revelé, non plus que lés hommes, le devons cacher fouyr dedens la terre" ("what God has given you and revealed to us women, no more than men should we hide it and bury it in the earth"; *Epistre* a3; "M[arie] D[entière]" 297; *Epistle* 53). Once again, by moving from "you" to "us women" and "we," Dentière positions Marguerite in a place where they share the responsibility of declaring their faith. The first-person plural barely softens the implied criticism that Marguerite had compromised her convictions by staying within the Catholic Church. That accusation was often directed toward Marguerite, most dramatically by Calvin five years later when he chastised her for what he called Nicodemism.

Although addressed to Marguerite, the *Epistle* was clearly intended for a much wider audience, including men as well as women. In the dedicatory address Dentière mentions the different women for whom she wrote:

> Non seulement pour vous, ma dame, ay voulu escrire cette Epistre, mais aussi pour donner courage aux aultres femmes detenues en captivité, affin qu'elles ne craignent point d'estre deschassées de leurs pays, parans et amys, comme moy, pour la parolle de Dieu. (*Epistre* a3)
>
> Not only for you, my Lady, did I wish to write this letter, but also to give courage to other women detained in captivity, so that they might not fear being expelled from their homelands, away from their relatives and friends, as I was, for the word of God. (*Epistle* 53)

She encourages women convinced by the Reform but living under the threat of persecution, "in captivity," to follow her example and leave France. Marguerite is implicitly included among those women. Along with those already converted to the Reformation, Dentière includes among her intended audience a second group of women:

> Et principallement pour lés paouvres femmelettes desirans sçavoir et entendre la verité, lesquelles ne sçavent quel chemin, quelle voye doibvent tenir. Et affin que desormais ne soyent en elles mesmes ainsi tormentées et affligées, ains plustost resjouyes, consolées, et esmeues à suyvir la verité, qui est Evangile de Jesus Christ. (*Epistre* a3v)
>
> And principally for the poor little women (*femmelettes*) wanting to know and understand the truth, who do not know what path, what way to take, in order that from now on they not be internally tormented and afflicted, but rather that they be joyful, consoled and led to follow the truth, which is the Gospel of Jesus Christ. (*Epistle* 53)

Dentière envisions with sympathy women who are troubled in their religious beliefs; she assures them briefly here that salvation is a gift offered freely by Jesus Christ to all who have faith in him, a conviction that she will return to in the body of the *Epistle*. The word *femmelettes* in the original French text prompts me to ask for reactions to that diminutive and to recommend several secondary readings that discuss women's status in the French Reformation (Head, "Religion"; Davis, *Society* 65–95; Douglass, "Use of Scripture" and "Women"; Roelker, "Appeal" and "Role"; Thompson).

In the copy of the *Epistle* now in the Bibliothèque Mazarine (Kemp and Desrosiers-Bonin), Dentière mentions that Marguerite was the godmother of one of her own daughters. That daughter was another motivation for her letter to Marguerite:

> Et aussi pour donner courage à ma petite fille vostre fillole de donner aux Imprimeurs une petite grammaire hebraique qu'elle a faict en

> françoys à l'utilité & proffit dés aultres petites filles. Et principallement pour ma Dame la princesse vostre fille, à laquelle elle est dirigée. (*Epistre* a3v)
>
> And also to give courage to my little daughter, your goddaughter, to give to the printers a little Hebrew grammar that she has made in French for the use and profit of other little girls, above all, for your daughter, my Lady the Princess, to whom it is directed. (*Epistle* 53)

In what circumstances Marguerite served as godmother to this little girl is just one of the many mysteries shrouding the relationship between the two women. Already in the mid-1520s Marguerite supported from afar some of the French in Strasbourg whom Dentière might have known there; Lefèvre d'Étaples and Gérard Roussel had sought refuge there while working on the translation of the Bible into French (Farge; Nauert; Heller; Reid; Kemp and Desrosiers-Bonin). Perhaps she had met Marguerite after leaving her convent but while still in France. The detail about the young daughter's creation of a Hebrew grammar in French intrigues students and shows the importance Reformers and Christian humanists such as Erasmus and Lefèvre d'Étaples attached to reading scripture in its original languages.

The "Defense of Women" (54–56) continues an important literary tradition: writings in praise of women, refuting the misogynistic writings of the Middle Ages. The women Dentière named all come from the Bible, from both the Old and the New Testament. We discuss the qualities that made these women exemplary and would encourage imitation from Dentière's contemporaries. The New Testament women enjoyed a privileged close relationship with Christ, one needing no male intermediaries. Dentière uses them explicitly as examples to authorize women as preachers:

> Quelle prescheresse a esté faicte plus grande que la Samaritaine, laquelle n'a point eu d'honte de prescher Jesus et sa parolle, le confessant ouvertement devant tout le monde, incontinent qu'elle a entendu de Jesus qu'il fault adorer Dieu en esperit et verité. Ou est celuy qui se peut vanter d'avoir eu la première manifestation de ce grand mystere de la resurrection de Jesus, sinon Marie Magdaleine, de laquelle il avoit jecté sept diables? et lés aultres femmes auxquelles plustost s'est declaré par son Ange, que non pas aux hommes, et commandé le dire, prescher, et declairer aux aultres? (*Epistre* a4v)
>
> What woman was a greater preacher than the Samaritan woman, who was not ashamed to preach Jesus and his word, confessing him openly before everyone, as soon as she heard Jesus say that we must adore God

> in spirit and truth? Who can boast of having had the first manifestation of the great mystery of the resurrection of Jesus, if not Mary Magdalen, from whom he had thrown out seven devils, and the other women, to whom, rather than to men, he had earlier declared himself through his angel and commanded them to tell, preach and declare it to others? (*Epistle* 55)

We know of two incidents when Dentière herself preached, each time meeting a hostile reception, once from Catholic nuns and once from Calvin himself (McKinley, Introduction 8–9, 19–20; Jussie, *Short Chronicle*). We look at excerpts from defenses by Giovanni Boccaccio, Christine de Pisan, and Henricus Cornelius Agrippa. Like Agrippa, Dentière points out the examples of evil men in the Bible, and she associates them with current leaders of the Catholic Church. Where Agrippa praised women's beauties, she emphasizes their virtues. Our discussion usually runs over into the next class meeting, when we also embark on the "Epistle" proper, the third section of the work.

This longest part of the work is also the most difficult for students to absorb. It ranges from affirming the teachings of the Reformed Church, including positions held by Calvin and Farel, to passionately attacking the Catholic Church. Its target is not only the pope and the Church in Rome but also the hierarchy of the clergy in France, including people whom Marguerite protected—and even Marguerite herself. It also attacks the Genevan authorities who had banished Calvin and Farel. In my edition I provide in footnotes the basic information that students need to follow this section. I also ask students in small groups to do some research to help the class understand passages where the following words are important: *canon law*; *shroud of Turin*; *Waldensians*; *transubstantiation*, *real presence*; *Nicodemism*; *Melchizedek*; and *Babylon*, for example. The *Heptameron* provides us with concrete examples that can illustrate different points made by the *Epistle*. I encourage students to recall those passages during our discussions. I stress four main doctrinal issues, including some where the *Heptameron* takes a position different from the one Dentière advocates (Backus, "Marie Dentière"; Denommé; Douglass, "Marie Dentière's"; Skenazi).

The first is the primacy of the Bible: from the beginning of the movement that became the Protestant Reformation, Holy Scripture, the word of God, was the authority on which the Reformed churches were founded. Later doctrines and practices initiated by Rome were dismissed. The *Heptameron* portrays regular reading of the Bible as part of the daily routine of the storytellers. They meet every morning for scriptural readings led by the widow Oisille, their spiritual guide, and they tell their stories in the afternoon. We learn in the prologues to the later days what biblical books Oisille has chosen to read. In their discussions the storytellers frequently quote verses from scripture. Biblical references fill the margins of the *Epistle*, and echoes of scripture resound within the text itself.

The second issue is faith in Jesus Christ alone. The "Epistle" proper opens with a stirring affirmation:

> Le Seigneur Dieu qui desire tous venir à la pure et vraye congnoissance de verité par un seul moyenneur Jesus Christ, sans acception de personne, moyennant que par vraye et vive foy lon luy demande l'intelligence d'icelle sans vaciller n'attendre que de luy seul. (*Epistre* a5v)
>
> The Lord God desires that all without exception come to the pure and true knowledge of truth through Jesus Christ alone by asking for that understanding only through a true and living faith, without wavering nor seeking anyone but him. (*Epistle* 56)

Behind that affirmation is a denial of two teachings of the Catholic Church that the Reformers considered corrupt. The emphasis on Jesus alone rejects the authority of the popes and the entire clergy, while the insistence on faith alone rejects the efficacy of good works in salvation. We have already found evidence in the *Heptameron* of the Reformation debate between faith and good works. Its stories (e.g., 30, 35, and 72) frequently illustrate the folly of thinking that by pious practices a Christian can earn salvation. The storytellers often mock such practices, and they present as cautionary tales stories of people who trust too much in their own ability to resist sin (stories 22, 30) (Miernowski; Thysell). The *Epistle* attacks the abuses of the Catholic Church that have supplanted faith in Christ alone:

> Ce neantmoins incontinent par oeuvres le nyent et renuncent ester leur Dieu, leur ayde, esperance, consolation et sauveur quand par aultre moyen que par luy seul veulent remission de peché, cerchans aultre salut, aultre confiance que en luy. Comme par œuvres, merites, religions, voyages, pelerinages, confessions auriculaires, messes, adorations d'idoles, argent donné pour indulgences et pardons, et à tout plein d'aultres mechantes inventions, ceremonies, et sacrifices que lés hommes ont controuvé: veu que par un seul sacrifice et seule oblation, nous a eternellement sainctifiez. (*Epistre* c5)
>
> In spite of all that, by their actions they quickly denied and renounced him as their God, their help, hope, consolation and savior when by

> means other than him alone they wanted to get remission for their sins, seeking salvation and trust other than in him: by works, merits, religions, journeys, pilgrimages, auricular confession, masses, adoration of idols, money given for indulgences and pardons and all kinds of other inventions, ceremonies and sacrifices that men have contrived—when it was by one sacrifice only and one oblation only that he sanctified us for all eternity. (*Epistle* 74–75)

The third issue I focus on is the Lord's Supper and the Catholic Mass: The *Epistle* is particularly virulent in its attack on the Catholic Mass. Its argument and language are very similar to the 1534 placards, considered blasphemous by the French Catholics. We know now that those placards were the work of a group of French Reformers led by Antoine Marcourt, who had settled in Neuchâtel and who almost certainly would have known Dentière and her husband and collaborated with them (Denommé). Both documents attack the notion that the Mass repeats the sacrifice of Christ and the belief that the priest changes the bread and wine into the "real presence" of Christ's body and blood. The Reformed Church replaced the Mass with the Lord's Supper. It understood that Jesus meant his actions at the Last Supper to be remembered in a service that commemorated them instead of presuming to repeat them. The *Epistle* explains the Reformers' belief that the bread and wine used in the Lord's Supper are a sign of Christ's body and blood rather than a miraculous "transubstantiation" (Ellwood). I explain that Farel and Calvin's position was different from that of Luther, different also from that of Zwingli. In the *Heptameron* Marguerite has the storytellers attend Mass as a regular part of their daily program. The readings of scripture conducted by Oisille begin each day and precede Mass, at times overshadowing it in the narrative, but there is no trace of the virulent animosity that the *Epistle* directs toward the Mass.

Fourth, I emphasize abuses of the Catholic clergy: among the passages developing the attack on the Mass are indignant outbursts against the Catholic hierarchy and against the temporal authorities in France who kept them in power and thereby supported them in their persecution of those suspected of heresy. Here the criticism targets "kings, princes, and lords," necessarily including while not naming Francis I.

> Qu'est ce que vous craignez lés cardinaux ny evesques, qu'avez en voz cours. Si Dieu est pour vous, qui sera contre vous? Pourquoy ne leur faites vous maintenir leur cause publiquement devant tout le monde? Ilz sont tant de docteurs, tant de sages, tant de grans clercs, tant

> d'universitez contre nous paouvres femmes, que sommes rejectées et mesprisées de tout le monde. (*Epistre* b2)
>
> What do you fear from the cardinals and bishops who are in your courts? If God is on your side, who will be against you? Why don't you make them support their case publicly, before everybody? They are just so many doctors, so many wise men, so many great clerics, so many universities against us poor women, who are rejected and scorned by everyone. (*Epistle* 61)

Dentière places Marguerite in an ambiguous position. Although one of the "poor women" persecuted by the universities, Marguerite was also in the circle of kings and princes.

The diatribe against the Roman Catholic hierarchy, especially the pope and those who support him, dominates the end of the *Epistle*. The Geneva Reformers saw in the history of the church under the popes a steady corruption of the teachings of Christ in the New Testament. They rejected the pious practices that the clergy had encouraged over the centuries—using holy water, going on pilgrimages, giving money for indulgences, venerating saints, fasting during Lent—as erroneous beliefs in the efficacy of good works rather than in faith alone, and they related them to the rituals of the Jewish law in the Old Testament (*Epistle* 70, 74). They expressed contempt for the clergy and certain religious orders, who, they felt, lived off the labor of the people and took concubines while refusing priests the right to marry (*Epistle* 68, 70). Their contempt extended to the devotion shown to certain saints, some of whom are ridiculed here (*Epistle* 74). They decried the persecutions of those whom the church viewed as heretics. The *Epistle* defends in particular the Waldensians, a sect condemned as heretics in 1215 that had survived in remote communities in the Alps (*Epistle* 71–73). In 1532 some of their leaders had met with Farel and had moved toward a union with the Reformers. Persecution of the group spread and would culminate in 1545 in an organized massacre of the Waldensians living in the Luberon region of Provence, a massacre authorized by Francis I (*Epistle* 71n37, 73n40).

These pages refer indirectly to historical events of the mid-1530s that reverberated in Geneva. Although the ostensible reason for addressing the *Epistle* to Marguerite in 1539 was to convey to her details of the expulsion of Farel and Calvin, other events may have provoked the Geneva Reformers and may help to explain their anger at the French court. Before 1539 Francis vacillated between rapprochement with Henry VIII of England, who encouraged Francis to follow his example and break with the pope, and with the pope himself. In spring 1538 Francis agreed to meet with his nemesis Charles V, the Holy Roman Emperor and a staunch Catholic, for peace negotiations mediated by Pope Paul III. Francis met twice with the pope in Nice in June and met with Charles in July. Marguerite accompanied her brother on that trip and participated in the customary ceremonial festivities marking such meetings (Knecht, *Renaissance Warrior*; Jourda 231–34). Those events could not have gone unnoticed in Geneva. The *Epistle*'s reference to the custom of kissing the pope's slipper as a gesture of reverence (78) raises the specter of that meeting as it attacks those who believed in reform but remained in the church. Already in 1537 Calvin had written to Gérard Roussel, Marguerite's almoner, castigating him for hypocritically remaining among the "papists" in order to avoid persecution and to receive the benefice that his bishopric of Oloron allowed him. Without naming him, Dentière refers to Roussel and those like him as "vermine sur la terre" ("vermin on earth"; *Epistre* c7v; *Epistle* 78) and entreats Marguerite to avoid them. Calvin was to continue his criticism of those whom he later called Nicodemites in a 1544 treatise, and he implicated Marguerite de Navarre among them in a letter addressed to her in 1545 (McKinley, Introduction 18; Calvin, *Letters* 1: 453–58). If the *Epistle* offended Marguerite or Francis, it did not prevent Antoine Froment from meeting with the king three years later in Lyon, according to a report from Froment to Calvin that Calvin mocked in a letter to Farel (McKinley, Introduction 17–18). Froment's name, the word for a kind of wheat in French, appears as an allusive signature in the last lines of the *Epistle* (87) and indicates that he had a collaborative role in the drafting of the work (Denommé).

As we read these closing pages, I ask the students to notice the words *woman* and *women* (*Epistle* 76, 77, 79, 80, 84), words that have not appeared since the "Defense of Women." Dentière anticipates animosity toward a woman who dares to criticize male church officials, both Catholic and Reformed. That animosity soon declared itself. The Geneva council that had expelled Calvin and Farel confiscated the book from the printer, Jean Girard, shortly after it appeared in April 1539 and apparently destroyed most of the copies. A Reformed pastor in Lausanne, Beatus Comte, advised in August of that year that the book be suppressed "parce que le titre annonce qu'une femme (dont ce n'est pas l'office de prophétiser dans l'Eglise) l'a dicté et composé, et que cela n'est pas vrai" ("because the title announces that a woman [who has no business prophesying in the church] dictated and composed it, and because that is not true"; qtd. in

Herminjard 333nn2–3; McKinley, Introduction 15). In 1546 a letter from Calvin to Farel ridiculed Dentière's public preaching. Now, increased interest in women's history and literary activity has led to new research on Marie Dentière and new assessments of her role in the Reformation. I like to end our discussion of the *Epistle* with a news item that I was not aware of when my translation went to press. On Reformation Sunday 2002, Marie Dentière's name was added to the Wall of the Reformers in Geneva, a major monument honoring recognized leaders of the Reformation (Graesslé, "Reformation Sunday").

Note

1. Quotations of the *Epistle* cite my edition.

Colette H. Winn

Variations on the Same Tune: The Love Lyrics of Louise Labé and Gabrielle de Coignard

Of all the Renaissance courses that I have taught at Washington University, my seminar Gender and Genre is by far the best attended. This seminar, which follows the French literature survey sequence required for French majors, is intended primarily for seniors. In the span of thirteen weeks students are exposed to seven or eight early modern women writers and different kinds of writing including advice books, letters, memoirs, novels, drama, and love and religious poetry. Each writing introduces them to a specific genre, literary tradition, or intellectual movement and shows them how women of the Renaissance placed themselves in relation to the male canon.

The Petrarchist tradition is exemplified by four French sonneteers. However, we begin by examining a few sonnets from Petrarch's *Canzoniere* so that students can learn to identify the themes, concepts, imagery, and rhetorical devices associated with Petrarchism. Then I distribute a few poems by Maurice Scève and Pierre de Ronsard and follow with more extensive readings from Louise Labé and Gabrielle de Coignard to demonstrate the influence Petrarch exerted over French poetry throughout the Renaissance. We read Labé's sonnet cycle in its entirety but only a few sonnets from Coignard's *Sonnets chrétiens* at first. Students always enjoy reading Labé's passionate love sonnets. However, they generally find Coignard's devotional poetry less appealing. This essay considers the pedagogical advantages of reading Coignard's spiritual sonnets alongside Labé's love poetry.

Coignard's spiritual sonnets are introduced immediately after Labé. By this time, students have no difficulty recognizing the essentials of Petrarchism. I usually begin by a remark of the sort, "Labé's *Œuvres* had an instantaneous success." Indeed, the 1555 Lyon edition by the renowned publisher Jean de Tournes was followed by three additional reprints in 1556. Then, to encourage students to explore my assumption further, I ask the question, "Who read Louise Labé in sixteenth-century France? Do you think Gabrielle de Coignard had read her works or at least known of them when she wrote her sonnets?" (on Labé's audience see Berriot-Salvadore, "Héritières" 93–99; Jones, "City Women" 299–309). Skeptical students ordinarily respond that this is unlikely because Labé and Coignard were born thirty years apart and into very different socioeconomic milieus. Furthermore, they lived in cities that were overall quite different and at some distance from each other.

I take this opportunity to point out the affinities between the two sonneteers, beginning with personal circumstances. I note for instance that they were both born at an opportune place and time, Labé in Lyon in the 1520s, Coignard in Toulouse in the 1550s. I remind students of Lyon's strategic geographic situation (at the crossroads between France and Italy) and of the role the city played in the early 1500s as a flourishing center of banking, trade, and printing and as the cultural capital of France. Lyon's cosmopolitanism was mostly responsible for the renewed interest in classicism from Italy and for an unusual openness to new ideologies (see Rigolot, *Louise Labé* 13–20). Then, pointing at Toulouse on a map of the time (see "Late 1500s"), I note that it was the chief city of southern France in the 1500s. Its parliament, which acted as the king's court of justice, ruled Languedoc. However, after 1572, Toulouse sided with the Catholic League and soon became a stronghold of the Catholic faith in a region heavily infiltrated by Calvinism (for a map showing the religious and political divisions of France in the late 1500s and the exposed position of Toulouse, see "Religious and Political Divisions"). Also, when the Portuguese began importing refined indigo from India, the woad (blue dye) trade collapsed, and the city experienced a major economic crisis (see Wolff). Toulouse remained nevertheless an important cultural center throughout the Renaissance. Its university, which was second in reputation only to that of Paris, attracted many bright masters and students from the whole kingdom and beyond. Toulouse also continued to host the *Jeux floraux* ("Floral Games"), a two-hundred-year-old poetry contest in which, every May, poets from Languedoc and various parts of France contended for the prize of gold and silver flowers given at the expense of the city.

Louise Labé was the daughter of a prosperous rope manufacturer and married into the same trade. Her father, who strongly believed in the benefits of learning, saw to it that Louise received an education that included the traditional feminine skills of singing and embroidery and the less usual disciplines of the martial arts, horseback riding, rhetoric, Italian, Spanish, and Latin. This allowed her to enter the cultural elite of Lyon, especially coteries like the so-called École Lyonnaise, the most influential literary group before La Pléiade. At the end of her works Labé included twenty-four poems written in her honor in Greek, Latin, Italian, and so on, which attest to her prestige among her contemporaries. As for Gabrielle de Coignard, she was the daughter of a wealthy lawyer in the parliament of Toulouse. She married Pierre de Mansencal, a local nobleman and the son of a president of the parliament, who soon became president of the parliament himself. He died in 1573, leaving Gabrielle a widow at the age of twenty-three with two young daughters to raise. For more than twenty years Gabrielle's father served as the president of the Floral Games. We know little of Gabrielle's life, though we may safely assume, judging from her socioeconomic background and her family connections, that she led a highly cultivated life. She did not participate in the Floral Games herself, but she most likely came in contact with the learned poets who contended in the annual competitions. In 1554 Pierre de Ronsard, to whom she refers in several of her sonnets (see, e.g., sonnets 1 and 8) and for whom she wrote an epitaph (this is the last of her sonnet sequence; see Winn, "Gabrielle"), was awarded an honorary prize, and for the first time a sonnet appeared in the records of the *Livre rouge*, the record of the proceedings of the annual Floral games (on Toulouse's Floral Games, see Dawson 1–87).

Labé believed women ought to "elevate their spirits above their distaffs and spindles" and demonstrate to men that they were capable of great intellectual achievements. She viewed writing as a source of self-worth and personal satisfaction, as well as "a vehicle of authentic remembrance, allowing a woman to reflect on specific moments or phases of her inner experience" (Lesko Baker 37; for an interesting reading of the *Epistre à M.C.D.B.L.*, see 11–40). Coignard seems to have begun writing as an outlet for grief. They both wrote poetry, but, whereas Labé saw her works in print during her lifetime, Coignard never did. Labé, in a dedicatory epistle to her young noblewoman friend Clémence de Bourges, claims that it was her friends who first suggested to her that she should publish her works. François Rigolot sheds light on the very unusual circumstances behind this publication: Labé was often compared with the Greek poet Sappho, and as such represented a great tourist attraction for Lyon (*Louise Labé* 31–67). Nevertheless, it was Labé herself who applied for the royal imprimatur for her book. Coignard, on the other hand, had little to do with the publication, in 1594, of her *Œuvres chrétiennes*, the only one of her works we know today. It was her daughters, Jane and Catherine de Mansencal, who felt some years after their mother's death that the public should know how this exemplary Christian woman spent her widowhood.

Labé's sonnets tell of a woman's passionate love for a man but give us no clear idea of his personality or character. Coignard uses a series of sonnets to express similar feelings for Christ, who is depicted as the savior of the faithful. Each poet sings the lover's praises, each writes of the greatness of love as well as of the conflicting impulses—hope and despair, desire and frustration—that love generates, causing great suffering.

At this point I pause to remark that while such affinities do not prove that Coignard knew of Labé's works, they nevertheless reveal a common source of inspiration. Obviously both women knew of Petrarch or at least of French poets like Maurice Scève and Pierre de Ronsard who, by that time, had already made a name for themselves in writing Petrarchan verses. Finally, to consider further the claims I have made about the two sonneteers, I invite students to examine a few poems I have carefully selected. I divide the class into small groups of two or three and assign to each group a set of thematically paired poems, one by Labé, one by Coignard. Students are asked first to identify the Petrarchan theme or motif treated by the French poets, then to look for parallels and differences between the two.

Note that Coignard's *Sonnets chrétiens* are now available in modern editions in both French (*Œuvres chrétiennes* [1995]) and English (*Spiritual Sonnets*). This translation is available as well online (http://home.infionline.net/~ddisse/coignard.html). In addition, the site, maintained by the Bibliothèque Nationale de France, gives access to the complete 1594 edition of Coignard's *Œuvres chrestiennes.* Also, several sites provide the French text of various sonnets with no biobibliographical references or annotations: Sonnets 10 and 15 (http://poesie.webnet.fr/auteurs/coignard.html), sonnets 1, 10, and 45 (http://www.florilege.free.fr/florilege/coignard/), sonnets 108, 56, 117, 115, 122, 126, 102, 10, 25, 15, and 85, with a biographical notice from Jeannine Moulin's *La poésie féminine* (http://www.biblisem.net/indexmed.htm#c).

The first set of poems shows how the two French poets reconfigure Petrarchan themes and tropes. Students usually respond enthusiastically.

Je vis, je meurs: je me brule et me noye.
J'ay chaut estreme en endurant froidure:
La vie m'est et trop molle et trop dure.
J'ay grans ennuis entremeslez de joye:

Tout à un coup je ris et je larmoye,
Et en plaisir maint grief tourment j'endure:
Mon bien s'en va, et à jamais il dure:
Tout en un coup je seiche et je verdoye.

Ainsi Amour inconstamment me meine:
Et quand je pense avoir plus de douleur,
Sans y penser je me treuve hors de peine.

Puis, quand je croy ma joy estre certeine,
Et estre au haut de mon desiré heur,
Il me remet en mon premier malheur.

(Labé 186)[1]

Ha! que je suis extreme en ma condition,
Je ne garde jamais le milieu de la voye:
Car en mes actions quelque part que je soye,
Je n'aye jamais le sel de la discretion.

Je suis ores trop douce, or' sans compassion,
Ores j'ay trop de pleurs, ores j'ay trop de joye,
Je ne me puis facher pour chose que je voye,
Et puis je suis esmeue à toute occasion.

Helas! qui domtera ces passions estranges?
Ce sera toy, bon Dieu, qui façonnes et changes,
Les cœurs plus inconstans en un ferme rocher.

Delivre moy, Seigneur, de l'orage et tempeste,
Qui pour me submerger s'eslance sur ma teste:
Car tu es mon espoir, ma nef, et mon nocher

(Coignard 77–79)[2]

I live, I die: I burn and I also
drown.
I'm utterly hot and all I feel is cold.
Life is too soft and too hard for me
to hold;
my joy and my heavy burden are
mixed in one.

I laugh at the same time that I
weep and frown;
The tarnish of grief has marred my
pleasure's gold;

My good flies away, but stays until
it's old;
I wither just as I find out that I've
grown.

This is how love guides me, so
changeably
That when I think the pain has me
controlled,
With my very next thought I find
that I am free.

Then, just as I trust in joy so
certainly
That the peak of a yearned-for hour
makes me bold,

He shows me my familiar grief
unfold.

(Labé 187)

Ah! I am extreme in my condition;
I never keep to the middle of the
road.
In my actions, no matter where
I am,
I never have the salt of discretion.

First I am too sweet, then I am
without compassion;
In one instant I have too many
tears, the next I have too much
joy.
I avoid getting angry over the
things I might see,
And then I am moved by the
slightest little thing.

Alas! Who will temper these strange
passions?
It will be You, beneficient God,
who fashion and change
The most inconstant hearts into
solid rock.

Deliver me, Lord, from the storm
and the tempest
That thrust themselves onto my
head to submerge me:

For You are my hope, my ship, and
my captain.

(Coignard 77–79)

Having studied Petrarch's sonnets 134 and 229 ("Pace non trovo et non ò da far guerra" and "Cantai, or piango; et non men di dolcezza") as well as Ronsard's *Amours,* volume 1, sonnet 12 ("J'espere et crain") the preceding weeks, students have no difficulty recognizing as the source of Labé's sonnet 8 and Coignard's sonnet 41 a common theme in Petrarchan lyrics: the incomprehensible changeability of the self in love. They also note major differences in the way this theme is rendered by the two French sonneteers and the unexpected development in Coignard's poem. While the tension between stability and change constitutes the basis of both sonnets, only the pattern of fluctuation, or alternation of opposites, is fully developed in Labé's poem. In Coignard's, on the other hand, hints of an eventual resolution of the tension surface in the sestet. Connected with this idea is the pattern of regularity that emerges from the rhyme scheme in Coignard's sonnet, three quatrains in which the first line rhymes with the last (*abba abba cc deed*), a pattern especially favored by the French poet Clément Marot. In sharp contrast, Labé's sonnet takes after Petrarch with a sestet on two rhymes (*abba abba cdc cdd*), which contributes to the general impression of disorder and irregularity expressed throughout the poem.

On the basis of syntax and events both sonnets divide into an octave and a sestet that may be further subdivided into two units: the first line and the remaining five lines. In each sonnet, the octave presents a series of alternations that describes the lover's fluctuations between joy and suffering. Specific to Labé are the series of images (hackneyed conventions of her time for the most part) to describe these opposites, the staccato of antitheses (life/death, fire/water, hot/cold, torment/joy, laugh/sobs, brief/longlasting, dry/green) and the frequency of alternation: the first line contains two alternations and the following lines one each. This, combined with alliterations (especially in the first quatrain), word repetitions, and syntactic parallelisms, contributes to the impression of doomed fatality. In Coignard's poem each alternation spreads over two lines, except for lines 5 and 6, which contain one alternation each. For images Coignard turns to the Bible ("the salt of discretion" on line 4 may be inspired by Prov. 1.4, 2.10–11, etc.) and, most likely, to Luis de Granada's *Le vray chemin* (see fol. 273a), a contemporary devotional manual from which she borrows heavily elsewhere in her works, and she engages in a more abstract psychological analysis contrasting various emotions like compassion and indifference, excessive sensitivity and the most complete detachment.

Labé uses the first line of the sestet both to sum up the situation presented in the quatrains ("Ainsi") and to reveal the source of the contradictions: "Amour." In Coignard's poem, this central line serves a different purpose. Beginning with an exclamation ("Helas"), which is immediately followed by a question to create a greater sense of poignancy, line 9 introduces a shift, already hinted at in line 4, from a worldly perspective to a spiritual perspective, from the first-person singular to the second-person singular, from the persona's painful contradictions to the eventual resolution of her inner conflict. In the following line the agent of change is identified: "Ce sera toy, bon Dieu."

In Labé's poem the remaining five lines of the sestet take us back to the pattern of contradiction. Although alternations occur with less frequency—only two alternations in four lines—several elements hint at the idea that the pattern of alternation is inescapable: the repetitiveness of words and syntax ("Et quand je pense" / "Puis quand je croy"), and especially the overall structure of the passage. Both lines 9 and 14 sum up the lines that precede them. At the same time they complete each other, which is evident from the use of the pronoun "Il" in line 14 to replace the subject "Amour" from line 9. In addition, they are like parentheses within which can be found the description of the situation in lines 10 through 13. The resulting effect of inescapability and the repetition throughout the passage of verbs like "penser" and "croire" suggest the image of the female self who is obsessively turning over thoughts of her desperate love and its contradictions.

Coignard, in the last part of her poem, further explores the possibility of resolve. However, there is still a sense of great uncertainty in these lines, which is accentuated by the use of the future tense in line 10, the imperative in line 12, and the constant shift in focus: from God, who is first depicted as a powerful agent of change in line 12 (this is underlined by the superlative and the antithesis: "plus inconstans" / "ferme"), to a powerless "I" to, once again, the Almighty to whom the "I" finally turns as her unique resort to regain peace and stability. Coignard relies here on the imagery of the storm at sea, which she borrows from the Bible. Obviously it was also used by Petrarch and his followers to depict the tumultuous nature of love and the sense of loss, submersion, and drowning associated with it. Students are reminded of Petrarch's sonnet 235, "Lasso, Amor mi transporta ov'ir non voglio," which they have read two weeks earlier. Despite the continuous shift in moods in the sestet (confusion, uncertainty, hope, wish, and supplication for help), the expression of faith, in the last line, heightened by the present tense and the image of the ship captain ("Car tu es mon espoir, ma nef, et mon nocher"), suggests that the return to stability is a real possibility.

In sum, human love (whatever its object may be) is treated here from a similar point of view. Both poets underline its ambivalent or contradictory nature, which is the cause of great suffering. Instead of the irresolvable tension between desire and frustration, hope and despair, joy and suffering, Coignard concentrates on her faith in God the Savior and her anticipation of the resolution of her inner conflict.

Other pairings, just as fruitful, may include the following:

Clere Venus, qui erres par les
Cieus,
Entens ma voix qui en pleins
chantera,
Tant que ta face au haut du Ciel
luira,
Son long travail et souci ennuieus.

Mon œil veillant s'atendrira bien
mieus,
Et plus de pleurs te voyant gettera.
Mieus mon lit mol de larmes
baignera,
De ses travaus voyant témoins tes
yeus.

Donq des humains sont les lassez
esprits
De dous repos et de sommeil espris.
J'endure mal tant que le Soleil luit:

Et quand je suis quasi toute cassee,
Et que me suis mise en mon lit
lassee,
Crier me faut mon mal toute la
nuit.

(Labé 180)

Listen, bright Venus—errant in
the air!
Listen to my clear voice move, as
I sing
For your face, shining so high
above everything,
About my long labor and my
exhausting care.

My eyes grow softer with the
night's long stare,
And as you look you'll see much,
much more weeping.
More tears will dampen this bed,
with your eyes watching,
Though they trouble the sight of
witnesses so rare.

Obscure nuit, laisse ton noir
manteau,
Va reveiller la gracieuse aurore,
Chasse bien loin le soin qui me
devore,
Et le discours qui trouble mon
cerveau.

Voicy le jour gracieux, clair et
beau,
Et le soleil qui la terre decore,
Et je n'ay point fermé les yeux
encore,
Qui font nager ma couche toute
en eau.

Ombreuse nuit, paisible et
sommeillante,
Qui sçais les pleurs de l'ame
travaillante,
J'ay ma douleur cachée dans ton
sein,

Ne voulant point que le monde le
sçache,
Mais toutefois je te pry' sans
relasche,
De l'apporter aux pieds du
Souverain.

(Coignard 48–49)

Dark night, take leave of your black
cloak;
Go awaken the gracious dawn.
Chase far way the care that
devours me
And the chatter that troubles my
mind.

The gracious day, beautiful and
bright, is here
With the sun that adorns the
earth,
And I have yet to close my eyes,
Which flood my bed with water.

Humans are weary now. Their
spirits sleep
In a gentle hold of rest that
pulls them deep.
But my pain will last as long as
the sky is bright,

And when, almost completely
broken, I
Am pulled to my tear-wet bed,
I'll plead and cry
With hurt that will hold me
through the whole long
night.
(Labé 181)

Shadowy night, slumberous and
quiet,
You who know the tears of the
laboring soul,
I have hidden my pain in your
breast,

Not wanting the world to know
of it.
Nonetheless, I implore you without
reprieve
To carry it to the feet of the
Sovereign One.
(Coignard 48–49)

We have previously studied Petrarch's Sonnet 34, Scève's dizain 100, and Ronsard's *Amours*, volume 1, sonnet 148. Thus, in the situation described here, my students immediately recognize a theme that is frequently evoked by Petrarch and his followers: the lover's passionate outcries during lonesome and troublesome nights. They also note the analogous division of the poems into octave and sestet with the rhyme scheme typical of the Marotic sonnet (*abba abba cc deed*), the basic technique of comparison and contrast used by both Labé and Coignard, and the apostrophe by which the two poems open.

At first the most significant difference apparent to them is, in Coignard's sonnet 10, the apostrophe to the "Obscure nuit," as opposed to Labé's apostrophe in sonnet 5 to "Clere Venus": the goddess of love who can be expected to sympathize with the lovesick but who is also the evening star that, at night, during the time of its special ascendancy, dominates the earth from on high. Although this would ordinarily be the occasion to discuss the place mythology occupies in these works, for fear of being sidetracked I keep momentarily to the text and, in order to encourage further thinking, I invite my students to compare the way in which each poet describes Night/Venus in the quatrains. They note that night, in both poems, is associated with sleeplessness (Labé, line 5; Coignard, line 7), misery, and intense suffering as indicated by words like "long travail," "souci ennuieus," "travaus" (Labé, lines 4, 8), "soin," "devore," "trouble" (Coignard, lines 3–4), as well as the striking image of the "tear-wet bed"—an image drawn from the Psalms (see, e.g., 6.6–7) but also frequently found in Petrarchan lyrics: "O letticciuol che requie eri et conforto / in tanti affanni: di che dogliose urne / ti bagna Amor" ("O little bed that used to be a rest and comfort among so many / labors, with what sorrowful urns does Love bathe you"; *Petrarch's Lyric Poems* 392–93). However, whereas, in Labé's poem, pain is described as a sort of emission from the body ("Entens ma voix qui en plains chantera"; "de pleurs gettera"; lines 2, 6), in Coignard's, it appears more like a phenomenon from within that affects both body and mind: "le soin qui me devore"; "le discours qui trouble mon cerveau" (lines 3–4). Furthermore, in Coignard's poem, night is linked with images of darkness and gloominess ("obscure nuit," the color black, the sinister black cloak) and is further contrasted with the reassuring brightness of dawn, which, the speaker hopes, will chase away her somber and frightening thoughts. Night never takes on this nightmarish aspect in Labé's octave. Instead, night remains bright and clear because of the presence of Venus. The goddess of love, watching over earthly lovers, serves both as a witness to the misery they endure during the lonesome hours of night and a reminder of the brighter and happier moments of love. Labé, it has been previously shown, represents the experience of love in terms of these oppositions throughout her work. Gazing at Venus's shining face and eyes (lines 3, 8) while reminding the lover of the beloved's enticing beauty, renews desire and the sense of loss simultaneously and makes the lover's suffering worse: "Mon œil veillant s'attendrira bien mieus / Et plus de pleurs te voyant gettera" (lines 5–6).

Both Labé and Coignard rely on the same technique of contrast in the sestets. In Labé's sonnet, the structural organization of the sestet (where the first two and the last four lines rhyme), reinforced by the couplet's punning rhymes ("esprits" / "espris"), renders more evident the opposition between the "I" and other human beings. At the end of the day all are tired ("lassez esprits," "lassee") and even more so the lover ("cassee") after her silent endurance while the sun shines: "J'endure mal tant que le Soleil luit" (I think the translator is mistaken when she writes: "But my pain will last as long as the sky is bright"). Thus, when night settles down, ordinary people rest in tranquility. Labé's speaker, too, wishes for peace, but she lies awake and finds no rest. In the end, though, night proves beneficial to all: while most human beings recover from the fatiguing activities of daytime, the suffering lover is finally able to find relief in the confines of her chamber, where she can freely express the pain that she has been compelled to contain in public. Some critics claim that the poem ends on a negative note (see, for instance, L. Harvey 72), but when one considers the importance Labé attaches to the ability to express her existence as a lover ("montrer signe d'amante" ["show signs of love"]; *Complete Poetry* 198, 199; see Sonnet 14), one can better appreciate the cathartic value of night evoked in this sonnet.

Similar qualities are attributed to night by Coignard in her sestet. In sharp contrast to the octave, where night is said to be dark and dismal, the sestet pictures it as quiet and slumberous: "paisible et sommeillante." No explanation is provided for this shift in perspective. Instead, the mysterious and intimate aspect of night is emphasized in the next lines by words like "ombreuse" and "cachée." Also highlighted is night's liberating power: nighttime brings release to the self, who is now beyond scrutiny. For Coignard, though, night is not only the sympathetic and compassionate witness described by Labé but also the intermediary between the creature and her creator. The sonnet closes with the picture of the poet offering her suffering to God in the secrecy of the night.

Filled with pain, night for both poets remains nevertheless an occasion for liberation and catharsis. Whereas Labé's speaker gives in to the freedom night affords her for affective expression, the source of her sense of self, as shown in sonnet 14, the devotional subject in Coignard's sonnet 10 welcomes nocturnal tranquility to achieve closer proximity to God.

Just as apt to produce discussion is the next pairing:

Tant que mes yeux pourront larmes espandre,
A l'heur passé avec toy regretter:
Et qu'aus sanglots et soupirs resister
Pourra ma voix, et un peu faire entendre:

Tant que ma main pourra les cordes tendre
Du mignart Lut, pour tes graces chanter:
Tant que l'esprit se voudra contenter
De ne vouloir rien fors que toy comprendre:

Je ne souhaitte encore point mourir.

Je ne puis plus chanter, je ne puis plus escrire,
J'ay le cœur oppressé, j'ay l'estomac pantoix,
Je ne puis r'appeller la parole et la voix,
Je ne puis remonster les cordes de ma lire.

J'ay les yeux esblouys, je lamente et souspire,
Je veux ores mourir sous la divine croix,
Je ne veux plus bouger de l'ombre de ce bois,
Je veux estre à jamais subjecte à son empire.

Mais quand mes yeus je sentiray
tarir,
Ma voix cassee, et ma main
impuissante,

Et mon esprit en ce mortel sejour
Ne pouvant plus montrer signe
d'amante:
Prirey la Mort noircir mon plus cler
jour.

(Labé 198)

While my eyes can still pour out
fountains of tears,
Mourning our shared hours, gone
now, so long gone;
While my slow sighs and sobs can
still bemoan
The loss of you in a voice someone
might hear;

While my hands can still caress this
lute to clear
Praises for any grace you might
have shown,
And while my spirit remembers to
bend alone
On you, on nothing that's outside
your sphere—

I'll never want to reach the point
of death!
Though when my eyes grow dry
and this Voicing breath
Is broken and my hand is
powerless,

And when my spirit takes its mortal
flight,
Beating with no more signs of
love—yes, then, I'll press
Death to come and cover my
clearest day with night.

(Labé 199)

Je voy le Sainct des Saincts sur la
terre eslever,
Je voy son sang bouillant, où je me
veux laver,
Je voy son corps divin, chargé de
cicatrices.

Je voy ses bras cloués qu'il tend aux
esgarez,
Je voy son cœur ouvert aux pauvres
alterez,
Je le voy trespasser pour l'amour de
nos vices.

(Coignard 106–07)

I can no longer sing; I can no
longer write;
My heart is oppressed; my stomach
is all aflutter;
I cannot recall any words or rouse
my voice;
I cannot raise the strings of my lyre.

My eyes are blurry; I lament and sigh;
I want now to die beneath the
divine Cross;
I no longer want to move from the
shadow of this wood;
I want to be subject to its empire
forever.

I see the Saint of Saints rise up on
the earth;
I see His boiling blood, in which I
want to wash myself;
I see His divine body, covered with
scars;

I see His arms pierced with nails
that He stretches toward the
lost ones;
I see His heart open to the thirsty
poor,
I see Him die because of our love
for our vices.

(Coignard 106–07)

Although at first students are unsure of the real subject of these sonnets, they can immediately identify several points of comparison. What attracts their attention is fairly predictable: the Petrarchan imagery of tears, sobs, and sighs; the importance attached to the senses, as shown by words like "yeux," "voix," and "main"; the "lire" (or "lut") motif, a common symbol of the early modern poet; and various parallelisms and repetitions that structure the meaning of the poems.

On the basis of the rhyme scheme, both Labé and Coignard follow in the footsteps of French theoreticians with a sonnet dividing into two quatrains (*abba abba*), a couplet (*cc*), and a quatrain (*dede* in Labé's poem, *deed* in Coignard's). On the basis of syntax and meaning, however, Labé's sonnet divides into a nine-line unit and a five-line unit. Line 9 receives special emphasis, connected as it is with both the three preceding adverbial clauses that modify it and the following subordinate clause, introduced by "Mais." The coordinating conjunction signals the opposition between two states of feeling on which the poem's meaning is constructed. The speaker's present ability to manifest love and, consequently, selfhood, hence her desire to live ("Je ne souhaitte encore point mourir"; line 9), is contrasted with her wish to die ("Prirey la Mort noircir mon plus cler jour"; line 14) when all means of expressing her existence as a lover are lost ("Ne pouvant plus montrer signe d'amante"; line 13). The subordinating conjunction "Tant que," repeated three times, implies that the current state of things is subject to change unless certain conditions are fulfilled, but obviously the speaker would like to see it last forever: this is conveyed by the future tense, the *enjambement* of lines 3 and 4, and the unusually long (eight lines) hypotactic unit.

Coignard's sonnet, constructed exclusively on repetitious verbal patterns, consists of three units: a five-line unit beginning with "Je ne puis" or "J'ai" plus a negatively charged past participle; a three-line unit opening with "Je veux" or "Je ne veux pas"; and a sestet marked by the repetition of "Je voy." Each unit depicts a state of feeling. Lines 1–5 describe the poet's generalized incapacity for creative expression or rather the loss of her creative faculties of voice and hand. The short juxtaposed sentences and the galloping rhythm, particularly in the first two lines that contain two short sentences each, reproduce the sensation of shortness of breath described in this stanza. The reason for the body's current incapacity is revealed in lines 6–8: will prompts the poet to renounce all things worldly in order to embrace more fully spiritual matters ("la divine croix"). In Ignatius of Loyola's *Exercices spirituels* (1548), from which Coignard draws here and elsewhere in her sonnets, will must cooperate with memory and understanding for successful meditation. Even though the alternation in lines 6–8 between "Je veux ores," "Je ne veux plus," and "Je veux estre à jamais" suggests the fluctuating instability of her will, the speaker insists on the fact that she is no longer who she was. Such metamorphosis leads to the wish to die ("Je veux ores mourir"), which is represented, on the physical level, as a deliberate step toward immobility ("Je ne veux plus bouger") and, on the spiritual level, as a willful self-abnegation out of her love for God ("Je veux estre à jamais subjecte à son empire")—a claim that seems to be contradicted by the prominence given to the "Je" in the poem (no fewer than eighteen occurrences). Indeed, the sestet depicts a crucified Christ, but the position of the first-person singular at the beginning of each verse suggests that the focus of attention continues to be the subject of the gaze ("*Je* voy") rather than its object.

Obviously the question of subjectivity is central to Labé's and Coignard's poems. In Labé's poem the first-person singular is relatively scarce (two occurrences), and each time it directs our attention to the subject's ability to feel ("je sentiray"), which is made equivalent to life itself ("Je ne souhaitte encore point mourir"). Over the pronoun "Je" Labé chooses the synecdoche, thus shifting the emphasis away from the subject onto her eyes, voice, hand, and mind. Indeed, what counts most for Labé's speaker is what lies in her power ("pourront," "pourra") and what she desires for her own contentment and well-being ("se voudra contenter"), that is, her ability and desire to communicate the drives, hopes, and contradictions of desperate love and to sing the praises of her beloved. Her quest for internal selfhood is made possible through this authentic self-expression and through interaction with ("avec *toy*"), commemoration of ("*tes* graces chanter"), and "containment" of ("riens fors que toy comprendre") the absent beloved. In Coignard's poem the constant focus on the self contrasts with Christ's altruistic love and self-sacrifice as evidenced by the images of the open arms ("tend aux"), the open side and kind heart ("ouvert aux," "trespasser pour l'amour de"), and the redeeming blood in line 10 ("sang . . . , où je me veux laver"). On the one hand, this fixation on the self, which is a form of self-absorption, shows how remote Coignard's speaker still is, despite the momentary act of sight evoked in the sestet, from her quest for *unio*. Indeed, union with the divine requires that the ego lose its separate identity. On the other hand, we cannot deny the fact that the attention is drawn, at least momentarily, to Christ's sufferings: the body with its open wounds and scars, the arms nailed to the cross, the blood splattering. In his *Exercices spirituels* Ignatius of Loyola urges the exercitant to imagine himself a witness of Christ's Passion and employ each of the five senses in turn in order to enter the scene more fully and achieve intimacy that saves. Reminiscent of Ignatius of Loyola's "exercices spirituels," the scene described in the sestet, with its gory detail and appeal to the senses and the speaker's bodily participation in Christ's suffering, seems to indicate progress toward the desired state of *unio.* Indeed the description of the speaker's indisposition and her wish to die expressed in line 6 should be read in conjunction with the sestet's references to Christ's suffering and his consent to die in the sinner's stead in line 14. Thus, the movement in Coignard's poem from negative to positive, from the body's complete shutdown in the first five lines to the momentary enlightenment in the sestet, seems to suggest that the speaker's goal of union with Christ is within her reach. In contrast, the opposite movement (from positive to negative) in Labé's poem gives greater intensity to the speaker's fear that someday she may no longer be capable of making creative use of her passion through her eyes, voice, hands, and mind. In the end, whereas Coignard's speaker voluntarily relinquishes her creative faculties in her attempt to achieve intimacy with God (see also sonnet 86, "Je veux quicter les vers, je veux laisser la muse / J'abandonne le lut, je ne veux plus chanter" ["I want to quit these verses, I want to leave the muse; / I am abandoning the lute; I shall not sing any longer"; 118–19]), Labé's speaker places the highest value on her ability to sing of her love as the key to the expansion of her selfhood (see Lesko Baker 145–53; Moore 94–124).

Other pairings that work effectively include Labé's sonnet 8 and Coignard's sonnet 44; Labé's sonnet 17 and Coignard's sonnet 79 or sonnet 92 or 96; Labé's sonnet 19 and Coignard's sonnet 19; and the anaphoric blazonlike poems in "ô" (Labé's sonnet 2 and Coignard's sonnet 25) or other laudatory pieces like Labé's sonnet 10 and 11 and Coignard's sonnets 62 and 70. Usually three to five examples suffice for students to find some comfort level with Coignard's poetry, but one may request a short paper as well. Topics that have worked well in my class include the use of mythology in Labé's sonnet 19 and Coignard's sonnet 19; the poets' attitudes toward writing and humanistic learning, based on a selection of sonnets from Coignard (for example 1, 2, 8, 14, 111, and 124) and Labé's *Epistre à M.C.D.B.L.*; their attitudes toward worldly concerns, the here and now, life and death (I suggest comparing Coignard's sonnets 3, 6, 11, 18, or 30 with Labé's sonnet 13 and 18); the treatment of the distaff motif in Coignard's sonnet 122 and Labé's *Epistre à M.C.D.B.L.* or the night motif in Labé's sonnet 9 and Coignard's sonnets 13, 17, 45, or 80.

In sum, without attempting to prove a direct influence, this comparative approach effectively illustrates the continued vogue Petrarchism enjoyed throughout the Renaissance and the many variations it generated in early modern France. Students can appreciate the ways in which each poet adapts Petrarchan conventions and the sonnet form to her own needs. Through her appropriation of these topoi Labé finds an empowering source for constructions of female agency and subjectivity. Coignard, on the other hand, uses Petarchan lyrics to articulate the contradictory emotions that accompany her spiritual quest. This is the first step in her search for union with the divine. In the second part of her works, she will abandon mundane poetry as exemplified by the popular Petrarchan sonnet in favor of an antipagan approach and forms like the stance, the hymn, and the *discours,* generally less subjective and therefore better suited to celebrate her divine lover. In comparison with Coignard, who wrote exclusively French sonnets as practiced by Marot and defined by Peletier du Mans (*abba abba cc deed* or *dede*), Labé appears to my students to be more inventive in how she explores the possibilities of contrast and symmetry among the different parts of the sonnet (*abba abba cdccdd*, etc.). Finally, students can now identify with little help common traits between Labé and Coignard such as the highly emotional and introspective nature of their poetry; the straighforwardness and sobriety of their writing (i.e., the absence of mythological trappings), as opposed to the male sonneteers they have read; the tendency to construct meaning on repetitious word patterns; and other characteristics belonging to oral language like apostrophes, interjections, exclamations, and so on. Obviously this comparative approach has increased my students' understanding and appreciation of Gabrielle de Coignard's sonnets. We can now further explore her *Œuvres chrétiennes* in the context of religious lyric.

Notes

1. Citations to Labé, in French and English translation, are from *Complete Poetry.*

2. The French and English translation of Coignard are from *Spiritual Sonnets.*

Deborah Lesko Baker

Teaching Louise Labé's Prose in Translation: The Dedicatory Letter and the *Debate of Folly and Love*

Although I long regarded my principal research and teaching field as that of early modern French lyric poetry and poetics, my intensive study of Louise Labé's verse carried with it an imperative that I explore with equal attention the two prose texts that constitute the bulk of her 1555 *Complete Works*: the two-page dedicatory letter to Mademoiselle Clémence de Bourges and the some two-thousand-line mythological prose dialogue, *The Debate of Folly and Love*. While working on a critical volume devoted to Labé's complete works, I experienced the difficulties presented by portions of the original French texts of these prose works, with their lengthy, convoluted, and often allusive sentences composed in the evolving grammar and lexicon of the sixteenth century. Getting past these issues well enough to stimulate appreciation in the classroom for Labé's prose works as important literary and cultural documents opened up yet a new challenge. Although I was able to spark some interest in the shorter polemical text of the letter, my efforts to introduce excerpts of the *Debate* revealed how hard it was for even advanced undergraduate French majors to engage this work.

I came to reconfront these challenges as I was involved in writing new translations of the prose texts for the first bilingual edition of Labé's complete works. During this process I concluded that for the anglophone public, in addition to critical scholarship, translation is a crucial resource for the understanding of Labé's prose texts—not only for those English speakers who do not read French but also for most of those who do.[1] Indeed, for many native English students with varying levels of competence in French, a careful analysis of the works in translation, in juxtaposition (more or less closely, as course context requires) with the original French, will produce the most satisfying learning experience.

I have developed a pedagogical approach that aims to integrate the study of the dedicatory letter with the *Debate* so as to demonstrate their intertextual subtlety and enliven their appeal. For I am convinced that the dedicatory letter and the *Debate*, despite their differences, are best studied and appreciated in close dialogue with each other, and I outline a thematic structure and set of textual examples through which this dialogical reading might be done. Such a reading reveals the internal coherence of Labé's works and makes the discovery of her writing not only more intellectually satisfying but more fun. For Labé is a gifted comic writer, and although the underpinnings of her discourse on female selfhood and male-female relations in both society and love can be profound and provocative, it is often their transmission through her comic wit—especially as enhanced by the translation of her original language into idiomatic English—that can make or break the experience of enjoying her works. Since my emphasis here is on teaching the texts in translation, I refer to and cite all passages in English.[2]

Context: Setting Up Part I of the Study

To pursue a productive reading of the dedicatory letter in dialogue with the *Debate*, my first step, after I assign a preliminary reading of the letter alone, is to contextualize Labé's prose and her feminism within the debate on the position of early modern women popularly termed the *querelle des femmes*. Using as my fundamental sources the classic essay by Joan Kelly "Early Feminist Theory and the *Querelle des Femmes*" and the opening chapters of two groundbreaking volumes, Constance Jordan's *Renaissance Feminism*, and Ann Rosalind Jones's *The Currency of Eros*, I structure my introduction to the *querelle* in three parts. First, I situate the notion and characteristics of an early modern feminism in relation to societal transitions between the Middle Ages and the Renaissance stemming from the changing position of the aristocracy and the rise of the middle class. Second, I provide a short history of the conflicted literary attitudes toward women coming out of the medieval courtly tradition on the one hand and the ecclesiastical and secular bourgeois traditions on the other. Third, I give an overview of the varied "defenses" of women in reaction to these attitudes up until Labé's time, focusing on the portrayal of women as exempla, on their presentation as courtly and Petrarchan stereotypes, and finally on profemale treatises on education, of which Labé's dedicatory letter is the first to be written by a French woman in the sixteenth century.

This situating of Labé's participation in the *querelle*'s defenses of women affords an excellent transition to a fuller introduction to the life, writings, and social positioning of the author herself, for which chapter 5 of Jones's book and the general introduction to the new bilingual edition of Labé's works (*Complete Poetry and Prose*) are helpful supports. As a prelude to the biographical presentation of Labé, I discuss Lyon as the cultural capital of France throughout much of the sixteenth century and as a city in which the rise of a bourgeois economy contributed to a flexibility in social class structure that opened opportunities in the public domain for certain women. I then review Labé's family background, education, domestic situation, and literary production in the context of issues faced by a woman who takes up the pen in response to the polemical debates surrounding her gender and her times. This background, accompanied by the assignment of a second reading of the dedicatory letter, serves as a segue to a discussion on what students have found most striking in this text overall, followed by an examination of the two principal thematic strands of its chronological development: the importance of education and study for women in the public sphere (section 1) and the importance of writing and self-expression for women in the private sphere (section 2). This examination sensitizes students to the contrasting narrative postures between which Labé alternates in her text (e.g., adherence to confrontation versus conventionality, advocacy of collective progress versus individual growth) as well as to the specific language she uses to structure each rhetorical stance. Once the strategies and stakes of the letter have been explored, portions of the *Debate* can then be assigned and illuminated with respect to the epistolary text.

Part I of the Study

The first part considers the challenging of gender roles in the public sphere. We read the dedicatory letter (section 1) and the *Debate* (discourses 1, 2, and 3). Although references to women's roles in the public and private spheres are interspersed throughout both of Labé's prose texts, it is helpful from a pedagogical perspective to note that the focus on women in public life occurs in roughly the first half of the dedicatory letter and in the first three discourses of the *Debate.* Our classwork thus centers on how the *Debate*'s theatrical presentation comically restages three crucial elements of Labé's social vision: her "call to arms" for women to pursue education so they can compete intellectually and practically with men; her critique of the long-standing conception of women as mere reflections of the male gaze; and her encouragement of solidarity among women and of mutually supportive partnerships between women and men.

We begin by exploring how the *Debate*'s first discourse—its opening encounter between Love and Folly at the door of Jupiter's palace—dramatically reenacts the confrontational gesture at the beginning of Labé's dedicatory letter against the obstacles to female education and expression put forth by men:

> *Folly.* From what I can see, I'll be the last to arrive at Jupiter's banquet, where I believe everyone's expecting me. But I see, too, so it seems, Venus's son, who is just as late as I am. I must *get past him*, so no one accuses me of being late and lazy.
>
> *Love.* Who is this *madwoman* pushing *past* me so rudely? What's her big hurry? If I'd seen you, I would have *stopped* you from *getting ahead* of me.
>
> *Folly.* You wouldn't have been able to *stop* me, young and weak as you are. So goodbye now, I'm going in to say that you're arriving at your own leisure.
>
> *Love.* Oh no you won't, because before you get away from me, I'll show you that you mustn't meddle with me.
>
> *Folly.* Let me go, and don't try to *stop* me, for it would be *shameful* of you to pick a fight with a woman.
>
> (47–48)

First, it is useful to examine the importance of Cupid's reference to Folly as "this *madwoman*" both in his opening line and when he repeats the insult a few lines later (49).[3] We discuss how this negatively charged reference highlights the female protagonist's transgressive rupture of social norms staged in her cutting in ahead of her male counterpart—an act that parallels Labé's demand for women to move forward in their pursuit of education. The opening exchange plays repeatedly on alternating actions of *moving ahead* and *blocking passage* as Folly pushes past Cupid and Cupid vows to stop her. Students will quickly recognize that these are the same verbs used by Labé to issue her social challenges in the letter, when in her jubilant opening address to her female Lyonnais co-citizen she speaks of how male law no longer can *stop* women from pursuing study and, later, how women might not only equal but *surpass* men in learning:

> Since the time has now come, Mademoiselle, when men's harsh laws no longer prevent women from applying themselves to study and learning, it seems to me that those who have the chance should take advantage of this well-deserved freedom—so fervently desired by our sex in the past—to pursue them, and to show men how *wrong* they were to deprive us of the benefit and *recognition* these things might have given us. . . . I cannot carry out on my own the sincere wish I have for our sex, to see it *surpass or equal* men not only in physical beauty, but in knowledge and virtue. . . . Beyond the acclaim our sex will receive, we will benefit the public good, since men will put more effort and study into valuable domains of knowledge in order to avoid the shame of seeing themselves surpassed by women, over whom they have always claimed to be *superior* in almost everything. (43)

Other elements of shared rhetoric between these passages from the letter and their reenactment in the first scene of the *Debate* soon become obvious. The "wrong" long done by men in blocking women from attaining "recognition" through study and the "shame" prospectively projected onto men should they be outmatched by women in intellectual endeavors are amusingly made concrete by Folly's admonition that Cupid should be ashamed to hold her back by doggedly continuing his aggressive quarrel. I also alert students to the broader problem of women's "recognition" by men raised in the *Debate* by Cupid's outraged opening question—which shows not only his view of Folly as a mad, unentitled transgressor but also his failure to know *who she is*. This question suggests from the very outset, even before Folly put out Love's eyes, that Love is, figuratively speaking, blind and that he will have a dual problem concerning knowledge in respect to others and in respect to himself. This dual problem is emphasized as the opening scene continues and the dialogue plays on the repetition of various forms of the verb "to know" or "to recognize":

> *Folly*. You're really showing how misguided you are to take so badly what I did to you in fun. *You simply don't know yourself for who you are* if you can't accept that I will have the upper hand if you get in my way. . . . Don't you see that you're just a little boy—so puny in size that I would hardly be afraid of you even if I had one arm tied around my back?

Love. Do you know who I am?
Folly. You are Love, Venus's son.
Love. So how is it that you act so boldly in front of me, when—however small I may seem to you—I am the most feared and dreaded among gods and men? And you, a woman *I don't even know*, dare to consider yourself greater than me? Your youth, your sex, and the way you act already prove you *wrong*, but even more than that your ignorance, which keeps you from *recognizing* the high rank that I hold. (49)

Like the mythical figure of Narcissus, Cupid does not *know himself* for who he really is and ironically rebukes Folly for not "recognizing" *his* superior rank. But in fact it is he who repeatedly refers to Folly as "a woman I don't even know" and conflates her female sex with "ignorance"—thus exposing his own failure to "recognize" *her* respective rank and reputation.

The issue of knowing women for who they really are and not just for how they are perceived and validated by men allows the class to transition to a key intertextual moment between the first part of the letter and discourse 2 of the *Debate*. In this short scene between now-blinded Cupid and his mother Venus, the famed goddess of love decries the impact of her son's sorry state on *her*: "And thus Folly, the most wretched *thing* of them all, has the power to rob Venus of the *greatest pleasure* she had in life—which was to have her son, Love, be able to *look at her. . . . My only source of wealth is my beauty*" (61). We discuss this melodramatic exclamation as embodying Labé's critique of the conventional omnipotence of the male gaze in valorizing female identity—referring back to her letter's plea for women to "adorn" themselves with their written ideas, "rather than with *chains, rings, and lavish clothing,* all of which we cannot truly consider our own except by social custom" (43). We pursue the link between Venus's desperate confession of a purely male-constructed identity and her move to attack and even dehumanize Folly in her opening words with a misogynist rhetoric that continues throughout the scene and spills into discourse 3—where her plea to Jupiter for vengeance culminates in her characterization of Folly as "the most despicable Fury that hell has ever known" (63).

The internalization by Venus of the omnipotent male gaze, as well as her vitriolic assault on Folly before the supreme figure in the patriarchal hierarchy, provides a dark imperative fueling Labé's impassioned case in her dedicatory letter for sustained solidarity among women in their pursuit of an independent female identity based on intellectual achievement. Furthermore, we can look at this third discourse as the point in the *Debate* where the letter's famous vision below of an appropriate public partnership between women and men is also negotiated:

> I can do no more than urge virtuous ladies to raise their minds a bit above their distaffs and spindles, and to dedicate themselves to making the world understand that *if we are not made* to be *in command*, we nevertheless should not be scorned as *partners*, *in domestic as in public affairs* by *those who rule* and demand obedience. . . . For this reason, we have to *spur one another on* to such a worthy undertaking. (43)

In discourse 3, we first discuss how Venus's antagonistic counterexample to the letter's proposed solidarity among women compels Folly to present the most positive posture possible before Jupiter's court as her case prepares to go to trial. We then examine how Folly follows Labé's rhetorical strategy in the letter of moderating her assertive stance by defering to masculine rule while working to form a favorable yet realistic partnership with the king and his other male deities. Folly states,

> "Noble and supreme Jupiter, I stand ready here to respond to whatever Love wishes to ask me. However, I have one request to make of you. . . . I beg you to allow one of the gods to speak for me and another for Love, so that the rank of the parties involved won't receive more consideration than the merits of the case . . . I beg you to *charge* someone to *protect* me and to *handle my defense*." (63)

Although it might seem at first glance that Folly is simply ceding her voice to a court-appointed attorney, she is in fact cleverly creating the most harmonious partnership possible with Jupiter and the court representative she selects (Mercury) and, moreover, through this request for intervention is ensuring that her public stature vis-à-vis Cupid will remain as equal and unprejudiced as possible. It is also useful to point out here that Folly's voice will *not* be totally absent from the trial proceedings, since when the case is actually argued in discourse 5, Folly will interrupt Mercury's oratory forcefully at several points to insert her own voice and contributions to her defense.

Context: Setting Up Part 2 of the Study

At this point of transition to the subsequent sections of both prose texts, it bears reminding students that in the quotation from Labé's letter (43), cited above, there is a plea for a partnership not only in public but in domestic affairs, which is an effective segue into an examination of how the author interrogates the private realms of love and self-expression. To make the most of this part of the study it is important (unless her lyric has been studied earlier) to provide a bit of background to Labé's poetry and poetics, specifically to the Petrarchan tradition within and against which she writes.[4] For the purposes of our study of the letter and the *Debate*, I focus on four features of that tradition: the inevitable inaccessibility of the female beloved, the anguished and conflicted psychological state of the self-turned male lover, the lover's view of his own desire as a moral failing and a dangerous force, and the perceived paralyzing effect of suffering on self-expression. Labé's exploitation and subversion of these features are then revealed in readings and class discussions of sonnet 1 (her view of desire), sonnet 8 (her acceptance of the emotional contradictions provoked by love), sonnet 14 (her embrace of ongoing self-expression, even in suffering), and sonnet 18 (her vision of attainable, mutual erotic, and spiritual love).

Part 2 of the Study

The second part focuses on the challenging of gender roles in the private sphere. The class reads the dedicatory letter (section 2) and the *Debate* (discourses 4 and 5). In returning to Labé's prose, we observe that after the focus on women in public life in the first half of the letter and discourses 1 through 3 of the *Debate*, there is generally a more concerted move to the realm of private experience in the second half of the letter and in discourses 4 and 5 of the *Debate*. At the outset we encounter something of a challenge in the juxtaposition of these portions of the two texts, since while the *Debate* explicitly invokes the problematics of both male-female love and verbal self-expression, the letter, at least at first glance, seems to elide the direct discussion of love in its emphasis on writing as a key to women's self-renewal and growth. Especially since students will just have studied examples of Labé's own love poetry in the Petrarchan context, an effective approach eventually to addressing this seeming divergence in emphasis is to begin by studying the highlights of the conversation on love between Cupid and Jupiter in the short discourse 4 of the *Debate*. Here, in responding to Jupiter's bewilderment over the young love god's adored status among human beings—despite the suffering love causes them—Cupid first provides an aphoristic assessment of his own worldly success: "The true greatness of Love lies in this: *when we love someone who treats us badly*" (67). I encourage students to see that in this sardonically amusing statement Cupid is actually invoking the fundamental dynamics of conventional Petrarchan love, which is based on a painful nonreciprocity between lover and beloved. We then link this dynamics of inequality and the disempowerment it produces to the extended comic critique of Petrarchan love made by Folly's representative, Mercury, in discourse 5, especially in his presentation of its renowned destabilizing effects:

> *To have a heart divided against itself; to be at peace one minute, at war the next*, and then at truce the next; to cover up and hide one's pain; to change expressions a thousand times a day; to feel the blood rush up and redden one's face, then suddenly drain away, to go in search of what torments us, while pretending to run away from it / and yet to dread finding it; for every laugh, to breathe a thousand sighs; to deceive oneself, to burn from afar, but to freeze up close; to stumble on our words and fall abruptly silent—aren't these all signs of someone no longer in control of his senses? (123)

However, discourses 4 and 5 of the *Debate* do not simply expose and critique the conventional imbalances and oxymora of Petrarchan love. We next explore the latter part of discourse 4, where, in commiserating with Jupiter's dissatisfaction over his inability to inspire love in the women he conquers, Cupid himself surprisingly sets forth an *alternative* view, one that likewise will be echoed by Mercury in discourse 5:

> *Love. . . . Love thrives best when things are equal. . . .* And then you will feel a kind of *satisfaction* unlike anything you have known in the past, and you will experience twice the pleasure. For there's every bit as much *pleasure* to be had in *being kissed and loved*, as in *kissing and loving*. (69 [discourse 4])
>
> *Mercury.* Once he's gotten started, the lover must do two things: he must let it be known he's in love, and *he must make himself loved in return*. (125 [discourse 5])

In examining Cupid's second declaration, I try to heighten students' awareness of the extent to which the love god is communicating contradictory messages with respect to his earlier statement. Specifically, with his newfound call for equality and his notion of doubled pleasure deriving from a completely reciprocated vision of love, Cupid (like Mercury) is putting into question his own conventional mythology, demonstrating the very un-Petrarchan model that Labé herself envisions in male-female love relations and asserts in her insistence on mutually expressed and fulfilled love, both physical and spiritual, in her most famous sonnet 18: "Then, *both* sweetly bent / on love, we'll enter joy through *doubleness*, / and we'll each have *two loving lives* to tend: / one in our single self, one in our friend" (207, lines 8–10).

At this juncture, it is a fertile moment to go back to the second part of the dedicatory letter to evaluate in what ways Cupid's and Mercury's "double" mythology of love possibly informs and illuminates Labé's valorization of female study, writing, and selfhood. The letter's transition between the public and private benefits of these pursuits sets up an intriguing comparison and a compelling new network of vocabulary:

> Yet if there is something else beyond fame and honor to recommend in the study of letters, the *pleasure* it typically provides ought to be an incentive to every one of us. This pleasure is different than in other diversions, for when people have gotten as much *enjoyment* from them as they want, they can boast of nothing except having passed the time. Study, to the contrary, brings with it a unique inner satisfaction that stays with us far longer. We take *joy* in the past, and it serves us better than the present, but the pleasures of the senses immediately slip away and never return, and the memory of them is sometimes as painful as the acts were sweet. (43, 45)

Students will quickly appreciate that the change in focus between external and internal validation is accomplished through the transcendence of fame by *pleasure* and that, according to the narrator, this very phenomenon of pleasure, elaborated by a series of quasi-synonymous terms (*enjoyment*, *satisfaction*, *joy*), stands to be greater and longer lasting in response to intellectual activities than other pursuits. Given the eroticized language used to describe and deflate the "pleasures of the senses," we discuss how Labé may well be referring here to the disappointments and pain of romantic connections, thus indirectly invoking (and illustrating) Cupid's aphorism in discourse 4 on the unbalanced dynamics of Petrarchan love.

We then pursue how Labé's specific encomium to female *writing* in the following lines actually weaves together the thematics of love and self-expression in a provocative fashion that recalls Cupid's own subsequent advocacy of mutually based and nurtured love:

> But when we happen to put our thoughts down in writing . . . by going back much later to what we wrote, we can nevertheless recapture the moment and state of mind we were in before. Then we experience twice the enjoyment, for we rediscover the *pleasure* we had in the past in the subject we were writing about. . . . And beyond this, the judgment that our second impressions allow us to make of our earlier ones repays us with an unparalleled *satisfaction*. (45)

Here the ongoing, almost hyperbolic deployment of eroticized language—especially the doubling of pleasure deriving from shared love (reminiscent of Cupid's second amatory "lesson" to Jupiter)—leads the students to recognize that in her letter Labé seeks to replicate *metaphorically* her vision of a fulfilled mutual love experience through the enriching and enduring relationship that a woman can forge with her own writing. This exciting new way of viewing a woman's role and her potential might even suggest a modification to Apollo's famous adage in his defense of Cupid in discourse 5: "In short, *the greatest pleasure there is, after love, is talking about it*" (85). Indeed perhaps for Labé the greatest pleasure of all, even more than putting forth new public and private models of interpersonal connections, lies in giving passionate *voice* to those connections.

Finally, I like to end my teaching of Labé's prose by insisting that the notion of desire, broadly defined, is as much of a catalyst and motor for her prose texts as it is for her much better known love poetry. For just as in her lyric she challenges the Petrarchan worldview by insisting on the expressive perpetuation of her erotic desire, however painful, as a condition for her very existence (sonnets 1 and 14), in her prose she challenges the social ethos and practice of her times by assimilating the desire of the female collective for a new kind of intellectual freedom ("this well-deserved freedom—so fervently *desired* by our sex in the past" [43, line 4]) and by "translating" her global conception of love as "nothing other than a desire for the pleasure of meeting and uniting with the object of our love" (123 [*Debate*, Discourse 5]) into a vision of fulfillment through communion with one's own thinking and writing as well as through relationships with others. As we see Mercury (the mouthpiece for Folly and by extension for Labé) declare in the final pages of the *Debate*, "Since Love is *desire*, or since whatever it might be, it can't exist without *desire*, we must acknowledge that once this passion takes hold of a man, *it alters and changes him*" (145). And so can desire—in all its forms—alter and change a woman, enabling her to redefine the goals and priorities of her gender in the public and private world—a notion that students can take with them from this dawn of early modern feminism into their twenty-first-century lives.

Notes

1. For a selection of critical sources in English with an in-depth focus on Labé's prose, see Benkov; Clark-Evans; Cottrell, "Problematics"; Jones, *Currency* 11–35; Jordan; Larsen, "Louise Labé's *Débat*"; Lesko Baker; Losse; Rigolot, "Gender versus Sex Difference"; and Yandell, *Carpe Corpus* 111–27.

2. The English translations are taken from my 2006 edition of *Louise Labé: Complete Poetry and Prose*. All italics are mine in this essay.

3. I will sometimes refer to Love by his more well-known name in English, Cupid. This variation is especially useful further on in the essay to clarify the distinction between "love" as a concept and "Love" ("Cupid") as the *Débat*'s male protagonist.

4. For a selection of background sources in English for the Petrarchan tradition, see the studies listed in the works cited by Braden, *Petrarchan Love*; Kennedy; Lesko Baker; and Moore.

Part IV

Current Resources

Colette H. Winn

Print Resources for Teaching and Further Study

The interest in French women writers of the Renaissance and Reformation has exploded alongside the vital feminist critique, in North America, that began in the late 1970s and the publication, in France, of important works devoted to texts by and about women starting in the mid 1980s (Guillerm et al.; Lazard, *Images*; Berriot-Salvadore, *Femmes*; Timmermans). Women writers, previously known only to bibliophiles, have since been exhumed, and a significant number of multigenre anthologies of works and modern editions as well as English translations of texts by individual women have become available for both the specialist and the less experienced reader. Many instructors have already begun to include works by early modern women writers in both their graduate and undergraduate courses. However, those who are contemplating incorporating women writers into their courses for the first time may need guidance navigating the extensive interpretive material and numerous new editions of works by these writers, with whom they may be less familiar. The purpose of the following discussion is to present an overview of resources currently available.

The Instructor's Library

Scholarly Editions

One of the greatest contributions of Évelyne Berriot-Salvadore's *Les femmes dans la société française de la Renaissance* lies in the abundance of primary sources that she has brought to light, some of them archival and some written by women. Many of the texts by women uncovered two decades ago by this French scholar are now available in modern editions. I here limit discussion to the authors studied in this volume.

Colette H. Winn's 1995 critical edition of Gabrielle de Coignard's *Œuvres chrétiennes* brings to the public the 129 *Sonnets spirituels*, which were reprinted in 1900, as well as longer devotional poems, which had not been reissued since 1613, the date of the third edition of the collection. Winn's introduction sets forth what little is known about this late-sixteenth-century poet from Toulouse; the publication history of her works; the cultural, literary, and religious contexts for her writing; and the poetic genres she cultivated. The notes to the text in Winn's edition, for the most part, elucidate ancient and biblical sources as well as historical events and indicate points of comparison with contemporary poets. With the exception of the punctuation, which has been modernized for the sake of legibility, the text has been little altered. A glossary of archaic words completes the edition.

In addition to Slatkine's 1977 reprint edition of Hélisenne de Crenne's 1560 *Œuvres*, which includes Claude Colet's revisions, several modern editions are now available. As opposed to the two 1968 editions of *Angoysses* (ed. Demats; Vercruysse), which reproduced only the first part of the novel, subsequent editions offer the text in its entirety. Christine de Buzon's 1997 edition of *Les angoysses douloureuses qui procedent d'amours* is based on the first edition of the novel, which appeared in 1538, and this edition includes an authoritative introduction, the original engravings, the variants of all sixteenth-century editions, copious notes, a summary of the novel, a mythological dictionary, and a useful glossary. Jean-Philippe Beaulieu's 2005 edition (*Angoisses*), in the low-cost paperback series produced by the press of the Université de Saint-Étienne, uses as its base the 1543 L'Angelier edition (*Œuvres*), the sole edition in which Crenne's stylistic particularities, notably her Latinisms, have been left intact. The orthography and punctuation have been modernized for greater legibility, but the flavor of the original language has been preserved, and a glossary of archaic usage is provided at the end of the volume. Whereas Buzon's edition is a must for the Hélisenne de Crenne scholar, Beaulieu's edition, which features a concise introduction, adequate notes, and mythological clarifications and is affordably priced, is specifically intended for the classroom. In his insightful preface, Beaulieu recounts the publication history of Crenne's works and discusses, among other things, the conflict between sensual love and morality in Crenne's works and the relation of the novel to the *Epistres* and the *Songe de madame Helisenne.*

Surprisingly, Hélisenne de Crenne's *Epistres familieres et invectives* appeared in a modern English translation (*Renaissance Woman*) before a modern French edition was made available. In the mid-1990s, however, two editions appeared: Jean-Philippe Beaulieu and Hannah Fournier's in 1995 and, the following year, Jerry C. Nash's. Both texts are based on the unedited version first published in 1539 by Denys Janot, and both compare it with later versions, whose spelling and punctuation were corrected, with Crenne's permission, by Claude Colet. The 1995 and 1996 editions are accompanied by a full scholarly apparatus: introductions (which should be read in tandem since they highlight different aspects of the letters), lists of textual variants, glossaries of contemporary usage, indexes of proper names, and selected bibliographies. Nash situates the letters especially in connection with the *querelle des femmes*, thus emphasizing their feminist overtones. Beaulieu and Fournier, on the other hand, focus on the ambiguities of the letters' style and fiction, which they view as an intentional element in the overall design of Crenne's work, and trace a progression in the characterization of the epistolary writer and her relations with her various correspondants. An edition of *Le songe*, by two eminent Crenne specialists, Jean-Philippe Beaulieu and Diane Desrosiers-Bonin, was published in 2007 by Champion.

All the known works of Madeleine and Catherine Des Roches, that is *Les œuvres*, *Les secondes œuvres*, and *Les missives*, are now available in meticulously annotated editions, thanks to the diligence of Anne R. Larsen. The reader will want to begin by consulting the introduction to *Les œuvres*, which contains the most complete biographical information, and commentaries on the learned milieu of sixteenth-century Poitiers, the literary context and background that inform the works, an account of the current state of research on the Des Roches, and a well-informed bibliography. The preface to *Les secondes œuvres* complements this general introduction by providing a thorough discussion of salon culture and its influence on Catherine's writing, the importance of Poitiers and its place in the Des Roches' works, literary and philosophical influences, and specific aspects of their poetry. For assessment of the epistolary genre, the Des Roches' contribution to it, and the particularities of the letter as they practice it (style, tone, function), see Larsen's preface to *Les missives.*

Pernette Du Guillet's *Rymes* has generated continued critical interest ever since the publication, in 1968, of the excellent edition of her work overseen by Victor E. Graham. Two subsequent editions have appeared: Élise Rajchenbach's (2006) and Christian Barataud and Danielle Trudeau's (2006). Both build upon the foundations laid by their predecessors (Saulnier, "Études"; *Rymes* [1968]) and benefit from over forty years of critical inquiry. Rajchenbach's introduction touches briefly on the question of authorship that has enlivened scholarly debates since the 2006 publication of Mireille Huchon's *Louise Labé: Une créature de papier* and explores in great detail Du Guillet's relations to her sources (Petrarchan and Marotic poetics, the *belle dame sans mercy* tradition, and Neoplatonist philosophy) and various aspects of her work like the aesthetics of the fragmentary and the episodic. Most helpful are the scrupulous annotations aimed at elucidating lexical and grammatical difficulties; the extensive bibliography, followed by a discography with the facsimile of contemporary musical partitions, which reminds us that several of these poems were set to music; several annexes; and a detailed concordance. Christian Barataud and Danielle Trudeau's 2006 edition is based on the original edition published by Jean de Tournes and Antoine Du Moulin in 1545 and on the second edition by Tournes in 1552. An abundant critical apparatus explains the language and the formal features of the poems, revealing how Du Guillet, far from being a shy disciple of Maurice Scève, subverts the Petrarchan paradigm and promotes a concept of love and poetry that enhances female dignity. The footnotes illuminate the many links that run through the collection, revealing the deep relationships that underlie an ostensible lack of organization. The commentary refers to the most recent European and North American criticism on Du Guillet and the decade that precedes the coming of the Pléiade. A glossary, an index of authors cited, a table of *incipit*, and a bibliography complement the text.

Marie de Gournay's complete works now exist in a two-volume, fully annotated, 2,080-page edition (*Œuvres complètes*). In the last two decades or so several of Gournay's works have been edited (see, for instance, François Rigolot's 1989 edition of Gournay's preface to the 1595 edition of the *Essays*; Constant Venesoen's 1993 edition of L'Égalité des hommes et des femmes. Le grief des dames, *suivis du* Promenoir de Monsieur de Montaigne; and

Jean-Claude Arnould's 1996 edition of *Le promenoir de Monsieur de Montaigne*). However, the critical edition of the complete works, compiled by a team of Gournay experts under the direction of Jean-Claude Arnould, is the first to contain in the latest revised version all of Gournay's published works between 1594 and 1641: her novel; poetry; treatises and epistles relating to contemporary debates on linguistic and poetic concerns; treatises on moral, social, and political issues; translations from Latin in prose and verse; and prefaces to Montaigne's essays with the translation of their citations. Its carefully established text with all the variants of previous editions; its thorough introductory presentation of Gournay's career and works; its extensive annotation, glossary, indexes, and complete bibliography are fitting vehicles for further serious study of these works.

Most of those who teach Louise Labé in French use François Rigolot's edition of the *Œuvres complètes*, first published in 1986 and reprinted in 2004. Its authoritative and elegantly written introduction, helpful notes, chronological table, glossary, and updated bibliography make it the best available. Furthermore, this is the only modern edition to include the poems written in homage to Labé by her contemporaries and appended to her 1555 *Œuvres*. Françoise Charpentier's edition of Labé's *Œuvres poétiques* (1983) contains Labé's dedicatory epistle, sonnets, and elegies as well as Pernette Du Guillet's *Rymes* and a selection from *Les blasons du corps féminin* and *Contreblasons*. The texts are followed by brief biographical notes. The introduction to these works is rather succinct, and so are the annotations. Most of these elucidate lexical difficulties, hence the absence of a glossary. A bibliography of secondary sources is sorely missing. However, the fact that the orthography and punctuation have been modernized and that this edition brings together several works in one reasonably priced volume make it an alternative choice in undergraduate courses where lots of authors are treated.

Gary Ferguson's 1997 thoroughly annotated edition of Anne de Marquets's *Sonets spirituels*, the first since the original publication of the work in 1605, contains the entire text, that is, all 480 sonnets and seventeen commendatory pieces, as well as a brief account of Anne de Marquets's life with a critical discussion of the history of the work and its most remarkable aspects, like the liturgical arrangement of the sonnet sequence, the style, the meditative techniques and their notable influences, the marked preference for the communal voice over the individual's, copious notes, a glossary of terms, and a useful bibliography.

The seminal importance of Marguerite de Navarre's *Heptameron* in the French literature canon is indicated by the number of modern critical editions that have appeared in the last forty years. On these please see Winn's *Approaches to Teaching Marguerite de Navarre's* Heptameron (3–5). Long neglected, Marguerite's theater and religious poetry have recently begun to receive the critical scrutiny they deserve. In 2000 Barbara Marczuk and her collaborators produced the first separate edition of *Les comédies bibliques*, with introductory commentary on the theological, literary, and stylistic features of these texts and substantial notes that identify a multiplicity of allusions. This edition makes available a body of texts that should prove valuable for introducing students to early-sixteenth-century theatrical forms and religious thought. At the present time, the full corpus of Marguerite's writings is being edited and examined by a French team of Marguerite experts under the leadership of Nicole Cazauran. Five copiously annotated volumes with full scholarly apparatus have appeared so far from Champion: Sabine Lardon's edition Pater Noster *et* Petit œuvre devot, based on manuscript 5109 from Paris's Bibliothèque de l'Arsenal; Simone de Reyff's edition of *Le triomphe de l'Agneau*; Geneviève Hasenohr and Olivier Millet's edition of Marguerite's *Théâtre*; Richard Cooper's edition of *Chrétiens et mondains, poèmes épars*; and Michèle Clément's edition of La complainte pour un détenu prisonnier *et* Les chansons spirituelles. Additional volumes are in progress.

We are greatly indebted to Éliane Viennot for her two impressive critical editions of Margaret of Valois's works. *Mémoires et autres écrits, 1574–1614* includes the *Declaration du roi de Navarre*, written by Margaret in April 1574 at her husband's request; her memoirs, published some thirteen years after her death; her *Discours docte and subtil*, written to the Jesuit father François Loriot in defense of women; and various poems published during the queen's lifetime. Particularly useful are the contextualization of these works, each being situated in the life of their author and, in the case of the *Discours*, in the longer tradition of the *querelle des femmes*, the analytical commentaries, and the extensive annotation elucidating historical events and characters, literary allusions, and linguistic usage. Like her memoirs, Marguerite's *Correspondance, 1569–1614*, addressed to the royal family, contemporary influential figures, close friends, and lovers, offers important insight into the political and cultural events of the time. Once again Viennot's authoritative introduction, with its judicious remarks on Margaret's writing habits; carefully established text; scrupulous notes; and attention to editorial detail remain a model of scholarship. Her edition comprises a total of 469 letters, 117 of which had never been published before. Viennot has retained for these previously unpublished letters only the original orthography and punctuation (the rest are modernized as they were in previous publications) and is therefore able to analyze the different styles and registers Margaret uses with her various correspondents.

Note that with a few exceptions, many of these editions have been published by the French publisher Honoré Champion. The number of scholarly editions of both early modern women and proto-feminist texts that have appeared in its prestigious Textes de la Renaissance series, headed by Claude Blum, and the subseries it started, Éducation féminine de la Renaissance à l'âge classique, under the direction of Winn (and now published by Classiques Garnier), is a testimony to Champion's commitment to the study of early modern women. In addition to the aforementioned, these include Madeleine de L'Aubespine, *Cabinet des saines affections*; Jean Bouchet, *Le jugement poetic de l'honneur femenin*; Gabrielle de Bourbon, *Œuvres spirituelles*; Renée Burlamacchi, *Descrittione della vita et morte del Sigr Michele Burlamachi gentilhuomo lucchese*; Marguerite de Cambis, *Epistre consolatoire de Messire Jean Boccace*; Catherine de Clermont, countess of Retz, *Album de poésies*; Jeanne Du Laurens, *Genealogie de Messieurs du Laurens*; Jean Du Pré, *Le palais des nobles dames*; Philippe Du Verger's *Le Verger fertile des vertus*; Marie Le Gendre, *Exercice de l'âme spirituelle*; Jean de Marconville, *De la bonté et mauvaistié des femmes*; Winn, *Protestations et revendications féminines*, which features, among others, Charlotte de Brachard's *Harengue*; Jacqueline de Miremont's *Apologie pour les dames*; Suzanne de Nervèse's *Apologie en faveur des femmes.* Champion has also published landmark scholarship on early modern women like Rigolot's *Louise Labé Lyonnaise ou la Renaissance au féminin* and Daniel Martin's *Signe(s) d'amante.* In addition, several important volumes have appeared in its Conference Proceedings series, like *Le royaume de fémynie* (Wilson-Chevalier and Viennot) and *Veufs, veuves et veuvage dans la France d'Ancien Régime* (Winn and Pellegrin).

In 2002 Viennot founded the La cité des dames series with the Université de Saint-Étienne's publishing house, and several works by early modern women writers are now also available in inexpensive editions specifically designed for the classroom. To date publications in the series include Anne of France, Les enseignements *d'Anne de France à sa fille suivis de l'* Histoire du siège de Brest; Hélisenne de Crenne's *Les angoisses douloureuses qui procèdent d'amour* (2005) and *Epîtres familières et invectives* and *Songe* (2008); Jeanne Flore's *Les contes amoureux par Madame Jeanne Flore*; and Margaret of Valois's *Mémoires et discours*. These editions, all by eminent specialists in the field, invariably include a biographical sketch; a well-informed presentation of the historical, cultural, and literary contexts; brief annotations relevant to an understanding of the text; a glossary of archaic usage; and a selective bibliography.

Editions of early modern women's writing have increased in number and variety. These editions are responsible for the substantial increase in scholarly attention devoted to women writers of the period. Clearly strides have been taken since the early 1990s and yet much remains to be done. The existing editions still are, for the most part, of major works, more conventional literary genres, and better-known figures. Thus, to take one example, we have now a variety of well-designed editions of Marguerite de Navarre's *Heptameron* for teaching purposes. On the other hand, the first modern editions of her plays and religious poetry that appeared in the late 1960s and early 1970s are just now being revisited. Whereas, at the present time, instructors can choose from several editions of Louise Labé's works, they still have to rely, because of the lack of a modern edition, on a 1973 facsimile text of Georgette de Montenay's *Emblemes, ou devises chrestiennes*, which has a useful but outdated introductory note by Christopher N. Smith—this in spite of recent assessments by literary critics of the importance of Montenay's work in the development of emblem literature and the numerous and diverse emblem studies that have appeared in the last two decades. Those interested in Marie Dentière will soon benefit from a scholarly edition prepared by a Canadian team including Diane Desrosiers-Bonin, William Kemp, and Isabelle C. Denommé. A critical edition of Marie de Romieu's *Premières œuvres poétiques*, which has not been republished since André Winandy's 1972 edition, and of her *Instruction pour les jeunes dames* is being prepared by Claude La Charité. In contrast, Nicole Estienne's *Les misères de la femme mariée* has not been revisited since being reprinted in Ilana Zinguer's *Misère et grandeur de la femme au XVIe siècle* in 1982, published by Slatkine.[1] In the last decade or so, Jeanne de Jussie has gained some notoriety thanks to several translations of her short chronicle in French, English, and German, but many other writers await rescue from undeserved obscurity. In the meantime instructors have recourse to printed literary anthologies of generally abbreviated works or of a small selection of writers or genre-based anthologies (see below).

It is to be hoped that more will rally to the cause of excavating buried and neglected texts. Many resources are now available: in addition to Berriot-Salvadore's list of works published by French women from 1497 to 1626 as well as her larger bibliography of manuscripts and printed primary sources (*Femmes* 540–67), interested publishers will want to consult William Kemp's catalogue raisonné of all works written or translated by women and printed in France before 1550, Pierre-Louis Vaillancourt and Dawn Smyth's *Les écrits féminins non fictionnels de la Renaissance,* Susan Broomhall's "French Women in Print, 1488 to 1599" (she lists close to 150 works written by eighty-five French women), and Roméo Arbour's *L'ère baroque en France. Répertoire chronologique des éditions de textes littéraires.* One potential source of information about women's lives and texts is compilations by earlier French bibliographers like François Grudé La Croix du Maine and Antoine Du Verdier's *Les bibliothèques françoises*, Hilarion de Coste's *Eloges et vies des roynes, princesses, dames et damoiselles illustres*, Marguerite Buffet's *Nouvelles observations sur la langue françoise . . . Avec les eloges des illustres sçavantes tant anciennes que modernes*, Joseph De La Porte and Jean-François de la Croix's *Histoire littéraire des femmes françoises*, and Marguerite Ursule Fortunée Briquet's *Dictionnaire historique, littéraire et bibliographique des Françaises et des étrangères naturalisées en France.* Printed manuscript catalogs for the major libraries such as the *Catalogue général des manuscrits français de la Bibliothèque Nationale de France,* the *Catalogue of Medieval and Renaissance Manuscripts in the Beinecke Rare Book and Manuscript Library, Yale University*, and the *Catalogue of Manuscripts in the Houghton Library, Harvard University* will also provide important resources. To this list can be added *Les Amazones,* a catalog of old and modern books by and about women with numerous original editions (www.galaxidion.com/amazones).

English Translations and Dual-Language Editions

As early modern women writers are incorporated in more humanities and interdisciplinary courses, cross-listed by departments of English, comparative literature, history, religious studies, gender and women's studies, and others, English translations of their works are needed. Thus, some publishers now specialize in English translations and dual-language editions. The Other Voice in Early Modern Europe series from the University of Chicago (now University of Toronto) Press was designed by Margaret L. King and Albert Rabil, Jr., to make available in reasonably priced English and bilingual editions a comprehensive and focused collection of European writings before 1700, both by women and for and about them. The quality of the translations and of the critical apparatus has been uniformly outstanding. Each volume in the series opens with the introduction by the series editors, King and Rabil, who briefly review the situation of women in early modern Europe. A general overview by each individual volume's editor follows, including adequate biographical and bibliographic information and a succinct yet thorough analysis of the work(s) translated, with a discussion of issues relating to the translation. Explanatory notes, usually limited to the clarification of literary allusions or historical events, principally address students and nonspecialists. Many important texts are now accessible to English-speaking students and scholars such as Henricus Cornelius Agrippa's *Declamation on the Nobility and Preeminence of the Female Sex*, Madeleine de L'Aubespine's *Selected Poems and Translations*, Anna Maria van Schurman's Whether a Christian Woman Should Be Educated *and Other Writings from Her Intellectual Circle*, Juan Luis Vives's *The Education of a Christian Woman*, as well as numerous Italian women writers of the Renaissance like Laura Cereta's *Collected Letters of a Renaissance Feminist*, Cassandra Fedele's *Letters and Orations*, Moderata Fonte's *The Worth of Women*, Veronica Franco's *Poems and Selected Letters*, and Tullia d'Aragona's *Dialogue on the Infinity of Love*. Among the authors treated in this volume the following are now available in this acclaimed series from the University of Chicago Press.

In addition to Gabrielle de Coignard's *Imitation de la victoire de Judith*, which was translated into English in 2000 by Colette H. Winn and Robert H. McDowell, a substantial part of her 1594 *Œuvres chrestiennes* is now also available to an English-speaking audience thanks to Melanie E. Gregg's scrupulous translation (*Spiritual Sonnets*). This is the first English translation of Coignard's *Spiritual Sonnets*. Most helpful for readers who possess a basic knowledge of French is the inclusion of the French originals on pages that face Gregg's translation. Gregg's clear and accessible presentation of the organization, major themes, versification, style, and language of the sonnets and of their religious and classical sources, as well as her updated bibliography and basic annotations make this an excellent choice for a teaching text.

Another addition to The Other Voice series is Marie Dentière's *Epistle to Marguerite de Navarre* and her *Preface to a Sermon by John Calvin*. The introduction to this volume conveys the sparse information available about Dentière's life and her particular situation in Calvinist Geneva and provides background on the theological controversies in Geneva and Strasbourg from which these works emerge and the specific issues to which Dentière was responding. What follows includes a discussion of the "defense of women"; issues of faith, works, and grace, which are more prevalent in the rest of the epistle; and the question of authorship. Did Dentière herself write the *Very Useful Epistle to the Queen of Navarre* or is this a work in collaboration with her husband, who, after all, shared her doctrinal and political positions? The translation is lively and accessible. Mary McKinley does an excellent job in capturing the tone, style, and spirit of the original. Explanatory notes, along with an extensive bibliography, assist the reader.

In 2000 Anne R. Larsen published an English translation of Catherine Des Roches's pastoral. Her more recent edition of the Dames Des Roches includes selections from their poetry, prose dialogues, and letters. The latter two are presented only in English; the translations of the poetry are in verse but are not rhymed. Larsen's translation retains the flavor of the originals while making the texts available to a modern reader. Her substantial introduction provides extensive biographical information as well as the contemporary historical and cultural background and discusses the "fortunes" of the Des Roches and important themes such as the mother-daughter bond, women's education, and so on. Annotations, reasonably complete without being burdensome to students, elucidate classical references. A glossary and an excellent bibliography of primary and secondary sources complete the scholarly apparatus.

One of the most recent additions to the series is Karen Simroth James and Marta Rijn Finch's edition and translation of Pernette Du Guillet's *Rhymes*. It includes the entire text of the 1545 Jean de Tournes edition as well as the three poems added in the 1552 edition, the preface by Antoine Du Moulin, a liminary poem by Jean de Tournes and lyric epitaphs by Maurice Scève and Jean de Vauzelles. Finch's English translations of the poems maintain the same rhyme scheme as the French with a parallel versification, capturing the rhythm, tone, and subtleties of meaning of the original. A substantial introduction addresses important features of Du Guillet's poetry and presents background information helpful to understanding the collection and its reception through time, with references to previous studies and recent French critical editions. Notes for each poem explain questions of interpretation raised in the translation process, lexical nuances, and key literary and mythological allusions.

Thanks to Richard Hillman and Colette Quesnel we now have a

great selection of Marie de Gournay's works. Their volume (Apology) includes four of Gournay's feminist pieces; her two well-known treatises with their last revisions (1641); *The Equality of Men and Women* and *The Ladies' Complaint*; her psychological novel, *The Promenade of Monsieur de Montaigne*; and her autobiographical apology, *The Apology for the Woman Writing*. The last two appear in Hillman and Quesnel's edition in English for the first time. The editors supply a general overview of Gournay's literary career, as well as individual introductions, explanatory notes, and a selective bibliography that includes references to modern editions and previous translations of Gournay's works, critical books, and articles for further reading.

Carrie Klaus's English translation of Jeanne de Jussie's *The Short Chronicle* is based on Helmut Feld's critical edition of the two extant sixteenth-century manuscripts of the *Petite chronique* (1996). In addition to a full translation of the manuscript presumed to be in Jussie's own hand, the volume includes an introduction to the Genevan Reformation, to Jussie, and to the Poor Clares, as well as a bibliography, notes, and index.

There have been several translations of Louise Labé's works: Graham Dunstan Martin's of her *Sonnets* (1972), Edith R. Farrell's of the complete works (1986), Anne-Marie Bourbon's of the *Debate of Folly and Love* (2000), to name a few. Recently published in The Other Voice in Early Modern Europe series, Deborah Lesko Baker's edition, *The Complete Poetry and Prose*, is the first bilingual edition of Labé's works and features the latest scholarly discussions of them. Annie Finch's translations of the *Elegies* and *Sonnets* are the first to incorporate Labé's original rhyme schemes, and Lesko Baker's translations of the prose aim to present the most accurate and idiomatic renditions of the *Dedicatory Letter* and the *Debate* to date. Lesko Baker also provides three substantial critical introductions to Louise Labé's life and legacy, to her prose and to her poetry, as well as extensive notes on all the translations. Sensitive and scholarly, these introductory commentaries should be read in conjunction with her earlier monograph on Labé, *The Subject of Desire*.

In commemoration of the tenth anniversary of the publication of the first volume of The Other Voice in Early Modern Europe series, editors Margaret L. King and Albert Rabil, Jr., added a complementary teaching volume for texts dealing with religion: *Teaching Other Voices: Women and Religion in Early Modern Europe*. Most valuable to readers of French literature will be the introductory overview by the editors of women's involvement in early modern Europe's religious struggles and aspirations, as well as the articles by Rouben Cholakian on Marguerite de Navarre's religious views, Mary B. McKinley on creative ways of bringing Marie Dentière's work into the classroom and helping students appreciate her rhetorical strategies ("Early Modern Teacher"), and Carrie F. Klaus on how to teach about monasticism and the pedagogical advantages to be gained by pairing Jeanne de Jussie's *Short Chronicle* with Arcangela Tarabotti's *Paternal Tyranny* ("Reading").

The bilingual edition of Marguerite de Navarre's *Selected Writings* was published in 2008 by Rouben C. Cholakian and Mary Skemp. This volume includes a representative sampling of Marguerite's prose and poetry, most of it never before translated into English. (Several of Marguerite's works are also available in separate volumes: The Coach *and* The Triumph of the Lamb; *The Mirror of the Sinful Soul*; a selection from her secular plays [*Théâtre* (2002)]; and *The Prisons.*)

Timothy Reiss is at work on a dual-language edition of Hélisenne de Crenne's *Complete Works.* Although these works, for the most part, already exist in English, there is a need for a comprehensive volume with a synthesizing overview of Hélisenne's œuvre and the numerous studies that it has generated in the past two decades. (As early as 1986, Marianna M. Mustacchi and Paul J. Archambault published an English translation of the *Personal and Invective Letters* along with a good overview of the epistolary tradition and Hélisenne's contribution [*Renaissance Woman*]). In 1996 the entire text of the *Angoysses douloureuses* was translated under the title *The Torments of Love*, by Lisa Neal and Steven Rendall. The translators have done a good job at maintaining the flavor of the original and elucidating difficult passages. Neal's study of the medieval dream tradition and English translation of the *Songe*, under the title *Lady Hélisenne's* Dream, appeared in Larsen and Winn, *Writings* 63–105.

A brief selection from Anne de Marquets's spiritual sonnets was translated by Gary Ferguson and Catherine Hampton. Some of Georgette de Montenay's *Emblems and Christian Devices*, translated by Régine Reynolds-Cornell, and Marie de Romieu's *Brief Discourse*, translated by Marian Rothstein, appeared in the same collection (see *Writings*). However, more needs to be done to bring these authors to the larger public.

New translations and bilingual editions of French women writers of the Renaissance and Reformation have helped increase the accessibility of primary texts beyond the French-speaking audience and have allowed instructors to introduce these texts in a variety of new and exciting courses. The Other Voice in Early Modern Europe series continues to play a seminal role in attaining these goals. Instructors will want to keep up to date on the University of Toronto Press's publication agenda for the series.

Anthologies of Texts in French and English

Reading the complete text is preferable but not always feasible in courses that try to cover a lot of material or in interdisciplinary courses. In such courses, an anthology can serve a useful purpose: while providing students access to a number of texts at relatively low cost, it enables them to place writers in their historical, cultural, and literary context and to compare different works. Even selective passages will allow exploration of important issues and themes. *Lettres de femmes: XVIe–XVIIIe siècle*, edited by Elizabeth Goldsmith and Colette H. Winn, offers several important sixteenth-century documents never published before. The reader will find copious excerpts from Marguerite de Navarre's correspondence with Francis I; Louise-Julienne, Elisabeth, and Amélie de Nassau's correspondence with their sister Charlotte-Brabantine; Louise de Coligny's correspondence with various family members from France and the Netherlands as well as texts in their entirety like Gaspard de Saillans's correspondence with his future wife Louise de Bourges (Louise, "Correspondance") and the anonymous 1564 *Epistre d'une damoiselle françoise à une sienne amie dame estrangere.* Destined for students, professors, and scholars, volume 1 of *Les femmes et la tradition littéraire*, edited by Vicki Mistacco, includes a general introduction, "Philomèle et les sœurs de Procné," which highlights recurring themes in women's writing and contends the Renaissance is a pivotal moment for this literature. Individual chapters on Pernette Du Guillet, Louise Labé, Hélisenne de Crenne, and Marguerite de Navarre feature substantial critical introductions along with extensive selections from their works to allow for in-depth analysis. Spelling is modernized, and the selections are annotated for vocabulary and literary allusions. Questions, both specific and general, on these readings are available from an online study guide.

Early modern women writers are often introduced in interdisciplinary courses and, therefore, are read in translation. Domna C. Stanton's bilingual anthology, *French Feminist Poems from the Middle Ages to the Present*, features thirty-seven poets with biographical, historical, and critical background information and extensive bibliographic notes. Norman R. Shapiro's *French Women Poets of Nine Centuries: The Distaff and the Pen* contains over six hundred poems from fifty-four different pens, from Marie de France to Albertine Sarrazin. Introductory essays by reputed scholars of each era's poetry are included along with biographical sketches and presentations of each poet's place in her period. Original texts and translations are conveniently presented on facing pages. *Women Writers of the Renaissance and Reformation*, edited by Katharina Wilson, offers short biographies and excerpts of "canonical" works by women writers from England, Germany, Italy, the Low Countries, and France. The French works excerpted include Marie Dentière's epistle to Marguerite de Navarre; Diane de Poitiers's selected poems and correspondence; Pernette Du Guillet's selected epigrams and chansons; Hélisenne de Crenne's *Angoysses douloureuses qui procedent d'amours* (chs. 1–6) and *Epistres invectives* 4; Louise Labé's "Epistle to M.C.D.B.L." and sonnets 2–10 and 12–13; Marguerite de Navarre's *Heptameron*, tales 1, 3, 51, and 52; and Madeleine and Catherine Des Roches's selected epistles and poetic works. *Writings by Pre-revolutionary French Women: From Marie de France to Elizabeth Vigée-Le Brun*, edited by Anne R. Larsen and Colette H. Winn, privileges whenever possible works in their entirety and generally less familiar texts such as Gabrielle de Coignard's *Imitation de la victoire de Judith*; Hélisenne de Crenne's Le songe *de Madame Hélisenne*; Marie de Gournay's *La copie de la vie de la Demoiselle de Gournay*; Marguerite de Navarre's *Le miroir de l'âme pécheresse*; Marie de Romieu's *Brief discours: L'excellence de la femme surpasse celle de l'homme, autant recreatif que plein de beaux exemples*; and Catherine Des Roches's *Bergerie*. Included also are substantial excerpts of Charlotte de Bourbon's *Lettres et documents*; Charlotte Arbaleste de Mornay's *Mémoires*; Anne de Marquets's *Sonets spirituels*; and Georgette de Montenay's *Emblemes ou devises chrestiennes*.

Noteworthy also is Frank J. Warnke's *Three Women Poets, Renaissance and Baroque: Louise Labé, Gaspara Stampa, and Sor Juan Inez de la Cruz*. This anthology contains information about each poet and her place in Renaissance and baroque history, with extensive critical references. The English translation is presented alongside the original. There is a real need for cross-cultural anthologies like Warnke's and Wilson's (*Women Writers*) to accommodate the increasing number of courses across the disciplines.

Biographical and Bibliographic Studies

"Canonical" writers like Marguerite de Navarre have been the subject of biographies so numerous that it would be impossible to enumerate all of them here (P. Cholakian and R. Cholakian's *Marguerite de Navarre: Mother of the Renaissance* is highly recommended) and so have such colorful figures as Louise Labé and Margaret of Valois (see, e.g., Berriot; Cameron; Lazard, *Louise Labé*; Sealy; and Viennot, *Marguerite de Valois*). For lesser-known authors Berriot-Salvadore's *Les femmes dans la société française de la Renaissance* will prove particularly useful. Women's works are carefully analyzed and used as tools along with relevant sixteenth-century texts in order to explicate the writer's life. Written in a lively and most engaging style, Madeleine Lazard's *Les avenues de fémynie* will no doubt appeal to undergraduate students and provide them with adequate biographical and bibliographic information. Roland H. Bainton's *Women of the Reformation in France and England* constitutes a rich source of information on Protestant women.

In addition to these more specialized works, students can be guided to the various dictionaries and encyclopedias that have recently appeared featuring early modern women writers and artists of all kinds. Reminiscent of the famous sixteenth-century *Bibliothèques* of La Croix du Maine and Du Verdier, they offer brief biographical sketches—more substantial, though, than their predecessors'—along with a list of works and a selective bibliography of secondary sources. Among these the following command special attention: *An Encyclopedia of Continental Women Writers*, edited by Katharina M. Wilson, provides important information on well-known and lesser-known figures in the form of critical essays by reputed specialists. *French Women Writers: A Bio-bibliographical Source*, edited by Eva Martin Sartori and Dorothy Wynne Zimmerman, also contains substantial authoritative essays on selected authors, among which are Pernette Du Guillet, Marie de Gournay, Hélisenne de Crenne, Louise Labé, and Marguerite de Navarre. Of particular interest as well is *The Feminist Encyclopedia of French Literature*, edited by Sartori, which includes several hundred alphabetically listed entries for authors, genres, literary movements, institutions, events, and organizations related to French literature. Alongside well-known authors, lesser-known figures like Marie de Cotteblanche, Anne de Rohan, Catherine de Partenay, and others receive special emphasis. The entire content of this encyclopedia is available at the online subscription-only database at *Questia*.

Among its recent publications the Edwin Mellen Press also shows Ingrid Akerlund's *Sixteenth-Century French Women Writers*, which includes chapters on Marguerite d'Angoulême, Anne de Graville, the Lyonnese school, Jeanne de Jussie, Marie Dentière, and Camille de Morel. The last three are mostly intended for the general reader: *Extraordinary Women of The Medieval and Renaissance World: A Biographical Dictionary*, edited by Carole Levin and others comprises seventy short biographies of women of diverse status, backgrounds, and occupations from the ninth to the seventeenth century. Great Britain is given special attention with twenty-two articles, whereas France only receives nine entries. The *Encyclopedia of Women in the Renaissance, Italy, France, and England*, edited by Diana Robin, Anne R. Larsen, and Carole Levin, contains authoritative profiles of most early modern women artists, leaders, scientists, doctors, writers, and religious and philosophical thinkers followed by suggested readings. Finally, *Daughters of Time: Two Thousand Notable Women from Antiquity to 1800*, edited by Vivian Gould, pays tribute to women of accomplishment (artists, philosophers, scientists, composers, theologians, writers, etc.) throughout history.

Background Studies

Instructors will most likely provide the historical, cultural, and literary background information necessary as they first introduce "the early modern woman" or a new author in their class, but they may also want to assign further readings to their students. For a synthetic overview of the history of women from the Middle Ages to the beginning of the modern era, with helpful bibliographies of secondary readings, Margaret L. King's *Women of the Renaissance* and Olwen Hufton's volume 1 of *The Prospect before Her: A History of Women in Western Europe* are recommended. Whereas King examines women of all classes and in three different but interrelated settings (the family, the Church, and in high culture), Hufton discusses the prospects for most young women in Europe during the early modern period, focusing on marriage, motherhood, widowhood, as well as deviant behavior and its consequences. Madeleine Lazard's works still remain valuable resources for an overview of the woman question in Renaissance France. Where *Images littéraires de la femme* does not sufficiently take into account concurrent advances in feminist and gender theory in England and North America, it has the merit of surveying the principal texts for, about, and by women and of addressing a number of important topics like the images and stereotypes of women in literature, the education of girls, life in the convent, the first literary salons, and so on, which, in the years following its publication, would become the focus of scrutiny of more specialized studies. Her more recent *Les avenues de fémynie: Les femmes et la Renaissance* treats the images as well as the reality of women and the conflict or discrepancy between the two. Of particular interest are the chapters on the role and work of lower-class women and various trades and professions for women, including prostitution—topics that had received little attention until her 2001 study—and chapters on the role of women in the Reformation and Counter-Reformation. On the same topic, Susan Broomhall's *Women and Religion in Sixteenth-Century France*, based on meticulous archival research and extensive review of primary documents such as secular and consistory court records, convent chronicles, testimony from witchcraft trials, family papers, and many detailed accounts of women's lives, will offer the more advanced student a fascinating examination of the role that religion played in women's life and the various manifestations of women's involvement in sixteenth-century religion. These range from the relations Catholic and Calvinist women entertained with their institutional churches to the role women played in religious politics and religious violence to their contributions to religious history and "visible religious practices."

For a learned presentation of the basic theory of sexual difference adhered to in Renaissance medicine, law, and theology, Ian Maclean's *The Renaissance Notion of Woman* remains the most brilliant example. Noteworthy also is Berriot-Salvadore's *Les femmes dans la société française de la Renaissance*, which compares the legal, educational, Reformed, and Catholic discourses on women with the reality of women's lives. Chapter 1 of Linda Timmermans's *L'accès des femmes à la culture* may also be assigned to give students a brief synthesis of Renaissance debates on the status, roles, and capabilities of women. Volume 1 of Maïté Albistur and Daniel Armogathe's *Histoire du féminisme français* offers comprehensive coverage of the *querelle des femmes*, its different stages, authors, and arguments, with a summary of the principal texts. This can be supplemented by Joan Kelly's "Early Feminist Theory and the *Querelle des Femmes*, 1475–1789" and excerpts from Constance Jordan's *Renaissance Feminism*, which will give students a broader European perspective on the question. Modernized excerpts of pamphlets can be found in Albistur and Armogathe's *Grief des femmes* and in volume 1 of Jean-Pierre Guillerm and others' *Le miroir des femmes*. The chronological table in volume 2 places these texts in relation to other contemporary writings. Students will no doubt enjoy comparing literary images and stereotypes of women with iconographical representations. A great resource on the subject is Sara F. Matthews Grieco's comprehensive study, *Ange ou diablesse. La représentation de la femme au XVIe siècle*, which details a wide range of representations from emblem books to single prints, fly leaves, and posters.

Students should be made aware of the various positions of contemporary critics regarding women's condition in sixteenth-century France. While some argue that women's condition somewhat improved over time (David Herlihy), others like Joan Kelly-Gadol ("Did Women Have a Renaissance?") maintain that the Middle Ages were a golden age for women and that the Renaissance, a great age of progress in knowledge and cultural achievement for man, brought about loss of rights and privileges for woman. A third position (Berriot-Salvadore, *Femmes*) claims that the Renaissance was a period of paradoxes and ambiguities for women marked by an overall increase in educational opportunities on the one hand and a decrease in economic power and expansion of legal and moral restrictions on the other hand. One of the best ways to give students an overall view of both the educational opportunities for women and patriarchal control is to assign a variety of readings including Broomhall's *Women and the Book Trade in Sixteenth-Century France* (ch. 1), Lazard's "Femmes, littérature, culture au XVIe siècle en France," Berriot-Salvadore's "Les femmes dans les cercles intellectuels de la Renaissance" and "Les femmes et les pratiques de l'écriture," as well as selected chapters from Ruth Kelso's *Doctrine for the Lady of the Renaissance*. Although it concerns Italian women, Lisa Jardine's "Women Humanists: Education for What?" also provides a pertinent account of humanist views on the education and the public role of women.

Broomhall's *Women and the Book Trade* and Ann Rosalind Jones's "Surprising Fame: Renaissance Gender Ideologies and Women's Lyric" are crucial to an understanding of women in the world of work. Whereas Broomhall explores the cultural context of women's publishing (women's modes of access to print culture, their involvement in a variety of book trades, specific publication strategies, and so forth), Jones describes the hostile milieu in which women had to work after being thrust into the masculine sphere of fame and eloquence and the strategies they employed to legitimize their authorship. On women's agency, one could assign one or two chapters from Gerda Lerner's *The Creation of Feminist Consciousness from the Middle Ages to Eighteen Seventy*. This book documents women's reactions to the patriarchal system of Western values by retracing their combat for intellectual emancipation, both singly and in networks or clusters, through motherhood, mysticism, and their own creativity. Finally, on the use of myths by early modern women as a means of self-expression, see

Tilde Sankovitch's *French Women Writers and the Book* and in particular chapters 2 and 3 on the Dames Des Roches and Marie de Gournay.

Critical Studies

Secondary readings, in some instructors' views, detract from students' experience of the text. These instructors feel that students should first become familiar with the text and have the opportunity to formulate their own critical judgment before sampling the vast array of critical orientations. Yet teachers in more advanced courses often require some familiarity with current critical issues in order to broaden students' horizons and allow them to develop different sets of questions designed to provoke exciting new insights.

As the literary canon opened up to accommodate new texts and authors, feminist criticism began to revise and extend the perspective and methodology that until then had been applied to the field of early modern studies. Natalie Zemon Davis's "Women's History in Transition: The European Case" and Joan Kelly-Gadol's "Did Women have a Renaissance?" prove useful to give students some sense of the evolution of feminist thought and women's history. Both studies promote the use of gender as a category of analysis. As early as 1976, Davis argued in favor of rereading the past from a gendered perspective. The following year, Kelly-Gadol's query, whether women had a Renaissance, also challenged, from the perspective of gender, the traditionally accepted periods of history and transformed the way critics studied women's history as an isolated phenomenon having no relationship to the history of men. *Gender and History in Western Europe,* Robert Shoemaker and Mary Vincent's reader, which arose out of the course Gender in European History, 1600–1950, is also helpful in pointing out historical subjects affected by gender and the current diversity of critical tools available to those interrogating the history and causes of gender differences (new historicism, literary and cultural theory, Marxism, deconstruction, psychoanalysis, etc.), as well as more specific questions of conceptualization and methodology. See in particular the general introduction and the introductory pieces to the different sections of the book. Joan Scott's piece in this volume, "Gender: A Useful Category of Analysis," is a provocative assessment of the theoretical problems involved in gender studies and their least and most fruitful applications. (Included in the same volume in the section on politics is also "Women on Top," Davis's early exploration of the symbolic significance, in early modern Europe, of the iconography of the disorderly woman and its subversive potential.)

Merry E. Wiesner's *Women and Gender in Early Modern Europe* is recommended for an informative and accessible introduction to the history of women and the construction of gender in the early modern period. With its clear exposition and limpid prose, present-day analogies to the historical material, and extensive bibliographies following each chapter, this book seems particularly well suited for our undergraduate students. Several studies included in Natalie Zemon Davis and Arlette Farge's *Renaissance and Enlightenment Paradoxes* will help students understand the meaning of the social construction of gender roles as they look at women in the varied contexts of work, marriage, and the family and the ways in which they experienced their status. *Rewriting the Renaissance: The Discourses of Sexual Difference in Early Modern Europe*, by Margaret W. Ferguson, Maureen Quilligan, and Nancy Vickers offers a broad sampling of perspectives on and approaches to sexuality and gender in early modern Europe. The essays, throughout, explore the marginalizing consequences of patriarchy for women and the ways in which individual women or groups of women subverted patriarchal dominance. On the relations of gender to issues of social power see Sheila ffolliott's study of Catherine de Médicis's need, after the death of Henry II, of an image to "authorize her power" ("Catherine" 230) and the subsequent creation of the image of a new Artemisia by the courtier Nicholas Houlel. Of particular interest to the student of French literature are also discussions by François Rigolot and Ann Rosalind Jones of Louise Labé's manipulation of the rhetoric of Renaissance love poetry. Whereas Rigolot seeks to define the various means by which Labé uses "gender deviations and ambiguities in speech patterns" ("Gender" 297) in order to reaffirm her identity as a female poet and lover, Jones analyzes "the contradictory rhetoric" to which Louise Labé and Veronica Franco were driven by their desire to rise socially ("City Women" 304). Also instructive on the impact of both gender and class on the emergence of the early women writers is Ann Rosalind Jones's cross-cultural study *The Currency of Eros: Women Love Lyric in Europe, 1540–1620.* The book first gives us background information with a discussion of the ideological climate, that is, the conflicting prescriptive models for comportment described by men for women in the courtesy literature of the day. Then eight English, French, and Italian female love poets, paired "according to parallels between their social situations and the forms of negotiation they invent" (8), are read in relation to predominantly masculine literary forms and discourses, notably Petrarchism and Neoplatonism, in order to demonstrate the strategies these women used to circumvent cultural barriers. This list does not purport to be comprehensive or exhaustive. For further critical readings, especially on specific approaches, see also the "Approaches and Methodologies" section of Part III of this volume.

Note

1. Nicole Estienne published under her married name, Mme Liebault.

Colette H. Winn

Professional Resources and Activities

If the field of early modern Frenchwomen studies developed at such a vigorous pace in the last thirty years, it is partly because of individual and collaborative scholarly initiatives such as the organization of specialized colloquia, the constitution of special-interest groups and professional organizations seeking to promote discussion of scholarly and pedagogical issues and to establish links with other national and international organizations with similar goals, and the creation of databases and Web sites making current resources available to the larger community of scholars (see Postolache and Winn, in this volume). It can also be explained by the commitment of various presses and academic journals to the essential task of making available to a growing readership of students and scholars works by women once forgotten or misread and significant scholarship about them. This section aims to provide instructors and young scholars with information they can use for both research and the classroom.

International Conferences and Colloquia

The last two decades have witnessed, in Europe and North America, a tremendous rise in the number of interdisciplinary conferences on French women of the early modern period beginning with Renaissance Woman / Renaissance Man: Studies in the Creation of Culture and Society at Yale in 1982 (for the proceedings, see Ferguson, Quilligan, and Vickers); Changing Perspectives on Women in the Renaissance, at the Center for Renaissance Studies at the Newberry Library in 1983 (Mary Rose); The Poetics of Gender in 1984 at Columbia's Maison Française, one of the series of annual colloquia initiated by Michael Riffaterre (for the proceedings, see Miller, *Poetics*, which features Ann Rosalind Jones's "Surprising Fame"); Women in the Renaissance, a series of colloquia at the Folger Shakespeare Library between 1985 and 1989; Femmes et Pouvoirs Sous l'Ancien Régime, in Paris in 1989 (Haase Dubosc and Viennot); Royaume de Fémynie: Pouvoirs, Contraintes, Espaces de Liberté des Femmes, de la Renaissance à la Fronde, in Blois in 1995 (Wilson-Chevalier and Viennot); Femmes Savantes, Savoirs des Femmes: Du Crépuscule de la Renaissance à l'Aube des Lumières, in Chantilly in 1995 (Nativel); La Femme Lettrée à la Renaissance / De Geleerde Vrouw in de Renaissance, at the Free University of Brussels in 1996 (Bastiaensen); Women's Writings in the French Renaissance, at Clare College, Cambridge, England, in 1997 (Ford and Jondorf); Des Femmes et des Livres: France et Espagne, XIVe–XVIIe Siècles, in Fontenay / Saint-Cloud, France, in 1998 (De Courcelles and Julián); Les Femmes et la Traduction du Moyen Age au XVIIIe Siècle, in Montréal in 2002 (Beaulieu, *D'une écriture*); MARGOT: Dix ans de Recherche sur les Femmes Écrivains de l'Ancien Régime: Influences et Confluences, in Waterloo, Ontario, in 2005 (Poirier, McWebb, Paré, and Russel); Émergence Littéraire des Femmes à Lyon à la Renaissance, 1520–1560, in Lyon in 2006 (Clément and Incardona); and Masculinities and Femininities in the Middle Ages and the Renaissance, Arizona Studies in the Middle Ages and the Renaissance Conference series, in Tempe in 2007 (Kiefer); *Ut Pictura Poesis* and the *Querelle des femmes*, in Edinburgh in 2007. While all of these were a one-time event followed, for the most part, by the publication of selected papers, other conferences have had a more enduring fortune, and two in particular have met with some regularity (every three or four years) since the early 1990s: Women in Old Régime France and Attending to Early Modern Women. Both of these will be of the utmost interest to the student of early modern French women.

Held in different countries, Women in Old Régime France brings together French and Anglo-American scholarly communities (including those in Great Britain, the United States, Canada, and Australasia). It highlights a particular theme, and selected proceedings are usually published. Themes include women as producers of texts and the rediscovery of these texts

(Beaulieu and Fournier, "Women"); women's strategies to access learning and negotiate their entry into print (Winn and Kuizenga); self-reflexion and self-representation in women's texts (Beaulieu and Desrosiers-Bonin, *Dans les miroirs*); ways in which cultural change affected women's lives and writings (Women in Cultural Change, in Charlottesville in 1999, organized by Mary McKinley, no proceedings); women's access to reading, reading practices, book acquisition, and so on (Brouard-Arends); women as actors and subjects of history (Steinberg and Arnould); and women and rhetoric (La Charité and Breitenstein).

While less internationally oriented, Attending to Early Modern Women, hosted by the Center for Reformation and Baroque Studies at the University of Maryland, College Park, attracts eminent as well as younger scholars of various disciplines. It explores varying aspects of the lives, roles, and writings of women in early modern societies. The first conference, which convened in 1990, focused on English women; the second, held in 1994, treated European women in general; the third, in 1997, adopted an even broader focus on the lives of women in Asia and the New World. The theme of the 2006 symposium, Attending to Early Modern Women and Men, reflects current interest in gender-oriented approaches. The 2009 meeting was Conflict and Concord. What makes this conference particularly appealing is its multidisciplinary and dialogistic nature. It usually features several plenary lectures by prominent American scholars (Natalie Zemon Davis, Sheila ffolliott, Lisa Jardine, Ann Rosalind Jones, Josephine A. Roberts, Merry Wiesner-Hanks) as well as numerous workshops designed to encourage productive debate on a variety of topics. The proceedings, which generally include the keynote essays, as well as summaries of the activities of the workshops with the questions raised in discussion and a select bibliography, will prove a highly valuable tool for both teaching and research.

It should finally be noted that entire sessions on French early modern women are regularly organized at the annual meetings of the Renaissance Society of America (www.rsa.org), the Sixteenth-Century Studies Conference (www.sixteenthcentury.org), and the Société Canadienne d'Études de la Renaissance/Canadian Society for Renaissance Studies (www.crrs.ca). Individual papers are usually included in topical or interdisciplinary sessions. Although there is no page specifically devoted to early modern women writers, one may also want to consult the official site of the French Society for the Study of the Sixteenth Century (SFDES), maintained by the Centre d'Études Supérieures de la Renaissance, Université François

Rabelais (www.cesr.univ-tours.fr) for upcoming colloquia, bibliographies, and access to journal articles. However, for upcoming colloquia, academic events, and forthcoming publications on French early modern women writers the Société Internationale pour l'Étude des Femmes de l'Ancien Régime (SIEFAR) remains the best and most reliable source of information.

Professional Associations

Several groups are now actively engaged in promoting research on early modern French women writers: SIEFAR; the Institut Émilie du Châtelet pour la Diffusion et le Développement des Recherches sur les Femmes, le Sexe et le Genre, or IEC (named after Gabrielle Émilie Le Tonnelier de Breteuil, marquise du Châtelet); the Moyen Âge et Renaissance: Groupe de Recherche—Ordinateurs et Textes, or MARGOT; the Groupe d'Analyse et de Recherche sur l'Écriture des Femmes à la Renaissance, or GARSE-XVI; Women in French, or WIF; the Society for the Study of Early Modern Women, or SSEMW; and the Association Mnémosyne.

SIEFAR is a network of scholars seeking to further scholarship on early modern women by bringing specialists and nonspecialists together, by maintaining an electronic discussion list and Web site in order to make available important scholarship and research in progress, and by sponsoring conferences and workshops (http://siefar.org or http://siefar.femmes.free.fr/). SIEFAR promotes a series of Web sites committed to research on early modern French women writers such as http://pagesperso-orange.fr/mnemosyne.association/, which is devoted to the discussion of the history of women; http://genrehistoire.fr/, which provides online free access to articles, reviews, and abstracts in French and English; and www.lafrancelesfemmesetlepouvoir.org/tabledesmatieres.html, which features Éliane Viennot's research on women and power (some articles available online).

MARGOT concerns itself with the recovery, editing, interpretation, and publication of works by women, especially those that are not easily available. The main purpose of this group is to make these texts available online. For example, it hosted the colloquium The Use of Technology for Teaching and Research on Early Modern Texts (see http://margot.uwaterloo.ca/).

Created in 2006 with the support of the Ile-de-France Regional Council, IEC promotes research on women and gender studies as well as interdisciplinary projects (www.mnhn.fr/iec or www.emilieduchatelet.org).

Subsidized by Québec's Fonds pour la Formation des Chercheurs et l'Aide à la Recherche, GARSE-XVI involves a small group of Canadian scholars of the French Renaissance. Its goals are limited to the pursuit of specific scholarly projects on French early modern women's writing: the establishment of a bibliographical repertory of printed editions and translations by French women of the first part of the sixteenth century; preparation of modern editions of various texts by women such as Marie Dentière's *La guerre et deslivrance de la ville de Genesve* (1536) and *L'epistre à la Royne de Navarre* (1539), Hélisenne de Crenne's *Le songe de Madame Helisenne*, and Marguerite d'Auge's *Les pitoyables et funestes regrets de M. d'Auge, 1600*; the further exploration of women's writing and their use of medieval and early modern rhetoric (www.arts.mcgill.ca/programs/french/groupes_garse.html).

A research group under the direction of Jean-Philippe Beaulieu, Diane Desrosiers-Bonin, and Claude La Charité is currently at work on "Les femmes et la rhétorique à la Renaissance française. Dire et se dire au féminin."

WIF seeks to promote research on and teaching of French and francophone women from all centuries by publishing a biannual newsletter, an annual refereed journal, as well as special volumes on a regular basis; by organizing an annual conference and by establishing a presence at the MLA's and the regional MLA's annual conferences; by maintaining an electronic discussion list; and by publishing the first National Women in French directory. Participation in the Women in French discussion group in both French and English is reserved to WIF subscribers (http://users.ipfw.edu/virtue/WIF/ or http://users.ipfw.edu/virtue/WIF/WIF-Chatlist.htm). (Results are available on *Yahoo* only, or one can copy and paste the URL into another search bar.)

SSEMW, which is an outgrowth of the Folger colloquium on Women of the Renaissance (1985–89), is the American counterpart to SIEFAR in that it shares many of the same objectives: it promotes the exchange of ideas in the field of early modern women, meets regularly, has a Web site and electronic discussion list, publishes a newsletter, sponsors sessions at conferences, and so on (www.ssemw.org/). However, SSEMW is less internationally oriented, and, even though it welcomes scholars and students from any discipline, it has a distinctly anglophone focus. The latter also holds true for other research groups like the Australian Research Council Network for Early European Research (www.neer.arts.uwa.edu .au/), which coordinates large-scale cross-disciplinary investigations in early European research (400–1850) and occasional projects on early modern women.

The Association Mnémosyne is the French section of the International Federation for Research in Women's History. Created at the initiative of the scholarly journal *Clio*, it seeks to encourage and promote research on women's history and genre studies in France. It is responsible for the foundation of *Genre & Histoire*, an electronic journal offering to all and especially to young scholars a wealth of resources such as selective bibliographies, articles, accounts of scholarly discussions, and so on (http:// perso.wanadoo.fr/mnemosyne.association/ or e-mail contact@mnemosyne .asso.fr).

Scholarships, Fellowships, and Awards

IEC subsidizes several doctoral and postdoctoral fellowships each year. SSEMW awards annual prizes for the best book, essay, or article; best collaborative project; and best graduate student conference presentation pertaining to women and gender in the early modern period (1450–1750). The Josephine Roberts Prize goes to the best edition, and there is also an award for the best translation.

Presses, Series, and Journals

Both Champion (Textes de la Renaissance) and Droz (Textes littéraires français) publish scholarly editions of early modern women and proto-feminist texts as well as current scholarship in their conference proceedings series. Classiques Garnier is now hosting the Textes de la Renaissance series under the direction of Claude Blum and a new series, Féminin-Masculin, has been inaugurated in 2010. The Parisian Indigo and Côté-femmes Éditions, funded by the Centre National du Livre, has published a significant number of books on writing by early modern women (mostly seventeenth and eighteenth centuries). Its Des femmes dans l'histoire series includes several early modern volumes like Jean de Marconville's *De la bonté et mauvaiseté des femmes* (with a preface by Françoise Koelher), and Louise Bourgeois Boursier's *Observations sur la stérilité, perte de fruits, fécon-*

dité, accouchements et maladies des femmes (with a preface by Françoise Olive), clearly addressed to the informed nonspecialist or general reader. The same series showcases a reprint of Fortunée Briquet's *Dictionnaire historique, littéraire et bibliographique des Françaises et des étrangères naturalisées en France.* In addition, *Dictionnaire des créatrices,* under the direction of Béatrice Didier and with the assistance of Daniel Martin as the editor for sixteenth-century women writers, appeared in 2010. The Medieval and Renaissance Texts and Studies at Arizona State University is specialized in the publication of critical editions, translations, and interdisciplinary studies in the Middle Ages and the Renaissance. Worthy of note is the English translation by Richard Hillman and Colette Quesnel of Marie de Gournay's *Preface to the Essays of Michel de Montaigne,* which appeared in 1998.

The Publications de l'Université de Saint-Étienne offers two series especially devoted to the teaching of early modern women and to satisfying the curiosity of the general public. La cité des dames series features texts by early modern women. In addition to the aforementioned texts, this series has also made available Marguerite de Navarre's *Inquisiteur,* Louise Labé's *Le débat de folie et d'amour,* and Catherine Des Roches's *Tobie, Bergerie, Placide et Sévère,* and *Iris et Pasithée* in a volume entitled *Théâtre de femmes de l'Ancien Régime, XVIe siècle.* This is the first of a five-volume project under the direction of the French and American experts Aurore Evain, Perry Gethner, and Henriette Goldwyn. The L'école du genre series welcomes works pertaining to the history of women in Old Regime France and the study of genres. Several important synthetic overviews have already appeared such as *Louise Labé 2005* (Alonso and Viennot); *Histoires d'historiennes* (Pellegrin); *Patronnes et mécènes en France à la Renaissance* (Wilson-Chevalier), *Émergence littéraire des femmes à Lyon à la Renaissance, 1520–1560* (Clément and Incardona); and *Femmes en fleurs, femmes en corps* (McClive and Pellegrin).

The University of Chicago Press has shown a similar commitment to the teaching of women's writing. In addition to its Other Voice in Early Modern Europe series, launched some twelve years ago, its Women in Culture and Society series, headed by Catharine R. Stimpson, has published several groundbreaking volumes on early modern women and the question of gender, among which are *Rewriting the Renaissance: The Discourse of Sexual Difference in Early Modern England,* edited by Margaret W. Ferguson, Maureen Quilligan, and Nancy J. Vickers; Joan Kelly's *Women, History, and Theory;* Margaret L. King's *Women of the Renaissance;*

Margaret W. Ferguson's *Dido's Daughters: Literacy, Gender, and Empire in Early Modern England and France*. It is unclear, however, what the current status of this series is.

Many university presses support work in the field of gender and early modern women's studies. Cambridge University Press, for example, has published groundbreaking scholarship in its Renaissance and Early Modern Studies series, such as Erica Longfellow's *Women and Religious Writing in Early Modern England*, Marjorie Keniston McIntosh's *Working Women in English Society, 1300–1620*, Sharon Cadman Seeling's *Autobiography and Gender in Early Modern Literature: Reading Women's Lives, 1600–1680*. As this brief list indicates, though, most of these publications concern the larger Europe or, more specifically, Britain. Several university presses feature series specifically devoted to the publication of works on women and to gender's studies, for example Oxford's Women's Studies Series; Princeton's Gender Studies; Harvard's Social Sciences: Gender Studies; Columbia's Gender and Culture; Indiana's Women of Letters; and Southern Illinois's *Ad Feminam*: Women and Literature. But publications on literature by early modern women remain sporadic. The Sixteenth Century Essays and Studies series also counts several key studies on the question of gender in the Renaissance among its publications: *The Politics of Gender in Early Modern Europe* (Brink, Coudert, and Horowitz) and *Privileging Gender in Early Modern England* (Brink).

However, compared with these, Ashgate's busy agenda suggests that currently it may well be the leading publisher in the history of early modern women. Its most recent list of publications includes many works of interest for students and scholars in this field: Naomi J. Miller and Naomi Yavneh, editors, *Maternal Measures: Figuring Caregiving in the Early Modern Period*; Susan Broomhall, *Women and the Book Trade in Sixteenth-Century France*; *Widowhood and Visual Culture in Early Modern Europe*, edited by Alison Levy; Barbara Stephenson, *The Power and Patronage of Marguerite de Navarre*; *Women and Early Modern Manuscript Culture*, edited by Jonathan Gibson and Victoria E. Burke; *Women's Letters across Europe, 1400–1700*, edited by Jane Couchman and Ann Crabb. In addition, Ashgate's Women and Gender in the Early Modern World series, under the direction of Allyson Poska and Abby Zanger, welcomes specialized monographs and collections of essays that explore the experiences of early modern women and the nature of gender in Europe, the Americas, Asia, and Africa. Recent volumes that have appeared in this series include Lianne McTavish, *Childbirth and the Display of Authority in Early Modern*

France; Julie Campbell, *Literary Circles and Gender in Early Modern Europe*; and Janine M. Lanza, *From Wives to Widows in Early Modern Paris.*

Reference works as well as English or dual-language anthologies of texts have been published by ABC-CLIO, The Edwin Mellen Press, Garland, Palgrave, and Routledge (Taylor and Francis Group) (see "Anthologies" in the last essay).

In the last two decades, several academic journals have published special issues on early modern French women: *L'esprit créateur* (*Writing in the Feminine in the Renaissance*, ed. Rigolot); *Études littéraires* (*Écrits de femmes à la Renaissance*, ed. Larsen and Winn); *Carrefour* (*Le beau au temps de la Renaissance* [ed. Beecher], which includes several papers on early modern women in literature and in art); *Papers on French Seventeenth Century Literature* (*L'éducation des filles sous l'Ancien Régime*, ed. Winn); *Littératures* (*L'écriture des femmes à la Renaissance française*, ed. Desrosiers-Bonin); *Dalhousie French Studies* (*Le mariage sous l'Ancien Régime*, ed. Carlin); *Renaissance and Reformation / Renaissance et Réforme* (*Collaboration et créativité au sein des "salons" et des foyers culturels de la Renaissance*, ed. Winn and Rouget); and *Tangence* (*Masques et figures du sujet féminin aux XVIe et XVIIe siècles*, ed. La Charité).

The main journals of early modern studies, like *Bibliothèque d'Humanisme et Renaissance, Renaissance Quarterly, The Sixteenth Century Journal*, and *Renaissance and Reformation / Renaissance et Réforme* regularly publish individual articles and reviews of books on early modern women writers. There also exists a number of refereed journals that specialize in women's history (*Journal of Women's History*); women's and gender studies (*Gender and History*); criticism about women in various fields, such as literature, history, art, anthropology, sciences, and so on (*Women's Studies*); historical, cultural, and interdisciplinary studies (*Clio, Histoire, Femmes, Société*); and feminist, multicultural, and interdisciplinary scholarship (*Signs*; *Frontiers*; *European Journal of Women's Studies*). However, refereed journals devoted solely to scholarship on early modern women are few. *Early Modern Women: An Interdisciplinary Journal* is one of a few that is entirely devoted to the interdisciplinary and global study of women and gender during the years 1400 to 1700. The journal *Early Modern Women* has published in 2009 an interdisciplinary forum, "Early Modern Women and Material Culture."

Tulsa Studies in Women's Literature considers articles on women's literature of all periods and nationalities and particularly encourages works in feminist critical and literary theory. *Women in French Studies* also welcomes submissions on early modern women, although its primary focus seems to be contemporary and francophone women writers. Its 2002 special issue, for instance, is devoted, for a good third, to discussing specific courses on and successful approaches to women writers of Old Regime France: Diane S. Wood offers information, techniques, and suggestions for a course on Hélisenne de Crenne ("Hélisenne"); Colette H. Winn describes a course she has been teaching on early modern women and the development of print culture ("Femmes et le développement"). Of interest also to the early modern scholar is "Rivalry, Cooperation, Conspiracy, and Patronage: Studies in the Dynamics of Women's Interaction in French Literature and Culture," edited by Julia Simms Holderness and Laurence M. Porter, forthcoming in *Women in French Studies. Women in French Studies* also publishes extensive critical bibliographies either of women writers or on a special topic. The bibliographies published so far feature essentially contemporary women writers, but this is for lack of submissions on earlier periods. Finally, *Atlantis / A Women's Studies Journal*, published twice a year by the Institute for the Study of Women at Mount Saint Vincent University, welcomes the submission of critical and creative works on the topic of women. Selective papers from the first colloquium on Women Writers in Old Regime France appeared in its special issue, *Femmes et textes sous l'Ancien Régime* (Beaulieu and Fournier).

Graziella Postolache and Colette H. Winn

Online Resources

Since the 1980s Renaissance studies has witnessed a reshaping of the canon and the inclusion in both graduate and undergraduate courses of works by women heretofore neglected or unknown. In tandem with this dramatic change in the literary curriculum, the twenty-first-century cyberrevolution has provided many new facilities for students and teachers. An increasing number of libraries and academic departments successfully maintain references, dictionaries, and texts on their official Web sites. Several scholarly projects make available rare books and archival documents. It is now possible to read online, in different formats, numerous *editio princeps* of French women writers of the Renaissance and Reformation that are difficult to obtain through interlibrary loan. Numerous Web sites provide information on the lives and works of early modern women, as well as relevant secondary literature, and give access to texts in their entirety or excerpts in French or in English.

There is still some disagreement among teachers and scholars about the use of the Internet. Sites disappear as fast as they come, and the information they provide is not always reliable. And yet sites with images offer a change of pace in the classroom, bring the century to life, and provide a stimulating cultural setting to the material studied. Sites with selected music, virtual trivia, quizzes, or interactive games contribute to more fun in the classroom and stimulate students' participation. Sites with portraits and frontispieces help instructors convey to their students a concrete sense of a writer's life and works. Sites offering women's writings can be especially useful for textual analysis. With a click of a mouse, the instructor can move from one excerpt to another and highlight orthography, stylistic characteristics, recurrent themes, or images and associations that are discussed in class. Web pages can also be an excellent source of historical information to which students can be referred after an introductory lecture on the background and contexts of a work. For a selection of sites on the early modern era, refer to Winn, *Approaches to Teaching Marguerite de Navarre's* Heptameron 13–15. The following pages aim to present some of the most useful sites for the study of early modern women writers. They can be used as general references in or outside the classroom. The section entitled "Individual Authors" includes a wide variety of resources and should be particularly useful for the instructors planning to incorporate early modern women writers in their curriculum.

General Data about Women's History

Comete. Revue de Littératures d'Ancien Régime provides free access to articles and book reviews, as well as a periodical update of current publications and conferences regarding the early modern period. Even though women are not the primary focus, much data can be found on early modern women and issues of gender, power, and jurisprudence (www.cometes.org/).

Cour de France offers important historical documents and scholarship on the French court from its beginning to the Revolution as well as many useful links (http://cour-de-France.fr).

Digital Librarian: A Librarian's Choice of the Best of the Web, maintained by Margaret Vail Anderson, provides access to helpful sites for the study of early modern women (http://www.digital-librarian.com).

The Digital Scriptorium, an image database of medieval and Renaissance manuscripts hosted by Columbia University Libraries, will be a precious tool for teaching and research (http://scriptorium.columbia.edu/).

Early Modern Literary Studies is an electronic review published three times a year with the support of the Humanities Research Center at Sheffield Hallam University. Of special interest is G. Ziegler's "Women Writers Online: An Evaluation and Annotated Bibliography of Web Resources." Note that this site also provides links to Renascence Editions in PDF files like Castiglione's *The Book of the Courtier* (http://extra.shu.ac.uk/emls/emlshome.html).

The Early Modern Women Database covers women in Europe and the Americas during the "long" early modern period (from the fourteenth to the nineteenth century) with links to databases arranged by languages, time periods, subjects, and titles (www.lib.umd.edu/ETC/LOCAL/emw/emw.php3).

Feminae: Medieval Women and Gender Index, maintained by Margaret Schaus at Haverford College, features Europe, North Africa, and the Middle East during the period between 450 and 1500. Access to journal articles, conference proceedings, and book reviews about women, sexuality, and gender is only available if one's institution subscribes to the resource (e.g., JSTOR) providing it (www.haverford.edu/library/reference/mschaus/mfi/whatis.html).

Fortune City provides general information on women writers by country, period, and names (http://members.fortunecity.com/jonhays/memorial.htm).

The Foundation for Early Modern Women's History World Wide Web Virtual Library, hosted by the International Institute of Social History in Amsterdam, offers over seven thousand bibliographic notices and articles pertaining to the early modern period, with an extensive list of archives, research institutions, museums, and associations from twenty-two countries with their corresponding Web site addresses (www.iisg.nl/w3vlwomenshistory/vlwhgeo.html#france).

La France, les femmes et le pouvoir is devoted to Éliane Viennot's work on women and power (www.lafrancelesfemmesetlepouvoir.org).

H-Women is an international discussion group that has been set up at Michigan State University to enable scholars of women's history to discuss research interests, teaching methods, and the state of historiography (www2.h-net.msu.edu/~women/).

Monastic Matrix is an ongoing collaborative site created by an international group of scholars of medieval history, religion, history of art, and archaeology that aims to document the participation of women in the religion and society of medieval Europe. This site should be of interest to anyone working on professional Christian women in Europe between 400 and 1600 (http://monasticmatrix.usc.edu/dematrice/).

The Project Gutenberg E-Book makes available works by and scholarship about women (www.gutenberg.org/catalog/world/results).

Salons de France, or *Salons français*, partially maintained by the École Normale Supérieure of Lyon (ENS), provides biographical information about women who presided over a salon in Old Regime France with useful links to other historical figures (www.aei.ca/~anbou/salonfranc.html).

Women's Review of Books features essays and in-depth reviews of new books by and about women (www.wcwonline.org/womensreview).

Biobibliographic Studies on Early Modern French Women Writers

Anyone seeking biobibliographic information on early modern women writers will want to begin by consulting the *Dictionnaire des femmes de l'Ancienne France* online. This site, maintained by the Société Internationale des Études des Femmes d'Ancien Régime (SIEFAR), will prove an excellent resource both on women writers from the Middle Ages to the French Revolution and on specialists in the field. It provides substantial accounts of individual authors in French and English, with references from authoritative dictionaries such as Hilarion de Coste's *Eloges et vies des roynes, princesses, dames et damoiselles illustres en pieté, courage et doctrine* (1630), Marguerite Buffet's *Eloges des illustres sçavantes tant anciennes que modernes* (1668), Pierre Joseph Boudier de Villemert's *Notice alphabétique des femmes célèbres* (1779), and Fortunée Briquet's *Dictionnaire historique, littéraire et bibliographique des Françaises et des étrangères naturalisées en France* (1804), a list of works, a selective bibliography, and iconography whenever possible. This is, however, an ongoing project, and some entries are still incomplete (http://siefar.org).

Les écrits féminins non fictionnels du Moyen Âge au XVIIIe siècle. Un inventaire raisonné makes available an annotated bibliography of nonfictional writings by women from the Middle Ages to the eighteenth century. Founded and maintained at the University of Ottawa by Marie-Laure Girou Swiderski in collaboration with several colleagues, this site currently includes women authors from the sixth to the fifteenth century. Entries comprise a brief biographical notice followed by a list of works and where they can be located, as well as a selective bibliography of critical studies (http://aix1.uottawa.ca/~margirou/Perspectives/Renaissance/renaissa.htm).

Women's Texts in French

The ARTFL French Women Project, maintained at the University of Chicago, currently contains works by some forty authors from the twelfth to the twentieth century. Access is limited to subscribing institutions (http://humanities.uchicago.edu/orgs/ARTFL/ or www.lib.uchicago.edu/efts/ARTFL/projects/FWW/index.html).

A Celebration of Women Writers, maintained by Mary Mark Ockerbloom at the University of Pennsylvania in collaboration with the *On-Line Books Page*, provides easy access to digitized texts by and about women writers as well as biographical and bibliographic information. So far this site features few texts by French women and an English translation of the *Heptameron* by Walter Kelly, with a foreword by the translator (http://digital.library.upenn.edu/women).

Gallica, the site maintained by the Bibliothèque Nationale de France, makes available many original editions of early modern women's works as well as nineteenth-century editions. The site has a search engine. For better and faster results, it is recommended to search authors by their last name only (http://gallica.bnf.fr).

Margot, organized by Hannah Fournier, Delbert Russell, and Peter Marteinson at the University of Waterloo, has produced a database of works by early modern French women and a selection of their Latin sources. These include Marie de Gournay's 1626 *L'ombre* and her 1641 *Les advis*; Marie de Cotteblanche's 1579 *Lettre à Mme Marguerite de Saluces, mareschalle de Termes*; Marie de Pech de Calages's 1661 *Judith*; and Jeanne de Cambry's 1655 *Traité de la reforme du mariage* (http://margot.uwaterloo.ca/margotFren/index.html).

The Renaissance in Print: Sixteenth-Century French Books in the Douglas Gordon Collection provides digital facsimiles of sixteenth-century printed books from the University of Virginia Douglas H. Gordon Collection as well as a network of resources designed to situate these books within their context. (For additional information, see James and McKinley, in this volume; www.lib.virginia.edu/small/exhibits/gordon/lit).

English Translations

Other Women's Voices, a very helpful site maintained by Dorothy Disse, contains several French early modern women's works in English translation, along with concise biographies, information on the historical background, secondary sources, essays, book reviews, and links to Internet sites, as well as portraits of the authors when available (http://home.infionline.net/~ddisse/index.html).

Secondary Literature and Additional Resources

The Early Modern French Women Writers Project, by Anne E. Duggan, Mary Skemp, and Michelle Miller provides extensive bibliographies, including general studies on literature and gender in early modern France and studies on individual Writers (http://etrc.lib.umn.edu/frenbib.htm).

Sunshine for Women offers bibliographies of women in print and lists various anthologies (www.pinn.net/~sunshine/biblio/antholgy.html and www.pinn.net/~sunshine/4dads/4dads5.html, for a tribute to feminist forefathers with links to excerpts from their works in English).

Women's Studies Digitization Project: Early Modern French Women, under the direction of Susan Stekel, contains biographies of early modern women, their publication history, secondary studies, as well as images. For direct access to their writings, the page is redirected to the *Early Modern French Women Writers Project* (http://etrc.lib.umn.edu/frenwom.htm and http://etrc.lib.umn.edu/frentxts.htm).

Individual Authors

Jeanne d'Albret

Gallica, under Albret or Bourbon, gives access to Jeanne d'Albret's correspondence with Antoine de Bourbon, and to her *Mémoires et poésies.* For a good biography in French and English with suggested readings, see *Siefar* and *Project Poissy* (www-rohan.sdsu.edu/~lavoicy/poissy/AlbretF.html, with portraits by Clouet). *Other Women's Voices* includes essays with numerous excerpts from Jeanne's letters and published works, five portraits, and several book reviews.

For an overview of Protestantism, major events, places, and important figures, students could be referred to the Web site for the Fédération Protestante de France (www.protestants.org) or the *Musée virtuel du protestantisme français* (www.museeprotestant.org, in French, English, and German). Also useful for a closer look at Protestant faith in the Bearn region and additional information on Jeanne d'Albret's religious views and political actions, see *Musée Jeanne d'Albret* (http://museejeannedalbret.com) and *Antithesis* (www.reformed.org/webfiles/antithesis/index.html). See especially the article by M. B. Manzer.

Oxford Journals gives access to R. J. Knecht's review of *Jeanne d'Albret et sa cour* (subscribers only).

Anne of France

The full text of the Chazaud edition of *Enseignements à sa fille* is now available on *Gallica*. In addition, biographical and bibliographic resources, information about the location of original works, as well as a brief description of these works can be found on *Les écrits féminins non fictionnels*. A useful site when teaching at the undergraduate level is *Histoire en Ligne* (www.histoire-en-ligne.com/spip.php?article429). It provides historical background in French regarding Anne of France's influence in the political sphere and her legacy as a successor to King Louis XI, as well as one portrait, but no reference is made to her *Enseignements*. For additional images and information about Anne of France's public role students could be referred to the site for the Ducal Palace of the Bourbons in Moulins (today the Anne de Beaujeu Museum; www.evene.fr/culture/lieux/musee-anne-de-beaujeu-3443.php.

Gabrielle de Coignard

Advanced students can now access the 1595 edition of the *Œuvres chrestiennes* on *Gallica*. They will find adequate historical background, bibliographic references, essays, and an English translation of both the *Sonnets spirituels* and the *Imitation de la victoire de Judith* on *Other Women's Voices*. Highly recommended is Paul Chilton's "Devout Humanism," available on *Google Books*.

Louise de Coligny

Siefar and *Les écrits féminins non fictionnels* provide sufficient biographical and bibliographic information in both French and English. However, for more complete documentation on the political background and the history of Protestantism in France, one may want to consult *Memo*'s piece on Louise de Coligny's husband, Guillaume d'Orange-Nassau (www.memo.fr/Dossier.asp?ID=493).

Hélisenne de Crenne

Advanced students can now consult on *Gallica* a variety of editions of Hélisenne de Crenne's works: the 1538 and 1541 editions of *Les angoysses douloureuses*, the 1550 edition of *Les epistres familieres*, and the 1543 edition of *Les œuvres.* In addition to these, Christine de Buzon's edition of *Les angoysses douloureuses* is now available in its entirety on *ARTFL French Women Project.* Bibliographic data and Lisa Neal's and Steven Rendall's English translation of Hélisenne's works as well as several helpful links can be found on *Other Women's Voices.* Students should be advised to read the introduction and first chapter of Diane S. Woods's *At the Crossroads of Renaissance Humanism and Feminism*, made available by *Google Books.* For those studying the *Epitres*, Jerry Nash's "Renaissance Misogyny, Biblical Feminism," now offered by *The Free Library*, is recommended.

Marie Dentière

Students may choose from a variety of short biographies: William Kemp's, in both French and English, on *Siefar*; Isabelle Graesslé's, in French only (see "Marie Dentière"), or Suzanne McCarthy, in English.

For further readings and an English translation of some of Dentière's works, students can be directed to *Other Women's Voices.* Of special interest is Jane Dempsey Douglass's "Glimpses of Reformed Women Leaders from Our History," on *Semper Reformanda.*

Madeleine and Catherine Des Roches

Students are now able to view various editions: the 1579 edition of *Les œuvres* on *Gallica*, the 1582 edition of *La puce de Madame des-Roches* on *The Renaissance in Print* (www2.lib.virginia.edu/rmds/portfolio/gordon); Catherine's poem, "La puce," begins on page 20. See also the 1583 edition of *Les Secondes œuvres* on both these sites. Students may want to begin their study by reading Anne R. Larsen's piece on *Siefar* ("Des Roches") or Kendall Tarte's on *Other Women's Voices* (http://home.infionline.net/~adisse/desroches.html) and Tarte's "Seductive Topographies." Access to Todd P. Olson's "La femme à la puce et la puce à l'oreille" is available with subscription to the *Project Muse.*

Pernette Du Guillet

The texts available online include the 1545 edition of the *Rymes* with the *Epitaphes de la gente et spirituelle Dame Pernette Du Guillet*, by Maurice

Scève and Jean de Vauzelles (*Gallica*), the 1546 edition (http://poesie.webnet.fr/auteurs/GUI.html), Joseph Aynard's edition on *The Early Modern French Women Writers Project* site, the Slatkine reprint of Pernette Du Guillet's *Poésies* (see André Socard's site, http://www.socard.fr/per00.htm), and individual poems, among which two poems exchanged by Scève and Du Guillet (see the project *Terres de femmes*, by Angèle Paoli [http://terresdefemmes.blogs.com/mon_weblog/2006/03/pernette_du_gui.html and http://terresdefemmes.blogs.com/mon_weblog/2006/05/jeu_dchange_pot.html]).

Élise Rajchenbach's piece on *Siefar* is recommended reading as well as the brief biography based on the entry from *The Feminist Encyclopedia of French Literature* (Sartori), which is made available by *The Early Modern French Women Writers Project.*

Charlotte Arbaleste de Mornay

Besides *Gallica*, which makes available the entire text of Henriette de Witt's 1868–69 edition of the *Mémoires*, *Other Women's Voices* is the most useful site. It provides excerpts in English as well as several links to illuminate the historical background. Among the documents available Catharine Randall's "Shouting Down Abraham" is highly recommended. Students will also find a brief biography by Nadine Kuperty-Tsur on *Siefar* as well as a brief notice on Charlotte's marriage to Philippe de Mornay and a useful genealogy on *Online Encyclopedia* by typing in the keywords *philippe* and *mornay* (http://encyclopedia.jrank.org).

Nicole Estienne (Mme Liebault)

See the biography in both French and English by Cathy Yandell with suggested readings on *Siefar* (one portrait mentioned).

Marie de Gournay

Students can now have access to many editions of Gournay's works: the 1626 edition of *L'ombre*; the 1634 and 1641 editions of *Les advis*, and several editions of the *Promenoir de Monsieur de Montaigne* on *Gallica*; *Peincture de Moeurs*, *Grief des dames*, and *Égalité des hommes et des femmes* on *Women-Philosophers* (www.women-philosophers.com/Marie-le-Jars-de-Gournay.html). *Égalité* is also available on *LITgloss*, with annotations by Soumia Boutkhil (http://wings.buffalo.edu/litgloss/gournay/text.shtml).

Students may choose from a variety of short biographies in French and English with a selective bibliography: Jean-Claude Arnould's, on *Siefar*; a publication history (http://etrc.lib.umn.edu/frenpub.htm gournay) and a bibliography (http://etrc.lib.umn.edu/frenbio.htm gournay) in English on *Early Modern French Women Writers* and *Women-Philosophers*, and Marie-Thérèse Noiset's piece in French on *Gournay sur Aronde*, with links of general interest (www.gournaysuraronde.com/histoire.html). Enlightening is the piece on Gournay's collaboration with Montaigne and interactions with different figures of her time (http://pagesperso-orange.fr/saphisme/s17/gournay.html).

Three additional sites will prove useful when teaching Gournay: *Sunshine for Women*, for a brief presentation of *Égalité des hommes et des femmes* and *Grief des dames*; *Early Modern French Women Writers* and *Other Women's Voices*, for an English translation of some of Gournay's works. *Other Women's Voices* provides as well access to essays by Jean-Claude Arnould, Natalie Zemon Davis, Katharine J. Lualdi, Orest Ranum, and Richard L. Regosin. Three portraits are available.

Jeanne de Jussie

For basic biographical information in both French and English, a brief summary of her works with the location of manuscripts and printed texts, and secondary sources, see Madeleine Lazard's notice on *Siefar* and *Les écrits féminins non fictionnels.* See *Other Women's Voices* for Carrie Klaus's English translation of *Petite chronique* and links to helpful sites online.

Louise Labé

Students have many texts from which to choose: the 1555 and 1556 editions of the *Euvres* (*Gallica*, *The Renaissance in Print*, and *Epistemon* [www.cesr.univ-tours.fr/Epistemon/cornucopie/Cornuc.asp], which includes a list of corrections to the Garnier-Flammarion edition); the Charles Boy edition (*Gallica*); Joseph Aynard's edition (see the Early Modern French Women Writers Project); and individual poems (see www.poesie.webnet.fr/). *Other Women's Voices* gives access to Annie Finch's and Deborah

Lesko Baker's English translations of Labé's works as well as useful links, essays, and book reviews.

In addition to the entry by Françoise Charpentier on *Siefar*, undergraduate students may be directed to Cécile Alduy's site (www.stanford.edu/dept/fren-ital/cgi-bin/rbp/?q=node/306), which contains a brief biographical notice, recommendations for further readings, a portrait and useful links to, for example, the debate around Mireille Huchon's *Créature de papier.* Two sites will be of great use to those who teach undergraduate or high school students: *Pearson Prentice Hall* provides a brief biography with a close reading of eight sonnets by André O. Hurtgen and pedagogical notes on how to use the material (www.phschool.com/curriculum_support/louise_labe/). *About.com* features French listening comprehension by Laura K. Lawless and contains a reading of "Je vis, je meurs," the poem in French with its English translation, and a glossary (http://french.about.com/od/listening/a/poetrypodcasts.htm). Those interested in gender studies may be referred to the bibliography provided by *The Early Modern French Women Writers Project.* More advanced students will benefit from the extensive bibliography available online (www2.ac-lyon.fr/enseigne/lettres/louise/biblio.html).

Anne de Marquets

Works by Anne de Marquets, available on *Gallica*, include the 1566 edition of her *Sonets, prieres et devises en forme de pasquins* and the 1605 edition of her *Sonets spirituels.* Two sites will prove useful for basic biographical and bibliographic information: *Siefar* with an article in both French and English by Gary Ferguson ("Marquets"; one portrait mentioned) and the *Poissy Project* (www-rohan.sdsu.edu/~lavoicy/poissy/Marquets.htm).

Georgette de Montenay

Both *Gallica* and *The Renaissance in Print* offer access to the 1571 edition of Georgette de Montenay's *Emblemes, ou devises chrestiennes.* A facsimile of Georgette de Montenay and Anna Roemer Visscher's *Cent emblemes chrestiens* has been made available by the *Emblem Project Utrecht* with a brief introduction, a concordance (www-rohan.sdsu.edu/~lavoicy/poissy/Marquets.htm), and all emblems (http://emblems.let.uu.nl/av1615_all_picturae.html).

For in-class presentations refer to the site maintained at the Bryn Mawr College Special Collections Library (www.brynmawr.edu/library/speccoll/guides/Emblems/demontenay.html.), where you will find a digital image of pages 54–55 of *Emblematum christianorum centuria*, and also to *French Emblems at Glasglow* (www.emblems.arts.gla.ac.uk/french/books.php?id=FMOa), which contains various images, including a portrait of Georgette de Montenay, and Alison Adams's well-documented introduction to Georgette de Montenay and sixteenth-century emblem books, with suggestions for further study. This reading should be supplemented by Daniel S. Russell's "Emblems" on the Newberry Library site (www.newberry.org/renaissance/consortium/russell-wade%20emblem.html).

Marguerite de Navarre

Available on *Gallica* are the 1559 edition of the *Heptameron* as well as several eighteenth- and nineteenth-century editions and the Michel François edition; both the 1531 and 1533 editions of *Le miroir de l'âme pécheresse* (the latter with the *Dialogue en forme de vision nocturne* and the *Discord*); and the Laudun edition of her *Lettres inédites, 1579–1606. The Renaissance in Print* provides selections from the *Heptameron* and *La Marguerite des princesses* with a brief presentation of Marguerite's life and her times (see James and McKinley, in this volume).

Most of Marguerite de Navarre's works now also exist in translation online. *Other Women's Voices* makes available Walter K. Kelly's 1855 translation of the *Heptameron* as well as excerpts from the Chilton's translation and from others works by Marguerite de Navarre like *Le Miroir de l'âme pécheresse*, *La comédie des quatre femmes*, *La coche*, *Le triomphe de l'agneau*, and *Les prisons.* Excerpts from Kelly's translation can also be found on *A Celebration of Women Writers*, and George Saintsbury's translation is made available by *Project Gutenberg*.

In addition to biographical and bibliographic data, essays, book reviews, and so forth, *Other Women's Voices* provides a wealth of visual material for the classroom (mainly from the Gordon Collection), including individual pages from several editions of various works, a color illustration from an early edition of *La coche*, and four portraits by Jean Clouet. Another useful site for class presentation is Michael Delahoyde's from Washington State University: you will find images and woodcuts from the first published editions of Marguerite's works, as well as a short biography in

English, a good overview of major works (no further readings suggested), and links to online texts from the Gordon Collection and a Renaissance index (www.wsu.edu/~delahoyd/renaissance/navarre.html).

Animation Renaissance Amboise is a fun source for checking who is who among the Valois; Marguerite de Navarre is portrayed essentially as a political figure (www.renaissance-amboise.com/dossiers). *Kings' College Women's History* may be used as a starting point about facts, scholarship, and Internet sites. It provides a short biography in English by Kimberly Fabbri with an annotated bibliography and links to secondary sources, and articles by Pierre Jourda, Marcel Tetel, and Kelly Walter (http://departments.kings.edu/womens_history/margueritN.html). For bibliographic data on Marguerite and gender in the Renaissance see *Early Modern French Women Writers*. Undergraduate students may be referred to the articles featured by *Fortune City* on Marguerite de Navarre as a queen, writer, humanist, and "mother of the Renaissance." Focusing on style and language in the *Heptameron*, Isabelle Garnier-Mathez's 2006 bibliography seems to be more appropriate for advanced students: see *The Centre d'Études Supérieures de la Renaissance* (www.cesr.univ-tours.fr/SFDES/SFDES/Navarrebiblio.doc). Instructors may want to consult Janet L. Smarr's course description of Women Writers in the Renaissance, which includes Marguerite de Navarre (www.umass.edu/complit/aclanet/ACLAText/illsmarr.html).

Marie de Romieu

The 1581 edition of *Les premières œuvres poétiques* and Prosper Blanchemain's 1878 edition of the *Œuvres poétiques* are now available online (see *Gallica*) as is the 1971 edition by André Winandy (*Google Books*). Students may be referred to Claude La Charité's biographical notice (in both French and English) on *Siefar*, with suggested readings, among which is Anne R. Larsen's "Paradox and the Praise of Women," the abstract for which can be found on http://escj.truman.edu/vol28abs.html.

Margaret of Valois

In addition to some of Margaret's letters, *Gallica* (http://gallica.bnf.fr) makes available several eighteenth- and nineteenth-century editions of her *Mémoires*. *The Project Gutenberg EBook Court Memoir* series gives an English translation of the full text of Margaret's *Memoirs*, edited by David

Widger. Volumes 1–3 are available on a mirror site for download (www.gutenberg.org/etext/3841). Links to a modernized version of Pierre de Bourdeille, sieur de Brantôme, *Discours sur la reyne de France et de Navarre* and to an English translation of Alexandre Dumas's *La reine Margot* are available on *Other Women's Voices*. As a point of departure, students may consult Éliane Viennot's piece on *Siefar* ("Marguerite").

Karen Simroth James and Mary B. McKinley

Rare Books and Web Pages

Introducing students to books printed in the sixteenth century can enhance any course in early modern France. Because women played an important role as readers, subjects, printers, and authors of early printed books (see Broomhall, *Women and the Book Trade*; Chang; Davis, "Women in the Crafts"), we routinely take our classes for a visit to the Albert and Shirley Small Special Collections Library, where they receive an orientation to books and their production in sixteenth-century France. We schedule that visit after the first four weeks of a fourteen-week semester, when students have already had an introduction to the period and have read a work or two in their Livre de Poche, Folio, or Garnier-Flammarion editions. We refer students in advance to two online glossaries of vocabulary useful for describing books from the first century of printing: "Petit glossaire du bibliophile" (*Galaxidion*: www.galaxidion.com/home/glossaire/index.php) and "ABC de bibliophilie" (*Bibliopolis*: www.bibliopolis.net/glossaire/glossair.htm). The latter, a Canadian site, provides English equivalents for each of its entries. We ask students to look up the most basic terms there: *la feuille* ("sheet"); *le feuillet* ("leaf"); *la page* ("page"); *le cahier* ("gathering" or "quire"); *la signature* ("signature"); *les pontuseaux* ("chain lines"); *les vergeures* ("wire lines"); *le filigrane* ("watermark"); *les caractères* ("letters"; "type"); *la gravure sur bois* ("woodcut engraving"); and so on. Henri-Jean Martin and Roger Chartier's beautifully illustrated history of the French book contains several relevant and informative articles, especially Jeanne Veyrin-Forrer's "Fabriquer un livre au XVIe siècle" and Natalie Davis's account of book production in Lyon ("Monde").

It is always a pleasure to watch students' reactions when, for the first time, they see and hold a book that sixteenth-century readers held and read. A frequent observation: "That type is weird—and hard to read!" About the 1542 Rabelais volumes: "They're so little!" The woodcuts ask for closer inspection. We urge students to turn the pages and to hold the books with a leaf open to the light—all with extreme care and clean hands, of course. They are delighted to discover for themselves the chainlines and watermarks. For many of them, the world of the sixteenth century becomes more immediate. The reaction is not universal. In a class of fifteen or twenty students, some of the eyes will begin to glaze over in the first few minutes, but in that same class there will be another group whose eyes shine with excitement. They turn the pages cautiously but eagerly. The light dawns that people living more than 450 years ago held and read this copy of Louise Labé's *Euvres*. Their eyes moved across the very lines that we are now seeing, and their fingers turned these very pages. Those students are hooked. They consult the Gordon catalog.[1] They return to the special collections library on their own. They ask to do a term paper on a topic that will involve more contact with those old books.

Not everyone has access to a collection of French books from the sixteenth century. That was the case at the University of Virginia before the Gordon books arrived in 1986. However, most college and university libraries own some books from the early age of printing, and librarians are usually happy to introduce students to them. A class trip to a nearby collection is well worth the effort. After a first physical experience of holding and examining a sixteenth-century book, virtual reality can lend support, helping to develop an awareness of early printing and the book trade that enriches our reading and discussions for the rest of the semester.

The Douglas Gordon Collection in the University of Virginia Library includes sixteenth-century editions of works by several women writers of the Renaissance and Reformation. It also offers numerous influential books written by men for and about women, works that reflect the historical contexts and cultural forces that shaped the women writers of the era. Many of these volumes are available online as part of *The Renaissance in Print: Sixteenth-Century French Books in the Douglas Gordon Collection* (www.lib.virginia.edu/rmds/portfolio/gordon/), a digital archive supported by funding from the Florence Gould Foundation and the National Endowment for the Humanities.

Along with the works of Louise Labé, Marguerite de Navarre, Madeleine and Catherine Des Roches, and Georgette de Montenay, *The Renaissance in Print* features digital facsimiles of a number of books representing sixteenth-century views on female nature, behavior, and education. The online archive includes devotional manuals for women (George de Esclavonie's *Le chasteau de virginite* [1515], for example, and *Cy comece vne petite instruction et maniere de vivre pour vne feme seculiere* [1530]), cosmetic recipes and medical advice (Le Fournier's *La decoration dhumaine nature* [1537]), the 1543 French edition of Juan Luis Vives's *Liure tres bon plaisant et salutaire de linstitution de la femme chrestienne*, important volumes of exempla (Boccaccio, Plutarch), and iconographic representations of women in popular emblem books of the period. These are digital facsimiles of original editions, displaying spelling and typographic conventions that are hurdles for the uninitiated. With a little preparation, however, those obstacles become teaching tools that allow students to interact with the real thing, albeit in a virtual environment.

Although the appearance of the sixteenth-century pages may at first seem a bit daunting to students, their comfort with digital media has made it easier than we anticipated for them to grasp the qualities of the original book. Students realize that they are looking at a faithful reproduction of the real thing, and the excitement of that encounter carries over into their reading and learning experience. Because students typically expect to have greater difficulty reading the original editions, they are often agreeably surprised to find that the challenge is manageable after a brief initial period of (dis)orientation. Once they get used to the unfamiliar typography and spelling, they appreciate the experience of reading the same pages that sixteenth-century readers did. That virtual connection often leads them into the special collections library for a closer encounter with the physical object and prompts them to sign up for courses on the history of the book and material bibliography in other departments. Even for short reading assignments, the experience of working with the book in its original format (or its digital representation) gives students a sense of engaging in serious scholarship. They feel at least temporarily empowered to bypass their anthologies or paperback editions and at the same time come away with a new appreciation for those modern editions with their notes and glossaries and familiar spelling.

From the beginning we have imagined an audience for *The Renaissance in Print* that includes both researchers and teachers. The site is a work in progress. Our first goal was to digitize a significant selection of the books and make them available on the Web. Visitors to the site can find a list of the books now available by clicking on the Index of Digitized Works link in the menu. An alphabetical list by author contains links to the digital facsimiles for each work. Our next task was to provide introductory information about the books and their authors, as well as suggestions for further reading. Colleagues from the United States, Canada, and Europe have generously contributed to those pages, and the network of reference materials continues to grow. The pages for Marguerite de Navarre, Louise Labé, Madeleine and Catherine Des Roches, and Georgette de Montenay have introductory material with links to the facsimiles of their books. We offer here a few ideas about how they might contribute to courses including those writers.

The introductory page for Marguerite de Navarre (www.lib.virginia.edu/rmds/portfolio/gordon/literary/marguerite/) gives a basic biographical overview, with links to pages devoted to the *Heptameron* (Prevost, 1560) and to the *Marguerites de la Marguerite des Princesses* in Jean de Tournes's beautiful first edition (1547), each with call numbers linking to the digital facsimiles of the works. The *Heptameron* images offer Benoist Prevost's ornate mannerist frame on the title page, as well as the inked signature of Thomas Smith, Queen Elizabeth I's ambassador to the French court. Perhaps it was Smith or a member of his family who wrote notes in the margins of the prologue and drew tiny sketches of the abbey of Saint Savin and of Oisille's psalter. The *Heptameron* page includes links to the electronic transcription of a modern edition on the *Gallica* Web site (http://gallica.bnf.fr) and to audio recordings of excerpts from selected stories on the *Portail Multimédia de Renaissance-France* (www.renaissance-france.org/multimedia/pages/pagmultimedia.html). (Here and elsewhere, we have not provided an exhaustive list of external links, choosing instead to highlight one or two online resources that we feel will be of greatest interest and use to teachers and students.) The *Heptameron* page includes two short transcriptions from the Gordon copy (the prologue and story 19) with links to a digital image of each page. Along with the transcriptions, students can consult the "conseils pour lire une édition ancienne" (tips on reading a sixteenth-century edition), provided by George Hoffmann.

Students reading the *Heptameron* can get a taste of Marguerite's poetry—the writing for which she was known during her lifetime—by browsing in the *Marguerites.* There they can read the verse "Au lecteur," in which Marguerite asks her reader in advance to excuse the rhythm and language of the poems, "Voyant que c'est d'une femme l'ouvrage" ("Seeing that it is the work of a woman"; image file 24; our trans.). We see the decorative initial letters, intricate jewels in Jean de Tournes's books, the italic type by Robert Granjon, and the woodcuts that Bernard Salomon created for *La coche.* The *Marguerites* page gives basic information about the work and links to the facsimiles of the two editions in the Gordon Collection—Jean de Tournes's elegant first edition, and the smaller 1558 edition, published by Jehan Ruelle in Paris.

A link on the Labé page sends us to the digital facsimile of *Euvres de Louïze Labé Lionnoise. Revues et corrigees par ladite dame* (Lyon: Tournes, 1556). This is the second of the two editions published by Jean de Tournes. The introduction to the volume (www.lib.virginia.edu/rmds/portfolio/gordon/literary/labe/) includes URLs for other key resources online, including the searchable transcription of the 1555 edition in the "Epistemon" database of the *Bibliothèques virtuelles humanistes* (www.bvh.univ-tours.fr/); the interactive examination of Labé's "Je vis, je meurs" on Marc Bizer's site, *Lyre entre les lignes* (http://www.laits.utexas.edu/rbtl/); and the text of the biographical entry for Louise Labé in Antoine Du Verdier's *Bibliothèque* (1584). Published nineteen years after the poet's death and thirty years after the publication of the *Euvres,* Du Verdier's brief account gives students an example of the reception of works by women writers. Mireille Huchon's recent book arguing that Labé as author of the *Œuvres* is a hoax, a collective joke foisted on the public by male writers, provokes students' curiosity and sends them back to the page images to weigh the evidence for themselves.

In her introduction to Madeleine and Catherine Des Roches (www.lib.virginia.edu/rmds/portfolio/gordon/literary/desroches/), Kendall Tarte provides an overview of the lives and works of that mother and daughter who animated cultural life in Poitiers during the Wars of Religion. Links on that main page send readers to additional information on *La puce de Madame Des-Roches* (1582) and *Les secondes œuvres de Mesdames des Roches de Poictiers, mere et fille* (1583) and to the facsimiles of the two books. They reveal a fascinating collaboration between mother and daughter as they offer a glimpse into early salon culture in a provincial city. Two prose dialogues in the *Secondes œuvres* address the subject of the education of women, one from the point of view of two older men ("Dialogue de Placide, et Severe") and the other from their daughters' perspective ("Dialogue d'Iris, et de Pasithée"). Addressing questions central to the *querelle des femmes* in these dialogues, Catherine Des Roches adopts a strong position in favor of women's independence that engages today's students.

The Gordon Collection also includes the first edition of the *Emblemes, ou, devises chrestiennes* (1571) of Georgette de Montenay (www.lib.virginia.edu/rmds/portfolio/gordon/emblem/montenay.html). Along with access to the digital facsimiles, the introductory page provides links to another copy of this emblem book and a reproduction of the 1584 edition on the Web site of the French emblems project at the University of Glasgow (www.emblems.arts.gla.ac.uk/french). One of eight French emblem books now offered by *The Renaissance in Print*, Montenay's invites comparison with them as well as with the deeply religious poetry of Marguerite de Navarre in *Les Marguerites de la Marguerite des Princesses.* Montenay declares in the dedication that hers is the first book of Christian emblems.

The beautiful engraved images by Pierre Woeiriot represent the use of copperplate engraving in printed books; this is the first French emblem book to use the new technique instead of woodcut illustrations. The engraved portrait of Montenay, present in some of the extant volumes, is dated 1567 and depicts the author at work, pen in hand, with an open music book and lute lying nearby. The pen and musical instrument represent the accomplishments of an educated woman, which here are dedicated entirely to spiritual concerns. The accompanying verses explain that the author uses her written words and voice to sing the praises of God. In her closing epistle, she offers her soul and her book to her *Seigneur*. The early date on the portrait lends support to the theory that Georgette de Montenay's work was ready for publication before 1571 but that its printing was delayed because of the turmoil of the French Wars of Religion, another topic well represented in the Gordon Collection.

The overview provided on the Books about Women page (www.lib.virginia.edu/rmds/portfolio/gordon/women/) can serve as an orientation or resource for a course on early modern women. It includes representative images from books written by men about women, and it provides links to those digital facsimiles. Students can browse Vives's *Institution de la femme chrestienne* and bring that author's prescriptions to a discussion of the *Heptameron*'s representation of women. Illustrations depicting the nature of women in the emblem books of Andreas Alciati or Gilles Corrozet complement those readings. Students can explore visual and verse depictions of women in domestic roles in the emblem books and compare them with discussions of women's household duties in Vives's manual or in Xenophon's *Mesnagerie.* They can read Vives's warnings against the dangers of female vanity in view of the recipes and instructions for makeup and hair color in André Le Fournier's *La decoration dhumaine nature.* That small 1537 volume, the product of François Juste, the same Lyonnais printer who published the 1542 *Pantagruel* and *Gargantua*, never fails to fascinate students. Its gothic typeface is daunting, but its table of contents is enticing. Warned in advance that it sometimes reverts to Latin, students can find instructions for increasing the milk of nursing mothers, enhancing their complexions, and curing kidney stones. Le Fournier even offers his readers advice on how to "faire triumpher la face de la personne qu'elle semblera n'avoir que xv ans" ("make the face of the person so improved that she will seem to be only fifteen years old"; our trans.).

We have also assembled a dossier page for "les femmes et les livres" (www.lib.virginia.edu/rmds/portfolio/gordon/women/dossier.html), which we find useful for introductory presentations or as the basis for in-class discussion. The dossier provides a brief outline illustrating widely held beliefs about women in the early modern period. Large thumbnails link each topic to full-page images that could be projected in the classroom. In the case of classrooms not equipped with projection equipment or a good Internet connection, *The Renaissance in Print* is set up so that students can easily find the recommended materials for assignments outside class.

We also provide links in *The Renaissance in Print* to several sites that we recommend to our students:

Le portail de la Renaissance, under the direction of Rémi Morel and Jean-Yves Pouilloux, provides information on many aspects of life and culture in sixteenth-century France (www.renaissance-france.org).

Lyon à la Renaissance features historical maps and background on culture, politics, and religion in Renaissance Lyon (www2.ac-lyon.fr/enseigne/lettres/louise/lyon/lyonren.html).

SIEFAR is the Web site of the Société Internationale pour l'Étude des Femmes de l'Ancien Régime and includes a biographical dictionary (www.siefar.org).

La muse Renaissante, by Marc Bizer, includes historical background on Renaissance France and an introduction to key literary figures and movements, plus a guided reading of a Labé sonnet (www.laits.utexas.edu/bizer).

Petit guide de la langue du XVIe siècle, by Marc Bizer, provides a brief introduction to Middle French (http://uts.cc.utexas.edu/~mbizer/fr355/guide.html).

Where do we go from here? As we write this article in spring 2008, over two hundred volumes are listed in the Index of Digitized Works on *The Renaissance in Print* site. We continue to add introductory reference materials for those books, which offer a window on sixteenth-century printing, literature, travel, architecture, social conventions, philosophy, devotion, religious conflict, and political developments. Metadata will eventually allow users to search the digitized collection by key bibliographic features, such as printers' marks, ornamental letters, and dedicatees. The next phase of the project will focus on creating searchable electronic texts corresponding to the digital facsimiles. Those resources will enhance the use of *The Renaissance in Print* for both teaching and research, allowing us and our students to search for topics and phrases of interest in multiple Gordon Collection volumes for, about, and by women.

Web pages will not replace books in our classrooms, but Internet sites that feature sixteenth-century printed pages can help us bring old books to life for our students. The use of online resources seems particularly appropriate for studying the period when the printed book was young. The Internet allows us to view a revolution in media culture that occurred five hundred years ago in the light of another one taking place today, one using technology that was new to some of us just twenty years ago but that our students find as comfortable as their favorite sweatshirts.

Note

1. To browse the catalog of the Gordon Collection on the University of Virginia Library Web site, go to the online catalog, VIRGO, at http://search.lib.virginia.edu. Type "Gordon" in the search box; select Call Number from the drop-down menu to the right, then click on the Search button. Narrow your search results by clicking on one of the facets on the left side of the screen. To see Gordon titles published in a particular year, enter "Gordon" plus the desired year in the search box, as follows: "Gordon 1540"; select Call Number from the drop-down menu to the right, and then click on the Search button. The records for Gordon books include links to the digital copy (if that copy has been digitized). To view the list of Gordon books currently available online in digital facsimiles, go to the home page of *The Renaissance in Print* (www.lib.virginia.edu/rmds/portfolio/gordon/) and click on the link for the Index of Digitized Works in the column on the right.

Notes on Contributors

Cécile Alduy is associate professor of French literature and director of the Center for Medieval and Early Modern Studies at Stanford University. She has published articles on Du Bellay, Marot, Scève, and La Boétie and on obscenity and pornography in French Renaissance literature, as well as the books *Politique des "Amours" : Poétique et genèse d'un genre français nouveau, 1544–1560* and *Maurice Scève*. Recent works include the *RenaissanceBodyProject*, a Web site on the representation of the body in early modern France. She is currently working on a critical edition of the *Blasons anatomiques du corps féminin*.

Jean-Philippe Beaulieu is professor of Renaissance French literature at the Université de Montréal. He has published articles and books on Hélisenne de Crenne and Marie de Gournay, the latest being a critical edition of *Le songe de madame Helisenne* (in collaboration with Diane Desrosiers-Bonin). He edited the anthology *D'une écriture à l'autre: Les femmes et la traduction sous l'Ancien Régime*. His current research includes a project on women and rhetoric in sixteenth- and seventeenth-century France.

Edith Benkov in professor of European studies and French at San Diego State University. Her primary area of research is premodern France, with a focus on gender studies. She has published articles on language and women, sexuality and cross-dressing, Marie de France, Christine de Pisan, Louise Labé, and Anne de Marquets. She is currently working on a bilingual edition of Anne de Marquets for the Other Voice series.

Laura B. Bergman is currently a lectrice at the Université de Limoges. She completed her master's degree at Texas Tech University with a thesis titled "L'imagerie du pouvoir féminin dans l'*Heptaméron* de Marguerite de Navarre." Her research interests include French Renaissance literature, late medieval and early modern European social history, and women's studies.

Susan Broomhall is Winthrop Professor of Early Modern History at the University of Western Australia. She is the author of *Women and the Book Trade in Sixteenth-Century France*; *Women's Medical Work in Early Modern France*; *Women and Religion in Sixteenth-Century France*; and, with Jennifer Spinks, *Early Modern Women in the Low Countries: Feminising Sources and Interpretations of the Past*. She is editor of volumes on women's identities and communities, emotions in the household, governing masculinities, policing and masculinities, and has edited, with Colette H. Winn, several modern editions of early modern women's writing.

Leah Chang is associate professor of French at George Washington University. She is the author of *Into Print: The Production of Female Authorship in Early Modern France.* She has also published essays on early modern France, including women writers, authorship and title pages, female printers, the early modern preface, and royal entry pamphlets.

Jane Couchman is professor emerita of French, humanities and women's studies and Senior Scholar at Glendon College, York University (Toronto). Her research deals with the letters of late-sixteenth- and early-seventeenth-century Huguenot women. She has published on Louise de Coligny, Catherine de Bourbon, Charlotte de Bourbon-Montpensier, and Éléonore de Roye. She edited, with Ann Crabb, *Women's Letters across Europe, 1400–1700: Form and Persuasion.*

Gary Ferguson is professor of French at the University of Delaware. He is the author of *Mirroring Belief: Marguerite de Navarre's Devotional Poetry* (1992) and of *Queer (Re)Readings in the French Renaissance: Homosexuality, Gender, Culture* (2008). He has published a critical edition of Anne de Marquets's *Sonets spirituels*, coedited and edited collections of essays on the *nouvelle* and on the representation of masculinity, and written articles on medieval and early modern French literature and culture dealing in particular with the history of religion, women's writing, and questions of gender and sexuality.

Carla Freccero is professor of literature, feminist studies, and history of consciousness at the University of California, Santa Cruz. Her most recent book is *Queer / Early / Modern.* She directs the Center for Cultural Studies at UCSC.

Nancy Frelick is associate professor of French at the University of British Columbia. She is the author of *Délie as Other: Toward a Poetics of Desire in Scève's* Délie (1994) as well as articles on French Renaissance literature, including the work of Scève, Montaigne, Rabelais, Louise Labé, Marguerite de Navarre, Marie de Gournay, Hélisenne de Crenne, and Jeanne Flore. Her work explores discourses of desire in early modern texts.

Zeina Hakim is assistant professor of French at Tufts University. She has published articles on Mademoiselle de Montpensier, Isabelle de Charrière, and Madame Roland, as well as on eighteenth-century writers, such as Rousseau, Diderot, and Marivaux. She is currently working on the aesthetic implications of make-believe and the poetics of fiction in eighteenth-century French memoir novels. Her book, *Fictions déjouées. Le récit en trompe-l'œil au dix-huitième siècle*, is forthcoming.

Karen Simroth James is director of *The Renaissance in Print* (Gordon Project) and lecturer in the Department of French at the University of Virginia. Her research and teaching interests include sixteenth-century French poetry, history of the book in early modern France, and Internet technology in the humanities. With Marta Rijn Finch, she recently published a bilingual edition of Pernette Du Guillet's *Complete Poems* in the Other Voice in Early Modern Europe series (2010).

Ann Rosalind Jones is Esther Cloudman Dunn Professor of Comparative Literature and director of the comparative literature program at Smith College. She is the author of *The Currency of Eros: Women's Love Lyric in Europe, 1540–1620*; editor and translator, with Margaret Rosenthal, of *The Poems and Selected Letters of Veronica Franco*; and, with Peter Stallybrass, author of *Renaissance Clothing and the Materials of Memory.* She has published articles on Louise Labé, Catherine Des Roches, sixteenth-century costume books in France, and 1970s French theorists of femininity. With Margaret Rosenthal, she recently completed an illustrated translation of Cesare Vecellio's *Habiti antichi et moderni di diverse parti del mondo.*

Carrie F. Klaus is associate professor of modern languages (French) at DePauw University. She has translated Jeanne de Jussie's *Petite chronique* (*Short Chronicle*) for The Other Voice in Early Modern Europe series and has published articles on Jussie; teaching early modern writers at the undergraduate level; and the eighteenth-century writer Cornélie Wouters, Baroness of Wasse. Her current research involves transnational women writers during the French Revolution.

Claude La Charité is Canada Research Chair in Literary History and professor in the Departement of Letters at the Université du Québec à Rimouski. He has published *La rhétorique épistolaire de Rabelais.* He edited special issues of *Tangence* (*Masques et figures du sujet féminin aux XVIe et XVIIe siècles*); *Renaissance and Reformation* (*Henri III, la rhétorique et l'Académie du Palais*); and *Dalhousie French Studies* (*Prégnance et polyvalence du modèle rhétorique sous l'Ancien Régime*). He also edited the collection *Gabrielle Roy traduite* (2006) and, with Marc André Bernier, an annotated edition of the *Mémoires* of Philippe Aubert de Gaspé (2007).

Anne R. Larsen is professor of French at Hope College. She has published editions of the Dames Des Roches's *Œuvres* (1993), *Secondes œuvres* (1998), *Missives* (1999), and *From Mother and Daughter: Poems, Dialogues, and Letters of the Dames des Roches* (2006); edited, with Colette H. Winn, *Renaissance Women Writers: French Texts, American Contexts* and *Writings by Pre-revolutionary French Women*; with Diana Robin and Carole Levin, *Encyclopedia of Women in the Renaissance: Italy, France, and England*; and, with Julie Campbell, *Early Modern Women and Transnational Communities of Letters* (2009). She is currently working on Anna Maria van Schurman and the seventeenth-century debate on the education of women.

Deborah Lesko Baker is professor and former chair of the French department at Georgetown University. She is the author of *The Subject of Desire: Petrarchan Poetics and the Female Voice in Louise Labé* (1996) and *Narcissus* *and the Lover: Recovery and Reinvention in Maurice Scève's "Délie,"* as well as articles on Renaissance poetry and mythic structures in literary texts. She is the editor and translator (with the poet Annie Finch) of the first bilingual critical edition of Louise Labé's *Complete Works.*

Mary B. McKinley is the Douglas Huntly Gordon Professor of French at the University of Virginia. She has written two books on Montaigne, coedited and contributed to *Critical Tales: New Studies of the* Heptameron *and Early Modern Culture* and edited and translated Marie Dentière's *Epistle to Marguerite de Navarre* and *Preface to a Sermon by John Calvin* for The Other Voice in Early Modern Europe series (2004).

Dora E. Polachek is visiting associate professor of French at Binghamton University. Her publications include the edited volume *Heroic Virtue, Comic Infidelity: Reassessing Marguerite de Navarre's* Heptameron, as well as articles on gender, power, sexuality, and the comic in the early modern period. She is currently working on projects on Brantôme and on the role of women during the French Wars of Religion.

Graziella Postolache earned her PhD in French from Washington University. Her doctoral dissertation concerns the dialogue as cultivated by early modern women writers from France and Italy. Her teaching interests include the pedagogy of Romance languages and literatures and gender and cultural studies.

François Rigolot is Meredith Howland Pyne Professor of French Literature, and former chair of the Department of French and Italian at Princeton University. He has written books on Louise Labé, Michel de Montaigne, and François Rabelais, as well as on problems of linguistics, poetics, and epistemology. He is the editor of Labé's *Œuvres*, Montaigne's *Journal de voyage*, Clément Marot's complete works, and Sainte-Beuve's *Causeries sur Montaigne.*

Brigitte Roussel, associate professor of French at Wichita State University, has focused her research on women writers and published articles on poets, novelists, and essayists of the medieval period, the French Renaissance, the nineteenth century, and contemporary Quebec in essay collections, conference proceedings, and journals.

Danielle Trudeau is professor of French at San José State University. Her publications include *Les inventeurs du bon usage* and critical editions of Pernette Du Guillet's *Rymes* and Bertrand de La Borderie's *Le discours du Voyage de Constantinople* and *L'amie de court.*

Kathleen Wilson-Chevalier is professor of art history at the American University of Paris. A specialist on the castle of Fontainebleau in the age of King Francis I, she has published on the decorative cycles of Fontainebleau (including a gendered reading of the Gallery), sixteenth-century prints, and the women around Francis I (Claude of France, Eleonor of Austria, the Duchess of Étampes). She recently edited *Patronnes et mécènes en France à la Renaissance.*

Colette H. Winn is professor of French at Washington University. Her publications include *The Dialogue in Early Modern France*; *Ronsard, figure de la variété*; *Veufs, veuves et veuvage dans la France d'Ancien Régime* (ed. with Pellegrin); *Approaches to Teaching Marguerite de Navarre's* Heptameron; *Vieillir à la Renaissance* (with Yandell). She has also published special issues on biblical exegesis in the sixteenth century, the education of women in Old Regime France, memory in early modern times, and early modern medicine.

Diane S. Wood is professor of French at Texas Tech University. She is the author of *Hélisenne de Crenne: At the Crossroads of Renaissance Humanism and Feminism* and articles on Hélisenne de Crenne, as well as the editor (with Paul Allen Miller) of *Recapturing the Renaissance: New Perspectives on Humanism, Dialogue, and Texts.* She is currently preparing a critical edition of Hélisenne's *Les eneydes.*

Leslie Zarker Morgan is professor of Italian and French in the Department of Modern Languages and Literatures at Loyola University Maryland. She has published an English translation of Ariosto's *Cinque Canti* and has edited *The Foreign Language Classroom: Bridging Theory and Practice*, with M. A. Haggstrom and J. A. Wieczorek; *Dante: Summa Mediaevalis*, with Charles Franco; *Approaches to Teaching the* Song of Roland, with William Kibler; *Epic Studies: Acts of the Seventeenth International Congress of the Société Rencesvals for the Study of Romance Epic* (a special issue of *Olifant*), with Anne Berthelot and others; and the Geste Francor: *Chansons de geste of Ms. Marc. Fr. XIII.* She is currently writing, with Jean-Claude Vallecalle, "Une nouvelle synthèse sur l'épopée franco-italienne."

Carla Zecher is director of the Center for Renaissance Studies at the Newberry Library, where she administers programming in medieval, Renaissance, and early modern studies for an international consortium of universities. She has taught French language and literature at Bates College and Coe College. She is the author of *Sounding Objects: Musical Instruments, Poetry, and Art in Renaissance France* and editor, with Gordon M. Sayre and Shannon Lee Dawdy, of *Regards sur le monde atlantique*, the memoir of Dumont de Montigny.

Works Cited

Adams, Alison. Introduction. *Georgette de Montenay's* Emblematum christianorum centuria / Cent emblemes chrestiens *(1584). French Emblems at Glasgow.* Glasgow U, n.d. Web. 3 Nov. 2009.

———. *Webs of Allusion: French Protestant Emblem Books of the Sixteenth Century.* Geneva: Droz, 2003. Print.

Adams, Alison, Stephen Rawles, and Alison Saunders. *A Bibliography of French Emblem Books of the Sixteenth and Seventeenth Centuries.* 2 vols. Geneva: Droz, 1999–2002. Print.

Agrippa, Henricus Cornelius. *Declamation on the Nobility and Preeminence of the Female Sex.* Trans. and ed. Albert Rabil, Jr. Bilingual ed. Chicago: U of Chicago P, 1996. Print. The Other Voice in Early Modern Europe.

———. *Sur la noblesse et l'excellence du sexe féminin, et de sa prééminence sur l'autre sexe.* 1537. Pref. Marie-Josèphe Dhavernas. Paris: Côté-femmes Éditions, 1990. Print.

Ajmar, Marta. "Exemplary Women in Renaissance Italy: Ambivalent Models of Behavior?" *Women in Italian Renaissance Culture and Society.* Ed. Letizia Panizza. Oxford: European Humanities Research Center, 2000. 244–64. Print.

Akerlund, Ingrid. *Sixteenth-Century French Women Writers: Marguerite d'Angoulême, Anne de Graville, the Lyonnese School, Jeanne de Jussie, Marie Dentière, Camille de Morel.* Lewiston: Mellen, 2003. Print.

Albistur, Maïté, and Daniel Armogathe, eds. *Le grief des femmes.* Paris: Hier et Demain, 1978. Print. Vol. 1. of *Anthologie des textes féministes du Moyen Âge à la Seconde République.*

———. *Histoire du féminisme français.* Vol. 1. Paris: Éditions des femmes, 1977. 2 vols.

Albret, Jeanne d'. *Lettre d'un cardinal envoyée à la royne de Navarre (le 18e jour d'aoust 1563). Ensemble la response d'icelle dame audit cardinal.* 18 Aug. 1563. Lyon: La Fons, 1564. Print.

———. *Lettres d'Antoine de Bourbon et de Jehanne d'Albret.* Ed. Achille-Lacroix de Rochambeau, Paris: Renouard, 1877. *Gallica.* Bibliothèque Nationale de France, n.d. Print; Web.

———. *Lettres de la Royne de Navarre au roy avec une ample declaration d'icelles.* La Rochelle: Berton, 1569. Print.

———. *Lettres de treshaute, tresvertueuse, et treschrestienne Princesse, Jane, royne de Navarre.* [La Rochelle: Berton], 1568. Print.

———. "Lettres diverses." *Bulletin de la Société d'Histoire du Protestantisme français* 2 (1854): 429; 5 (1857): 147; 11 (1862): 271; 15 (1866): 398, 400; 16 (1867): 63; 75 (1926): 389; 76 (1927): 37; 77 (1928): 21. Print.

———. Mémoires et poésies, *publiés par le baron de Ruble.* Paris: Huart, 1893. *Gallica.* Bibliothèque Nationale de France, n.d. Print; Web.

Albret, Jeanne d', and Marguerite de Navarre. "Epîtres en vers inconnues des historiens de ces princesses et des éditeurs de leurs œuvres." *Dernier voyage de la reine de Navarre Marguerite d'Angoulême avec sa fille Jeanne d'Albret aux bains de Cauterets (1549)*. Ed. Félix Frank. Toulouse: Privat, 1897. Print.

Alonso, Béatrice, and Éliane Viennot, eds. *Louise Labé, 2005*. 2 vols. Saint-Étienne: PU de Saint-Étienne, 2004. Print. L'école du genre. Nouvelles recherches.

Althusser, Louis. *Essays on Ideology*. London: Verso, 1984. Print.

———. "Ideology and Ideological State Apparatuses (Notes toward an Investigation)." *"Lenin and Philosophy" and Other Essays*. Trans. Ben Brewster. London: New Left, 1971. Print.

Altman, Janet Gurkin. "Women's Letters in the Public Sphere." *Going Public: Women and Publishing in Early Modern France*. Ed. Elizabeth C. Goldsmith and Dena Goodman. Ithaca: Cornell UP, 1995. 98–101. Print.

Amboise, Catherine d'. *Poésies*. Ed. Catherine M. Müller. Montréal: CERES, 2002. Print.

———. *Traicté de morale sur la fortune*. MS naf 19738. Bibliothéque Nationale de France, Paris.

Anne of France. Enseignements *à sa fille suivis de l'*Histoire du siège de Brest. Ed. Tatiana Clavier and Éliane Viennot. Saint-Étienne: PU de Saint-Étienne, 2006. Print. La cité des dames 4.

———. *Les enseignements d'Anne de France à sa fille Susanne de Bourbon*. Ed. A.-M. Chazaud, with original drawings by M. A. Queyroy. Moulins: Desroziers, 1878. *Gallica*. Bibliothèque Nationale de France, n.d. Print; Web.

Aragona, Tullia d'. *Dialogue on the Infinity of Love*. Ed. and trans. Rinaldina Russell and Bruce Merry. Chicago: U of Chicago P, 1996. Print. The Other Voice in Early Modern Europe.

———. *Sweet Fire: Tullia d'Aragona's Poetry of Dialogue and Selected Prose*. Ed. and trans. Elizabeth A. Pallitto. New York: Braziller, 2005. Print.

Arbour, Roméo. *L'ère baroque en France. Répertoire chronologique des éditions de textes littéraires*. 4 vols. Geneva: Droz, 1977–85. Print.

Archibald, Elizabeth. *Incest and the Medieval Imagination*. Oxford: Clarendon, 2001. Print.

Aristotle. *De la génération des animaux*. Trans. Pierre Louis. Paris: Les Belles Lettres, 1961. Print.

———. *Poétique*. Trans. Michel Magnien. Paris: Livre de Poche, 1994. Print.

Armstrong, Elizabeth. *The French Book-Privilege System: 1498–1526*. Cambridge: Cambridge UP, 1990. Print.

Arnould, Jean-Claude. "Gournay, Marie Le Jars, dite Marie de (1566–1645)." *Dictionnaire de la Siefar*. Siefar, 2003. Web. 18 Oct. 2010.

Aubigné, Théodore-Agrippa d'. *Œuvres complètes*. Ed. Henri Weber, Jacques Bailbé, and Marguerite Soulié. Paris: Gallimard, 1969. Print.

Backus, Irena. "Les Clarisses de la rue Verdaine / The Poor Clares of the Rue Verdaine." *Le guide des femmes disparues / Forgotten Women of Geneva*. Ed. Anne-Marie Käppeli. Geneva: Metropolis, 1993. 309–25. Print.

———. "Marie Dentière: Un cas de féminisme théologique à l'époque de la Réforme." *Bulletin de la Société de l'Histoire du Protestantisme Français* 137.2 (1991): 177–95. Print.

Bainton, Roland H. "The Role of Women in the Reformation: Introduction to the Following Three Papers." *Archiv für Reformatioengeschichte* 63 (1972): 141–42. Print.

———. *Women of the Reformation in France and England.* Minneapolis: Augusburg, 1973. Print.

Bakhtin, Mikhail. *The Dialogic Imagination: Four Essays by M. M. Bakhtin.* Ed. Michael Holquist. Trans. Caryl Emerson and Holquist. Austin: U of Texas P, 1981. Print.

Banks, Kathryn. "Situating the Masculine: Gender, Identity, and the Cosmos in Scève's *Délie,* Ficino's *De amore,* and Leone Ebreo's *Dialoghi.*" *Masculinities in Sixteenth-Century France.* Ed. Philip Ford and P. White. Cambridge: Cambridge UP, 2006. 61–84. Print.

Barataud, Christian, and Danielle Trudeau. Introduction. Du Guillet, *Rymes.*

Barthes, Roland. "La mort de l'auteur." *Essais critiques* IV. *Le bruissement de la langue.* Paris: Éditions du Seuil, 1984. 61–67. Print.

———. *Le plaisir du texte.* Paris: Éditions du Seuil, 1973. Print.

Bassanese, Fiora. *Gaspara Stampa.* Boston: Twayne, 1983. Print.

Bastiaensen, Michel, ed. *La femme lettrée à la Renaissance / De geleerde vrouw in de Renaissance.* Brussels: Peeters, 1997. Print.

Baudrier, Henri-Louis. *Bibliographie lyonnaise. Recherches sur les imprimeurs, libraires, relieurs et fondeurs de lettres de Lyon au XVIe siècle.* 13 vols. Lyon: Lib. Ancienne d'Auguste Brun, 1895–1921. Geneva: Slatkine, 1999. Print.

Beaulieu, Jean-Philippe. "La *Dispositio* du recueil épistolaire. Unité et variété dans les *Epistres* d'Hélisenne de Crenne." *Écrire et conter.* Ed. Marie-Claude Malenfant and Sabrina Vervacke. Saint-Nicholas: PU Laval, 2003. 37–52. Print.

———. "Les données chevaleresques du contrat de lecture dans les *Angoysses douloureuses* d'Hélisenne de Crenne." *Études françaises* 32.1 (1996): 71–83. Print.

———, ed. *D'une écriture à l'autre. Les femmes et la traduction sous l'Ancien Régime.* Ottawa: PU d'Ottawa, 2004. Print. Regards sur la traduction.

———. "Erudition and Aphasia in Hélisenne de Crenne's *Les angoysses douloureuses qui procedent d'amours.*" *L'esprit créateur* 29.3 (1989): 36–42. Print.

———. "Lettre de femme, voix d'homme? Jeux identitaires et effets de travestissement dans la treizième épître familière d'Hélisenne de Crenne." *Tangence* 84 (2007): 31–47. Print.

———. "Marie de Gournay ou l'occultation d'une figure auctoriale." *Renaissance and Reformation* 24.2 (2000): 23–34. Print.

———. "Postures épistolaires et effets de *dispositio* dans la correspondance entre Marguerite d'Angoulême et Guillaume Briçonnet." *Études françaises* 38.3 (2002): 43–54. *Érudit.* 1 Sept. 2010. Web.

———. "Relire Marie de Gournay, sans Montaigne?" *Terrae incognitae de l'écriture féminine.* Ed. Marie-Laure Girou Swiderski. New York: Legas, 2004. 73–83. Print.

Beaulieu, Jean-Philippe, and Diane Desrosiers-Bonin. "Allégorie et épistolarité. Les jetées de l'érudition féminine chez Hélisenne de Crenne." *Revue d'histoire littéraire de la France* 99.6 (1999): 1155–67. *Cairn.* 1 Sept. 2010. Print, Web.

———, eds. *Dans les miroirs de l'écriture.* Montreal: Paragraphes, 1998. Print.

———, eds. *Hélisenne de Crenne. L'écriture et ses doubles.* Paris: Champion, 2004. Print.

Beaulieu, Jean-Philippe, and Hannah Fournier, eds. *Femmes et textes sous l'Ancien Régime.* Spec. issue of *Atlantis: Women's Studies Journal* 19.1 (1993): 1–145. Print.

———. "'Les interests du sexe': Dédicataires et réseaux de sociabilité chez Marie de Gournay." *Renaissance and Reformation* 28.1 (2004): 47–59. Print.

———, eds. "Women and Texts in Pre-revolutionary France" / "Femmes et textes sous l'Ancien Régime." *Atlantis* 19.1 (1993): 1–145. Print.

Beaune, Colette, and Élodie Lequain. "Femmes et histoire en France au XVe siècle: Gabrielle de la Tour et ses contemporains." *Médiévales* 38 (2000): 111–36. Print.

Beauvalet-Boutouyrie, Scarlett. *Être veuve sous l'Ancien Régime*. Paris: Belin, 2001. Print.

Beecher, Donald, ed. *Le beau au temps de la Renaissance*. Spec. issue of *Carrefour* 17.2 (1995): 3–128. Print.

Béguin, Sylvie, Jean Guillaume, and Alain Roy. *La galerie d'Ulysse à Fontainebleau*. Paris: PU de France, 1985. Print.

Bell, Susan Groag. *The Lost Tapestries of* The City of Ladies: *Christine de Pizan's Renaissance Legacy*. Berkeley: U of California P, 2004. Print.

Bembo, Pietro. *Gli Asolani*. Trans. Rudolf B. Gottfried. Bloomington: Indiana UP, 1954. Print.

Benkov, Edith Joyce. "The Remaking of Love: Louise Labé's *Débat de folie et d'amour*." *Symposium* 46.2 (1992): 94–104. Print.

Benson, Pamela Joseph. *The Invention of the Renaissance Woman: The Challenge of Female Independence in the Literature and Thought of Italy and England*. University Park: Pennsylvania State UP, 1992. Print.

Berriot, Karine. *Louise Labé: La belle rebelle et le françois nouveau. Essai, suivi des* Œuvres complètes. Paris: Éditions du Seuil, 1985. Print.

Berriot-Salvadore, Évelyne. *Un corps, un destin. La femme dans la médecine de la Renaissance*. Paris: Champion, 1993. Print.

———. "Évocation et représentation du mariage dans la poésie féminine." Jones-Davies 210–27.

———. *Les femmes dans la société française de la Renaissance*. Geneva: Droz, 1990. Print.

———. "Les femmes dans les cercles intellectuels de la Renaissance. De la fille prodige à la précieuse." *Mélanges Petti-Ferrandi. Études corses, études littéraires*. Paris: Le Cerf, 1989. 210–37. Print.

———. "Les femmes et les pratiques de l'écriture de Christine de Pisan à Marie de Gournay. 'Femmes sçavantes et savoir féminin.'" *Réforme, Humanisme, Renaissance* 16 (1983): 52–69. Print.

———. "Les héritières de Louise Labé." *Louise Labé. Les voix du lyrisme*. Ed. Guy Demerson. Saint-Étienne: Éditions du CNRS, PU de Saint-Étienne, 1990. 93–106. Print.

Billon, François de. *Le fort inexpugnable de l'honneur du sexe feminin*. Introd. M. A. Screech. New York: Johnson, 1970. Print.

Bimbenet-Privat, Michèle. "Catherine de Médicis et ses orfèvres: Autorité, précision, exigence." Wilson-Chevalier, *Patronnes* 545–56.

Blaisdell, Charmarie Jenkins. "Calvin's Letters to Women: The Courting of Ladies in High Places." *Sixteenth Century Journal* 13.3 (1982): 67–84. Print.

Blanc, Pierre. "Parallèle de Louise Labé et de Gaspara Stampa ou le sonnet et l'amour entre la France et l'Italie. Pour une approche contrastive des échanges culturels franco-italiens." *Franco-italica, serie storico-letteraria* 1 (1992): 25–55. Print.

Blumenberg, Hans. *The Legitimacy of the Modern Age*. Trans. Robert M. Wallace. Cambridge: MIT P, 1983. Print. Trans. of *Die Legitimität der Neuzeit*.

Boccaccio, Giovanni. *Le livre de Jehan Bocasse de la louenge et vertu des nobles et cleres dames, translate et imprimé novellement à Paris*. Paris: Vérard, 1493. Print.

Boehrer, Bruce Thomas. *Monarchy and Incest in Renaissance England: Literature, Culture, Kinship, and Kingship*. Philadelphia: U of Pennsylvania P, 1992. Print.

Boucher, Jacqueline. *Présence italienne à Lyon à la Renaissance*. Lyon: Éditions Lyonnaises d'Art et d'Histoire, 1995. Print.

———. *Vivre à Lyon au XVIe siècle*. Lyon: Éditions Lyonnaises d'Art et d'Histoire, 2001. Print.

Bouchet, Jean. *Le jugement poetic de l'honneur femenin*. Ed. Adrian Armstrong. Paris: Champion, 2006. Print. Textes de la Renaissance 101.

Boudier de Villemert, Pierre-Joseph. *Notice alphabétique des femmes célèbres*. Amsterdam: Monory, 1779. Print.

Bourbon, Catherine de. *Lettres et poésies*. Ed. Raymond Ritter. Paris: Champion, 1927. Print.

Bourbon, Gabrielle de. *Œuvres spirituelles*. Ed. Évelyne Berriot-Salvadore. Paris: Champion, 1999. Print. Textes de la Renaissance 26.

Bourbon-Montpensier, Charlotte de. "Charlotte de Bourbon, Princess of Orange. Lettres et Documents (1565–1582)." Ed. and trans. Jane Couchman. Larsen and Winn, *Writings* 107–22.

Bourgeois, Louis. *Louise Labé (1523?–1566) et les poètes de son temps*. Lyon: LUGD, 1994. Print.

Bourras, Émile. "Essai sur Marie de Romieu." *Revue du Vivarais* 9 (1901): 404–15, 456–66, and 507–21. Print.

Boursier, Louise Bourgeois. Observations sur la stérilité, perte de fruits, fécondité, accouchements et maladies des femmes et enfants nouveau-nés *suivi de* Instructions à ma fille. 1609. Pref. Françoise Olive. Paris: Côté-femmes Éditions, 1992. Print.

Braden, Gordon. "Gaspara Stampa and the Gender of Petrarchism." *Texas Studies in Literature and Language* 38.2 (1996): 115–39. Print.

———. *Petrarchan Love and the Continental Renaissance*. New Haven: Yale UP, 1999. Print.

Brantôme, Pierre de Bourdeille, seigneur de. *Les dames galantes*. Ed. Maurice Rat. Paris: LGF, 1990. Print.

———. *Recueil des dames, poésies et tombeaux*. Ed. Étienne Vaucheret. Paris: Gallimard, 1991. Print. Bibliothèque de la Pléiade.

———. *Tales of Fair and Gallant Ladies*. Trans. Lowell Bair. Illus. Sheila Beckett. New York: Bantam, 1958. Print.

Brézé, Jacques de. *La chasse, les dits du bon chien Souillard et les Louanges de Madamme Anne de France*. Ed. Gunner Tilander. Lund: C. Bloms Boktryck, 1959. Print.

Brink, Jean R., ed. *Privileging Gender in Early Modern England*. Kirksville: Sixteenth Century Journal P, 1993. Print. Sixteenth Century Essays and Studies 23.

Brink, Jean R., Allison P. Coudert, and Maryanne C. Horowitz, eds. *The Politics of Gender in Early Modern Europe*. Kirksville: Sixteenth Century Journal P, 1989. Print. Sixteenth Century Essays and Studies 12.

Briquet, Marguerite Ursule Fortunée. *Dictionnaire historique, littéraire et bibliographique des Françaises et des étrangères naturalisées en France*. Paris: Treuttel and Würtz, 1804. Print.

———. *Dictionnaire historique, littéraire et bibliographique des Françaises et des étrangères naturalisées en France*. Paris: Indigo et Côté-femmes, 1997. Print.

Brisson, Marie. "Quelques mots sur Louise Labé." *Club des poètes*. Web. 5 Feb. 2010.

Broomhall, Susan. "'Burdened with Small Chidren': Women Defining Poverty in Sixteenth Century Tours." Couchman and Crabb 223–37.

———."French Women in Print, 1488 to 1599." *Bibliographical Society of Australia and New Zealand Bulletin* 22.4 (1998): 195–231. Print.

———. "'In My Opinion': Charlotte de Minut and Female Political Discussion in Print in Sixteenth-Century France." *Sixteenth Century Journal* 31.1 (2000): 25–45. *JSTOR*. Web. 18 Apr. 2008.

———. "Lettres de Louise-Julienne, d'Elisabeth et d'Amélie de Nassau à Charlotte-Brabantine de Nassau (1595–1601)." Goldsmith and Winn, *Lettres* 135–78.

———. *Women and Religion in Sixteenth-Century France*. New York: Palgrave, 2006. Print.

———. *Women and the Book Trade in Sixteenth-Century France*. Aldershot: Ashgate, 2002. Print.

Brouard-Arends, Isabelle, ed. *Lectrices d'Ancien Régime*. Rennes: PU de Rennes, 2003. Print.

Brown, Cynthia J. "Le mécénat politique d'Anne de Bretagne et la politique du livre." Wilson-Chevalier, *Patronnes* 195–224.

———. *Poets, Patrons, and Printers: Crisis of Authority in Late Medieval France*. Ithaca: Cornell UP, 1995. Print.

———. "The Reconstruction of an Author in Print: Christine de Pizan in the Fifteenth and Sixteenth Centuries." Desmond, *Christine de Pizan and the Categories* 215–35.

Brown-Grant, Rosalind. "The *Epistre Othéa*: An Ethical and Allegorical Alternative to the *Roman de la Rose*?" *Christine de Pizan and the Moral Defence of Women: Reading beyond Gender*. Cambridge: Cambridge UP, 1999. 52–88. Print.

Brownlee, Kevin. *Poetic Identity in Guillaume de Machaut*. Madison: U of Wisconsin P, 1984. Print.

Bruneau, Marie-Florine. "Psychoanalysis and Its Abject: What Lurks behind the Fear of the Mother." *Studies in Psychoanalytic Theory* 1.2 (1992): 24–38. Print.

Buffet, Marguerite. *Nouvelles observations sur la langue françoise. . . . Avec les eloges des illustres sçavantes tant anciennes que modernes*. Paris: Cusson, 1668. Print.

Burckhardt, Jacob. *Der Kultur der Renaissance in Italien*. Leipzig: Seemann, 1885. Print.

Burlamacchi, Renée. *Descrittione della vita et morte del Sigr Michele Burlamachi gentilhuomo lucchese. Les femmes et l'histoire familiale (XVIe–XVIIe siècle)*. Ed. Susan Broomhall and Colette H. Winn. Paris: Champion, 2008. 7–73, 75–135. Print. Textes de la Renaissance 130.

Butler, Judith. *Antigone's Claim: Kinship between Life and Death*. New York: Columbia UP, 2000. Print.

———. *Bodies That Matter: On the Discursive Limits of "Sex."* New York: Routledge, 1993. Print.
———. *Gender Trouble: Feminism and the Subversion of Identity.* New York: Routledge, 1990. Print.
———. *The Psychic Life of Power: Theories in Subjection.* Stanford: Stanford UP, 1997. Print.
Buzon, Christine de. Introduction. Crenne, *Angoysses* 7–41.
———. "Les miroirs d'Hélisenne de Crenne." Beaulieu and Desrosiers-Bonin, *Hélisenne de Crenne* 71–81.
———. "Roman et passions: L'implicite dans *Les angoysses douloureuses* (1538) d'Hélisenne de Crenne." *Female Saints and Sinners / Saintes et Mondaines (France 1450–1650).* Ed. Jennifer Britnell and Ann Moss. Durham: U of Durham P, 2002. 197–218. Print.
Cabos, Alban. *Guy du Faur de Pibrac. Un magistrat poète au XVIe siècle, 1529–1584.* Paris: Champion, 1922. Print.
Calvin, Jean. *Come out from among Them: "Anti-Nicodemite" Writings of John Calvin.* Trans. Seth Skolnitsky. Dallas: Protestant Heritage, 2001. Print.
———. "Excuse à messieurs les Nicodémites sur la complaincte qu'ilz font de sa trop grand'rigueur." *Calvin: Three French Treatises.* Ed. Francis M. Higman. London: Athlone, 1970. 131–53. Print.
———. *Letter of John Calvin.* Ed. Jules Bonnet. 2 vols. New York: Franklin, 1972. Print.
Cambis, Marguerite de. *Epistre consolatoire de Messire Jean Boccace envoyee au Signeur Pino de Rossi* (1556). Ed. Colette H. Winn. Paris: Champion, 2003. Print. Textes de la Renaissance 68.
Cameron, Keith. *Louise Labé: Feminist and Poet of the Renaissance.* New York: Berg, 1990. Print. Berg Women's Series.
Campbell, Julie. *Literary Circles and Gender in Early Modern Europe: A Cross-Cultural Approach.* Aldershot: Ashgate, 2006. Print. Women and Gender in the Early Modern World.
Carlin, Claire, ed. *Le mariage sous l'Ancien Régime.* Spec. issue of *Dalhousie French Studies* 56 (2001): 3–166. Print.
Cassagnes-Brouquet, Sophie. *Un manuscrit d'Anne de Bretagne.* La vie des femmes célèbres *d'Antoine Dufour.* Rennes: Éditions Ouest-France, 2007. Print.
Cassirer, Ernst. *Individuum und Kosmos in der Philosophie der Renaissance.* Leipzig: Teubner, 1927. Print.
Castiglione, Baldassare. *The Book of the Courtier.* Trans. Charles Singleton. Ed. Daniel Javitch. New York: Norton, 2002. Print.
Catalogue général des manuscrits français de la Bibliothèque Nationale de France. Ed. Henri Omont et al. 18 vols. Paris: Leroux, 1868–1902. Print.
Catalogue of Manuscripts in the Houghton Library, Harvard University. 8 vols. Alexandria: Chadwyck-Healey, 1986–87. Print.
Catalogue of Medieval and Renaissance Manuscripts in the Beinecke Rare Book and Manuscript Library, Yale University. Ed. Barbara A. Shailor. 2 vols. Binghamton: Medieval and Renaissance Texts and Studies, 1984–92. Print.
A Catholic Dictionary of Theology. London: Nelson, 1962– .

Catullus. *The Poems of Catullus.* Ed. Robert Rowland. Trans. James Michie. Bilingual ed. New York: Random, 1969. Print.

Cavallo, Sandra, and Lyndan Warner, eds. *Widowhood in Medieval and Early Modern Europe.* New York: Pearson, 1999. Print. Women and Men in History.

Cazauran, Nicole. "La trentième nouvelle de l'*Heptaméron* ou la méditation d'un 'exemple.'" *Mélanges de littérature du Moyen Âge au XXe siècle offerts à Mlle Jeanne Lods.* Vol. 1. Paris: École Normale Supérieure de Jeunes Filles, 1978. 617–52. Print. 2 vols.

Cereta, Laura. *Collected Letters of a Renaissance Feminist.* Ed. and trans. Diana Robin. Bilingual ed. Chicago: U of Chicago P, 1997. Print. The Other Voice in Early Modern Europe.

Cerquiglini, Jacqueline. *"Un engin si soutil": Guillaume de Machaut et l'écriture au XIVe siècle.* Paris: Champion, 1985. Print.

Champollion-Figeac, Aimé. *Poésies du roi François Ier, de Louise de Savoie, duchesse d'Angoulême, de Marguerite, reine de Navarre, et correspondance intime du roi avec Diane de Poitiers et plusieurs autres dames de la cour.* 1847. Geneva: Slatkine, 1970. Print.

Chang, Leah. *Into Print: The Production of Female Authorship in Early Modern France.* Newark: U of Delaware P, 2008. Print.

Charpentier, Françoise. "Louise Labé." *Dictionnaire de la Siefar.* Siefar, 2005. Web. 29 Oct. 2010.

———. "Projet poétique, travail poétique dans les *Rymes* de Pernette Du Guillet: Autour de trois quatrains." *Poétique et narration. Mélanges offerts à Guy Demerson.* Ed. François Marotin and Jacques-Philippe Saint-Gérand. Paris: Champion, 1993. 143–55. Print.

Chartier, Roger. *Histoire de la vie privée.* Ed. Philippe Ariès and Georges Duby. Paris: Éditions du Seuil, 1979. Print.

Chilton, Paul A. "Devout Humanism." Hollier 253–58.

Chodorow, Nancy. *The Reproduction of Mothering: Psychoanalysis and the Sociology of Gender.* Berkeley: U of California P, 1979. Print.

Cholakian, Patricia F., and Rouben C. Cholakian. *Marguerite de Navarre: Mother of the Renaissance.* New York: Columbia UP, 2006. Print.

Cholakian, Rouben C. "Marguerite de Navarre: Religious Reformist." King and Rabil 98–109.

Christine de Pisan. *The Book of the City of Ladies.* Trans. Earl Jeffrey Richards. Fwd. Marina Warner. New York: Persea, 1982. Print.

———. *Le chemin de long estude de Dame Christine de Pise.* Pref. Étienne Groulleau. Paris: Groulleau, 1549. Print.

Churchill, Laurie J., Phyllis R. Brown, and Jane E. Jeffrey, eds. *Women Writing Latin from Roman Antiquity to Early Modern Europe.* 3 vols. New York: Routledge, 2002. Print.

Cixous, Hélène. "Le rire de la Méduse." *L'arc* 61 (1975): 39–54. Print.

Cixous, Hélène, Madeleine Gagnon, and Annie Leclerc. *La venue à l'écriture.* Paris: Union Générale d'Éditions, 1977. Print.

Clark-Evans, Christine. "The Feminine Exemplum in Writing: Humanist Instruction in Louise Labé's Letter Preface to Clémence de Bourges." *Exemplaria* 6.1 (1994): 205–21. Print. Rpt. in Alonso and Viennot 91–106.

Clément, Michèle, and Janine Incardona, eds. *Émergence littéraire des femmes à Lyon à la Renaissance, 1520–1560. Actes du colloque de Lyon (2006).* Saint-Étienne: PU de Saint-Étienne, 2008. L'école du gentre.

Coignard, Gabrielle de. *Imitation of the Victory of Judith.* Trans. Colette H. Winn and Robert H. McDowell. Larsen and Winn, *Writings* 171–211.

———. *Œuvres chrestiennes de feu dame Gabrielle de Coignard.* Tournon: Faure, 1595. *Gallica.* Bibliothèque Nationale de France, n.d. Print; Web.

———. *Œuvres chrétiennes.* Ed. Colette H. Winn. Geneva: Droz, 1995. Print. TLF 453.

———. *Spiritual Sonnets: A Bilingual Edition.* Ed. and trans. Melanie E. Gregg. Chicago: U of Chicago P, 2004. Print. The Other Voice in Early Modern Europe.

Coligny, Louise de. *Correspondance de Louise de Coligny, princesse d'Orange.* Ed. Paul Marchegay et Léon Marlet. Paris, 1887. Geneva: Slatkine, 1970. Print.

———. "Lettres de Louise de Coligny, princesse d'Orange, aux membres de sa famille aux Pays-Bas et en France (1573–1620)." Ed. Jane Couchman. Goldsmith and Winn 89–134.

Colonna, Vittoria. "Provo tra duri scogli e fiero vento." Stortoni and Lillie 58–59.

"Le con de la pucelle." Labé, *Œuvres poétiques* 152–53.

Conley, Tom. "Feminism, *Écriture*, and the Closed Room: The *Angoysses douloureuses qui procèdent d'amours.*" *Symposium* 27.4 (1973): 322–32. Print.

Coste, Hilarion de. *Eloges et vies des roynes, princesses, dames et damoiselles illustres en pieté, courage et doctrine.* Paris: Cramoisy, 1630. Print.

Cotgrave, Randle. *A Dictionarie of the French and English Tongues.* 1611. Columbia: U of South Carolina P, 1950. Print.

Cottrell, Robert D. "Female Subjectivity and Libidinal Infractions: Hélisenne de Crenne's *Angoysses douloureuses qui procèdent d'amours.*" *French Forum* 16.1 (1991): 5–19. Print.

———. *Grammar of Silence: A Reading of Marguerite de Navarre's Poetry.* Washington: Catholic U of America P, 1986. Print.

———. "Hélisenne de Crenne's *Le Songe.*" Winn and Kuizenga 187–206.

———. "The Problematics of Opposition in Louise Labé's *Débat de folie et d'amour.*" *French Forum* 12.1 (1987): 27–42. Print.

Couadau, Marie-Louise. "Clémence Isaure ou l'invention d'un mythe méridional." *Revue des sciences humaines et de la littérature de la France du Sud* 2 (1987): 48–51. Print.

Couchman, Jane. "Charlotte de Bourbon's Correspondence: Using Words to Implement Emancipation." Winn and Kuizenga 101–15.

———. " 'Give Birth Quickly and Then Send Us Your Good Husband': Informal Political Influence in the Letters of Louise de Coligny." Couchman and Crabb 163–84.

———. "Models for Women in the Letters of Huguenot Noblewomen, 1560–1620." *Creating Women: Notions of Femininity from 1350–1700.* Ed. Konrad Eisenbickler and Manuela Scarci. Toronto: Centre for Reformation and Renaissance Studies, forthcoming.

———. "La vertu féminine et les relations franco-anglaises: La traduction anglaise de l'*Epistre . . . sur la mort d[e] . . . Leonore de Roye, Princesse de Condé. . . .* " Beaulieu, *D'une écriture* 121–37.

———. "What Is 'Personal' about Sixteenth-Century French Women's 'Personal' Writings?" *Atlantis* 19.1 (1993): 16–22. Print.

Couchman, Jane, and Ann Crabb, eds. *Women's Letters across Europe, 1400–1700: Form and Persuasion*. Aldershot: Ashgate, 2005. Print.

Cox, Virginia. *The Renaissance Dialogue: Literary Dialogue in Its Social and Political Contexts, Castiglione to Galileo*. Cambridge: Cambridge UP, 1992. Print.

———. "Women Writers and the Canon in Sixteenth-Century Italy." *Strong Voices, Weak History: Early Modern Women Writers and the Canon in England, France, and Italy*. Ed. Pamela Benson and Victoria Kirkham. Ann Arbor: U of Michigan P, 2005. 14–31. Print.

Craveri, Benedetta. *The Age of Conversation*. Trans. Teresa Waugh. New York: New York Rev. of Books, 2005. Print.

Crenne, Hélisenne de. *Les angoisses douloureuses qui procèdent d'amour*. Ed. Jean-Philippe Beaulieu. Saint Étienne: PU de Saint-Étienne, 2005. Print. La cité des dames 2.

———. *Les angoysses douloureuses qui procedent d'amours*. Paris: Janot, 1538. *Gallica*. Bibliothèque Nationale de France, n.d. Print; Web.

———. *Les angoysses douloureuses qui procedent d'amours*, roman. 1538. Ed. Paule Demats. Paris: Les Belles Lettres, 1968. Print.

———. *Les angoysses douloureuses qui procedent d'amours*. Paris: Sergent, 1541. *Gallica*. Bibliothèque Nationale de France, n.d. Print; Web.

———. *Les angoysses douloureuses qui procedent d'amours (Première partie)*. 1560. Ed. Jérôme Vercruysse. Paris: Minard-Lettres Modernes, 1968. Print.

———. *Les angoysses douloureuses qui procedent d'amours*. Ed. Christine de Buzon. Paris: Champion, 1997. Print. Textes de la Renaissance 13.

———. *Complete Works*. Ed. and trans. Timothy Reiss. Bilingual ed. Chicago: U of Chicago P, forthcoming. Print. The Other Voice in Early Modern Europe.

———. *Les epistres familieres de ma dame Helisenne: De nouveau vuës et corrigées oultre les precedentes impressions*. Paris: Groulleau, [1550]. *Gallica*. Bibliothèque Nationale de France, n.d. Print; Web.

———. *Les epistres familieres et invectives de ma dame Helisenne*. Paris: Janot, 1539. Print.

———. *Les epistres familieres et invectives de ma dame Helisenne*. Ed. Jean-Philippe Beaulieu and Hannah Fournier. Montréal: PU de Montréal, 1995. Print.

———. *Les epistres familieres et invectives*. Ed. Jerry C. Nash. Paris: Champion, 1996. Print. Textes de la Renaissance 8.

———. *Les epîtres familières et invectives. Le songe*. Ed. Jean-Philippe Beaulieu. Saint-Étienne: PU de Saint-Étienne, 2008. Print. La cité des dames 7.

———. *Lady Hélisenne's Dream*. Trans. Lisa Neal. Larsen and Winn, *Writings* 63–105.

———. *Les œuvres de ma dame Helisenne*. Paris: L'Angelier, 1543. *Gallica*. Bibliothèque Nationale de France, n.d. Print; Web.

———. *A Renaissance Woman: Hélisenne's Personal and Invective Letters*. Ed. and trans. Marianna M. Mustacchi and Paul J. Archambault. Syracuse: Syracuse UP, 1986. Print.

———. *Le songe*. Ed. Jean-Philippe Beaulieu. Paris: Indigo et Côté-femmes, 1995. Print.

———. Le songe *de madame Helisenne*. 1540. Trans. Lisa Neal. Larsen and Winn, *Writings* 63–105.

———. Le songe *de madame Helisenne*. Ed. Jean-Philippe Beaulieu and Diane Desrosiers-Bonin. Paris: Champion, 2007. Print. Textes de la Renaissance 127.

———. *The Torments of Love*. Trans. Lisa Neal and Steven Rendall. Minneapolis: U of Minneapolis P, 1996. Print.

Crespin, Jean. *Histoire des vrays tesmoins de la verité l'Evangile qui de leur sang l'ont signée, depuis Jean Hus jusques au temps présent*. Geneva: Crespin, 1570. Print.

Crété, Liliane. *Le protestantisme et les femmes. Aux origines de l'émancipation*. Geneva: Labor, 1999. Print.

Croizat, Yassana C. "'Living Dolls': François Ier Dresses His Women." *Renaissance Quarterly* 60 (2007): 94–130. Print.

Crouzet, Denis. *Le haut cœur de Catherine de Médicis. Une raison politique aux temps de la Saint-Barthélemy*. Paris: Albin-Michel, 2005. Print.

Curione, Cecelio Secundo. *Pasquillorum tomi duo: Quorum primo versibus ac rhythmis, altero soluta oratione conscripta quamplurima continentur*. [Basel: Oporinus], 1544. Print.

———. *Pasquillus Ecstaticus et Marphorius*. Basel, 1544. Print.

Dangerous Beauty. Dir. Marshall Herskovitz. Written by Jeannine Dominy. Prod. Herskovitz, Edward Zwick, Arnon Milchan, Sarah Caplan. Warner Bros., 1998. Videocassette.

Daston, Lorraine, and Katharine Park. "The Hermaphrodite and the Orders of Nature: Sexual Ambiguity in Early Modern France." *Premodern Sexualities*. Ed. Louise Fradenburg and Carla Freccero. New York: Routledge, 1996. 117–36. Print

———. *Wonders and the Order of Nature, 1150–1750*. New York: Zone, 2001. Print.

Dauvois, Nathalie. *Le sujet lyrique à la Renaissance*. Paris: PUF, 2000. Print.

Davis, Natalie Zemon. "La femme 'au politique.'" Davis and Farge 175–90.

———. "Le monde de l'imprimerie humaniste: Lyon." Martin and Chartier 255–77.

———. *The Return of Martin Guerre*. Cambridge: Harvard UP, 1983. Print.

———. *Society and Culture in Early Modern France*. Stanford: Stanford UP, 1975. Print.

———. "Women in the Crafts in Sixteenth-Century Lyon." *Feminist Studies* 8.1 (1982): 47–80. Print. Rpt. in *Women and Work in Pre-industrial Europe*. Ed. Barbara A. Hanawalt. Bloomington: Indiana UP, 1986. 172–77.

———. "Women on Top." Shoemaker and Vincent 285–306.

———. "Women's History in Transition: The European Case." *Feminist Studies* 3.3-4 (1976): 83–103. Print.

Davis, Natalie Zemon, and Arlette Farge, eds. *Renaissance and Enlightenment Paradoxes*. Cambridge: Belknap–Harvard UP, 1993. Print. Vol. 3 of *A History of Women in the West*. Georges Duby and Michelle Perrot, gen. eds. 5 vols.

Dawson, Jean Charles. *Toulouse in the Renaissance*. New York: Columbia UP, 1923. Print.

Debaisieux, Martine. "'Des dames du temps jadis': Fatalité culturelle et identité féminine dans *Les angoysses douloureuses*." *Symposium* 41.1 (1987): 28–41. Print.

———. "Subtilitez féminines: L'art de la contradiction dans l'œuvre d'Hélisenne de Crenne." *Études littéraires* 27.2 (1994): 25–37. Print.

De Courcelles, Dominique, and Carmen Val Julián, eds. *Des femmes et des livres: France and Espagnes, XIVe–XVIIe siècle*. Paris: École des Chartres, 1999. Print. Études et rencontres 4.

De Gendt, Anne Marie. "*Aucuns petis enseignemens*: 'Home-Made' Courtesy Books in Medieval France." Drijvers and MacDonald 279–98.

Delaborde, Jules. *Charlotte de Bourbon, princesse d'Orange*. Paris: Fischbacher, 1888. Print.

———. *Éléonore de Roye, princesse de Condé, 1535–1564*. Paris: Sandoz 1876. Print.

Delaney, Susan. "Lyric Dialogue in the 'Ring' Poems of Pernette Du Guillet and Maurice Scève." *French Review* 68.4 (1995): 822–29. Print.

De La Porte, Joseph, and Jean-François de la Croix. *Histoire littéraire des femmes françoises. . . . Contenant un précis de la vie, et une analyse . . . des ouvrages des femmes qui se sont distinguées dans la littérature française*. 5 vols. Paris: Lacombe, 1769. Print.

Delumeau, Jean, ed. *Le rôle des femmes dans la transmission de la foi*. Paris: Cerf, 1992. Print.

Denommé, Isabelle C. "La vision théologique de Marie d'Ennetières et le 'groupe de Neuchâtel.'" *Le livre évangélique en français avant Calvin*. Ed. Jean-François Gilmont and William Kemp. Turnhout: Brepols, 2004. 179–97. Print.

Dentière [d'Ennetières], Marie. Epistle to Marguerite de Navarre *and* Preface to a Sermon by John Calvin. Ed. and trans. Mary McKinley. Bilingual ed. Chicago: U of Chicago P, 2006. Print. The Other Voice in Early Modern Europe.

———. *Epistre tresutile faicte et composée par une femme Chrestienne de Tornay. Envoyée à la royne de Navarre seur du roy de France. Contre les Turcz, Iuifz, infideles, faulx Chrestiens, Anabaptistes, et Lutheriens*. Anvers [Geneva]: Lempereur [Jean Girard], 1539. Print.

———."M[arie] D[entière] à Marguerite de Navarre." *Correspondance des réformateurs dans les pays de langue française. Recueillie et publiée avec d'autres lettres relatives à la Réforme et des notes historiques et biographiques*. 1866–97. Ed. A.-L. Herminjard. Vol. 5. Nieuwkoop: De Graaf, 1965. 295–304. Print. 9 vols.

———. *Œuvres de Marie d'Ennetières*. Ed. Diane Desrosiers-Bonin, William Kemp, and Isabelle Crevier Denommé. Geneva: Droz, forthcoming.

[Dentière, Marie?]. *La guerre et deslivrance de la ville de Genesve*. Ed. Albert Rilliet. Geneva: Schuchardt, 1881. Print.

Derrida, Jacques. "Structure, Sign, and Play in the Discourse of the Human Sciences." *Writing and Difference*. Trans. Alan Bass. Chicago: U of Chicago P, 1978. 278–93. Print.

Dersofi, Nancy. "Laura Terracina." *Italian Women Writers: A Bibliographical Sourcebook*. Ed. Rinaldina Russell. Westport: Greenwood, 1994. 422–30. Print.

Desmond, Marilyn, ed. *Christine de Pizan and the Categories of Difference*. Minneapolis: U of Minnesota P, 1998. Print.

———. "Christine de Pizan: Gender, Authorship, and Life-Writing." *The Cambridge Companion to Medieval French Literature*. Ed. Simon Gaunt and Sarah Kay. Cambridge: Cambridge UP, 2008. 123–35. Print.

Des Roches, Catherine Fredonnoit. *Pastoral*. Trans. Anne R. Larsen. Larsen and Winn, *Writings* 159–69.

———. *Tobie, Bergerie, Placide et Sévère, Iris et Pasithée. XVIe siècle*. Ed. Aurore Evain, Perry Gethner, and Henriette Goldwyn. Saint-Étienne: PU de Saint-Étienne, 2006. Print. Vol. 1 of *Théâtre de femmes de l'Ancien Régime*. Èliane Viennot, gen. ed. La cité des dames 5.

Des Roches, Madeleine Neveu, and Catherine Des Roches Fredonnoit. *Dialogue between Placide and Severe*. Des Roches and Des Roches, *From Mother* 217–29.

———. *From Mother to Daughter*. Ed. and trans. Anne R. Larsen. Bilingual ed. Chicago: U of Chicago P, 2006. Print. The Other Voice in Early Modern Europe.

———. *La puce de Madame Des-Roches*. Paris: L'Angelier, 1582. *The Renaissance in Print*. U of Virginia Lib., n.d. Print; Web. 3 Sept. 2010.

———. *Les missives*. Ed. Anne R. Larsen. Geneva: Droz, 1999. Print. TLF 515.

———. *Les missives de Mesdames des Roches de Poitiers, Mere et fille, avec le* Ravissement de Proserpine *prins du Latin de Clodian*. Paris: L'Angelier, 1586. Print.

———. *Les œuvres*. Ed. Anne R. Larsen. Geneva: Droz, 1993. Print. TLF 428.

———. *Les œuvres de Mesdames Des Roches, de Poitiers, mere et fille*. Paris: L'Angelier, 1579. Print. *Gallica*. Bibliothèque Nationale de France, n.d. Print; Web.

———. *Les secondes œuvres*. Ed. Anne R. Larsen. Geneva: Droz, 1998. Print. TLF 497.

———. *Les secondes œuvres de Mesdames Des Roches de Poictiers, mere et fille*. Poitiers: Courtoys, 1583. *Gallica*, Bibliothèque Nationale de France, n.d. Print; Web.

———. *Les secondes œuvres de Mesdames des Roches de Poictiers, mere et fille*. Poitiers: Courtoys, 1583. *The Renaissance in Print*. U of Virginia Lib., n.d. Print; Web.

Desrosiers-Bonin, Diane, ed. *L'écriture des femmes à la Renaissance française*. Spec. issue of *Littératures* 18 (1998): 7–22. Print.

Diane of Poitiers. "Diane de Poitiers: The Woman behind the Legend." Ed. and trans. Sandra Sider. Wilson, *Women Writers* 158–76.

———. *Lettres inédites*. Ed. Georges Guiffrey. Paris, 1866. Geneva: Slatkine, 1970. Print.

Dictionnaire des créatrices. Ed. Béatrice Didier, Mireille Calle-Gruher, and Antoinette Fouque. Paris: Éditions des femmes-Antoinette Fouque, 2010. Print.

Dinnerstein, Dorothy. *The Mermaid and the Minotaur: Sexual Arrangements and Human Malaise*. New York: Harper, 1976. Print.

Dixon, Laurinda S. *Perilous Chastity: Women and Illness in Pre-Enlightenment Art and Medicine*. Ithaca: Cornell UP, 1995. Print.

Donahue, Charles, Jr. "The Canon Law on the Formation of Marriage and Social Practice in the Later Middle Ages." *Journal of Family History* 8.2 (1983): 144–56. Print.

Doody, Margaret A. *The True Story of the Novel*. New Brunswick: Rutgers UP, 1997. Print.

Douglass, Jane Dempsey. "Glimpses of Reformed Women Leaders from Our History." *Semper Reformanda*. World Alliance of Reformed Churches, n.d. Web. 4 Nov. 2009.

———. "Marie Dentière's Use of Scripture in Her Theology of History." *Biblical Hermeneutics in Historical Perspective: Studies in Honor of Karlfried Froehlich on His Sixtieth Birthday*. Grand Rapids: Eerdmans, 1991. 227–44. Print.

———. "Women and the Continental Reformation." *Religion and Sexism: Images of Women in the Jewish and Christian Traditions*. Ed. Rosemary R. Ruether. New York: Simon, 1974. 292–318. Print.

Drijvers, Jan Willem, and Alasdair A. MacDonald, eds. *Centres of Learning. Learning and Location in Pre-modern Europe and the Near East.* Leiden: Brill, 1995. Print.

Du Bellay, Joachim. *La deffence et illustration de la langue françoyse.* Ed. Henri Chamard. Paris: Didier, 1948. Print.

———. La deffence et illustration de la langue françoyse *et* L'Olive. Ed. Jean-Charles Monferran. Geneva: Droz, 2008. 65–185. Print.

———. *Œuvres poétiques.* Ed. D. Aris and F. Joukovsky. Vol. 2. Paris: Bordas, 1993. Print. Classiques Garnier.

Dufour, Antoine. *Vies des femmes célèbres.* MS XVII. Musée Dobrée, Nantes.

Du Guillet, Pernette. *Complete Poems: A Bilingual Edition.* Ed. Karen Simroth James. Trans. Marta Rijn Finch. Toronto: CRRS Pubs., Center for Reformation and Renaissance Studies, 2010. Print. The Other Voice in Early Modern Europe.

———. *Poésies.* Ed. Jean-Louis-Antoine Coste. 1830. Geneva: Slatkine, 1970. Print.

———. *Rymes.* Ed. Joseph Aynard. *Les poètes lyonnais: Précurseurs de la Pléiade.* Paris: Brossard, 1924. 141–53. *Early Modern French Woman Writers.* U of Minnesota, n.d. Print; Web.

———. *Rymes.* Ed. Victor E. Graham. Geneva: Droz, 1968. Print. TLF 152.

———. *Rymes (1545).* Ed. Élise Rajchenbach. Geneva: Droz, 2006. Print. TLF 583.

———. *Rymes.* Ed. Christian Barataud and Danielle Trudeau. Paris: Champion, 2006. Print. Textes de la Renaissance 129.

———. *Rymes de D. Pernette du Guillet, Lyonnoize.* Lyon: Tournes, 1552. *Les grands classiques.* Poésie Française, 1996–2009. Print; Web.

———. *Rymes de gentile, and vertueuse dame D. Pernette du Guillet, Lyonnoise.* Lyon: Tournes, 1545. *Gallica.* Bibliothèque Nationale de France, n.d. Print; Web.

Du Laurens, Jeanne. *Genealogie de Messieurs du Laurens.* 1631. *Les femmes et l'histoire familiale (XVIe-XVIIe siècle).* Ed. Susan Broomhall and Colette H. Winn. Paris: Champion, 2008. 7–73, 137–72. Print. Textes de la Renaissance 130.

Du Monin, Jean-Édouard. "A Mademoyselle de Romieu, Sonnet Foeminin, sur son Discours." Romieu, *Premières œuvres* [1878] 7–8.

Duplessis-Mornay, Philippe. *Mémoires et correspondance de Duplessis-Mornay . . . depuis l'an 1571 jusqu'en 1623. Édition complète . . . précédée des mémoires de Madame de Mornay sur la vie de son mari . . . .* 12 vols. 1824. Geneva: Slatkine, 1969. Print.

Du Pré, Jean. *Le palais des nobles dames.* Ed. Brenda Dunn-Lardeau. Paris: Champion, 2007. Print. Textes de la Renaissance 115.

Duval, Edwin. "Maurice Scève and the Feminized Lover of Courtly-Petrarchan Lyric." Renaissances. Stanford U, Stanford. 9 Nov. 2006. Address.

Du Verger, Madame, and Philippe Du Verger. *Le Verger fertile des vertus.* Paris: Jacquin, 1595. Print.

———. *Le Verger fertile des vertus. Composé par defuncte Madame du Verger augmenté et amplifié par Philippe Du Verger sa fille, femme d'un procureur de la cour.*

Ed. Susan Broomhall and Colette H. Winn. Paris: Champion, 2004. Print. Textes de la Renaissance 85.

"Early Modern Women and Material Culture." *Early Modern Women* 4 (2009): 135–246. Print.

Ebreo, Leone. *Dialoghi d'amore.* Piscataway: Gorgias, 2010. Print.

———. Dialogues d'amour, *the French Translation Attributed to Pontus de Tyard and Published in Lyon, 1555, by Jean de Tournes.* Ed. T. Anthony Perry. Chapel Hill: U of North Carolina P, 1974. Print.

———. The Philosophy of Love / Dialoghi d'amore *by Leone Ebreo.* Trans. F. Friedeberg-Seeley and Jean H. Barnes. Introd. Cecil Roth. London: Soncino Soc., 1937. Print.

Eichberger, Dagmar, ed. *Women of Distinction. Margaret of York / Margaret of Austria.* Mechelen: Davidsfonds, 2005. Print. Exhibition catalog.

Eisenstein, Elizabeth. *The Printing Press as an Agent of Change.* Vol. 1. Cambridge: Cambridge UP, 1979. Print.

Ellwood, Christopher. *The Body Broken: The Calvinist Doctrine of the Eucharist and the Symbolization of Power in Sixteenth-Century France.* New York: Oxford UP, 1999. Print. Oxford Studies in Historical Theology.

Epistre d'une damoiselle françoise à une sienne amie dame estrangere, sur la mort d'excellente et vertueuse Dame, Leonor de Roye, Princesse de Condé. N.p.: n.p., 1564. Print.

"*Epistre d'une damoiselle françoise à une sienne amie dame estrangere* (1564)." Ed. Colette H. Winn. Goldsmith and Winn 179–222.

Erasmus, Desiderius. *The Essential Erasmus.* Trans. John P. Dolan. 1964. New York: New Amer. Lib., 1983. Print.

Estienne, Charles. *De Dissectione Partium Corporis Humani Libri Tres.* Paris: Colin, 1545. Print.

Evain, Aurore. "Les reines et princesses de France, mécènes, patronnes et protectrices du théâtre au XVIe siècle." Wilson-Chevalier, *Patronnes* 59–99.

Evans, Dylan. *An Introductory Dictionary of Lacanian Psychoanalysis.* London: Routledge, 1996. Print.

Ezell, Margaret. *The Patriarch's Wife: Literary Evidence and the History of the Family.* Chapel Hill: U of North Carolina P, 1987. Print.

Farge, James K. "Marguerite de Navarre, Her Circle, and the Censors of Paris." *International Colloquium Celebrating the Five-Hundredth Anniversary of the Birth of Marguerite de Navarre.* Ed. Régine Reynolds-Cornell. Birmingham: Summa, 1995. 15–28. Print.

Febvre, Lucien. *Amour sacré, amour profane. Autour de* L'heptaméron. Paris: Gallimard, 1944. Print.

Fedele, Cassandra. *Letters and Orations.* Ed. and trans. Diana Robin. Bilingual ed. Chicago: U of Chicago P, 2000. Print. The Other Voice in Early Modern Europe.

Feld, Helmut. "Einleitung." Jussie, *Petite chronique* xiii–lxxv.

———. "Jeanne de Jussie: Der Stand der Jungfräulichkeit und das große Gut der Ehe." *Frauen des Mittelalters: Zwanzig geistige Profile.* Ed. Feld. Cologne: Böhlau, 2000. 309–25. Print.

Felman, Shoshana. *Jacques Lacan and the Adventure of Insight: Psychoanalysis in Contemporary Culture.* Cambridge: Harvard UP, 1987. Print.

———. "To Open the Question." *Literature and Psychoanalysis.* Spec. issue of *Yale French Studies* 55-56 (1977): 5–10. Print.

The Feminist Encyclopedia of Italian Literature. Ed. Rinaldina Russell. Westport: Greenwood, 1997. Print.

Ferguson, Gary. "Biblical Exegesis and Social and Theological Commentary in the *Sonets spirituels* of Anne de Marquets." *L'exégèse biblique au seizième siècle.* Ed. Colette H. Winn. Spec. issue of *Œuvres et critiques* 20 (1995): 111–21. Print.

———. "Le chapelet et la plume, ou, quand la religieuse se fait écrivain: Le cas du prieuré de Poissy (1562–1621)." *Nouvelle revue du seizième siècle* 19.2 (2001): 83–100. Print.

———. "The Feminisation of Devotion: Gabrielle de Coignard, Anne de Marquets, and François de Sales." Ford and Jondorf 187–206.

———. Introduction. Marquets, *Sonets spirituels* [1997] 9–73.

———. "Marquets, Anne de (1533?–1588)." *Dictionnaire de la Siefar.* Siefar, 2003. Web. 18 Oct. 2010.

———. "Rules for Writing: The 'Dames de Poissy.'" *The Cloister and The World: Early Modern Convent Voices.* Ed. Thomas M. Carr, Jr. *EMF: Studies in Early Modern France* 11 (2007): 44–58. Print.

Ferguson, Margaret W. *Dido's Daughters: Literacy, Gender, and Empire in Early Modern England and France.* Chicago: U of Chicago P, 2003. Print.

———. "Recreating the Rules of the Games: Marguerite de Navarre's *Heptaméron.*" *Creative Imitation: New Essays on Renaissance Literature in Honor of Thomas M. Greene.* Ed. David Quint. Binghamton: State U of New York at Binghamton, Center for Medieval and Renaissance Studies, 1992. 153–87. Print.

Ferguson, Margaret, Maureen Quilligan, and Nancy Vickers, eds. *Rewriting the Renaissance: The Discourses of Sexual Difference in Early Modern Europe.* Fwd. Catharine R. Stimpson. Chicago: U of Chicago P, 1986. Print. Women in Culture and Soc.

Feugère, Léon. *Les femmes poètes au XVIe siècle.* Paris: Didier, 1860. Print.

ffolliott, Sheila. "Catherine de' Medici as Artemisia: Figuring the Powerful Widow." Ferguson, Quilligan, and Vickers 227–41.

———. "La reine mécène idéale de la Renaissance: Catherine de Médicis définie par elle-même ou définie par les autres?" Wilson-Chevalier, *Patronnes* 455–66.

Ficino, Marsilio. *Commentary on Plato's* Symposium. Trans. Sears Jane. Columbia: U of Missouri, 1944. Print.

Flore, Jeanne. *Les contes amoureux par Madame Jeanne Flore.* Ed. Régine Reynolds-Cornell. Saint Étienne: PU de Saint-Étienne, 2006. Print. La cité des dames.

Fogel, Michèle. *Marie de Gournay. Itinéraires d'une femme savante.* Paris: Fayard, 2004. Print.

Fonte, Moderata. *The Worth of Women.* Ed. and trans. Virginia Cox. Bilingual ed. Chicago: U of Chicago P, 1997. Print. The Other Voice in Early Modern Europe.

Ford, Philip. "Morel, Camille de (1547–1611)." *Dictionnaire de la Siefar.* Siefar, 2009. Web. 24 Sept. 2010.

Ford, Philip, and Gillian Jondorf, eds. *Women's Writings in the French Renaissance:*

Proceedings of the Fifth Cambridge French Renaissance Colloquium. Cambridge: Cambridge UP, 1999. Print. Cambridge French Colloquia.

Forster, Leonard Wilson. *The Icy Fire: Five Studies in European Petrarchism*. London: Cambridge UP, 1969. Print.

Fortia, Maria de. "A tres-noble et tres-vertueuse Dame, Madame de Fresnes." Marquets, *Sonets* [1997] 77–78.

Foucault, Michel. *Histoire de la sexualité I: La volonté de savoir*. Paris: Gallimard, 1976. Print.

———. *The History of Sexuality*. Trans. Robert Hurley. Vol. 1. New York: Vintage, 1980. Print.

———. "Qu'est-ce qu'un auteur?" *Bulletin de la société française de philosophie* 63 (1969): 75–104. Print.

———. "What Is an Author?" *Language, Counter-memory, Practice: Selected Essays and Interviews*. Trans. Donald F. Bouchard and Sherry Simon. Ithaca: Cornell UP, 1977. 113–38. Print.

Fournier, Hannah S. "La voix textuelle des *Sonets spirituels* d'Anne de Marquets." *Études littéraires* 20 (1987): 77–92. Print.

Fraenkel, Béatrice. *La signature. Genèse d'un signe*. Paris: Gallimard, 1992. Print.

Franchetti, Anna Lia. *L'ombre discourante de Marie de Gournay*. Paris: Champion, 2006. Print.

Franco, Veronica. *Poems and Selected Letters*. Ed. and trans. Ann Rosalind Jones and Margaret F. Rosenthal. Bilingual ed. Chicago: U of Chicago P, 1998. Print. The Other Voice in Early Modern Europe.

Freccero, Carla. "Archives in the Fiction: The Rhetoric of the Law in Marguerite de Navarre's *Heptameron*." *Rhetoric and Law in Early Modern Europe*. Ed. Lorna Hutson and Victoria Kahn. New Haven: Yale UP, 2001. 73–94. Print.

———. "1527: Margaret of Navarre." Hollier, *New History* 145–48.

———. "Marguerite de Navarre and the Politics of Maternal Sovereignty." *Women and Sovereignty*. Ed. Louise Olga Fradenburg. Spec. issue of *Cosmos* 7 (1992): 132–49. Print.

———. "Patriarchy and the Maternal Text: The Case of Marguerite de Navarre." *Renaissance Women Writers: French Texts / American Contexts*. Ed. Anne Larsen and Colette H. Winn. Detroit: Wayne State UP, 1994. 130–40. Print.

———. "Practicing Queer Philology with Marguerite de Navarre: Nationalism and the Castigation of Desire." Goldberg, *Queering the Renaissance* 107–23.

———. "Queer Nation, Female Nation." *Feminism in Time*. Ed. Margaret Ferguson and Marshall Brown. Spec. issue of *Modern Language Quarterly* 65.1 (2004): 29–47. Print.

———. "Rewriting the Rhetoric of Desire: Marguerite de Navarre's *Heptaméron*." *Contending Kingdoms: Historical, Psychological, and Feminist Approaches to the Literature of Sixteenth-Century England and France*. Ed. Marie-Rose Logan and Peter Rudnytsky. Detroit: Wayne State UP, 1991. 298–312. Print.

———. "Unwriting Lucretia: 'Heroic Virtue' and the *Heptaméron*." Polachek, *Heroic Virtue* 77–89.

———. "Voices of Subjection: Maternal Sovereignty and Filial Resistance in and around Marguerite de Navarre's *Heptaméron*." *Yale Journal of Law and the Humanities* 5.1 (1993): 147–57. Print.

Frelick, Nancy. "Contagions of Love: Textual Transmission." *Imagining Contagion in Early Modern Europe.* Ed. Claire L. Carlin. London: Palgrave, 2005. 47–62. Print.

———. "Images captivantes: Louise Labé Amazone." *Dix ans de recherches sur les femmes écrivains de l'Ancien Régime. Influences et confluences. Mélanges offerts à Hannah Fournier.* Ed. Guy Poirier. Sainte-Foy: PU Laval, 2008. 127–46. Print.

———. "Lacan, Courtly Love, and Anamorphosis." *The Court Reconvenes: Courtly Literature across the Disciplines.* Ed. Barbara K. Altmann and Carleton W. Carroll. Cambridge: Brewer, 2003. 107–14. Print.

French Emblems at Glasgow. Ed. Alison Adams et al. U of Glasgow. Web. 9 May 2008.

"Gabrielle de Coignard (c. 1500–1586)." *Other Women's Voices.* Ed. Dorothy Disse. 17 Feb. 2010. Web. 9 Mar. 2010.

"Gabrielle de Coignard (?–1594)." *Poésie Française.* 2009. Web. 9 Mar. 2010.

Gaillard, Gabriel-Henri. *Rhétorique françoise à l'usage des jeunes demoiselles.* Paris: Bauche, 1762. Print.

Galand-Hallyn, Perrine. "Le statut du sujet dans les théories de la représentation antiques et humanistes." *Éthos et pathos. Le statut du sujet rhétorique (Actes du colloque international de Saint-Denis, 19–21 juin 1997).* Ed. François Cornilliat and Richard Lockwood. Paris: Champion, 2000. 37–52. Print.

Galand-Hallyn, Perrine, and Fernand Hallyn, "'Recueillir des brouillars': Éthique de la silve et poétique du manuscrit trouvé." *Le poète et son œuvre, de la composition à la publication. Actes du colloque de Valenciennes, 20–21 mars 1999.* Ed. Jean-Eudes Girot. Geneva: Droz, 2004. 9–35. Print.

Galen. "The Soul's Dependence on the Body." *Selected Works.* Ed. and trans. P. N. Singer. Oxford: Oxford UP, 1997. 150–76. Print.

Gallop, Jane. *Around 1981: Academic Feminist Literary Theory.* New York: Routledge, 1991. Print.

Gambara, Veronica. "Mentre da vaghi e giovenil pensieri." Stortoni and Lillie 28–29.

Ganter, Edmond. *Les Clarisses de Genève: 1473-1535-1793.* Geneva: Société Catholique d'Histoire, 1949. Print.

Garin, Eugenio. *La cultura filosofica del Rinascimento italiano.* 1961. Florence: Sansoni, 1979. Print.

Garrisson, Janine. *Les protestants au XVIe siècle.* Paris: Fayard, 1988. Print.

Gascon, Richard. *Grand commerce et vie urbaine au XVIe siècle: Lyon et ses marchands (environs de 1520-environs de 1580).* Paris: SEVPEN, 1971. Print. Civilisations et sociétés 22.

Gelis, F. de. *Histoire critique des Jeux Floraux* (1912). Geneva: Slatkine, 1981. Print.

Gendre, André. "Naissance des échanges polémiques à la veille des guerres civiles: Anne de Marquets et son adversaire protestant." *Bibliothèque d'humanisme et Renaissance* 62.2 (2000): 317–57. Print.

George, Edward V. "Luisa Sigea (1522–1560): Iberian Scholar-Poet." Churchill, Brown, and Jeffrey 3: 167–87.

Gibson, Jonathan, and Victoria E. Burke, eds. *Women and Early Modern Manuscript Culture.* Aldershot: Ashgate, 2004. Print.

Goldberg, Jonathan, ed. *Queering the Renaissance.* Durham: Duke UP, 1994. Print.

———. *Sodometries: Renaissance Texts, Modern Sexualities.* Stanford: Stanford UP, 1992. Print.

Goldsmith, Elizabeth C. *Writing the Female Voice: Essays on Epistolarity.* Boston: Northeastern UP, 1989. Print.

Goldsmith, Elizabeth C., and Colette H. Winn, eds. *Lettres de femmes: XVIe–XVIIIe siècle.* Paris: Champion, 2005. Print. Textes de la Renaissance 89.

Gottlieb, Beatrice. "The Meaning of Clandestine Marriage." *Family and Sexuality in French History.* Ed. Robert Wheaton and Tamara K. Hareven. Philadelphia: U of Pennsylvania P, 1980. 49–83. Print.

Gould, Vivian, ed. *Daughters of Time: Two Thousand Notable Women from Antiquity to 1800.* Charleston: BookSurge, 2006. Print.

Gournay, Marie le Jars de. *Les advis, ou, les presens de la Demoiselle de Gournay.* Paris: Du Bray, 1634. *Gallica.* Bibliothèque Nationale de France, n.d. Print; Web.

———. *Les advis ou les presens de la demoiselle de Gournay.* Paris: Du Bray, 1641. *Gallica.* Bibliothèque Nationale de France, n.d. Print; Web.

———. Apology for the Woman Writing *and Other Works.* Ed. and trans. Richard Hillman and Colette Quesnel. Chicago: U of Chicago P, 2002. Print. The Other Voice in Early Modern Europe.

———. *Égalité des hommes et des femmes.* 1622. Pref. Milagros Palma. Paris: Côté-femmes Éditions, 1989. Print.

———. L'Égalité des hommes et des femmes. Le Grief des dames, *suivis du* Promenoir de Monsieur de Montaigne. Ed. Constant Venesoen. Geneva: Droz, 1993. Print. TLF 433.

———. *Imitation of the Life of Damoiselle de Gournay.* Trans. Élyane Dezon-Jones. Larsen and Winn, *Writings* 237–41.

———. *Œuvres complètes.* Ed. Jean-Claude Arnould et al. 2 vols. Paris: Champion, 2002. Print. Textes de la Renaissance 51.

———. *L'ombre de la damoiselle de Gournay, œuvre composée de meslanges.* Paris: Libert, 1626. *Gallica.* Bibliothèque Nationale de France, n.d. Print; Web.

———. "Préface de Marie de Gournay à l'édition de 1595 des *Essais.*" Ed. François Rigolot. *Montaigne Studies: An Interdisciplinary Forum* 1 (1989): 7–60. Print.

———. *Preface to the Essays of Michel de Montaigne by His Adoptive Daughter, Marie le Jars de Gournay.* Trans. Richard Hillman and Colette Quesnel. Tempe: Medieval and Renaissance Texts and Studies, 1998. Print.

———. *Le proumenoir de Monsieur de Montaigne.* Ed. Jean-Claude Arnould. Paris: Champion, 1996. Print. Textes de la Renaissance 51.

Graesslé, Isabelle. "Marie Dentière (1490–1560)." *Mur des réformateurs.* Les Églises réformées de Suisse Romande. Web. 5 Nov. 2009.

———. "Reformation Sunday." *Reformed World* 53.1 (2003): 50–53. Print.

———. "Vie et légendes de Marie Dentière." *Bulletin du centre Protestant d'études* 55.1 (2003): 1–31. Print.

Grafton, Anthony, and Lisa Jardine. *From Humanism to the Humanities: Education and the Liberal Arts in Fifteenth- and Sixteenth-Century Europe.* Cambridge: Harvard UP, 1986. Print.

Granada, Luis de. *Le vray chemin et adresse pour acquerir et parvenir à la grace de Dieu, et se maintenir en icelle, par le moyen et compagnie de l'oraison et contemplation en la loy et amour de Dieu.* Trans. François de Belleforest. Paris: Guillaume de la Noue, 1579. Print.

Grand-Dewyse, Camille. "Le triomphe d'une *mater familias*: Antoinette de Bourbon, duchesse de Guise, et une plaque émaillée de Léonard Limosin." Wilson-Chevalier, *Patronnes* 419–31.

Gratian. *Decretum Gratiani.* Ed. J. P. Migne. Paris: Garnier, 1912. Print.

Graville, Anne of. *Romant des deux amans Palamon et Arcita, et de la belle et saige Emilia.* Paris: Bibliothèque de l'Arsenal, 1566. Print.

The Greek Anthology. Ed. W. R. Paton. London: Heinemann, 1980. Print.

Grévin, Jacques. *Portraicts anatomiques de toutes les parties du corps humain gravez en taille douce, . . . ensemble l'abbrégé d'André Vésale.* Paris: Wechel, 1569. Print.

Guillard, Charlotte. Preface. *Lexicon graecolatinum, ingenti vocum accessione Jacobi Tusani.* By Jacques Toussain. Vol. 1. Paris: Guillard and Merlin, 1552. N. pag. Print.

Guillerm, Jean-Pierre, et al., eds. *Le miroir des femmes.* 2 vols. Lille: PU de Lille, 1983. Print.

Gutton, Jean-Pierre. *Guide de Lyon Renaissance âge classique, 1500–1789.* Lyon: Éditions Lyonnaises d'Art et d'Histoire, 1995. Print.

Haase-Dubosc, Danielle, and Éliane Viennot, eds. *Femmes et pouvoirs sous l'Ancien Régime.* Paris: Rivages, 1991. Print.

Halperin, David. *How to Do the History of Homosexuality.* Chicago: U of Chicago P, 2002. Print.

———. *"One Hundred Years of Homosexuality" and Other Essays on Greek Love.* New York: Routledge, 1990. Print.

Hampton, Timothy. *Literature and Nation in the Sixteenth Century: Inventing Renaissance France.* Ithaca: Cornell UP, 2001. Print.

Hanley, Sarah. "Family and State in Early Modern France: The Marriage Pact." *Connecting Spheres: Women in the Western World, 1500 to the Present.* Ed. Marilyn Boxer and Jean Quataert. New York: Oxford UP, 1987. 53–63. Print.

———. "La loi salique." *Encyclopédie politique et historique des femmes: Europe, Amérique du Nord.* Ed. Christine Fauré. Paris: P U de France, 1996. 11–30. Print.

———. "The Monarchic State in Early Modern France: Marital Regime Government and Male Right." *Politics, Ideology, and the Law in Early Modern Europe: Essays in Honor of J. H. M. Salmon.* Ed. Adrianna Bakos. Rochester: U of Rochester P, 1994. 107–26. Print.

Hartman, Geoffrey. "The Voice of the Shuttle: Language from the Point of View of Literature." *Beyond Formalism.* New Haven: Yale UP, 1970. Print.

Harvey, Elizabeth D. "Ventriloquizing Sappho: Ovid, Donne, and the Erotics of the Feminine Voice." *Criticism* 30.2 (1989): 115–38. Print.

Harvey, Lawrence E. *The Aesthetics of the Renaissance Love Sonnet. An Essay on the Art of the Sonnet in the Poetry of Louise Labé.* Geneva: Droz, 1962. Print.

Head, Thomas. "A Propagandist for Reform: Marie Dentière." Wilson, *Women Writers* 260–83.

———. "The Religion of the *Femmelettes*: Ideals and Experience among Women in Fifteenth- and Sixteenth-Century France." *That Gentle Strength: Historical Perspectives on Women in Christianity.* Ed. Lynda Coon, Katherine Haldane, and Elisabeth Sommer. Charlottesville: UP of Virginia, 1991. 149–75. Print.

Heller, Henry. "Marguerite de Navarre and the Reformers of Meaux." *Bibliothèque d'Humanisme et Renaissance* 33 (1971): 271–301. Print.

Herlihy, David. "Did Women Have a Renaissance? A Reconsideration." *Medievalia et Humanistica: Studies in Medieval and Renaissance Culture* 13 (1985): 1–22. Print.

Herminjard, A.-L., ed. *Correspondance des Réformateurs dans les pays de langue française. Recueillie et publiée avec d'autres lettres relatives à la Réforme et des notes historiques et biographiques.* Vol. 5. Nieuwkoop: De Graaf, 1965. Print. 9 vols.

Hicks, Eric. *Le débat sur* Le roman de la rose: *Christine de Pisan, Jean Gerson, Jean de Montreuil, Gontier et Pierre Col.* Paris: Champion, 1977. Print.

Higgott, Suzanne, and Isabelle Biron. "Marguerite de France as Minerva: A Sixteenth-Century Limoges Painted Enamel by Jean de Court in the Wallace Collection." *Apollo* 159.504 (2004): 21–30. Print.

Hindman, Sandra L. *Christine de Pizan's "Epistre Othéa."* Toronto: Pontifical Inst. of Mediaeval Studies, 1986. Print.

Hirsch, Marianne, and Evelyn Fox Keller, eds. *Conflicts in Feminism.* New York: Routledge, 1990. Print.

History of Europe: The Periodical Historical Atlas, 1100 to 1200—High Resolution Maps. Euratlas, n.d. Web. 5 Feb. 2010.

Hollier, Denis, ed. *A New History of French Literature.* Cambridge: Harvard UP, 1989. *Google Books.* Web. 5 Nov. 2009.

Holt, Mack P. *Renaissance and Reformation Europe, 1500–1648.* Oxford: Oxford UP, 2002. Print. Short Oxford History of France.

The Holy Bible Containing the Old and New Testaments and the Apocrypha. Cambridge: Cambridge UP, n.d. Print.

Hosington, Brenda M. "Elizabeth Jane Weston (1581–1612)." Churchill, Brown, and Jeffrey 3: 217–45.

Huchon, Mireille. *Louise Labé, Une créature de papier.* Geneva: Droz, 2006. Print.

Hufton, Olwen. *The Prospect before Her: A History of Women in Western Europe.* Vol. 1: 1500–1800. New York: Knopf, 1995. Print.

———. "Women, Work, and Family." *Renaissance and Enlightenment Paradoxes.* Ed. Natalie Zemon Davis and Arlette Farge. Cambridge: Harvard UP, 1993. 15–45. Print. Vol. 3 of *A History of Women in the West.* Dir. Georges Duby and Michèle Perrot.

Hunkeler, Thomas. *Le vif du sens. Corps et poésie selon Maurice Scève.* Geneva: Droz, 2003. Print.

Huot, Sylvia. *From Song to Book.* Ithaca: Cornell UP, 1987. Print.

———. "Seduction and Sublimation: Christine de Pizan, Jean de Meun, and Dante." *Romance Notes* 25 (1985): 361–73. Print.

Hutson, Lorna, ed. *Feminism and Renaissance Studies.* Oxford: Oxford UP, 1999. Print. Oxford Readings in Feminism Series.

Ignatius of Loyola. *Exercices spirituels.* Ed. François Courel. Paris, 1960. Print.

Impressions: Une petite histoire des techniques graphiques. Musée de l'Imprimerie de Lyon. BBF, 2000. CD-Rom.

Irigaray, Luce. *Ce sexe qui n'en est pas un.* Paris: Minuit, 1977. Print.

———. *This Sex Which Is Not One.* Trans. Catherine Porter, with Carolyn Burke. Ithaca: Cornell UP, 1985. Print.

Isley, Marjorie. *A Daughter of the Renaissance: Marie le Jars de Gournay.* The Hague: Mouton, 1963. Print.

Jackson, Richard A. "Peers of France and Princes of the Blood." *French Historical Studies* 7.1 (1971): 27–46. Print.

Jaffe, Irma. *Shining Eyes, Cruel Fortune: The Lives and Loves of Italian Renaissance Women Poets.* New York: Fordham UP, 2002. Print.

Jardine, Lisa. "Women Humanists: Education for What?" Grafton and Jardine 29–57.

Jauss, Hans Robert. *Pour une esthétique de la réception.* Trans. Claude Maillard. Paris: Gallimard, 1990. Print.

Johnson, Alfred Forbes. "Books Printed at Lyons [sic] in the Sixteenth Century." *Library* 4th ser. 3.3 (1922): 145–74. Print.

———. *French Sixteenth-Century Printing.* With Fifty Illus. New York: Scribner's, 1928. Print. Periods of Typography.

Jones, Ann Rosalind. "Assimilation with a Difference: Renaissance Women Poets and Literary Influence." *Yale French Studies* 62 (1981): 135–53. Print.

———. "City Women and Their Audiences: Louise Labé and Veronica Franco." Ferguson, Quilligan, and Vickers 299–316.

———. *The Currency of Eros: Women's Love Lyric in Europe, 1540–1620.* Bloomington: Indiana UP, 1990. Print.

———. "Pernette Du Guillet: The Lyonnais Neoplatonist." Wilson, *Women Writers* 219–31.

———. "Surprising Fame: Renaissance Gender Ideologies and Women's Lyric." Miller, *Poetics* 74–95.

Jones, Ann Rosalind, and Nancy Vickers. "Canon, Rule, and Restoration Renaissance." *The Politics of Tradition: Placing Women in French Literature.* Ed. Joan Dejean and Nancy K. Miller. Spec. issue of *Yale French Studies* 75 (1988): 9–25. Print.

Jones-Davies, M. T., ed. *Le mariage au temps de la Renaissance.* Paris: Klincksieck, 1993. Print.

Joplin, Patricia K. "The Voice of the Shuttle Is Ours." *Stanford Literature Review* 1.1 (1984): 25–33. Print.

Jordan, Constance. *Renaissance Feminism: Literary Texts and Political Models.* Ithaca: Cornell UP, 1990. Print.

Joubert, Laurent. Traité du ris, *suivi d'un dialogue sur la cacographie française.* 1579. Geneva: Slatkine, 1973. Print.

Joukovsky-Micha, Françoise. *Poésie et mythologie au XVIe siècle. Quelques mythes de l'inspiration chez les poètes de la Renaissance.* Paris: Librairie Nizet, 1969. Print.

Jourda, Pierre. *Marguerite d'Angoulême, Duchesse d'Alençon, Reine de Navarre (1492–1549). Étude biographique et littéraire.* 2 vols. Paris: Champion, 1930. Print.

Jussie, Jeanne de. *Kleine Chronik.* Ed. and trans. Helmut Feld. Mainz: Zabern, 1996. Print.

———. *Le levain du Calvinisme, ou commencement de l'heresie de Geneve. Faict par Reverende Soeur Jeanne de Jussie, lors religieuse de Saincte Claire de Geneve, et apres sa sortie Abbesse au Convent d'Anyssi.* Chambéry: Du Four, 1611. Print.

———. *Petite chronique.* Ed. Helmut Feld. Mainz: Zabern, 1996. Print.

———. *The Short Chronicle: A Bilingual Edition.* Ed. and trans. Carrie F. Klaus. Chicago: U of Chicago P, 2006. Print. The Other Voice in Early Modern Europe.

Kaplan, Cora. *Sea Changes: Culture and Feminism.* London: Verso, 1986. Print.

Kellogg, Judith L. "Transforming Ovid. The Metamorphosis of Female Authority." Desmond, *Christine de Pizan* 181–94.

Kelly, Joan (*see also* Joan Kelly-Gadol). "Early Feminist Theory and the *Querelle des Femmes,* 1475–1789." *Signs* 8 (1982): 2–28. Print. Rpt. in Kelly, *Women* 65–109.

———. *Women, History, and Theory: The Essays of Joan Kelly.* Fwd Catharine R. Stimpson. Chicago: U of Chicago P, 1984. Print. Women in Culture and Soc.

Kelly-Gadol, Joan (*see also* Kelly, Joan). "Did Women Have a Renaissance?" *Becoming Visible: Women in European History.* 1976. Ed. Renate Bridenthal, Claudia Koonz, and Susan M. Stuard. Boston: Houghton, 1977. 137–64. Print.

Kelso, Ruth. *Doctrine for the Lady of the Renaissance.* 1956. Urbana: U of Illinois P, 1978. Print.

Kemp, William. "D'Ennetières [Dentière], Marie (1495–1561)." *Dictionnaire de la Siefar.* Siefar, 2003. Web. 1 Nov. 2010.

———. "Textes composés ou traduits par des femmes et imprimés en France avant 1550: Bibliographie des imprimés féminins (1488–1549)." *Littératures: L'écriture des femmes à la Renaissance française.* Ed. Diane Desrosiers-Bonin. Montreal: McGill U, 1998. 151–220. Print. Éditions littéraires 18.

Kemp, William, and Diane Desrosiers-Bonin. "Marie d'Ennetières et la petite grammaire hébraïque de sa fille d'après la dédicace de l'*Epistre* à Marguerite de Navarre." *Bibliothèque d'Humanisme et Renaissance* 60.1 (1998): 117–34. Print.

Kennedy, William J. *Authorizing Petrarch.* Ithaca: Cornell UP, 1994. Print.

Kiefer, Frederick, ed. *Masculinities and Femininities in the Middle Ages and Renaissance. Proceedings of the ACMRS, Tempe, AZ, 2007.* Belgium: Brepols, forthcoming. Arizona Studies in the Middle Ages and the Renaissance Conference 23.

King, Margaret L. *Women of the Renaissance.* Chicago: U of Chicago P, 1991. Print.

King Margaret L., and Albert Rabil, Jr., eds. *Teaching Other Voices: Women and Religion in Early Modern Europe.* Chicago: U of Chicago P, 2007. Print.

Klapisch-Zuber, Christiane. *Women, Family, and Ritual in Renaissance Italy.* Trans. Lydia G. Cochrane. Chicago: U of Chicago P, 1985. Print.

Klaus, Carrie F. "Architecture and Sexual Identity: Jeanne de Jussie's Narrative of the Reformation of Geneva." *Feminist Studies* 29.2 (2003): 279–97. Print.

———. "Reading Jeanne de Jussie's *Short Chronicle* with First-Year Students." King and Rabil 127–36.

———. "Volume Editor's Introduction." Jussie, *Short Chronicle* 1–28.

Klibansky, Raymond, Erwin Panofsky, and Fritz Saxl. *Saturn and Melancholy: Studies in the History of Natural Philosophy, Religion, and Art.* London: Nelson, 1964. Print.

Knecht, R. J. Rev. of *Jeanne d'Albret et sa cour. Actes du colloque international de Pau 17–19 mai 2001,* by Évelyne Berriot-Salvadore, Philippe Chareyre, and Claudie Martin-Ulrich. *French Studies* 60 (2006): 100–01. *Oxford Journals.* Oxford UP. Web. 6 Nov. 2009.

———. *Renaissance Warrior and Patron: The Reign of Francis I.* Cambridge: Cambridge UP, 1994. Print.

Krause, Virginia. "Confessions d'une héroïne romanesque: *Les angoysses douloureuses* d'Hélisenne de Crenne." Beaulieu and Desrosiers-Bonin, *Hélisenne de Crenne* 19–34.

Kristeva, Julia. *Powers of Horror*. New York: Columbia UP, 1982. Print.

Kritzman, Lawrence. *The Rhetoric of Sexuality and the Literature of the French Renaissance*. Cambridge: Cambridge UP, 1991. Print.

Kuin, Roger, and Anne Lake Prescott. "The Wrath of Priapus: Rémy Belleau's 'Jean qui ne peult' and Its Traditions." *Comparative Literature Studies* 37.1 (2000): 1–17. Print.

Kuperty-Tsur, Nadine. "Charlotte Arbaleste." *Dictionnaire de la Siefar*. Siefar, 2003. Web. 12 Nov. 2010.

Kushner, Eva, ed. *Le dialogue à la Renaissance: Histoire et poétique*. Geneva: Droz, 2004. Print.

Labé, Louise. *Complete Poetry and Prose: A Bilingual Edition*. Ed. and prose trans. Deborah Lesko Baker. Poetry trans. Annie Finch. Chicago: U of Chicago P, 2006. *Other Women's Voices*. Web. 7 Apr. 2011.

———. *Complete Works*. Trans. and ed. Edith R. Farrell. Introd. C. Frederick Farrell, Jr., and Edith R. Farrell. Troy: Whitson, 1986. Print.

———. *Le débat de folie et d'amour. XVIe siècle*. Ed. Éliane Viennot. Saint-Étienne: PU de Saint-Étienne, 2006. 375–446. Print. Vol. 1 of *Théâtre de femmes d'Ancien Régime*. Aurore Evain, Perry Gethner, and Henriette Goldwyn, gen. eds. La cité des dames 5.

———. *Debate of Folly and Love*. Trans. Anne-Marie Bourbon. Fwd. Deborah Lesko Baker. New York: Lang, 2000. Print.

———. *Euvres de Louise Labé Lyonnoise*. Lyon: Tournes, 1555. *Gallica*. Bibliothèque Nationale de France, n.d. Print; Web.

———. *Euvres de Louise Labé Lyonnoise. Revues et corrigees par ladite dame*. Lyon: Tournes, 1556. *The Renaissance in Print*, U of Virginia Lib., n.d. Print; Web.

———. *Euvres de Louïze Labé Lionnoise. Revues et corrigees par ladite dame*. Lyon: Tournes, 1556. *Gallica*. Bibliothèque Nationale de France, n.d. Print; Web.

———. *Œuvres*. Ed. Joseph Aynard. *Les poètes lyonnais: Précurseurs de la Pléiade*. Paris: Bossard, 1924. Print. *The Early Modern French Women Writers Project*. Web. 6 Nov. 2009.

———. *Œuvres*. Ed. Charles Boy. 1887. Facsim. ed. Geneva: Slatkine, 1981. *Gallica*. Bibliothèque Nationale de France, n.d. Print; Web.

———. *Œuvres complètes*. Ed. François Rigolot. Paris: Garnier-Flammarion, 1986. Print.

———. *Œuvres complètes*. Ed. François Rigolot. Paris: Garnier-Flammarion, 2004. Print.

———. *Œuvres poétiques. Précédée des* Rymes *de Pernette du Guillet. Avec un choix de blasons du corps féminin*. Ed. Françoise Charpentier. Paris: Poésie-Gallimard, 1983. Print.

———. *S'ensuivent les Blasons anatomiques du corps feminin*. 1543. Paris: L'Angelier, 1550. Print.

———. *S'ensuivent les Blasons anatomiques du corps feminin*. Bruxelles: Gray, 1866. Print.

———. *Sonnets*. Introd. and commentaries by Peter Sharratt. Trans. Graham Dunstan Martin. Austin: U of Texas P, 1972. Print. Edinburgh Bilingual Lib. 7.

La Borderie, Bertrand de. *L'amie de court*. Ed. Danielle Trudeau. Paris: Champion, 1997. Print.

Lacan, Jacques. *The Four Fundamental Concepts of Psycho-analysis.* Trans. Alan Sheridan. New York: Norton, 1981. Print.

———. *Mon enseignement.* Paris: Éditions du Seuil, 2005. Print.

La Charité, Claude. "Le 'Brief discours que l'excellence de la femme surpasse celle de l'homme' (1581) de Marie de Romieu: Le genre du discours en vers ou le paradoxe désamorcé." *Littératures* 24, forthcoming.

———. "'Ce male vers enfant de ta verve femelle': Les destinataires féminins de la lyrique amoureuse de Marie de Romieu." *Nouvelle revue du XVIe siècle* 18.2 (2000): 81–94. Print.

———. "La décade féminine de Marie de Romieu." Brouard-Arends 317–30.

———, dir. *Femmes, rhétorique et éloquence sous l'Ancien Régime.* Saint-Étienne: PU de Saint-Étienne, forthcoming. Nouvelles recherches.

———. "Marie de Romieu et l'écriture androgyne: Les marques de généricité du sujet lyrique dans *Les premieres Œuvres poetiques* (1581)." *Sextant* 17-18 (2002): 213–34. Print.

———, ed. *Masques et figures du sujet féminin aux XVIe et XVIIe siècles.* Spec. issue of *Tangence* 77 (2005): 3–167. Print.

———. *La rhétorique épistolaire de Rabelais.* Québec: Nota Bene, 2003. Print.

———. "Romieu, Marie de." *Dictionnaire de la Siefar.* Siefar, 2004. Web. 1 Nov. 2010.

La Charité, Claude, and Renée-Claude Breitenstein, eds. "Traités sur l'excellence des femmes, XVIe–XVIIIe siècles." Saint-Étienne: PU de Saint-Étienne, forthcoming. Cité des dames 11.

La Croix du Maine, François Grudé, sieur de. *Premier volume de la bibliotheque du sieur de la Croix du Maine.* Paris: L'Angelier, 1584. Print.

La Croix du Maine, François Grudé, and Antoine Du Verdier. *Les bibliothèques françoises de La Croix du Maine et de Du Verdier sieur de Vauprivas. . . .* Ed. Rigoley de Juvigny. 6 vols. 1772–73. Graz: Akademische Druck, 1969. Print.

Lagarde, André, and Laurent Michard. *XVIe siècle.* Vol. 2. Paris: Bordas, 1962. Print.

Lanza, Janine M. *From Wives to Widows in Early Modern Paris: Gender, Economy, and Law.* Aldershot: Ashgate, 2007. Print. Women and Gender in the Early Modern World.

Larousse, Pierre. *Grand dictionnaire universel du XIXe siècle.* Vol. 4. Paris: Administration du Grand Dictionnaire Universel, 1865–78. Print.

Larsen, Anne R. "Catherine de Roches, *Epistre à sa mere.*" *Allegorica* 7.2 (1982): 58–64. Print.

———. "Des Roches, Catherine Fradonnet, dame (1542–1587)." *Dictionnaire de la Siefar.* Siefar, 2004. Web. 18 Oct. 2010.

———. "'Un honneste passetems': Strategies of Legitimation in French Renaissance Women's Prefaces." *L'Esprit Créateur* 30.4 (1990): 11–22. Print.

———. Introduction. Des Roches and Des Roches, *From Mother* 243–49.

———. "Louise Labé's *Débat de folie et d'amour:* Feminism and the Defense of Learning." *Tulsa Studies in Women's Literature* 2.1 (1983): 43–55. Print.

———. "Paradox and the Praise of Women: From Ortensio Lando and Charles Estienne to Marie de Romieu." *Sixteenth Century Journal* 28.3 (1997): 759–74. Print.

———. Preface. Des Roches and Des Roches, *Les missives* 9–49.

Larsen, Anne R., and Colette H. Winn, eds. *Écrits de femmes à la Renaissance.* Spec. issue of *Études littéraires* 27.2 (1994). 5–19. Print.

———, eds. *Renaissance Women Writers: French Texts / American Contexts.* Detroit: Wayne State UP, 1994. Print.

———, eds. *Writings by Pre-revolutionary French Women: From Marie de France to Elizabeth Vigée-Le Brun.* New York: Garland, 2000. Print.

"Late 1500s–Early 1600s, France—The Religious Wars." *Maps ETC.* Educational Technology Clearinghouse, U of South Florida. 2006. Web. 9 Mar. 2010.

L'Aubespine, Madeleine de. *Cabinet des saines affections.* Ed. Colette H. Winn. Paris: Champion, 2001. Print. Textes de la Renaissance 39.

———. *Selected Poems and Translations: A Bilingual Edition.* Ed. and trans. Anna Kłosowska. Chicago: U of Chicago P, 2007. Print. The Other Voice in Early Modern Europe.

Lavaud, Jacques. "Quelques poésies oubliées de Nicole Estienne." *Revue du seizième siècle* 18 (1931): 341–51. Print.

Lazard, Madeleine. *Les avenues de fémynie: Les femmes et la Renaissance.* Paris: Fayard, 2001. Print.

———. "Deux sœurs ennemies, Marie Dentière et Jeanne de Jussie: Nonnes et réformées à Genève." *Les réformes: Enracinements socio-culturels.* Ed. B. Chevalier and C. Sauzat. Paris: La Maisnie, 1985. 233–49. Print.

———. "Femmes, littérature, culture au XVIe siècle en France." Haase-Dubosc and Viennot 101–19. Rpt. in *Joyeusement vivre et honnêtement penser. Mélanges offerts à Madeleine Lazard.* Ed. Marie-Madeleine Fragonard and Gilbert Schrenck. Paris: Champion, 2000. 311–28. Print.

———. *Images littéraires de la femme à la Renaissance.* Paris: PUF, 1985. Print.

———. "Jussie, Jeanne de." *Dictionnaire de la Siefar.* Siefar, 2003. Web. 18 Oct. 2010.

———. *Louise Labé.* Paris: Fayard, 2004. Print.

———. *Pierre de Bourdeille, seigneur de Brantôme.* Paris: Fayard, 1995. Print.

Lecoq, Anne-Marie. *François Ier imaginaire. Symbolique et politique à l'aube de la Renaissance française.* Paris: Macula, 1987. Print.

Le Fournier, André. *La decoration dhumaine nature, & aornement des dames.* Lyon: Juste, 1537. *The Renaissance in Print.* U of Virginia Lib., 29 June 2005. Print; Web.

Legaré, Anne-Marie. "Charlotte de Savoie's Library and Illuminators." *Journal of the Early Book Society* 4 (2001): 32–87. Print.

Le Gendre, Marie. *Exercice de l'âme spirituelle.* Ed. Colette H. Winn. Paris: Champion, 2001. Print. Textes de la Renaissance 38.

Lequain, Élodie. "Anne de France et les livres: La tradition et le pouvoir." Wilson-Chevalier, *Patronnes* 155–68.

Lerner, Gerda. *The Creation of Feminist Consciousness from the Middle Ages to Eighteen-Seventy.* New York: Oxford UP, 1993. Print.

Lesko Baker, Deborah. *The Subject of Desire: Petrarchan Poetics and the Female Voice in Louise Labé.* West Lafayette: Purdue UP, 1996. Print.

Le Sourd, Auguste. *Recherches sur Jacques et Marie de Romieu: Poètes vivarois.* Villefranche: Imprimerie du Réveil du Beaujolais, 1924. Print.

L'Estrange, Elizabeth. "Le mécénat d'Anne de Bretagne." Wilson-Chevalier, *Patronnes* 169–93.

———. "Sainte Anne et le mécénat d'Anne de France." Wilson-Chevalier, *Patronnes* 135–54.

Lévi-Strauss, Claude. *The Elementary Structures of Kinship*. Trans. and ed. James Harle Bell, John Richard von Sturmer, and Rodney Needham. Boston: Beacon, 1969. Print.

———. *Les structures élémentaires de la parenté*. Paris: Mouton, 1967. Print.

Levin, Carole, et al. *Extraordinary Women of the Medieval and Renaissance World: A Biographical Dictionary*. Westport: Greenwood, 2000. Print.

Levy, Alison, ed. *Widowhood and Visual Culture in Early Modern Europe*. Aldershot: Ashgate, 2003. Print.

Lewalski, Barbara. *Writing Women in Jacobean England*. Cambridge: Harvard UP, 1993. Print.

Liebault, Mme (Nicole Estienne). *Les misères de la femme mariée, où se peuvent voir les peines et tourmens qu'elle reçoit durant sa vie, mis en forme de stances, par Mme Liebaut*. Paris Mesnier, [c. 1600]. Print.

———. *Les misères de la femme mariée, où se peuvent voir les peines et tourmens qu'elle reçoit durant sa vie, mis en forme de stances, par Mme Liebaut*. Zinguer 32–40.

Loats, Carol L. "Gender, Guilds, and Work Identity: Perspectives from Sixteenth-Century Paris." *French Historical Studies* 20.1 (1997): 15–30. Print.

Lochrie, Karma. *Heterosyncrasies: Female Sexuality When Normal Wasn't*. Minneapolis: U of Minnesota P, 2005. Print

Longfellow, Erica. *Women and Religious Writing in Early Modern England*. Cambridge: Cambridge UP, 2004. Print.

Losse, Deborah N. "Women Addressing Women: The Differentiated Text." Larsen and Winn, *Renaissance Women Writers* 23–37.

Louange du muliebre et femynin sexe. MS Fr. 2242. Bibiliothèque Nationale de France, Paris.

Louise de Bourges. "Correspondance de Louise de Bourges et de Gaspard de Saillans (1569)." Ed. Anne R. Larsen. Goldsmith and Winn 33–88.

Loviot, Louis. "Hélisenne de Crenne." *Revue des livres anciens* 2 (1917): 137–45. Print.

Luciani, Isabelle. "Jeux Floraux et 'humanisme civique' au XVIe siècle: Entre enjeux de pouvoir et expérience du politique." *L'humanisme à Toulouse (1480–1596). Actes du colloque international de Toulouse, mai 2004*. Ed. Nathalie Dauvois. Paris: Champion, 2006. 301–35. Print.

Lyon, Site Historique. Patrimoine Mondial. Dir. Georges Combe. France 3 Rhône Alpes Auvergne Rotary, 2000. Videocassette.

Lyons, J. D., and Mary B. McKinley. *Critical Tales: New Studies of the* Heptameron *and Early Modern Culture*. Philadelphia: U of Pennsylvania P, 1993. Print.

MacDonald, A. A. "The Renaissance Household as Centre of Learning." Drijvers and MacDonald 289–98.

Maclean, Ian. *The Renaissance Notion of Woman: A Study of the Fortunes of Scholasticism and Medical Science in European Intellectual Life*. Cambridge: Cambridge UP, 1980. Print.

Mann, Nicholas, "The Origins of Humanism." *The Cambridge Companion to Renaissance Humanism*. Cambridge: Cambridge UP, 1996. 1–19. Print.

Mansencal, Jane de, and Catherine de Mansencal. "Aux dames devotieuses." Coignard, *Œuvres* [1995] 129–31.

Manzer, Marilyn B. "Reformed Royalty: The Strength of Queen Jeanne d'Albret." *CRTA: Center for Reformed Theology and Apologetics.* Covenant Community Church of Orange County, 1990. Web. 6 Nov. 2009.

Marconville, Jean de. *De la bonté et mauvaiseté des femmes.* 1564. Pref. Françoise Koelher. Paris: Côté-femmes, 2003. Print.

———. *De la bonté et mauvaistié des femmes.* Rouen: Belis, 1573. Print.

———. *De la bonté et mauvaistié des femmes.* Ed. Richard A. Carr. Paris: Champion, 2000. Print. Textes de la Renaissance 35.

[Marcourt, Antoine]. *Articles veritables sur les horribles, grandz, et importables abuz de la Messe papale: Inventée directement contre la saincte Cene de Jesus Christ* [Neuchâtel: Vingle, 1534]. *La Diffusion de la Réforme en France, 1520–1565.* Ed. Francis Higman. Geneva: Labor, 1992. 72–75. Print.

Margaret of Valois. *Correspondance, 1569–1614.* Ed. Éliane Viennot. Paris: Champion, 1998. Print. Textes de la Renaissance 23.

———. *Mémoires de Marguerite de Valois . . . auxquels on a ajouté son éloge, celui de M. de Bussy, et* La fortune de la cour. Ed. J. Godefroy. Liège: Broncart, 1713. *Gallica.* Bibliothèque Nationale de France, n.d. Print; Web.

———. *Mémoires de Marguerite de Valois, reine de France et de Navarre. Mémoires de Jacques-Auguste de Thou, depuis 1553 jusqu'en 1600. Collection complète des mémoires relatifs à l'histoire de France.* Paris: Foucault, 1823. *Gallica.* Bibliothèque Nationale de France, n.d. Print; Web.

———. *Mémoires de Marguerite de Valois suivis des anecdotes inédites de l'histoire de France pendant les XVIe et XVIIe siècles tirées de la bouche de M. le garde des sceaux Du Vair et autres.* Ed. Ludovic Lalanne. Facsim. ed. Paris: Jannet, 1858. Print. Bibliothèque Elzévirienne 40.

———. *Mémoires et autres écrits, 1574–1614.* Ed. Éliane Viennot. Paris: Champion, 1999. Print. Textes de la Renaissance 31.

———. *Mémoires et discours.* Ed. Éliane Viennot. Saint Étienne: PU de Saint-Étienne, 2004. Print. La cité des dames.

———. Mémoires et lettres de Marguerite de Valois, *suivi de* La ruelle mal assortie, dialogue d'amour entre Marguerite de Valois et sa bête de somme. Ed. M. Guessard. Paris: Renouard, 1842. *Gallica.* Bibliothèque Nationale de France, n.d. Print; Web.

Margolin, Jean-Claude. *Anthologie des humanistes européens de la Renaissance.* Paris: Gallimard, 2007. Print.

Marguerite de Navarre. *Les chansons spirituelles.* Ed. Georges Dottin. Geneva: Droz, 1971. Print. TLF 178.

———. *Chrétiens et mondains, poèmes épars.* Ed. Richard Cooper. Paris: Champion 2001. Print. Vol. 8 of *Œuvres complètes.* Nicole Cazauran, gen. ed. Textes de la Renaissance 131.

———. The Coach *and* The Triumph of the Lamb. Trans. Hilda Dale, with Simone de Reyff. Exeter: Elm Bank, 1999. Print.

———. *Les comédies bibliques.* Ed. Barbara Marczuk. With Beata Skrzeszewska and Piotr Tylus. Geneva: Droz, 2000. Print. TLF 531.

———. La complainte pour un détenu prisonnier *et* Les chansons spirituelles. Ed. Michèle Clément. Paris: Champion, 2001. Print. Vol. 9 of *Œuvres complètes.* Nicole Cazauran, gen. ed. Textes de la Renaissance 34.

———. *Contes et nouvelles de Marguerite de Valois, reine de Navarre, faisant suite aux Contes de J. Bocace.* London, 1784. Print.

———. *Contes et nouvelles de Marguerite de Valois, reine de Navarre, mis en beau langage accommodé au goût du temps.* Amsterdam: Gallet, 1698–1708. Print.

———. *Correspondance, 1521–1524 avec Guillaume Briçonnet.* Ed. Christine Martineau and Michel Veissière. 2 vols. Geneva: Droz, 1975–79. Print.

———. *Dialogue en forme de vision nocturne entre tres noble et excellente princesse Madame Marguerite de France . . . et l'âme saincte de defuncte Madame Charlotte de France, . . . Le miroir de l'âme pécheresse, . . . Discord estant en l'homme par la contrarieté de l'esprit et de la chair, et sa paix par vie spirituelle. Une oraison à Nostre Seigneur Jésus Christ.* Alençon: Du Bois, 1533. *Gallica.* Bibliothèque Nationale de France, n.d. Print; Web.

———. *The Heptameron.* Ed. and trans. Paul A. Chilton. Middlesex: Penguin, 1984. *Other Women's Voices.* Print; Web.

———. *L'heptaméron.* Ed. Michel François. 1967. Paris: Garnier, 1975. Paris: Bibliopolis, 1998–99. *Gallica.* Bibliothèque Nationale de France, n.d. Print; Web.

———. *L'heptaméron.* Ed. Gisèle Mathieu-Castellani. Paris: Lib. Générale Française, 1999. Print. Livre de Poche Classique.

———. *L'heptaméron.* Ed. Renja Salminen. Geneva: Droz, 1999. Print. TLF 94.

———. *The Heptameron.* Trans. Walter Kelly. London: Published for the Trade, n.d. *Celebration of Women Writers.* Ed. Mary Mark Ockerbloom. U of Pennsylvania, n.d. Web. 10 Nov. 2009.

———. *L'heptaméron des nouvelles de très haute et très illustre princesse Marguerite d'Angoulême reine de Navarre.* Ed. P. L. Jacob. Paris: Delayais, 1861. Print.

———. *L'heptaméron des nouvelles: De très illustre et trèsexcellente princesse Marguerite d'Angoulême, royne de Navarre.* Paris: Prevost, 1559. *Gallica.* Bibliothèque Nationale de France. Web. 7 Apr. 2011.

———. *L'heptameron des nouvelles de tresillustre et tresexcellente Princessse Marguerite de Valois, Royne de Navarre.* Paris: Prevost, 1560. *The Renaissance in Print.* U of Virginia Lib, n.d. Print; Web.

———. The Heptameron *of the Tales of Margaret of Navarre.* Trans. George Saintsbury. London: Navarre Soc., 1922. *Project Gutenberg,* n.d. Print; Web.

———. *L'inquisiteur, Le malade, Trop, Prou, Peu, Moins, . . .* Ed. Nancy Erickson Bouzrara and Catherine Masson. Saint-Étienne: PU de Saint-Étienne, 2006. Print. Vol. 1 of *Théâtre de femmes de l'Ancien Régime.* La cité des dames 5: XVIe siècle: Marguerite de Navarre. A. Evain et al., gen. eds.

———. *Lettres de Marguerite d'Angoulême, soeur de François Ier, reine de Navarre.* Ed. François Génin. Paris: Renouard, 1841. New York: Johnson, [1965]. Print.

———. "Lettres de Marguerite de Navarre à François Ier (1521–46)." Ed. Patricia Francis Cholakian and Rouben C. Cholakian. Goldsmith and Winn 3–32.

———. *Lettres inédites de Marguerite de Valois: Tirées de la bibliothèque impériale de Saint-Pétersbourg: 1579–1606, publiées pour la Société historique de Gascogne par Philippe Lauzun.* Paris: Champion, 1886. *Gallica.* Bibliothèque Nationale de France, n.d. Print; Web.

———. *Les Marguerites de la Marguerite des Princesses.* Lyon: Tournes, 1547. Print. *The Renaissance in Print.* U of Virginia Lib, n.d. Print; Web.

———. *Les Marguerites de la Marguerite des Princesses.* Paris: Ruelle 1558. Print. *The Renaissance in Print.* U of Virginia Lib., n.d. Print; Web.

———. *Le miroir de l'âme pécheresse, ouquel elle recongnoist ses faultes et pechez, aussi ses graces et benefices à elle faictz par Jesuchrist son époux.* Alençon: Du Bois, 1531. Print. *Gallica.* Bibliothèque Nationale de France, n.d. Print; Web.

———. *Le miroir de treschrestienne princesse Marguerite de France, royne de Navarre, duchesse d'Alençon et de Berry, ouquel elle voit son néant et son tout.* Paris: Augereau, 1533. Print. *Gallica.* Bibliothèque Nationale de France, n.d. Print; Web.

———. *The Mirror of the Sinful Soul.* Trans. Melanie E. Gregg. Larsen and Winn, *Writings* 35–61.

———. *Nouvelles lettres de la reine de Navarre, adressées au roi son frère.* Paris: Renouard, 1842. Print.

———. Pater Noster *et* Petit œuvre devot. Ed. Sabine Lardon. Paris: Champion, 2001. Print. Vol. 1 of *Œuvres complètes.* Nicole Cazauran, gen. ed. Textes de la Renaissance 33.

———. *The Prisons.* Ed. Hilda Dale. U of Reading: Whiteknights, 1989. Print.

———. *Selected Writings: A Bilingual Edition.* Ed. and trans. Rouben Cholakian and Mary Skemp. Chicago: U of Chicago P, 2008. Print. The Other Voice in Early Modern Europe.

———. *Théâtre.* Ed. Geneviève Hasenohr and Olivier Millet. Paris: Champion, 2002. Print. Vol. 4 of *Œuvres complètes.* Nicole Cazauran, gen. ed. Textes de la Renaissance 61.

———. *Le théâtre profane.* Ed. Verdun-L. Saulnier. Geneva: Droz, 1965. Print. TLF 3.

———. *Théâtre profane: The Nine "Secular" Plays.* Trans. Régine Reynolds-Cornell. Carleton: Dovehouse, 2002. Print.

———. *Le triomphe de l'Agneau.* Ed. Simone de Reyff. Paris: Champion, 2001. Print. Vol. 3 of *Œuvres complètes.* Nicole Cazauran, gen. ed. Textes de la Renaissance 42.

Marino, Laura. *Le donne di Roma. Dalla fondazione della città a Roma capitale.* 2nd ed. Roma: Tascabili Economici Newton, 1997. Print.

Marot, Clément. *Œuvres complètes.* Ed. François Rigolot. Vol. 1. Paris: Flammarion, 2007. Print.

———. *Œuvres poétiques.* Ed. Gérard Defaux. 2 vols. Paris: Garnier, 1993. Print.

———. "Le tétin." Labé, *Œuvres poétiques* 147–48, 168–69.

Marquets, Anne de. *Les divines poesies de Marc Antoine Flaminius.* Paris: Chesneau, 1568. Print.

———. *Sonets, prieres et devises en forme de pasquins pour l'assemblée de messieurs les prelats et docteurs, tenue à Poissy, M.D.LXI.* Paris: Morel, 1562. Gendre, "Naissance."

———. *Sonets, prieres et devises en forme de pasquins, pour l'assemblée de Messieurs les Prelats & Docteurs, tenue a Poissy, M.D.LXI.* Paris: Morel, 1566. *Soeur Anne de Marquets.* Poissy Project, San Diego State U, n.d. Print; Web.

———. *Sonets, prieres et devises en forme de pasquins, pour l'assemblée de Messieurs les Prelats & Docteurs, tenue à Poissy, M.D.LXI.* Paris: Morel, 1566. *Gallica.* Bibliothèque Nationale de France, n.d. Print; Web.

———. *Sonets spirituels de feüe très vertueuse et très-docte dame Sr Anne de Marquet religieuse à Poissi, sur les dimanches et principales solemnitez de l'année.* Paris: Morel, 1605. *Gallica.* Bibliothèque Nationale de France, 6 Nov. 2009. Print; Web.

———. *Sonets spirituels . . . sur les dimanches et principales solemnitez de l'année.* 1605. Ed. Gary Ferguson. Geneva: Droz, 1997. Print. TLF 481.

———. *Sonets spirituels.* Trans. Gary Ferguson and Catherine Hampton. Larsen and Winn, *Writings* 213–23.

Martin, Daniel. *Signe(s) d'amante. L'agencement des* Euvres *de Louïze Labé Lionnoize.* Paris: Champion, 1999. Print.

Martin, Henri-Jean, and Roger Chartier, eds. *Le livre conquérant: Du Moyen-Âge au milieu du XVIIe siècle.* Paris: Promodis, 1982. Print. Vol. 1 of *Histoire de l'édition française.* 4 vols.

Martin-Ulrich, Claudie. *La* Persona *de la princesse au XVIe siècle: Personnage littéraire et personnage politique.* Paris: Champion, 2004. Print.

Matarasso, Pauline. *Queen's Mate: Three Women of Power in France on the Eve of the Renaissance.* Aldershot: Ashgate, 2001. Print.

Mathieu-Castellani, Gisèle. *La quenouille et la lyre.* Paris: Corti, 1998. Print.

Matos, Luis de. *Les Portugais en France au XVIe siècle.* Coimbra: Par Ordem da Universidade, 1952. Print.

Matthews Grieco, Sara F. *Ange ou diablesse. La représentation de la femme au XVIe siècle.* Paris: Flammarion, 1991. Print.

———. "Corps, apparence et sexualité." Davis and Farge 59–94.

———. "Georgette de Montenay: A Different Voice in Sixteenth-Century Emblematics." *Renaissance Quarterly* 47.4 (1994): 793–871. Print.

McCarthy, Suzanne. "Marie Dentière: Defense of Women." *Suzanne's Bookshelf.* 29 Jan. 2009. Web. 6 Nov. 2009.

McCartney, Elizabeth. "In the Queen's Words: Perceptions of Regency Government Gleaned from the Correspondence of Catherine de Médicis." Couchman and Crabb 207–22.

McClive, Cathy, and Nicole Pellegrin, eds. *Femmes en fleurs, femmes en corps: Sang, santé, sexualités, du Moyen Âge aux lumières.* Saint-Étienne: PU de Saint-Étienne, 2008. L'école du genre.

McFarlane, Ian, ed. *The* Délie *of Maurice Scève.* London: Cambridge UP, 1966. Print.

McIntosh, Marjorie Keniston. *Working Women in English Society, 1300–1620.* Cambridge: Cambridge UP, 2005. Print.

McKinley, Mary B. "The Absent Ellipsis: The Edition and Suppression of Marie Dentière in the Sixteenth and the Nineteenth Century." Winn and Kuizenga 85–99.

———. "The Early Modern Teacher: Marie Dentière: An Outspoken Reformer Enters the French Literary Canon." King and Rabil 113–26.

———. Introduction. Dentière, *Epistle* 1–39.

———. "Marie Dentière: An Outspoken Reformer Enters the French Literary Canon." *Sixteenth Century Journal* 37.2 (2006): 401–12. Print.

———."Telling Secrets: Sacramental Confession and Narrative Authority in the *Heptaméron.*" Lyons and McKinley 146–71.

McLeod, Glenda K., ed. *The Reception of Christine de Pizan from the Fifteenth through the Nineteenth Centuries: Visitors to the City.* Lewiston: Mellen, 1991. Print.

McManus, Barbara F. "Whose Voice Is It Anyway? Teaching Early Women Writers." *Crossing Boundaries: Attending to Early Modern Women.* Ed. Jane Donawerth and Adele Seeff. Newark: U of Delaware P, 2000. 227–40. Print.

McTavish, Lianne. *Childbirth and the Display of Authority in Early Modern France.* Aldershot: Ashgate, 2005. Print. Women and Gender in the Early Modern World.

Médicis, Catherine de'. *Lettres de Catherine de Médicis.* Ed. Hector de la Ferrière and Baguenault de Puchesse. 10 vols. Paris: Imprimerie Nationale, 1880–1909. Print.

Medioli, Francesca. "An Unequal Law: The Enforcement of *Clausura* before and after the Council of Trent." *Women in Renaissance and Early Modern Europe.* Ed. Christine Meek. Dublin: Four Courts, 2000. 136–52. Print.

Mentzer, Raymond A., Jr. "La place et le rôle des femmes dans les églises réformées." *Archives de sciences sociales des religions* 46.113 (2001): 119–32. Print.

Michahelles, Kerrie-Rue. "Apprentissage du mécénat et transmission matrilinéaire du pouvoir. Les enseignements de Catherine de Médicis à sa petite-fille Christine de Lorraine." Wilson-Chevalier, *Patronnes* 557–76.

Miernowski, Jan. "Fiction and Ritual in the *Heptameron.*" Winn, *Approaches* 106–12.

Miller, Nancy K. "Arachnologies: The Woman, the Text, and the Critic." Miller, *Poetics* 270–95.

———, ed. *The Poetics of Gender.* New York: Columbia UP, 1986. Print.

Miller, Naomi J., and Naomi Yavneh, eds. *Maternal Measures: Figuring Caregiving in the Early Modern Period.* Aldershot: Ashgate, 2000. Print.

Minut, Charlotte de. "A nostre Sainct Pere le Pape sixte cinquiesme de ce nom." G. Minut, *Morbi gallos* 3–18.

———. "Epistre à la royne [Catherine de' Medici]." G. Minut, *De la beauté* 3–19.

Minut, Gabriel de. *De la beauté.* Lyon: Honorat, 1587. *Gallica.* Bibliothèque Nationale de France, n.d. Print; Web.

———. *Morbi gallos infestantis salubris curatio et sancta medicina, hoc est, malorum, quae intestinum crudeleque gallorum bellum inflammant, remedium.* Lyon: Honorat, 1587. Print.

Miremont, Jacqueline de. *Apologie pour les dames.* 1602. Winn, *Protestations* 67–141.

Mistacco, Vicki, ed. *Les femmes et la tradition littéraire: Anthologie du Moyen Âge à nos jours.* 2 vols. New Haven: Yale UP, 2006. Print. Vol. 1: XIIe–XVIIIe siècle; Vol. 2: XIXe-XXIe siècle.

Montaigne, Michel de. "De la vanité." *Œuvres complètes.* Ed. Albert Thibaudet and Maurice Rat. Paris: Gallimard, 1962. 922–80. Print. Bibliothèque de la Pléiade.

———. "Sur des vers de Virgile." *Les essais de Montaigne.* Ed. Pierre Villey. 2 vols. Paris: PUF, 1978. 2: 840–97. Print.

Montenat, Benoît. *Traité de la conformité des prophètes et sibylles avec les douzes articles de la foi.* 1505. MS Fr. 949. Bibliothèque Nationale de France, Paris.

Montenay, Georgette de. *Emblematum christianorum centuria / Cent emblemes chrestiennes.* Zurich: Froschover, 1584. *French Emblems at Glasgow*, n.d. Print; Web.

———. *Emblemes ou devises chrestiennes.* Lyon: Marcorelle, 1571. *The Renaissance in Print.* U of Virginia Lib., n.d. Print; Web.

———. *Emblemes, ou devises chrestiennes.* 1571. Ed. Christopher N. Smith. Menston: Scolar, 1973. Print. Continental Emblem Series 15.

———. *Emblemes ou devises chrestiennes, composees par Damoiselle Georgette de Montenay.* Lyon: Marcorelle, 1567. Print.

———. *Emblemes ou devises chrestiennes.* Lyon: Marcorelle, 1571. *The Renaissance in Print.* U of Virginia Lib., n.d. Web.

———. *Emblemes ou devises chrestiennes, composees par Damoiselle Georgette de Montenay.* La Rochelle: Dinet, 1620. Print.

———. *Emblems and Christian Devices.* Trans. Régine Reynolds-Cornell. Larsen and Winn, *Writings* 123–36.

———. *Livre d'armoiries en signe de fraternité (edit 1619).* 1619. Paris: Aux Amateurs de Livres, 1987. Print.

Moore, Mary B. *Desiring Voices: Women Sonneteers and Petrarchism.* Carbondale: Southern Illinois UP, 2000. Print.

Morata, Olympia. *The Complete Writings of an Italian Heretic.* Ed. and trans. Holt N. Parker. Chicago: U of Chicago P, 2003. Print. The Other Voice in Early Modern Europe.

———. *Orationes, dialogi, epistolae, carmina, tam latina quam graeca: Cum eruditorum de ea testimoniis et laudibus. Hippolytae Taurellae elegia elegantissima.* Basel: Pernam, 1562. Print.

Mornay, Charlotte Arbaleste de. *Mémoires de Madame de Mornay.* Ed. Madame de Witt. 2 vols. Paris: Renouard, 1868–69. *Gallica.* Bibliothèque Nationale de France, n.d. Print; Web.

Mosse, George L. *Nationalism and Sexuality: Middle-Class Morality and Sexual Norms in Modern Europe.* Madison: U of Wisconsin P, 1985. Print.

Moulin, Antoine du. Preface. Du Guillet, *Rymes* [1545] a2r–a4r.

Moulin, Jeannine. *La poésie féminine.* Paris: Seghers, 1966. Print.

Muchembled, Robert. *Passions de femmes au temps de la reine Margot, 1553–1615.* Paris: Éditions du Seuil, 2003. Print.

Müller, Catherine M. "Anne de Graville lectrice de *Maistre Allain.* Pour une réécriture stratégique de la *Belle dame sans mercy.*" Brouard-Arends 231–41.

Müller, John P., and William J. Richardson. *The Purloined Poe: Lacan, Derrida, and Psychoanalytic Reading.* Baltimore: Johns Hopkins UP, 1988. Print.

Munns, Jessica, and Penny Richards. "Antoinette de Bourbon, première duchesse de Guise, et Rémy Belleau: Construction d'un tombeau, création d'un mythe." Wilson-Chevalier, *Patronnes* 401–17.

Musée de l'imprimerie de Lyon. Musée de L'imprimerie de Lyon, n.d. Web. 15 Aug. 2010.

Nash, Jerry C. "Constructing Hélisenne de Crenne: Reception and Identity." *"Por le soie amisté": Essays in Honor of Norris J. Lacy.* Ed. Keith Busby and Catherine M. Jones. Amsterdam: Rodopi, 2000. 371–83. Print.

———. "Renaissance Misogyny, Biblical Feminism, and Hélisenne's *Epistres familieres et invectives.*" *Renaissance Quarterly* 50 (1997): 379–410. *The Free Library.* Gale, 1997. Web. 6 Nov. 2009.

Nassau, Louise-Julienne de, Elisabeth de, et Amélie de. "Lettres de Louise-Julienne, d'Elisabeth et d'Amélie de Nassau à Charlotte-Brabantine de Nassau (1595–1601)." Ed. Susan Broomhall. Goldsmith and Winn 135–78.

Nativel, Colette, ed. *Femmes savantes, savoirs des femmes. Du crépuscule de la Renaissance à l'aube des Lumières.* Geneva: Droz, 1999. Print.

Nauert, Charles. "Marguerite de Navarre, Lefèvre d'Étaples, and the Growth of Christian Humanism in France." Winn, *Approaches* 38–43.

Nelson, Eric. "The Problem of the Prince." *The Cambridge Companion to Renaissance Philosophy.* Ed. James Hankins. Cambridge: Cambridge UP, 2007. 319–37. Print.

Nolde, Dorothea. "Violence et pouvoir dans le mariage. Le rapport conjugal à travers les procès pour meurtre du conjoint devant le Parlement de Paris, 1580–1620." Wilson-Chevalier and Viennot 121–33.

Noonan, John T., Jr. "Marriage in the Middle Ages: 1. Power to Choose." *Viator: Medieval and Renaissance Studies* 4 (1973): 419–34. Print.

Nugent, Donald. *Ecumenism in the Age of the Reformation: The Colloque de Poissy.* Cambridge: Harvard UP, 1974. Print.

Odde, Laurent. "Les coulisses du pouvoir: Châteaux, jardins et fêtes. Quelques aspects du mécénat (transgressif) de Catherine de Médicis." Wilson-Chevalier, *Patronnes* 481–510.

Olson, Todd P. "La femme à la puce et la puce à l'oreille: Catherine des Roches and the Poetics of Sexual Resistance in Sixteenth-Century French Poetry." *Journal of Medieval and Early Modern Studies* 32.2 (2002): 327–42. *Project Muse.* Web. 9 Nov. 2009.

Orth, Myra D. "Louise de Savoie et le pouvoir du livre." Wilson-Chevalier and Viennot 71–90.

———. "'Madame Sainte Anne': The Holy Kinship, the Royal Trinity, and Louise of Savoy." *Interpreting Cultural Symbols: Saint Anne in Medieval Society.* Ed. Kathleen Ashley and Pamela Sheingorn. Athens: U of Georgia P, 1990. 199–227. Print.

———. "Manuscrits pour Marguerite." *Marguerite de Navarre, 1492–1992: Actes du colloque international de Pau 1992.* Ed. Nicole Cazauran and James Dauphiné. Mont-de-Marsan: Éditions Universitaires, 1995. 85–105. Print.

Ovid. Heroides *and* Amores. Trans. Grant Showerman. Cambridge: Harvard UP, 1977. Print.

———. [Epistres d'Ovide]. Trans. Octavien de Saint-Gelais. MS Fr. 875. Bibliothèque Nationale de France, Paris.

———. *Metamorphoses.* Trans. Frank Justus Miller. Cambridge: Harvard UP, 1984. Print.

The Oxford Dictionary of the Christian Church. Ed. F. L. Cross. 3rd ed. Ed. E. A. Livingstone. Oxford: Oxford UP, 1997. Print.

The Oxford Encyclopedia of the Reformation. Ed. Hans Hillerbrand. 4 vols. Oxford: Oxford UP, 1995. Print.

Palazzo Davanzati. Home page. Ministero per i Beni e le Attività Culturali, 2007. Web. 6 Oct. 2010.

Parker, Andrew, Mary Russo, Doris Sommer, and Patricia Yaeger, eds. *Nationalisms and Sexualities.* New York: Routledge, 1992. Print.

Parr, Catherine. *Œuvres spirituelles.* Ed. Guy Bedouelle. Paris: Champion, 2006. Print. Textes de la Renaissance 106.

Parthenay, Catherine de. *Ballets allégoriques en vers, 1592–1593.* Ed. Raymond Ritter. Paris: Champion, 1927. Print.

Pascal, Eugénie. "La lectrice devenue scriptrice. Lecture épistolaire dans les réponses d'Elisabeth à Charlotte-Brabantine de Nassau." Brouard-Arends 409–18.

———. "Princesses épistolières au tournant du XVIe au XVIIe siècle: Consommatrices de culture, mécènes et/ou propagandistes?" Wilson-Chevalier, *Patronnes* 101–31.

Pasquinate romane del cinquecento. Ed. Valerio Marucci, Antonio Marzo, and Angelo Romano. 2 vols. Rome: Salerno Editrice, 1983. Print.

Patterson, Annabel. "The Royal Romance." *Censorship and Interpretation: The Conditions of Writing and Reading in Early Modern England.* Madison: U of Wisconsin P, 1984. 159–90. Print.

Peletier du Mans, Jacques. *Art poétique. Traités de poétique et de rhétorique de la Renaissance.* Ed. Francis Gayot. Paris: Lib. Générale Française, 1990. Print. Livre de Poche Classique.

Pellegrin, Nicole, ed. *Histoires d'historiennes.* Saint-Étienne: PU de Saint-Étienne, 2006. Print. L'école du genre.

Pellegrini, Carlo. "Il Petrarca nella cultura francese." *Tradizione italiana e cultura europea.* Messina: D'Anna, 1947. 3–18. Print. Biblioteca di Cultura Contemporanea 13.

Pelletier, André, and Françoise Bayard. Illus. Jean Prost. *Histoire de Lyon en bande dessinée.* 2nd ed. Lyon: Éditions Lyonnaises d'Art et d'Histoire, 1998. Print.

Perrier, Simone. "Le corps de la sentence: Les *Emblèmes Chrestiens* de Georgette de Montenay." *Littérature* 78 (1990): 54–64. Print.

———. Introduction. Montenay, *Livre d'armoiries* n. pag.

Petrarch, Francesco. *Canzoniere.* Trans. J. G. Nichols. New York: Routledge, 2002. Print.

———. *Canzoniere / Le Chansonnier.* Ed. Pierre Blanc. Paris: Garnier, 2004. Print. Classiques Garnier.

———. *Petrarch's Lyric Poems. The* Rime sparse *and Other Lyrics.* Trans. and ed. Robert M. Durling. Cambridge: Harvard UP, 1976. Print.

Piéjus, Marie-Françoise. "La création au féminin dans le discours de quelques poétesses du XVIe siècle." *Dire la création: La culture italienne entre poétique et poïétique.* Ed. D. Budor. Lille: PU de Lille, 1994. 79–90. Print.

Plato. *The Symposium.* Trans. Christopher Gill. London: Penguin, 1999. Print.

Poirier, Guy, Christine McWebb, François Paré, and Delbert W. Russel, eds. *Margot. Dix ans de recherche sur les femmes écrivains de l'Ancien Régime. Influences et confluences.* Mélanges offerts à Hannah Fournier. Québec: PU de Laval, forthcoming.

Polachek, Dora E. "À la recherche du spirituel: L'Italie et les *Dames Galantes* de Brantôme." *Romanic Review* 94.1-2 (2003): 227–43. Print.

———, ed. *Heroic Virtue, Comic Infidelity: Reassessing Marguerite de Navarre's* Heptaméron. Amherst: Hestia, 1993. Print.

———. "Le mécénat meurtrier, l'iconoclasme et les limites de l'acceptable: Anne d'Este, Catherine-Marie de Lorraine et l'anéantissement d'Henri III." Wilson-Chevalier, *Patronnes* 433–54.

Postel, Guillaume. *Les tres-merveilleuses victoires des femmes du Nouveau-Monde.* Ed. Gustave Brunet. Geneva: Slatkine, 1970. Print.

Quilligan, Maureen. *The Allegory of Female Authority: Christine de Pizan's* Cité des dames. Ithaca: Cornell UP, 1991. Print.

———. "Incest and Agency: The Case of Elizabeth I." *Generation and Degeneration: Tropes of Reproduction in Literature and History from Antiquity to Early Modern Europe.* Ed. Valeria Finucci and Kevin Brownlee. Durham: Duke UP, 2001. 209–31. Print.

Rabelais, François. *The Complete Works.* Trans. Donald M. Frame. Berkeley: U of California P, 1991. Print.

———. *Gargantua. Œuvres complètes.* Vol. 1. Ed. Pierre Jourda. Paris: Garnier, 1962. 1–210. Print.

———. *Pantagruel. Œuvres complètes.* Ed. Mireille Huchon. Paris: Gallimard, 1994. 209–337. Print.

Rajchenbach, Élise. "Pernette du Guillet (v. 1520–1545)." *Dictionnaire de la Siefar.* Siefar, 2007. Web. 18 Oct. 2010.

Ramunni, Girolamo. Rev. of "Impressions, Cédérom, Musée de l'imprimerie." *La revue pour l'histoire du CNRS* 1 (1999): n. pag. Web. 9 Nov. 2009.

Randall, Catharine. "Shouting Down Abraham: How Sixteenth-Century Huguenot Women Found Their Voice." *Renaissance Quarterly* 50 (1997) 411–42. *Questia.* Gale, Cengage Learning, 2010. Web. 1 Nov. 2010.

Rang, Brita. "A 'Learned Wave': Women of Letters and Science from the Renaissance to the Enlightenment." *Perspectives in Feminist Political Thought in European History: From the Middle Ages to the Present.* Ed. Tjitske Akkerman and Siep Stuurman. London: Routledge, 1998. 50–66. Print.

Rapley, Elizabeth. *A Social History of the Cloister: Daily Life in the Teaching Monasteries of the Old Regime.* Montreal: McGill-Queen's UP, 2001. Print.

Réach-Ngô, Anne. "La mise en livre des narrations de la Renaissance: Écriture éditoriale et herméneutique de l'imprimé." Diss. U Paris IV-Sorbonne, 2005. Print.

Read, Kirk D. "Writing in the Feminine in the Renaissance." *Writing in the Feminine in the Renaissance.* Ed. François Rigolot. Spec. issue of *L'Esprit Créateur* 30.4 (1990): 106–11. Print.

Reid, Jonathan. *King's Sister, Queen of Dissent: Marguerite de Navarre (1492–1549) and Her Evangelical Network.* 2 vols. Leiden: Brill, 2009. Print.

Les religieuses dans le cloître et dans le monde des origines à nos jours. Actes du 2e colloque international du CERCOR, Poitiers, 1988. Saint-Étienne: PU de Saint-Étienne, 1994. Print.

Les religieuses enseignantes, XVIe-XIXe siècles. Angers: PU d'Angers, 1981. Print.

"Religious and Political Divisions of France, 1585–1598." *Le poulet gauche.* 1 Jan. 2004. Web. 9 Mar. 2010.

RenaissanceBodyProject. Ed. Cécile Alduy. Stanford U, 2007. Web. 22 Feb. 2010.

Renaut, Alain. *L'ère de l'individu. Contribution à une histoire de la subjectivité.* Paris: Gallimard, 1989. Print.

Reno, Christine. "Feminist Aspects of Christine de Pizan's *Epistre d'Othéa à Hector.*" *Studi Francesi* 71 (1980): 271–77. Print.

Retz, Catherine de Clermont, countess of. *Album de poésies, Ms. fr. 25455 de la BnF.* Ed. Colette H. Winn and François Rouget. Paris: Champion, 2004. Print. Textes de la Renaissance 87.

Reynier, Gustave. *Le roman sentimental avant l'*Astrée. Paris: Colin, 1908. Print.

Reynolds, Anne. "Cardinal Oliviero Carafa and the Early Cinquecento Tradition of the Feast of Pasquino." *Humanistica Lovaniensia* 34 (1985): 178–208. Print.

Reynolds-Cornell, Régine. "*Les misères de la femme mariée*: Another Look at Nicole Liebault and a Few Questions about the Woes of the Married Woman." *Bibliothèque d'Humanisme et Renaissance* 64 (2002): 37–54. Print.

Richards, Earl Jeffrey. "Christine de Pizan and the Question of Feminist Rhetoric." *Teaching Language through Literature* 22 (1983): 15–24. Print.

———. "The Medieval *Femme Auteur* As a Provocation to Literary History." McLeod 101–26.

Richardson, Lula McDowell. *The Forerunners of Feminism in the French Literature of the Renaissance from Christine of Pisan to Marie de Gournay.* Baltimore: Johns Hopkins UP, 1929. Print.

Ridé, Jacques. "Martin Luther et le mariage." Jones-Davies 229–39.

Rieu, Josiane. "Pernette du Guillet: Poétique et réflexivité dans les *Rymes* (1545)." Beaulieu and Desrosiers-Bonin, *Dans les miroirs* 33–47.

Rigolot, François. "Écrire au féminin à la Renaissance: Problèmes et perspectives." *L'esprit créateur* 30.4 (1990): 3–10. Print.

———. "Gender versus Sex Difference in Louise Labé's Grammar of Love." Ferguson, Quilligan, and Vickers 287–98.

———. "Louise Labé and the 'climat lyonnois.'" *French Review* 71.3 (1998): 405–13. Print.

———. *Louise Labé Lyonnaise ou la Renaissance au féminin.* Paris: Champion, 1997. Print.

———. *Poétique et onomastique: L'exemple de la Renaissance.* Geneva: Droz, 1977. Print.

———. "Rabelais, Misogyny, and Christian Charity: Biblical Intertextuality and the Renaissance Crisis of Exemplarity." *PMLA* 109.2 (1994): 225–37. Print.

———, ed. *Writing in the Feminine in the Renaissance.* Spec. issue of *L'esprit créateur* 30.4 (1990): 3–111. Print.

Rigolot, François, and Kirk D. Read. "Discours liminaire et identité littéraire. Remarques sur la préface féminine au XVIe siècle." *Versants* 15 (1989): 75–98. Print.

Robb, Nesca. *Neoplatonism of the Italian Renaissance.* 1935. New York: Octagon, 1968. Print.

Robin, Diana. *Publishing Women: Salons, the Presses, and the Counter-Reformation in Sixteenth-Century Italy.* Chicago: U of Chicago P, 2007. Print.

Robin, Diana, Anne R. Larsen, and Carole Levin. *Encyclopedia of Women in the Renaissance, Italy, France, and England.* Santa Barbara: ABC-CLIO, 2006. Print.

Rochemore, Jacques de, trans. *Propos amoureux contenans le discours des amours et mariage du seigneur Clitophant et damoiselle Leusippe.* Lyon: Rigaud, 1573. Print.

Rocher, Gregory de. *Rabelais's Laughters and Joubert's* Traité du ris. University: U of Alabama P, 1979. Print.

Roelker, Nancy L. "The Appeal of Calvinism to French Noblewomen in the Sixteenth Century." *Journal of Interdisciplinary History* 2.4 (1972): 391–418. Print.

———. "The Role of Noblewomen in the French Reformation." *Archiv für Reformationgeschichte* 63 (1972): 168–94. Print.

Romier, Lucien. "Lyons and Cosmopolitanism at the Beginning of the French Renaissance." *French Humanism, 1470–1600.* Ed. Werner L. Gundersheimer. New York: Harper, 1969. 90–109. Print.

Romieu, Marie de. *A Brief Discourse: That Woman's Excellence Surpasses That of Man, as Recreative as It Is Full of Fine Examples.* Trans. Marian Rothstein. Larsen and Winn, *Writings* 137–49.

———. *Les premières œuvres poétiques.* Ed. Prosper Blanchemain. Paris: Librairie des Bibliophiles, 1878. Print. *Gallica.* Bibliothèque Nationale de France, n.d. Print; Web.

———. *Les premières œuvres poétiques.* Ed. André Winandy. Geneva: Droz, 1972. Print. TLF 186.

———. *Les premières œuvres poétiques de Madamoiselle Marie de Romieu Vivaroise.* Paris: Breyer, 1581. Print. *Gallica.* Bibliothèque Nationale de France, n.d. Print; Web.

———. *Œuvres complètes.* Ed. Claude La Charité. Paris: Classiques Garnier, forthcoming.

Ronsard, Pierre de. *Les amours.* Ed. Henri Weber and Catherine Weber. Paris: Garnier, 1963. Print.

———. Les amours *de Pierre de Ronsard Vandomoys. Œuvres complètes.* Ed. Paul Laumonier. Vol. 4. Paris: Hachette, 1925. Print. 18 vols.

———. *Œuvres complètes.* Ed. Gustave Cohen. Paris: Gallimard, 1950. Print. Bibliothèque de la Pléiade.

———. *Selected Poems.* Trans. Malcolm Quainton and Elizabeth Vinestock. Harmondsworth: Penguin, 2002. Print. 2 vols.

Roper, Lyndal. *The Holy Household: Women and Morals in Reformation Augsburg.* Oxford: Oxford UP, 1989. Print.

Rose, Marc. *Authors and Owners: The Invention of Copyright.* Cambridge: Harvard UP, 1993. Print.

Rose, Mary Beth. *Changing Perspectives on Medieval and Renaissance Women.* Syracuse: Syracuse UP, 1985. Print.

Roth, Henri. "Une femme auteur du 16e siècle: Jeanne de Jussie." *Revue du Vieux Genève* 19 (1989): 5–13. Print.

Rubin, Gayle. "The Traffic in Women: Notes on the 'Political Economy' of Sex." *Toward an Anthropology of Women.* Ed. Rayna Reiter. New York: Monthly Review, 1975. 157–210. Print.

Rubin, Gayle, and Judith Butler. "Sexual Traffic." *Differences: A Journal of Feminist Cultural Studies* 6.2-3 (1994): 62–99. Print.

Ruggiero, Guido. *The Boundaries of Eros: Sex Crime and Sexuality in Renaissance Venice.* New York: Oxford UP, 1985. Print.

Rumeurs à propos des mœurs de Louise. Site de Lettres de l'Académie de Lyon. Académie de Lyon. Web. 5 Feb. 2010.

Russell, Daniel S. "Emblems: Their Development and Context in European Material Culture." Newberry Lib. Web. 9 Nov. 2009.

Russell, Rinaldina, and Bruce Merry. Introduction. Aragona, *Dialogue* 21–48.

Sabatier, Robert. *Histoire de la poésie française. La poésie du seizième siècle.* Paris: Michel, 1975. Print.

Sachs, Hannelore. *The Renaissance Woman.* Trans. Marianne Herzfeld. Rev. ed. D. Talbot Rice. New York: McGraw, 1971. Print.

Sankovitch, Tilde A. *French Women Writers and the Book: Myths of Access and Desire*. Syracuse: Syracuse UP, 1988. Print.

Sappho. *If Not, Winter: Fragments of Sappho*. Trans. Anne Carson. New York: Knopf, 2002. Print.

Sartori, Eva Martin, ed. *The Feminist Encyclopedia of French Literature*. Westport: Greenwood, 1999. Print.

Sartori, Eva Martin, and Dorothy Wynne Zimmerman, eds. *French Women Writers: A Bio-bibliographical Source*. 1991. Lincoln: U of Nebraska P, 1994. Print.

Sasu, Voichita. "Idéologie amoureuse dans le lyrisme féminin français du XVIe siècle." *La femme à la Renaissance*. Ed. Kazimier Kupisch. Lodz: Acta Universitatis Lodziensis, 1985. 151–74. Print.

Saulnier, Verdun-Louis. "Études sur Pernette Du Guillet et ses *Rymes*." *Bibliothèque d'Humanisme et Renaissance* 4 (1944): 7–119. Print.

———. *Maurice Scève*. Paris: Klincksieck, 1948–49. Print.

———. "Quelques nouveautés sur Hélisenne de Crenne." *Bulletin de l'Association Guillaume Budé* 23.4 (1964): 459–63. Print.

Sauvage, Odette. "Sintra, poème latin de Luisa Sigea." *Arquivos do Centro Cultural Português* 4 (1972): 560–70. Print.

Sawday, Jonathan. *The Body Emblazoned: Dissection and the Human Body in Renaissance Culture*. London: Routledge, 1994. Print.

Scève, Maurice. *Délie, object de plus haute vertu*. Paris: Sabon, 1544. Print.

———. *Microcosme*. Ed. Enzo Giudici. Paris: Vrin, 1976. Print.

Scherer, Jacques. *La dramaturgie classique en France*. Paris: Nizet, 1973. Print.

Schiff, Mario. *La fille d'alliance de Montaigne. Marie de Gournay*. 1910. Geneva: Slatkine, 1979.

Schurman, Anna Maria van. *Anne Marie de Schurman, femme savante (1607–1678). Correspondance*. Ed. Constant Venesoen. Paris: Champion, 2004. Print. Textes de la Renaissance 80.

———. Whether a Christian Woman Should Be Educated *and Other Writings from Her Intellectual Circle*. Trans. and ed. Joyce L. Irvin. Bilingual ed. Chicago: U of Chicago P, 1998. Print. The Other Voice in Early Modern Europe.

Scott, Joan. "Gender: A Useful Category of Analysis." Shoemaker and Vincent 42–65.

Sealy, Robert J. *The Myth of the Reine Margot: Toward the Elimination of a Legend*. New York: Lang, 1994. Print.

Sébillet, Thomas. *Art poëtique françoys*. Paris: Corrozet, 1548. Print.

Sedgwick, Eve Kosofsky. *Between Men: English Literature and Male Homosocial Desire*. New York: Columbia UP, 1985. Print.

———. *Epistemology of the Closet*. Berkeley: U of California P, 1990. Print.

Seeling, Sharon Cadman. *Autobiography and Gender in Early Modern Literature: Reading Women's Lives, 1600–1680*. Cambridge: Cambridge UP, 2006. Print.

Shapiro, Norman R., ed. *French Women Poets of Nine Centuries: The Distaff and the Pen*. Baltimore: Johns Hopkins UP, 2008. Print.

Sheingorn, Pamela. "The Wise Mother: The Image of St. Anne Teaching the Virgin Mary." *Gesta* 32.1 (1993): 69–80. Print.

Shemek, Deanna. *Ladies Errant: Wayward Women and Social Order in Early Modern Italy*. Durham: Duke UP, 1998. Print.

Shepardson, Nikki. "Gender and the Rhetoric of Martyrdom in Jean Crespin's *Histoire des vrays tesmoins*." *Sixteenth Century Journal* 35.1 (2004): 155–74. Print.

Shoemaker, Robert, and Mary Vincent, eds. *Gender and History in Western Europe*. London: Arnold, 1998. Print.

Shorter, Edward. *A History of Women's Bodies*. New York: Basic, 1982. Print.

Sider, Sandra. "Diane de Poitiers: The Woman behind the Legend." Wilson, *Women Writers* 158–76.

Simonin, Michel. *Vivre de sa plume au XVIe siècle; ou, La carrière de François de Belleforest*. Geneva: Droz, 1992. Print.

Skenazi, Cynthia. "Marie Dentière et la prédication des femmes." *Renaissance and Reformation / Renaissance et Réforme* 21.1 (1997): 5–18. Print.

Smarr, Janet Levarie. *Joining the Conversation: Dialogues by Renaissance Women*. Ann Arbor: U of Michigan P, 2005. Print.

Snyder, Jon R. *Writing the Scene of Speaking: Theories of Dialogue in the Late Italian Renaissance*. Stanford: Stanford UP, 1989. Print.

Solterer, Helen. *The Master and Minerva: Disputing Women in French Medieval Culture*. Berkeley: U of California P, 1995. Print.

Sommers, Paula. "Marguerite de Navarre as Reader of Christine de Pizan." McLeod 71–82.

Stampa, Gaspara. *The Complete Poems: The 1554 Edition of* Le Rime. Ed. and trans. Troy Tower and Jane Tylus. Chicago: Chicago UP, 2010. Print.

———. *Rimes d'amour*. Trans. Sophie Basch. Paris: La Différence, 1992. Print. Orphée.

———. *Selected Poems*. Ed. and trans. Laura Anna Stortoni and Mary Prentice Lillie. New York: Italica, 1994. Print.

Stanton, Domna C., ed. *French Feminist Poems from the Middle Ages to the Present: A Bilingual Anthology*. New York: Feminist, 1986. Print. The Defiant Muse.

Steinberg, Sylvie, and Jean-Claude Arnould, dir. *Les femmes et l'écriture de l'histoire (1400–1800)*. Rouen: PUs de Rouen et du Havre, 2008. Print.

Stephenson, Barbara. *The Power and Patronage of Marguerite de Navarre*. Aldershot: Ashgate, 2004. Print.

———. "'Pregnant with 100,000 Soldiers': The Correspondence of Marguerite de Navarre and François Ier." Couchman and Crabb 185–205.

———. "'La protection de vostre faveur': Le patronage humaniste de Marguerite de Navarre." Wilson-Chevalier, *Patronnes* 303–19.

Stevenson, Jane. "Female Authority and Authorization Strategies in Early Modern Europe." *"This Double Voice": Gendered Writing in Early Modern England*. Ed. Danielle Clarke and Elizabeth Clarke. New York: St. Martin's, 2000. 16–40. Print.

———. *Women Latin Poets: Language, Gender, and Authority from Antiquity to the Eighteenth Century*. Oxford: Oxford UP, 2005. Print.

Stier, Jane. "The Role of Women Religious Active in Education and Other Apostolates during the Renaissance: An Historical Study." Diss. Catholic U of Amer., 1966. Print.

Stortoni, Laura Anna, and Mary Prentice Lillie, eds. and trans. *Women Poets of the Italian Renaissance: Courtly Ladies and Courtesans*. New York: Italica, 1997. Print.

Szkilnik, Michelle. "Mentoring Noble Ladies: Antoine Dufour's *Vies des femmes célèbres.*" *The Cultural and Political Legacy of Anne de Bretagne: Negotiating Convention in Books and Documents.* Ed. Cynthia J. Brown. Cambridge: Brewer, 2010. 65–80. Print.

Tarte, Kendall. "Seductive Topographies: The Languages of Landscape in *La puce de Madame Des Roches.*" *Romanic Review* (2004): n. pag. Web. 9 Nov. 2009.

Tarugi, Luisa Rotondi Secchi, ed. *Petrarca e la cultura europea.* Milano: Nuovi Orizzonti, 1997. Print. Mentis Itinerarium.

Taylor, Charles. *Sources of the Self: The Making of the Modern Identity.* Cambridge: Harvard UP, 1989. Print.

Taylor, Gordon Rattray. *Sex in History.* 1954. New York: Vanguard, 1970. Print.

Thibault, Pascale. *Les manuscrits de la collection d'Anne de Bretagne.* Blois: Les Amis de la Bibliothèque de Blois, 1991. Print.

Thompson, John Lee. "Calvin and Marie Dentière." *John Calvin and the Daughters of Sarah: Women in Regular and Exceptional Roles in the Exegesis of Calvin, His Predecessors, and His Contemporaries.* Geneva: Droz, 1992. 40–45. Print.

Thysell, Carol. *The Pleasures of Discernment: Marguerite de Navarre as Theologian.* London: Oxford UP, 2000. Print. Oxford Studies in Historical Theology.

Timmermans, Linda. *L'accès des femmes à la culture (1598–1715). Un débat d'idées de Saint François de Sales à la marquise de Lambert.* Paris: Champion, 1993. Print.

Tolley, Thomas. "States of Independence: Women Regents as Patrons of the Visual Arts in Renaissance France." *Renaissance Studies* 10.2 (1996): 237–58. Print.

Toulmin, Stephen. *Cosmopolis: The Hidden Agenda of Modernity.* New York: Free, 1991. Print.

The Translation of a Letter Written by a French Gentilwoman to an Other Gentilwoman Straunger, Her Frind [sic], upon the Death of the Most Excellent and Vertuous Ladye, Elenor of Roye, Princess of Condé. London: Daye, 1564. Print.

Turbide, Chantal. "Catherine de Médicis, mécène d'art contemporain: L'hôtel de la Reine et ses collections." Wilson-Chevalier, *Patronnes* 511–26.

Vaillancourt, Luc. *La lettre familière au XVIe siècle. Rhétorique humaniste de l'épistolaire.* Paris: Champion, 2003. Print.

Vaillancourt, Pierre-Louis, and Dawn Smyth. *Les écrits féminins non fictionnels de la Renaissance.* Ottawa: Legas, 2003. Print.

Vesalius, Andreas. *De Humani Corporis Fabrica Libri Septem.* Basel: Oporinus, 1543. Print.

Veyrin-Forrer, Jeanne. "Fabriquer un livre au XVIe siècle." Martin and Chartier 336–69.

Vial, Mireille. Rev. of *Impressions, une petite histoire des techniques graphiques.* By Musée de l'Imprimerie. *BBF.* Bulletin des Bibliothèques de France, n.d. Web. 9 Nov. 2009.

Viala, Alain. *Naissance de l'écrivain.* Paris: Éditions de Minuit, 1985. Print.

Vickers, Nancy J. "Diana Described: Scattered Women and Scattered Rhyme." *Writing and Sexual Difference.* Ed. E. Abel. Chicago: U of Chicago P, 1982. 95–108. Print.

La vie de Louise Labé. Site des lettres de l'Académie de Lyon. Académie de Lyon, n.d. Web. 5 Feb. 2010.

Viennot, Éliane. *La France, les femmes et le pouvoir: Une recherche en histoire politique*. 26 May 2009. Web. 17 Nov. 2009.

———. "Louise attaquée! Louise Labé est-elle une créature de papier . . . ?" *Siefar*. Siefar, 2009. Web. 6 Oct. 2010.

———. "Marguerite de France, duchesse de Valois, reine de Navarre et de France ["reine Marguerite," "reine Margot"] (1553–1615)." *Dictionnaire de la Siefar*. Siefar, 2002. Web. 18 Oct. 2010.

———. *Marguerite de Valois. La reine Margot*. Paris: Éditions Perrin, 2005. Print. Collection Tempus 109/111.

Ville de Paris: Population History Analysis and Data. Demographia. Wendell Cox Consultancy, 2001. Web. 15 Aug. 2010.

Virtual Museum of Printing-Press. AMI-Associação Museu da Imprensa, n.d. Web. 15 Aug. 2010.

Vives, Juan Luis. *The Education of a Christian Woman*. Ed. and trans. Charles Fantazzi. Bilingual ed. Chicago: U of Chicago P, 2000. Print. The Other Voice in Early Modern Europe.

Wareham, T. E. "Christine de Pisan's *Livre des faits d'armes et de chevalerie* and Its Fate in the Sixteenth Century." *Seconda Miscellanea di Studi e Ricerche sul Quattrocentro Francese*. Ed. Franco Simone, Jonathan Beck, and Gianni Mombello. Chambéry: Centre d'Études Franco-Italien, 1981. 135–42. Print.

Warnke, Frank J., ed. and trans. *Three Women Poets, Renaissance and Baroque: Louise Labé, Gaspara Stampa, and Sor Juan Inez de la Cruz*. Lewisburg: Bucknell UP, 1987. Print.

Watt, Jeffrey R. "The Impact of the Reformation and Counter-Reformation." *Family Life in Early Modern Times, 1500–1789*. Ed. David I. Kertzer and Marzio Barbagli. New Haven: Yale UP, 2001. 125–54. Print. Vol. 1 of *The History of the European Family*.

Wayne, Valerie. "Advice for Women from Mothers and Patriarchs." *Women and Literature in Britain, 1500–1700*. Ed. Helen Wilcox. Cambridge: Cambridge UP, 1996. 56–79. Print.

Wieck, Roger S. "The Primer of Claude de France and the Education of the Renaissance Child." *The Cambridge Illuminations: The Conference Proceedings*. Ed. Stella Panayotova. Cambridge: Fitzwilliam Museum, 2007. 267–77. Print.

Wiesner, Merry E. *Women and Gender in Early Modern Europe*. Cambridge: Cambridge UP, 1993. Print. New Approaches to European History.

———. "Women's Defense of Their Public Role." *Women in the Middle Ages and the Renaissance: Literary and Historical Perspectives*. Ed. Mary Beth Rose. Syracuse: Syracuse UP, 1986. 1–27. Print.

Will, Samuel F. "Camille de Morel: A Prodigy of the Renaissance." *PMLA* 51.1 (1936): 83–119. Print.

Willard, Charity Cannon. *Christine de Pizan: Her Life and Works*. New York: Persea, 1984. Print.

Wilson, Katharina M., ed. *An Encyclopedia of Continental Women Writers*. New York: Garland, 1991. Print.

———. *Women Writers of the Renaissance and Reformation*. Athens: U of Georgia P, 1987. Print.

Wilson-Chevalier, Kathleen. "Art Patronage and Women (including Habsburg) in the Orbit of King Francis I." *Renaissance Studies* 10.4 (2002): 474–524. Print.

———. "Introduction: Les espaces des patrones et mécènes." Wilson-Chevalier, *Patronnes* 7–42.

———, ed. With Eugénie Pascal. *Patronnes et mécènes en France à la Renaissance.* Saint-Étienne: PU de Saint-Étienne, 2007. Print. L'école du genre.

Wilson-Chevalier, Kathleen, and Éliane Viennot, eds. *Le royaume de fémynie. Pouvoirs, contraintes, espaces de liberté des femmes, de la Renaissance à la Fronde.* Paris: Champion, 1999. Print.

Wimsatt, W. K., and Monroe C. Beardsley. *The Verbal Icon: Studies in the Meaning of Poetry.* New York: Noonday, 1954. Print.

Winn, Colette H., ed. *Approaches to Teaching Marguerite de Navarre's* Heptameron. New York: MLA, 2007. Print. Approaches to Teaching World Literature.

———. *The Dialogue in Early Modern France, 1547–1630: Art and Argument.* Washington: The Catholic U of Amer. P, 1993. Print.

———, ed. *L'éducation des filles sous l'Ancien Régime, in Memory of Linda Timmermans.* Spec. issue of *Papers on French Seventeenth Century Literature* 24.46 (1997): 3–136. Print.

———. "La femme écrivain au XVIe siècle. Écriture et transgression." *Poétique* 84 (1990): 435–52. Print.

———. "Femmes et culture en Vivarais. 'Le phénomène Marie de Romieu.'" *Revue du Vivarais* 107.1 (2003): 59–76. Print.

———. "Les femmes et le développement de la culture du livre." *French and Francophone Women, 16th–21st Centuries.* Ed. Marie-Christine Weidmann Koop and Catherine R. Montfort. Spec. issue of *Women in French Studies* (2002): 10–24. Print.

———. "Gabrielle de Coignard, 'Sur la mort de Ronsard' (1594)." *Ronsard, figure de la variété. En mémoire d'Isidore Silver.* Ed. Winn. Geneva: Droz, 2002. 251–63. Print. THR 368.

———. "Mère / fille / femme / muse: Maternité et créativité dans les œuvres des Dames des Roches." *Travaux de littérature* 4 (1991): 53–68. Print.

———. "Perception spatiale dans *Les angoysses douloureuses* d'Hélisenne de Crenne." *Degré second* 9 (1985): 1–14. Print.

———, ed. *Protestations et revendications féminines. Textes oubliés et inédits sur l'éducation féminine (XVIe-XVIIe siècle).* Paris: Champion, 2002. Print. Textes de la Renaissance 50.

———. "La symbolique du regard dans *Les angoysses douloureuses qui procèdent d'amours* d'Hélisenne de Crenne." *Orbis literarum* 40.3 (1985): 207–27. Print.

Winn, Colette H., and Donna Kuizenga, eds. *Women Writers in Pre-revolutionary France: Strategies of Emancipation.* New York: Garland, 1997. Print.

Winn, Colette H., and Nicole Pellegrin, eds. *Veufs, veuves et veuvage dans la France d'Ancien Régime.* Paris: Champion, 2003. Print.

Winn, Colette H., and François Rouget, eds. *Collaboration et créativité au sein des "salons" et des foyers culturels de la Renaissance.* Spec. issue of *Renaissance and Reformation / Renaissance et Réforme* 28.1 (2004): 5–83. Print.

Winn, Mary Beth. "Louise de Savoie, ses enfants et ses livres: Du pouvoir familial au pouvoir d'État." Wilson-Chevalier, *Patronnes* 251–81. Print.

Wolff, Philippe, dir. *Histoire de Toulouse.* Toulouse: Privat, 1967. Print.

Wood, Diane S. *Hélisenne de Crenne: At the Crossroads of Renaissance Humanism and Feminism.* Madison: Fairleigh Dickinson UP, 2000. Print.

———. "Hélisenne de Crenne (c.1500–c.1552)." *French and Francophone Women, 16th–21st Centuries.* Ed. Marie-Christine Weidmann Koop and Catherine R. Montfort. Spec. issue of *Women in French Studies* (2002) 25–38. Print.

Wroth, Mary. *The Poems of Lady Mary Wroth.* Ed. Josephine A. Roberts. Baton Rouge: Louisiana State UP, 1983. Print.

Yandell, Cathy. *Carpe Corpus: Time and Gender in Early Modern France.* Newark: U of Delaware P, 2000. Print.

———. "Estienne, Nicole, ép. Liebault ou Liebaut [<<Olympe Liebault>>](1542?–1588?)." *Dictionnaire de la Siefar.* Siefar, 2003. Web. 18 Oct. 2010.

———. "Raconter le temps: La réflexivité dans *Les Misères de la femme mariée* de Nicole Estienne." Beaulieu and Desrosiers-Bonin, *Dans les miroirs* 49–60.

Yenal, Edith. *Christine de Pisan: A Bibliography of Writing by Her and about Her.* Metuchen: Scarecrow, 1989. Print.

Zancan, Marina. *Il doppio itinerario della scrittura. La donna nella tradizione letteraria italiana.* Torino: Einaudi, 1998. Print.

Ziegler, Georgianna. "Women Writers Online: An Evaluation and Annotated Bibliography of Web Resources." *Early Modern Literary Studies* 6.3 (2001): n. pag. *Early Modern Literary Studies.* Ed. Lisa Hopkins. 2001. Web. 10 Nov. 2009.

Zinguer, Ilana. *Misères et grandeur de la femme au XVIe siècle.* Geneva: Slatkine, 1982. Print.

Zum Kolk, Caroline. "Le mécénat de Catherine de Médicis d'après sa correspondance." Wilson-Chevalier, *Patronnes* 467–80.

Zumthor, Paul. *La lettre et la voix.* Paris: Éditions du Seuil, 1987. Print.

Zvereva, Alexandra. "Catherine de Médicis et les portraitistes français." Wilson-Chevalier, *Patronnes* 527–44.

Index

Modern Language Association of America
Options for Teaching

Teaching French Women Writers of the Renaissance and Reformation. Ed. Colette H. Winn. 2011.

Teaching Seventeenth- and Eighteenth-Century French Women Writers. Ed. Faith E. Beasley. 2011.

Teaching Law and Literature. Ed. Austin Sarat, Cathrine O. Frank, and Matthew Anderson. 2011.

Teaching British Women Playwrights of the Restoration and Eighteenth Century. Ed. Bonnie Nelson and Catherine Burroughs. 2010.

Teaching Narrative Theory. Ed. David Herman, Brian McHale, and James Phelan. 2010.

Teaching Early Modern English Prose. Ed. Susannah Brietz Monta and Margaret W. Ferguson. 2010.

Teaching Italian American Literature, Film, and Popular Culture. Ed. Edvige Giunta and Kathleen Zamboni McCormick. 2010.

Teaching the Graphic Novel. Ed. Stephen E. Tabachnick. 2009.

Teaching Literature and Language Online. Ed. Ian Lancashire. 2009.

Teaching the African Novel. Ed. Gaurav Desai. 2009.

Teaching World Literature. Ed. David Damrosch. 2009.

Teaching North American Environmental Literature. Ed. Laird Christensen, Mark C. Long, and Fred Waage. 2008.

Teaching Life Writing Texts. Ed. Miriam Fuchs and Craig Howes. 2007.

Teaching Nineteenth-Century American Poetry. Ed. Paula Bernat Bennett, Karen L. Kilcup, and Philipp Schweighauser. 2007.

Teaching Representations of the Spanish Civil War. Ed. Noël Valis. 2006.

Teaching the Representation of the Holocaust. Ed. Marianne Hirsch and Irene Kacandes. 2004.

Teaching Tudor and Stuart Women Writers. Ed. Susanne Woods and Margaret P. Hannay. 2000.

Teaching Literature and Medicine. Ed. Anne Hunsaker Hawkins and Marilyn Chandler McEntyre. 1999.

Teaching the Literatures of Early America. Ed. Carla Mulford. 1999.

Teaching Shakespeare through Performance. Ed. Milla C. Riggio. 1999.

Teaching Oral Traditions. Ed. John Miles Foley. 1998.

Teaching Contemporary Theory to Undergraduates. Ed. Dianne F. Sadoff and William E. Cain. 1994.

Teaching Children's Literature: Issues, Pedagogy, Resources. Ed. Glenn Edward Sadler. 1992.

Teaching Literature and Other Arts. Ed. Jean-Pierre Barricelli, Joseph Gibaldi, and Estella Lauter. 1990.

New Methods in College Writing Programs: Theories in Practice. Ed. Paul Connolly and Teresa Vilardi. 1986.

School-College Collaborative Programs in English. Ed. Ron Fortune. 1986.

Teaching Environmental Literature: Materials, Methods, Resources. Ed. Frederick O. Waage. 1985.

Part-Time Academic Employment in the Humanities: A Sourcebook for Just Policy. Ed. Elizabeth M. Wallace. 1984.

Film Study in the Undergraduate Curriculum. Ed. Barry K. Grant. 1983.

The Teaching Apprentice Program in Language and Literature. Ed. Joseph Gibaldi and James V. Mirollo. 1981.

Options for Undergraduate Foreign Language Programs: Four-Year and Two-Year Colleges. Ed. Renate A. Schulz. 1979.

Options for the Teaching of English: Freshman Composition. Ed. Jasper P. Neel. 1978.

Options for the Teaching of English: The Undergraduate Curriculum. Ed. Elizabeth Wooten Cowan. 1975.